PUBLIC FINANCE, PLANNING AND ECONOMIC DEVELOPMENT

Public Finance, Planning and Economic Development

Essays in Honour of Ursula Hicks

edited by
WILFRED L. DAVID, D.Phil. (Oxon.)
Associate Professor of Economics, University of Delaware

Macmillan

First published 1973 by
THE MACMILLAN PRESS LTD
London and Basingstoke
Associated companies in New York Dublin
Melbourne Johannesburg and Madras

SBN 333 14660 3

Printed in Great Britain by
A. WHEATON & COMPANY
Exeter

To
Ursula Kathleen Hicks
Teacher, Scholar, Public Servant and Friend

Contents

Introduction

This volume of essays is dedicated to Ursula Hicks, economist, teacher, scholar and friend. During the course of her career she has travelled widely, delighting to visit the countries from which her students came. She has frequently advised their countries on economic and fiscal policy, often together with her husband, Professor J. R. Hicks, the 1972 Nobel Laureate in Economics. For eighteen years she was the principal teacher of Public Finance in Oxford, lecturing regularly and conducting a graduate seminar in Public Policy, as well as tutoring and supervising a continual stream of undergraduate and graduate students of Economics. Although Lady Hicks has now retired from her official position, she continues to teach and advise, being especially concerned with young economists from the less developed countries. The contents of this volume bear witness to her wide interests and influence in both the practical and academic sides of her subject.

Ursula Kathleen Hicks (*née* Webb) was born in Dublin, Ireland. She received her early education at a very well-known girls' secondary school (Alexandra School), afterwards going to Roedean, Brighton. From there she went up to Oxford, reading Modern History at Somerville College, where her tutor was the late Lady Woodward (wife of Sir Llewellyn Woodward). On graduating from Oxford, apart from a brief experience in the Ministry of Agriculture she felt compelled, as an only child, to return home to look after her parents, her father being very ill. She found time, however, during these years to do a good deal of work for the Workers' Educational Association, in Kent and Sussex, whither her parents had moved. This experience aroused her interest both in economics in general, and in local government and finance in particular. After the death of her father she enrolled at the London School of Economics. There she remained for seven years, as an undergraduate, graduate student and eventually lecturer in the Economics Department, under Professor Lionel (later Lord) Robbins. It was a stimulating period at L.S.E. with a brilliant group of young economists, many of whom later made their mark, particularly Nicholas Kaldor, Abba Lerner and Marian Bowley (now Professor at University College, London). As a young teacher, John Hicks (whom she subsequently married) was the natural leader of the group.

In 1935 John Hicks was appointed to a Fellowship at Caius College, Cambridge, and the couple, now married, moved there early in 1936. It was not to be for long, however. In 1938 John Hicks received a call to the Jevons Chair of Political Economy in Manchester. During the war Ursula Hicks was asked to take over the headship of the Economics Department in Liverpool University. This was an extremely interesting assignment, notwithstanding the difficult experience of that much bombed city. Soon after the end of the war the Hickses moved back to Oxford; John Hicks had been a scholar of Balliol, so that it was a home-coming for both of them. In 1947 John Hicks took up a Fellowship in the newly founded Nuffield College, the first of the mixed graduate colleges in Oxford. Ursula Hicks was appointed to the newly created post of University Lecturer in Public Finance. In spite of not infrequent journeys abroad, Oxford has been their home until retirement (and after). John Hicks became Drummond Professor of Political Economy in 1953. On the foundation of Linacre College in 1962 Ursula became a foundation Fellow. In these posts both are now emeritus. Queen's University, Belfast, has awarded Ursula a D.Sc. Econ., while the Institute of Social Studies at The Hague (where she lectured annually for many years) has made her a Fellow of that Institute.

It is impossible to do justice to Ursula Hicks's various contributions in this short introductory essay; but since there is no doubt that she has made a lasting mark in the fields of both theoretical and practical economics, some mention must be made of her chief activities. Her major contribution has of course been in the field of public finance and public policy. The methodology of public finance, the history of fiscal economics, growth and fiscal policy, the political economics of mutual understanding between developed and underdeveloped countries, budgetary classification, public authority budgeting and accounting processes, financial administration and development planning, have all received extensive and incisive treatment by her.

Running all through her work is the insistence on the need for an inter-disciplinary approach to the problems under consideration. This is reflected in her ability to combine, in a very exciting and clear manner, a concrete anatomy of economic problems with a 'treatment' analysis under selective criteria. Within such a framework, the inherent approach has been one of building a bridge between positive public finance, i.e. public finance as a theoretical subdiscipline of economic science, and normative public finance as reflected in sound historical knowledge and the recognition of certain 'non-economic' criteria and variables such as the socio-cultural milieu and the political situation, as being of paramount importance. Ursula Hicks is certainly a member of that select and distinguished circle of economists who have been able to achieve a fruitful synthesis between the requirements of theoretical rigour on the one hand and the ramifications of economic reality on the other.

The seminal aspects of her methodology can be observed as far back as 1938 with the publication of her first book, *The Finance of British Government 1920–36*. It is based on her thesis at the London School of Economics and is a thorough study of the subject based on ten years of detailed research. Further, it marked the first attempt by a scholar to quantify the major aspects of British public finance. To my mind, this work established on a firm footing her basic method of approach, one of marrying sound theoretical insight and logic to an intensive and extensive historical and political common sense. During the next decade she was primarily concerned with the consolidation and extension of this method of analysis, a period in which she also concentrated on a cross-polity investigation of local finance, thereby contributing to the fostering of mutual understanding between the developed and the underdeveloped nations. At this time she was specifically concerned with the analysis of the ideal types of grants for equalisation of wealth and financial needs, for a stable system of local tax on land and buildings and their valuation with appropriate periodicity and without arbitrariness. It is also worthy of note that during this phase she emphasised, based on the criteria of social benefits, that there should be a harmonious relationship between economic efficiency and political self-government, emphasising also the positive role of the central government by means of appropriate policy devices such as grants under national criteria, the valuation of the local rate based on free market rents, and similar measures.

These ideas can be seen permeating her researches of the late 1930s and early 1940s, when she moved into the field of macro-economic analysis. Two works which had a strong impact on her at this stage were John Maynard Keynes's paper, 'Britain's Income and Economic Potential' (*Economic Journal*, Dec. 1939), and her husband's *Social Framework* (Oxford, 1942). In the *E.J.* paper, Keynes pioneered the use of the national income approach to economic accounting as a policy tool rather than as a measure of social welfare, and this was developed to a high degree of sophistication by Sir John Hicks in his *Social Framework* and in journal articles on the subject. Making use of tools developed within this national income framework, Lady Hicks turned her attention to an examination of 'The Terminology of Tax Analysis', and in that vintage *Economic Journal* paper of 1946 she proceeded to demonstrate the possibility of treating public finance from the macro-economic angle. She emphasised the practical usefulness of making a distinction between an *income tax*, assessed on the basis of income receipts, and an *outlay tax*, assessed on the basis of expenditure, in preference to the traditional distinction between direct and indirect taxes. Related to this was the further important distinction between the *formal incidence* of taxes, which refers to statistical estimates of tax payments by income groups, and *effective incidence*, which relates to the economic effects of taxation.

Her academic position was firmly established with the publication of *Public Finance* in 1947, a work which not only broke new ground among the available texts on public finance, but still remains one of the best elementary texts in the field. This is evidenced by the fact that since its original appearance in 1947 it has run into several editions and has been reprinted ten times. Her long and deep interest in achieving a synthesis between normative and positive public finance reaches the high-water mark here.

Briefly, the work consists of an analysis of the administrative roles and economic functions of fiscal structures controlled by the government sector in the national economy, presents a detailed treatment of the effects and incidence of taxation, the relationship between welfare and consumer surplus – a new interpretation of the principles of taxation – by application of the distinction of taxes and incidence theory mentioned earlier, and contains a useful summary of analyses of fiscal policies in combination with macro-economic problems, i.e. fiscal activity and the national economy, the possibility of fiscal planning, and the development of a national accounting system. The treatment of these subjects was further expanded in a second edition (1955) and a third edition (1968), in which greater attention was paid to the problems of the less developed countries.

Among these were the idea of the welfare state, the problem of the control of the national debt, and the analysis of growth and development.

Lady Hicks's great interest in underdeveloped countries dates from 1950. It arose out of invitations to lecture at the Delhi School of Economics and to act on an Advisory Commission in Nigeria. In 1954 she was a member of the rather unique husband-and-wife Commission on Taxation in Jamaica. In the late 1950s and early 1960s she was assisting the Nigerian Federation in problems of revenue allocation between the Federal and Regional Governments. In particular, she took part in presenting the Eastern Regional Government's case to the Raisman Fiscal Commission of 1958 and the Binns Fiscal Commission of 1964. In 1962 Lady Hicks was again in the Caribbean investigating on behalf of the Colonial Office the prospects of federation among the smaller islands.

The fruits of such endeavours were reflected not only in the later editions of *Public Finance* but also in her subsequent work, especially *Development from Below*, first published in 1961. She has always made it a rule not to venture anything substantial about a country which is not known to her personally. *Development from Below* therefore bears the imprint of extensive fieldwork in East and West Africa, and also her wide experience in the practical fiscal field gained through extensive travel and, as previously mentioned, advising and lecturing in many countries. This work contains an authoritative discussion of state–local relationships.

One of Lady Hicks's major contributions lies in the application of the theories of fiscal policy and the financial approach to the problems of the less developed countries. This aspect of her work is illustrated in her *Development Finance: Planning and Control* (Oxford, 1965). In passing, an interesting terminological point made in the early pages of this book is that today's Third World economies should be categorised as 'development countries' because of the interest and involvement of international agencies such as the United Nations in their advancement, thereby emphasising the important, but often forgotten, point that development should not be conceived on a purely national and nationalist basis, but involves far-reaching international dimensions requiring mutual understanding, respect and co-operation between the advanced nations and their less fortunate partners. *Development Finance*, which represents a long-run analysis of planning for stable growth, is one of the best available studies of the development process from the fiscal and financial angles.

In addition to her work in the major areas of public finance and fiscal policy mentioned above, some note should also be made of her work in the field of federal finance. This aspect has been well reviewed in the papers by Sastri and Edwards in this volume, and to which the bibliographical references appearing at the end of this collection of essays attest.

This short commentary on certain basic themes running through the complex of Lady Hicks's work would be incomplete unless explicit reference is also made to at least one other aspect of her intellectual and academic involvement. First, Lady Hicks was a co-founder (with Abba Lerner and Paul Sweezy) of the *Review of Economic Studies*, and remained Managing Editor for a period of twenty-eight years from 1933 to 1961. That this publication has made its mark as one of the leading journals in the field of economics, and its continued success as a major academic journal, is to a large extent due to Ursula Hicks's skilful management of its affairs and her careful selection of the various papers which were to appear in its pages.

These decades of continuous high-level productivity were nurtured by the most lasting and fruitful partnership with her husband, John Richard Hicks (knighted in 1964), one of the most brilliant and eminent economic theorists of our time, whose work earned him the 1972 Nobel Prize in Economics. The fruits of their collaboration fill the pages of books, learned journals, official reports, and the minds of students, scholars and public officials. Anyone who comes into contact with this remarkable pair of personalities must become aware of a complementarity which, over time and in a dynamic sense, has certainly contributed much to world academic welfare.

Lady Hicks's energy is evidenced by the fact that she has always been able to spare time from her busy academic schedule to perform a wide variety of official duties. When not lecturing, writing or just giving counsel to some student at Oxford, she has been visiting and lecturing at foreign universities, serving on important fiscal commissions, or advising governments on matters of economic policy. She has held Visiting Professorships at Chicago and Harvard (1946), Delhi (1950 and 1969–70), Osaka (1960), Buenos Aires (1962), Northwestern and Purdue (1965) and the Australian National University (1967).

In 1968 the Hickses were in Tehran making proposals for the reform of the Economics Department at the University there at the request of the Iranian Government. In 1969 they made a lecture tour of Centres of Advanced Economic Study in India under the auspices of the Indian Universities Grants Commission; 1970 saw attendance at the Economics Seminar in Mexico City at which the participants included Wassily Leontieff, John Kenneth Galbraith and Joan Robinson; also in 1970 and in 1971 they were touring and lecturing at various Italian universities.

As a member of fiscal and other advisory missions Lady Hicks has served in India and Nigeria (1950), Jamaica (1954), Uganda and the Caribbean (1962) and Nigeria (1964). She has also been consultant to world organisations such as the World Bank. In 1967 a new interest opened for Lady Hicks as a result of being asked to write a paper on the finance of urban renewal and development at a centennial conference in Toronto. In the most recent years urban problems in both advanced and less developed countries have occupied a great deal of her attention.

The experience amassed from these missions has made her more qualified than most to match the rigours of high theory with sound common sense, to create effective links between positive and normative economics, and to stress at all times the need for an interdisciplinary approach to growth and development. This was one of the phenomena which struck me most of all while I was attending her lectures and seminars at Oxford.

As a student of development problems, I have always found this aspect of her work most interesting and satisfying. The academic world is replete with 'development experts' who have never visited any of the countries about which they purport to have expert knowledge. On the contrary, Ursula Hicks has deservedly carved out a name for herself in the field of development economics, as she has been able to combine a lively academic mind with constant travel and study of the relevant developmental problems *in situ*. In turn, the knowledge and experience gained by taking constant microscopic observations of these problems have formed the basis of continuous intellectual inquiries, and have tended to enhance the long respect for her views on the Economics of Discontent.

Many generations of Oxford graduates recall with pleasure and nostalgia the lucid expression of developmental ideas at the Institute of Commonwealth Studies, situated at the junction of the Banbury

Road and St Giles in Oxford. The Institute boasts a smart lodging-house – Queen Elizabeth House – which was built for students, scholars and public officials from Commonwealth countries. Aided by Lady Hicks's presence, the atmosphere has always been a pleasant interplay and cumulative interaction of customs, languages, politics and economics. Lady Hicks has been held in the highest esteem by successive generations of Commonwealth students who have studied at this institution. Mention must also be made of her work at Linacre College, which has become the foremost international graduate centre at Oxford. Ursula Hicks's friendly presence has undoubtedly made its mark there. Students at both institutions repeatedly express surprise at her profound knowledge of the problems facing their own societies. Her ability to replace dogma by sound empirical cognition, added to her unending desire of always wanting to learn more about overseas countries from the students themselves, has endeared her to all.

Oxford maintains its pre-eminence as one of the foremost institutions of higher learning in the world today, not only because of the high quality of teaching and research which goes on within its walls, but much more importantly because of the community life and spirit which has been the essence of its existence. By means of its collegiate life, the student is given the opportunity of developing every aspect of his personality. In contributing to this dual but integrated feature of university life, Lady Hicks was *don par excellence*, at all times keeping a watchful eye on the balanced progress and happiness of her students, especially those from foreign countries. Whether at Nuffield, the Institute of Commonweath Studies or Linacre, she always did her utmost to ensure that nothing stood in the way of the advancement of those entrusted to her care, by showing immense personal concern for each one, and by making sure that they gained the optimal benefit from Oxford life. For myself, the most important and pleasant years of my academic and personal life were experienced while I was her pupil.

University of Delaware, WILFRED L. DAVID
U.S.A.
June 1972

Part One
PUBLIC FINANCE: SOME THEORETICAL AND CONCEPTUAL ISSUES

1

Cost–Benefit Analysis in Developing Countries: The Evaluation of Projects Financed by Aid and External Loans*

MARTIN S. FELDSTEIN

I AM particularly pleased to have the opportunity of including this paper in a volume of essays in honour of Ursula Hicks. The problems of public finance in developing countries have long been a primary interest of Lady Hicks. Moreover, Lady Hicks was one of my supervisors in Oxford in 1962–3 when, as part of a thesis for the degree of Bachelor of Letters, I first presented the method of investment analysis which the current paper extends to developing countries with externally financed investments.

Section I reviews the basic method of public expenditure evaluation in the context of a closed economy. This simplified setting permits a clearer statement of the appropriate treatment of the effect of public spending on private investment and of the payment of wages in excess of the opportunity cost. Section II extends the analysis to a country that engages in foreign trade with an overvalued domestic currency and significant import tariffs. The result is an important extension of the consumer surplus shadow price rule of Harberger [10] and Schydlowsky [17]. It shows the interdependence between the problem of intertemporal aggregation, the opportunity cost of private investment and the shadow price of foreign exchange. The method developed in these two sections is then applied (Section III) to the analysis of projects financed by foreign aid and external loans. A by-product of this analysis is a method of determining the 'value' to the recipient country of a subsidised loan.

I. THE EVALUATION OF PUBLIC INVESTMENT: A BRIEF REVIEW

The economic welfare of a nation depends ultimately on the level of

* I am grateful for discussions with D. M. Schydlowsky and L. Taylor.

consumption, both private and public, that its citizens enjoy. Investment is important not as an end in itself but because it creates a future stream of consumption. The correct evaluation of a public project therefore has two aspects. First, it is necessary to estimate the total effect that the project has on private consumption. This includes not only the actual inputs and outputs of the project but also the effects of financing the project: the immediate reductions in private consumption and the indirect reductions of future consumption through reductions in private investment. Second, it is necessary to combine these changes in consumption at different dates into a single measure of the value of the project. This process of aggregating changes in consumption can, under certain conditions, be expressed as discounting to calculate a present value. The appropriate discount rate is an important policy parameter in any economy. It must reflect the judgement of politically responsible authorities about the relative desirability of consumption in different years. It is important to stress that this discount rate, generally referred to as the social time preference rate, is a normative policy parameter and not necessarily equal to the rate of return on private investment. It should in general depend on the level of consumption and its rate of growth.[1]

The operational implications of regarding public investment as a change in the time stream of consumption can best be explained by considering three cases of increasing complexity. The following seven assumptions will be made in all three cases:

1. Resources are fully employed and prices are stable.
2. Small redistributions of income leave social welfare unchanged.
3. All magnitudes are known with certainty.
4. Commodity markets are perfect so that market prices reflect social costs.
5. There are no collection costs or deadweight losses associated with tax revenues.
6. There is no external borrowing.
7. Monetary considerations can be ignored; more specifically, the demand and supply of money is interest-inelastic.

The special problem of a substantial labour surplus, which violates assumptions 1 and 4, will be analysed at the end of this section.

Consider a project that lasts T years, producing benefits b_t in year t and incurring costs c_t. Assume that this project has no effect on private investment or other public spending, i.e. that all benefits accrue to consumers and all costs are financed by sales to consumers or taxes that reduce consumption. Then it is clear that the value of the project is simply the discounted value of the net benefits, $b_t - c_t$, discounting at the social time preference rate, d:[2]

$$V = \sum_{t=0}^{T} \frac{b_t - c_t}{(1+d)^t}. \tag{1}$$

The project is worth doing if V exceeds zero; between two mutually exclusive projects, the one with the higher V should be chosen.

This calculation makes no reference to the project's cash expenditure (e_t) and sales revenues (r_t).[3] It is useful as a background to the more general cases considered below to express the annual net benefit as the consumers' surplus associated with the outputs ($b_t - r_t$) plus the 'surplus' associated with the inputs ($e_t - c_t$) minus the value that consumers forgo in taxes to pay the deficit on the project ($e_t - r_t$). The value of the project is thus

$$V = \sum_{t=0}^{T} \frac{(b_t - r_t) + (e_t - c_t) - (e_t - r_t)}{(1+d)^t}. \tag{2}$$

It is clear that the revenues and expenditures in (2) cancel each other so that (2) reduces to the simpler expression of (1).

We now drop the assumption that the project does not affect private investment. If part of the project's deficit is financed by a tax that reduces private investment,[4] the calculation of equations (1) and (2) must be modified. Reducing private investment is equivalent to removing the stream of consumption that would result from that investment. The value of the private investment is therefore the present value of the consumption to which it would have led. This present value is calculated by discounting at the social time preference rate (d), since that is the appropriate rate for aggregating consumption at different dates.

For example, if the marginal rate of return on private investment is ρ and all of these future profits are consumed, one 'peso' of investment today leads to a perpetual stream of ρ pesos each year in the future. The present value of this consumption stream is ρ/d; thus if $d = 0{\cdot}06$ and $\rho = 0{\cdot}15$, a peso of private investment would be equivalent in value to 2·5 pesos of consumption. More generally, future profits lead to future investment which in turn leads to both future consumption and further investment. As long as the rate of saving is less than socially optimal, i.e. as long as ρ exceeds d, a peso of investment will have greater welfare value than a peso of consumption. We shall denote the value or shadow price of investment, i.e. the present value of the consumption that is generated directly and indirectly, by S.[5]

The consumption value of the taxes levied to finance the project's deficit in any year can now be calculated using the shadow price of private investment, S. If the proportion of marginal taxes that falls on investment is p and the proportion that falls on consumption is $1\text{-}p$, the consumption value of a one-peso increase in taxes is $[(1\text{-}p) + p\,S]$ pesos, i.e. a consumption component of $(1\text{-}p)$ and an investment value of $p\,S$. In year t the project incurs a deficit of $e_t - r_t$ with a consumption equivalent value of $(e_t - r_t)\ [1\text{-}p + p\ S]$. The net benefit of the project in year t is therefore the consumers' surplus associated with the output $(b_t - r_t)$ plus the surplus associated with the inputs $(e_t - c_t)$ minus the consumption value of the taxes levied to cover the deficit $(e_t - r_t)\ [1\text{-}p + p\ S]$. Since the forgone investment has been valued in terms of consumption, this annual net benefit is also a 'consumption value' so that net benefits in different years can be discounted at the social time preference rate. The present value of the project is therefore

$$V = \sum_{t=0}^{T} \frac{(b_t - r_t) + (e_t - c_t) - (e_t - r_t)\ [1\text{-}p + p\ S]}{(1 + d)^t}. \tag{3}$$

By rearranging terms this can be rewritten more simply as

$$V = \sum_{t=0}^{T} \frac{(b_t - c_t) - (S - 1)\ p\ (e_t - r_t)}{(1 + d)^t}. \tag{4}$$

Note that the annual net benefit in equation (4) can be interpreted as follows: $(b_t - c_t)$ is the direct benefit of the project if financing is ignored, $p\ (e_t - r_t)$ is the reduction in private investment, and $(S - 1)$ is the 'excess value' of resources devoted to investment over their value in consumption.

The logic of equation (4) can be extended to the case in which part of the project's deficit is financed by reducing public expenditure elsewhere. Let g be the proportion of the project's deficit financed in this way, and let G be the 'consumption equivalent' shadow price of marginal government spending. The existence of a government budget constraint, i.e. the inability to reduce private consumption and increase government spending until the two forms of spending produce equal value at the margin, implies that G exceeds 1. The actual value of G will depend on the specific expenditures that are marginal in the government budget and, if they are public investments that entail subsequent profits, the currently anticipated reinvestment opportunities.[6] If p continues to denote the proportion of the deficit that is financed by a reduction in investment, and $1\text{-}p\text{-}g$ the proportion that is financed by a reduction in consumption, the consumption equivalent cost of financing the deficit is $(e_t - r_t)\ [1\text{-}p\text{-}g + p\ S + g\ G]$. Proceeding as before, the project value is[7]

$$V = \sum_{t=0}^{T} \frac{(b_t - c_t) - (e_t - r_t)\,[p\,(S-1) + g\,(G-1)]}{(1+d)^t}. \qquad (5)$$

Until now the discussion has implicitly assumed that there is no unemployment and that the wage rate measures the marginal product of labour. In many developing countries this assumption would lead to very inappropriate conclusions. There is often substantial unemployment or employment in the agricultural sector with a marginal product very much below the wage rate in the industrial sector. Given the artificially high industrial wage rate,[8] the level of industrial employment is effectively limited by the size of the capital stock. Government purchases of labour therefore directly or indirectly draw labour from low-productivity agriculture, while government purchases of industrial products withdraw that output from other uses. The prices of industrial products therefore measure their opportunity cost[9] even though the wage paid to labour exceeds the agricultural marginal product of labour.[10]

The implications of this situation for project evaluation are clear. The resource cost of the project (c_t) should be calculated using the market price of goods purchased by the project, but the wage rate for labour should be replaced by the marginal product of agricultural labour.[11] The expenditure (e_t) must of course be calculated using the actual wage rates. If the level of saving is optimal ($S = 1$), the expenditure is irrelevant and the effective cost of labour (the 'shadow price of labour') is the marginal product of agricultural labour, a. If saving is suboptimal ($S > 1$) and the project's deficit is financed by a tax that falls partially on investment ($p > 0$), the correct shadow price of labour exceeds the pure resource cost, a. More specifically, if the wage rate is denoted by w, equation (5) implies that the shadow price of labour is $a + w\ [p\ (S-1) + g\ (G-1)]$. This is of course automatically taken into account by the application of equation (5).[12]

II. EXTENSIONS TO AN OPEN ECONOMY WITH A FIXED EXCHANGE RATE[13]

Because developing nations often import a substantial fraction of their capital equipment and intermediate products, it is important to ask: if some of the inputs[14] of the project are to be imported, how should their costs be calculated? The answer to this question also provides the basis for valuing project outputs that are either to be exports or to be import substitutes.[15] It will also be used in the next section to analyse projects financed by aid and external loans.

The correct answer differs from country to country, depending on the particular way in which its international trade is organised: whether the exchange rate is fixed or flexible, whether there is import licensing, what mix of tariffs has been imposed, etc. In every case the basic principle of evaluation is the same: the social cost of government import spending is the present value of the change in domestic consumption that it causes. This includes both the direct impact on consumption and the present value of any future changes in consumption. The same rule also applies to exports and import substitutes. Although this statement of principle may seem trivial, it is important to emphasise two things: first, the present value of domestic consumption is the basic standard of evaluation; and second, the evaluation must reflect the changes that are predicted to occur and not what might occur if the economy were managed differently.[16]

To illustrate the application of this principle, I shall concentrate on the case of a country with a fixed exchange rate. I shall begin with the assumption that there are fixed tariffs and no import licensing. I shall then consider the implications of import licensing and, in particular, the gain (reduction in social cost) that this additional policy instrument permits.

Consider an economy whose domestic currency is the peso, and whose exchange rate is one peso equals one dollar. The currency is overvalued, but a balance of payments equilibrium is achieved by an import tariff of 100 θ per cent.[17,18] As part of an investment project the government spends 100 dollars on imports. The government must therefore take action to reduce import spending by consumers and investors of 100 $(1 + \theta)$ pesos. The policy used to achieve this import reduction must not cause domestic price inflation because, with a fixed exchange rate, that would cause a further balance of payments deficit.

These two 'targets', a reduction in import demand of 100 $(1 + \theta)$ and no change in domestic demand, can be achieved by the use of any two 'instruments' that have different effects on domestic demand and imports.[19] Assume that the government uses its two instruments to change the levels of consumption and investment.[20] Let m_c be the proportion of marginal consumer expenditure that is on imports (i.e. the ratio of consumers' marginal propensity to import to their marginal propensity to consume) and m_i the proportion of investors' marginal expenditure that is on imports.[21] Let the change in consumption due to the government policy be C and the change in investment be I. The requirements of external and internal balance imply

$$m_c C + m_i I = -100(1 + \theta) \qquad (6)$$
$$(1 - m_c)C + (1 - m_i)I = 0$$

or, equivalently,

$$C = 100(1 - m_i)(1 + \theta) / (m_i - m_c) \qquad (7)$$
$$I = -100(1 - m_c)(1 + \theta) / (m_i - m_c).$$

If the marginal import component of investment exceeds the marginal import component of consumption ($m_i > m_c$), the policy must increase consumption ($C > 0$) and decrease investment ($I < 0$).[22]

If there is no special shortage of saving, i.e. if an extra peso of investment has the same value as an equal peso of consumption, the social value of the changes in consumption and investment is simply the reduction in aggregate spending, $-(C + I)$. Equation (7) implies $C + I = 100(1 + \theta)$, i.e. the social cost of the government's import expenditure of 100 dollars is 100 $(1 + \theta)$ pesos, the amount that consumers and investors would pay (because of the tariff) for imports of 100 dollars.[23] However, if there is a shortage of saving so that the value of one peso of investment is worth S pesos of consumption, the social cost of the government import is $-[C + S \cdot I]$ or, in terms of equation (7),

$$-[C+S\cdot I]=\frac{-(1-m_i)+S(1-m_c)}{(m_i-m_c)}\cdot 100\ (1+\theta)\quad (8)$$

or, equivalently,

$$-[C+S\cdot I]=\left[1+(S-1)\frac{(1-m_c)}{(m_i-m_c)}\right](1+\theta)\ 100.\qquad (9)$$

Equation (9) brings out clearly the way in which the social cost of government import spending exceeds the direct value of the foreign exchange ($100\ (1+\theta)$) to the extent that importing is more investment-intensive and is of greater social value than consumption.[24] The quantitative importance of this may be very substantial. Even if S is as low as 2, m_i as high as 0·5 and m_c as low as 0·1, the extra social cost is $100\ (S-1)\ (1-m_c)\ (1+\theta)/(m_i-m_c)=225\ (1+\theta)$.

The widespread use of direct import controls makes it important to investigate their implications for project evaluation. Since the use of import licensing for consumption and investment goods provides two additional policy instruments, it can permit the government to make imports at lower social cost. Import licensing implies that the goods that can be purchased for one dollar are worth more than $1+\theta$ pesos to consumers and investors. Let D represent the value of a licence to import $(1+\theta)$ pesos' worth of consumption goods. Similarly, let J be the value of a license to import $(1+\theta)$ pesos of investment goods.

When the government spends 100 dollars on imports it must reduce import licences by 100 dollars. Let CL be the proportion of this 100-dollar reduction that is for licences to import consumer goods. The government must also take measures to prevent domestic demand from increasing. Using C and I again to denote the total changes in consumption and investment, the requirement for internal balance can be stated simply as

$$C+I=-\ 100\ (1+\theta)\qquad (10)$$

i.e. total spending must fall by the same amount as import spending in order to leave domestic demand unchanged.

The social value of these changes in domestic and imported consumption and investment may be stated in terms of D, J and S. Since C is the total 'increase' (perhaps negative) in consumption and $CL\cdot 100\ (1+\theta)$ is the reduction in imported consumption, $C+100\cdot CL\cdot(1+\theta)-100\cdot CL\ (1+\theta+D)=C-D\cdot 100\cdot CL\ (1+\theta)$.

For example, if total consumption were unchanged but the amount $100 \cdot CL\ (1 + \theta)$ was switched from imported to domestic goods, there would be a loss of $D \cdot 100 \cdot CL\ (1 + \theta)$. If a peso of investment has social value S and a dollar's worth of imported investment goods is as valuable to private investors as $(1 + \theta + J)$ pesos' worth, a dollar of investment imports has a social value of $(1 + \theta + J)\ S$ pesos. The value of the change in investment is (with I denoting 'increases' in investment) $S\ [I + 100\ (1 - CL)\ (1 + \theta) - 100\ (1 - CL)\ (1 + \theta + J)]$ or $S\ [I - J \cdot 100 \cdot (1 - CL)\ (1 + \theta)]$.[25] The total value of changes in consumption and investment is therefore

$$C - D \cdot 100 \cdot CL\,(1 + \theta) + S\,[I - J \cdot 100\,(1 - CL)\,(1 + \theta)] \qquad (11)$$

or, substituting for C from the domestic balance relation (equation (10)) and rearranging,

$$(S - 1) \cdot I + (SJ - D)\,100\,(1 + \theta) \cdot CL - (SJ + 1)\,100\,(1 + \theta). \qquad (12)$$

Note that (12) measures the 'value' of the changes resulting from the government purchase; the social cost is this value multiplied by -1. Although the government is in principle free to choose any values of I and CL, the choice is in practice constrained by political or other economic considerations. The expression in (12) permits the evaluation of alternative feasible policies. For example, if the government leaves aggregate investment and investment imports unchanged ($I = 0$ and $CL = 1$), the social cost is $(1 + D)\ (1 + \theta)\ 100$. In contrast, if the external balance is achieved by substituting domestic for imported investment ($I = 0$, $CL = 0$), the social cost is $(1 + SJ)\ (1 + \theta)\ 100$. This result emphasises the important fact that although private investors only put a premium of J on the right to import, the social value of imported investment is greater than J.

An examination of additional cases, e.g. the use of specific tariff changes or the result of inflation, could be developed along similar lines. It is more appropriate at this point to stop with the current results and apply them to the problem of evaluating projects financed by foreign aid and external finance.

III. EVALUATION OF PROJECTS FINANCED BY AID AND EXTERNAL LOANS

Sections I and II both emphasised that the cash expenditures and receipts of a project can be as important in evaluation as the direct use of resources and the direct output of benefits. This is particularly true for the potential balance of payments effects of project imports and exports. The framework that has been outlined above for combining real magnitudes and cash flows in project evaluation provides the key to the correct treatment of the financial flows associated with foreign aid and loans.

A simple example will illustrate the general principle. Consider a project that imports equipment costing 100 dollars, financing this import by a foreign loan bearing an interest rate of 6 per cent. The loan is to be repaid by a single payment of 200 dollars after twelve years; there are no interest or principal payments before that date. What is the correct measure of the social cost of this equipment?

In the year (t_0) of importing the equipment and making the loan, there is no effect on domestic consumption and investment and therefore no immediate social cost. The cost only occurs twelve years later (t_{12}), when funds must be raised to repay the loan and to reduce private demands for foreign exchange by 200 dollars. The social cost *then* of the loan repayment is the same as the cost of importing 200 dollars of equipment. Section II (equation (9)) showed that, in the case of fixed exchange rates and no import licensing, the shadow price per dollar of imports is $(1 + \theta)\ [1 + (S - 1)\ (1 - m_c)/(m_i - m_c)]$, where θ is the rate of tariff on imports, m_c is the marginal proportion of consumption that is imported, m_i is the marginal proportion of investment that is imported and S is the shadow price of private investment, i.e. the present value of the consumption that is produced per peso of investment. The social cost of the 200-dollar loan repayment is thus $200\ (1 + \theta)\ [1 + (S - 1)\ (1 - m_c)/(m_i - m_c)]$. Since this is evaluated in terms of 'equivalent consumption', its present value at t_0 is found by discounting this value at the social time preference rate (d). The social cost as at t_0 of the equipment purchased and corresponding loan is therefore $200\ (1 + \theta)\ [1 + (S - 1)\ (1 - m_c)/(m_i - m_c)]\ (1 + d)^{-12}$. For convenience I shall denote the shadow price per dollar of imports by F. If, for example, the following reasonable values are assumed:

$$\theta = 0{\cdot}50,\ S = 2,\ m_c = 0{\cdot}2,\ m_i = 0{\cdot}6$$

the value of $F = (1 + \theta)\ [1 + (S - 1)\ (1 - m_c)/(m_i - m_c)]$ is 4·5 pesos. The social cost of the 100-dollar purchase and corresponding loan is thus $200F\ (1 + d)^{-12}$ pesos. If $d = 0{\cdot}06$, the social cost is 450 pesos.[26]

This example illustrates two important principles. First, the rate of interest on the external loan is not relevant to the discounting of benefits and costs. It enters the analysis only through its influence on the amounts that the government must repay. All discounting is done by the social time preference rate after all quantities have been converted to equivalent consumption values. Second, it is clear that the cost of the expenditure-and-associated-loan can be calculated by evaluating the expenditure and the loan separately and adding the two results.[27] The social cost of the import spending at t_0 is $100F$ pesos. The value of the loan consists of a 'benefit' of 100 dollars with value $100F$ pesos at t_0 and a 'cost' of $200F$ pesos at t_{12}. The present value of the loan is therefore $100F - 200F\ (1 + d)^{-12} = 100F\ (1 - 2\ (1 + d)^{-12})$. Adding the value of the expenditure and the value of the loan yields a total value of $-200F(1 + d)^{-12}$. Although this example contains exactly offsetting imports and loans in the first year, the principle is quite general. The value of a project can be calculated by evaluating the project as if it were domestically financed and adding to this the value of any tied loan and grant. The next paragraph therefore sets out the formula, corresponding to equation (4) of Section I for a closed economy, that can be used to evaluate a domestically financed project in an open economy. The remainder of the section discusses the evaluation of an external loan.

Consider a project that lasts T years. In year t the project absorbs c_t of domestic resources and m_t of imported resources. The output of the project is now more complicated to describe. Let x_t be the marginal revenue (in pesos) of exports produced by the project, let q_t be the value of import replacements produced by the project and let v_t be the value of the additional output sold or given to domestic users. Further, let e_t be the government's expenditures for domestic resources; m_t is the expenditure for imported resources. Finally, r_t is the marginal revenue of domestic sales (corresponding to $q_t + v_t$) and x_t is the marginal revenue of foreign sales. The value of the project at time t is then the consumers' surplus associated with the additional domestic sales[28] $(v_t - r_t)$ plus the surplus associated with the domestic inputs $(e_t - c_t)$ minus the consumption value of the taxes levied to cover the domestic expenditure deficit $(e_t - r_t)$ $[1 - p + p\,S]$ plus the value of the excess of exports over imports, $(x_t + q_t - m_t)F$. Since all four terms are stated as equivalent consumption values, they can be added and discounted to the present at the social time preference rate. The value of the project is thus

$$V = \sum_{t=0}^{T} \frac{v_t - c_t - p\,(S-1)\,(e_t - r_t) + F\,(x_t + q_t - m_t)}{(1+d)^t} \tag{13}$$

where $F = (1 + \theta)\,[1 + (S - 1)\,(1 - m_c)/(m_t - m_c)]$. Since F is likely to be substantially greater than 1, this gives preference to projects with export earnings or low import content.

The value of a grant-and-loan aid package depends on the value of F and d in the recipient country and the basic characteristics of the grant and loan. A grant-and-loan aid package can be described in terms of the proportion of each dollar received that is to be treated as a grant, the rate of interest and the time schedule of repayments. Let γ be the grant proportion and r the interest rate on the loan component. To be specific, assume that the loan is to be repaid in equal annual payments for N years, starting at the end of year 1. The annual payments, a, must satisfy

$$\sum_{t=1}^{N} a\,(1 + r)^{-t} = 1 - \gamma \tag{14}$$

or

$$a = (1 - \gamma)\,r\,[1 - (1 + r)^{-N}]^{-1}. \tag{15}$$

The value to the recipient of the grant–loan package (per dollar) is the value of the original receipt (one dollar at value F) minus the discounted value of the annual repayments (each of which is a dollars at value $a\,F$). Denoting this value per dollar of financing as L, we have

$$\begin{aligned} L &= F - a\,F \sum_{t=1}^{N} (1 + d)^{-t} \\ &= F - a\,F\,[1 - (1 + d)^{-N}]d^{-1}. \end{aligned} \tag{16}$$

Substituting for a yields

$$L = F\{1 - (1-\gamma)(r/d)[1-(1+d)^{-N}][1-(1+r)^{-N}]^{-1}\}. \quad (17)$$

It is clear from equation (17) that the value of the foreign exchange shadow price ($F > 0$) does not influence whether a loan *per se* has a positive or negative value. F does affect the magnitude of L and therefore influences whether an investment-cum-loan package has positive or negative value.

Equation (17) can also be used to show that alternative grant-and-loan packages with the same present value to the donor can have different values to the recipient. More specifically, in the case in which annual payments are constrained to be constant, changes in the length of the repayment period do affect the relative values to donor and recipient, while changes in the loan interest rate (r) and the grant proportion (γ) do not. To see this, assume that the donor calculates the cost of a loan by discounting future repayments at a rate i that exceeds the subsidised rate r. Then the present value to the donor of the repayments per dollar of loan–grant may be denoted

$$\text{PV}(i) = a \sum_{t=0}^{T} (1+i)^{-t} \quad (18)$$

or, substituting from equation (15) for a and evaluating the sum,

$$\text{PV}(i) = (1-\gamma)(r/i)[1-(1+r)^{-N}]^{-1}[1-(1+i)^{-N}]. \quad (19)$$

Similarly, the present value to the recipient of the repayments may be denoted

$$\text{PV}(d) = a\,F \sum_{t=0}^{T} (1+d)^{-t} \quad (20)$$

A similar substitution yields

$$\text{PV}(d) = F(1-\gamma)(r/d)[1-(1+r)^{-N}]^{-1}[1-(1+d)^{-N}]. \quad (21)$$

The ratio of the present value to the recipient and the present value to the donor is therefore

$$\frac{\text{PV}(d)}{\text{PV}(i)} = F \cdot \frac{i}{d} \cdot \frac{1-(1+i)^{-N}}{1-(1+d)^{-N}} \quad (22)$$

It is clear from equation (22) that the ratio of present values is not influenced by the relative sizes of grant and subsidised loan (γ) or by the loan interest rate (r). The time to maturity is the only loan parameter that affects the relative present values; with $i > d$, it is possible to increase the recipient's value for any given donor value by keeping the repayment period short, i.e. essentially for using grants instead of subsidised loans.

IV. SUMMARY

This paper began by reviewing the method for public-sector project evaluation in an economy with suboptimal private investment. The basic principle of this method is that a project should be valued by the present value of the changes in consumption that result from the project, both directly and indirectly. In particular, the method of financing a project is important because it influences the amount of concurrent private investment.

This approach was extended in Section II to the evaluation of projects in an open economy. The case of a fixed exchange rate was examined explicity. Alternative measures of the shadow price of foreign exchange can be shown to depend on the shadow price of domestic private investment.

Section III applied these principles to the evaluation of projects financed by external grants and loans. The value of a project financed by tied external loans and grants is equal to the sum of the value of that project if domestically financed and the value of the loan–grant package. Specific methods are presented for calculating these two components.

NOTES

1. More formally, if MRS is the marginal rate of substitution between consumption in years $t + 1$ and t, the discount rate, d, is equal to MRS $- 1$. For detailed discussions of the meaning and use of the social time preference rate, see Feldstein [6, 7, 8] and Marglin [13].

2. For simplicity, the discount rate will be assumed to remain constant.

3. It is clear that revenues may differ from benefits if the output is distributed without charge or, more generally, at a price that is less than the maximum that individuals would pay. Cash expenditures (e_t) may differ from social costs (c_t) even when resources are fully employed, if the project imposes externalities or uses resources for which it need not pay.

4. The case in which part of the deficit is financed by borrowing is not considered here; see Feldstein [8].

5. See Feldstein [5] and Marglin [13] for detailed discussions of the calculation of this shadow price. The ideas are latent in early papers by Eckstein [4], Galenson and Leibenstein [9] and Steiner [18].

6. See Marglin [15] and Little and Mirrlees [12] for two different approaches to evaluating G.

7. The assumption that p and g are constant simplifies notation but is of no substantive importance. To relax the assumption it is only necessary to write p_t and g_t in equation (5). The nature of public budgeting is such that g may be high in the first year of a project and low thereafter.

8. It is 'artificially high' because it exceeds the marginal product of labour in agriculture. For the moment it is not relevant whether this reflects union strength, minimum wage legislation or the effect of the higher cost of urban living on the labour supply curve.

9. For an exception to this in the context of open economies, see Balassa and Schydlowsky [3].

10. The problem of valuing inputs is fundamentally different and more complex when unemployment is of the Keynesian type. Non-labour inputs purchased by a project can then be produced with otherwise unemployed labour and idle capital. As Acharya [1] has shown, the input–output method of Haveman and Krutilla [11] is internally inconsistent. It also tries to use a static model to study what is essentially a problem of lags in adjustment and ignores the positive Keynesian multiplier effects.

11. There are two exceptions. First, specifically skilled labour may actually earn a wage that does not exceed its opportunity cost. Second, industrial employment may cause the individual to incur additional costs of a 'consumption' variety; if a is the marginal product of agricultural labour, h the level of consumption of the marginal agricultural worker and k the minimum wage at which that worker would be willing to work in industrial employment, the 'resource' cost of the labour should be valued at $k - (h - a)$, i.e. the worker's supply price minus his previous excess of consumption over production.

12. This result is related to the approach presented in Little and Mirrlees [12].

13. See Bacha and Taylor [2] for a valuable summary, criticism and extension of earlier discussions of the foreign exchange shadow price for use in project analysis. After this paper was completed, a copy of Sandmo and Dreze [16] came to my attention. Although they deal with the same general questions as the current paper, the analyses and results are not really comparable. In particular, Sandmo and Dreze consider only a two-period model. Even in a closed economy this leads to an incorrect decision rule in terms of discounting by a weighted average of interest rates. (For a detailed critique of this type of method, See Feldstein [8].)

14. This includes not only direct imports but also indirect imports used in the production of domestic goods that are used in the project.

15. The measurement of import substitutes should in principle include the direct effect of substitution for a domestically produced good with imported components. The extent to which this type of calculation (and that required by note 14 above) can be done in practice depends on the availability of detailed input–output data.

16. It is therefore inappropriate to value foreign exchange at the rate that would prevail in an optimally managed economy (as suggested by Bacha and Taylor [2]) when the economy is actually far from that point. For a more general discussion of the confusion between 'ideal opportunity cost' and 'predicted opportunity cost', see Feldstein [8].

17. The special problems of different tariff rates on different commodities would increase the complexity of the analysis without changing the basic logic.

18. This need not be a suboptimal policy for the economy. It is equivalent to correctly valuing the currency and imposing a uniform export tariff. Such a policy could be optimal for a country that exports a single commodity for which demand is less than perfectly elastic.

19. The terminology of 'targets' and 'instruments', as well as the specific result about two targets and two instruments, is of course due to Tinbergen [19].

20. The instruments may be two different taxes as discussed in the previous section, or a mix of fiscal and monetary policy.

21. It will be assumed that these propensities are not affected by the project and its financing.

22. If $m_i = m_c$, the two targets cannot be achieved by changing investment and consumption.

23. This is equivalent to the rule proposed by Harberger [10] and Schydlowsky [17].

24. In principle, of course, the government could achieve both domestic and foreign balance without changing investment if it has two instruments that permit it to alter two forms of consumption (with different import contents) and a third instrument to make compensating changes to keep investment constant.

25. Note that, even if aggregate investment is unchanged ($I = 0$), a shift from imported to domestic investment goods imposes a social cost the value of which depends on S.

26. The case of indirect import controls will not be considered explicity, but expression (12) of Section II could be used to define a value of F and the corresponding calculations could be developed.

27. The loans and grants are of course relevant only if they would not have been made in the absence of the project.

28. The import replacement does not constitute *additional* domestic sales and is therefore grouped with the changes in external demand.

REFERENCES

[1] Acharya, S., 'Unemployment, Excess Capacity, and Benefit–Cost Investment Criteria: A Comment', *Review of Economics and Statistics*, LIII 1 (Feb. 1971) 103–5.

[2] Bacha, E., and Taylor, L., 'Foreign Exchange Shadow Prices in Chile: Conflicting Theories and Comparative Evaluations', *Quarterly Journal of Economics*, LXXXV (May 1971) 197–224.

[3] Balassa, B., and Schydlowsky, D., 'Effective Tariffs, Domestic Cost of Foreign Exchange, and the Equilibrium Exchange Rate', *Journal of Political Economy*, LXXVI (May/June 1968) 348–60.

[4] Eckstein, O., 'Investment Criteria for Economic Development and the Theory of Intertemporal Welfare Economics', *Quarterly Journal of Economics*, LXXI (Feb. 1957) 56–85.

[5] Feldstein, M. S., 'Net Social Benefit Calculation and the Public Investment Decision', *Oxford Economic Papers*, XVI (Mar. 1964) 114–31.

[6] ——, 'The Social Time Preference Discount Rate in Cost–Benefit Analysis', *Economic Journal*, LXXIV (June 1964) 360–79.

[7] ——, 'The Derivation of Social Time Preference Rates', *Kyklos*, XVIII (1965) 277–86.

[8] ——, 'Financing in the Evaluation of Public Expenditure' in W. Smith *et al.* (eds.) *Essays in Public Finance and Stabilization Policy* (forthcoming).

[9] Galenson, W., and Leibenstein, H., 'Investment Criteria, Productivity, and Economic Development', *Quarterly Journal of Economics*, LXIX (Aug. 1955) 79–85.

[10] Harberger, A. C., 'Survey of Literature of Cost–Benefit Analysis for Industrial Project Evaluation', paper presented at the United Nations Inter-Regional Symposium in Industrial Project Evaluation (Prague, 1965).

[11] Haveman, R., and Krutilla, J. 'Unemployment, Excess Capacity and Benefit–Cost Investment Criteria', *Review of Economics and Statistics*, XLIX (Nov. 1967) 654–5.

[12] Little, I. M. D., and Mirrlees, J. A., *Manual of Industrial Project Analysis in Developing Countries*, vol. II: *Social Cost–Benefit Analysis* (Paris: O.E.C.D., 1969).

[13] Marglin, S. A., 'The Social Rate of Discount and the Optimal Rate of Investment', *Quarterly Journal of Economics*, LXXVII (Feb. 1963) 95–111.

[14] ——, 'The Opportunity Costs of Public Investment', *Quarterly Journal of Economics*, LXXVII (May 1963) 274–89.

[15] ——, *Approaches to Dynamic Investment Planning* (Amsterdam: North-Holland Publishing Company, 1963).

[16] Sandmo, A., and Dreze, J., 'Discount Rates for Public Investment in Closed and Open Economies', CORE Discussion Paper No. 7025 (Louvain, Belgium, Aug. 1970).

[17] Schydlowsky, D. M., 'On the Choice of a Shadow Price for Foreign Exchange', Economic Development Report No. 108, Development Advisory Service, Harvard University (Cambridge, Mass., 1968).

[18] Steiner, P. O., 'Choosing among Alternative Public Investments in the Water Resource Field', *American Economic Review*, XLIX (Dec. 1969) 893–916.

[19] Tinbergen, J., *On the Theory of Economic Policy* (Amsterdam: North-Holland Publishing Company, 1963).

2

Public Goods and Multi-Level Government*

JOHN G. HEAD

I. INTRODUCTION

ONE of the most striking features of the public finance literature of the past two decades has been the development of the modern theory of public goods, due largely to the pioneering contributions of Musgrave, Samuelson and Buchanan.[1] Most of the relevant analysis has been devoted to such problems as the clarification of the basic theoretical concepts, the demonstration of market failure in public goods supply and the possibility of centralised political provision. Some attempt has, however, been made, led by Tiebout, Williams, Breton and Buchanan, to develop the implications of the theory for multi-level government.[2] It is the aim of the present paper to explore some of these implications.

We shall begin, in Section II, with a brief discussion of the public goods concept. In Section III we shall discuss some implications for optimal fiscal decentralisation in the absence of spillovers. In Section IV we shall explore the fiscal co-ordination problems which arise when public goods benefits spill over. In Section V we shall discuss the special problem of grants to poor unit governments. Section VI contains a brief discussion of some of the wider implications of the theory.

II. THE CONCEPT OF PUBLIC GOODS

A pure public good, in the original formulations of Samuelson and Musgrave, is one which must be consumed in equal amounts by all. The Polaris submarine deterrent provides a good example. Such a good has two main characteristics. The first is 'joint supply', in the special sense that, once it is supplied to one person, equal quantities of identical-quality services can be made available to

* My interest in this topic began with a paper I prepared while a member of Lady Hicks's seminar on 'The Economic Functions of Government' at Oxford, 1955–7. I am indebted to Geoff Brennan and Tom McGuire for helpful comments.

other persons without limit at no extra cost. The second is 'impossibility of exclusion': if the service is supplied to one person, it *cannot be withheld* from any other person wishing to consume it. A third characteristic, of somewhat less importance in the present context, is non-rejectability: once the service is supplied, it must be fully and equally consumed by all, including those who would if possible reject it.

It is easy to show that the market mechanism must fail dramatically in the supply of a pure public good, owing mainly to the problem of impossibility of exclusion. The joint supply characteristic also creates complicated differential pricing requirements, which no decentralised market mechanism can handle effectively. Political provision offers, by comparison, significant advantages, notably a crude exclusion device in the form of the tax power, though significant problems undoubtedly remain.[3]

The concept of a pure public good clearly represents an extreme polar case of limited empirical significance. The concept can, however, readily be generalised; and similar, though less dramatic, conclusions regarding market failure and political provision can be shown to hold for impure public goods.

The Samuelsonian joint supply characteristic can be generalised in two distinct dimensions. In the first place it is common for the benefits of a joint good to taper off in some pattern from the point of input, such as fire protection which diminishes with distance from the fire station. Other examples readily spring to mind in such areas as police services, emergency hospital services, reactional services, etc. For a given population distributed in a given pattern over a given area, the benefits from such a service are not equal, as with the Polaris submarine deterrent, but vary with distance from the input unit. The location of the input unit, such as the fire station, the hospital or the park, may be fixed, especially in the short run, but is in general variable, at least in the long run. Different consumers and producers will also be variously affected by other characteristics of the input unit; a given police force may be better trained and equipped to deal with some types of crime than with others.[4]

The joint supply characteristic can be generalised in a second and quite distinct dimension, as we envisage a steady increase in the population of a given area with no change in the general pattern of distribution. For a fixed facility (fire brigade, hospital establishment, park service, etc.) of given capacity, it is evident that, in contrast to the Polaris submarine deterrent, it is *only up to a certain point* that the same standard of service can be supplied to additional persons without extra cost. Beyond that point, congestion sets in and the standard of service deteriorates.[5]

The second public goods characteristic of 'impossibility of exclusion' is easily seen to be a special and extreme case of the general Pigovian concept of external economies.[6] This characteristic can therefore readily be generalised to cover empirically more significant cases such as that in which prices could readily be charged for *some but not all* of the benefits of a particular service. Examples might include the 'vocational' as against the 'cultural' benefits of educational services, and public health services such as a vaccination programme. The externalities involved will generally have both spatial and other dimensions. In the case of education, for example, the cultural externalities may spill over into neighbouring areas as a result of migration.

By means of these various generalisations the public goods concept can be expanded to encompass a broad spectrum of services all exhibiting important joint supply or non-exclusion characteristics, and posing varying but significant market failure problems and possibilities for public provision.

III. PUBLIC GOODS AND FISCAL DECENTRALISATION

Different levels of government are distinguished conventionally by the scope of the geographical area over which their respective jurisdictions extend. Central government jurisdiction extends by definition over the entire area under consideration. Regional governments administer non-overlapping subsections of the 'country'. Local governments exercise responsibility over non-overlapping areas within a region. Such governments are variously denominated in practice under different systems, federal and unitary, and in principle a much more elaborately tiered structure can readily be imagined.[7] In practice, of course, non-economic factors have exercised considerable influence on the precise structure of multi-level government, and constitutional and other rigidities impede change. Assuming away all these problems, it is, however, interesting to consider how a system of multi-level government should be structured from the point of view of ensuring an efficient supply of the many varieties of public goods, pure and impure. For the purposes of the present section we shall assume artificially that the benefits from public goods supply in a given jurisdiction do not extend (are neither sold nor spill over) to neighbouring jurisdictions.

In this context the crucial dimensions of the public goods concept are clearly those relating to area and population. In the case of a pure public good such as the Polaris submarine deterrent, provision should clearly be assigned to a single unit of government with jurisdiction over the entire area and population under consideration. The service does not taper off with area covered, and additional persons can be supplied at no extra cost. *Per capita* cost is therefore minimised by central government provision. (Even this, of course, is no absolute minimum, since with a pure public good *per capita* cost falls without limit and optimum population size is literally infinite.[8]) Pareto-optimal provision clearly also requires full knowledge of individual preference functions by the central planning agency. The preference-revelation problems involved in practice are a familiar theme in the modern public goods literature.[9]

In a world polarised between pure public goods and pure private goods, it is therefore evident that multi-level government has no economic place. Private goods should be provided by decentralised market institutions and public goods by centralised political institutions, chosen to ensure the best possible approximation to full preference revelation. As we have already seen, however, the pure public good concept is of very limited empirical significance. When the concept is generalised along the lines suggested in Section II, we find a considerable variety of 'impure' goods for which public provision may be appropriate.

When we depart from the pure public goods concept, a possible case for lower-level or 'multi-branch' provision is not difficult to construct. This is perhaps most clearly seen in a simple case in which a given and *completely immobile* population with the same tastes and incomes is distributed uniformly over a given area. Assume a very simple polar case of a regional or local public good, which is purely public only over a *limited area* (which we shall assume to be a simple fraction of the total area of the country). The same level of service can be extended to additional households, and over a wider area, up to this given limit without extra cost. Beyond this limited area the benefit 'tapers off' suddenly to zero. In such a case the public good must be provided by a number of regional or local governments (or 'branches', if provision is assigned initially to a single agency).

The country should simply be divided into non-overlapping jurisdictions of a size equal to the technologically fixed benefit area for the public good. In this way the *per capita* cost of providing a uniform Pareto-optimal level of service throughout the country is clearly minimised.

Somewhat more realistically, we might alternatively assume no rigid area limit to the extension of benefits, but suppose instead that some extra cost is necessarily involved as a given and uniform level of service is extended to additional households over a wider area. Following Tiebout, it might, for example, be assumed that *per capita* cost per unit of service (unit cost per resident) falls initially as a larger area and population are covered, but subsequently rises, owing, for example, to the impact of transport costs. Combining this relationship with, say, a conventional ∪-shaped relationship between unit cost and service level (for given area and population), a cost surface is obtained from which, with the aid of the preference functions, the *least-cost jurisdiction* for the optimal level of service can readily be determined.[10] (It is assumed that there is no spillover of benefit beyond the boundaries of the least-cost jurisdiction.) Again, a lower-level government or multi-branch agency will be required to provide a uniform Pareto-optimal level of service throughout the country.

It is not difficult to generalise this second example to cover the empirically much more significant case in which the level of service over the benefit area is not uniform but tapers off from some point of input, as in the case of fire protection or recreational services. With given cost and demand conditions, the maximisation of surplus in relation to cost will require the establishment of a number of service branches distinguished by points of input (e.g. anti-missile sites, fire stations, police stations, hospitals, parks, etc.) at regular intervals over the area under consideration. Each local branch would ideally provide the same tapering pattern of service over a least-cost jurisdiction for that Pareto-optimal standard of service.[11]

When the simplifying assumptions of uniform tastes, incomes and population distribution are relaxed, the country-wide uniformities in Pareto-optimal service standards and least-cost jurisdictions disappear. Higher standards of service should be provided in high-taste, high-income areas; and the ideal jurisdiction will vary in size, depending upon the precise cost function for the particular service, from one part of the country to another. Within a given jurisdiction the possibilities of discrimination in the case of 'tapering' services should be fully exploited to provide a higher level of service to clusters of high-taste, high-income households by appropriate location of the relevant input units (fire station, park, etc.).[12]

It should be noted that with the taste, income and area homogeneities previously assumed, there is no clear case for any *genuine delegation of political decision-making powers* to the local governments or branches, which need merely administer centralised decisions regarding the level of service provision.[13] We have so far justified only decentralised 'production', not decentralised 'provision' in the strict public finance sense. When these uniformities are relaxed and effective preferences vary widely, the resulting problems may well justify genuine decentralisation of political decision-making. In particular, preference-revelation problems, together with constitutional or quasi-constitutional rigidities, such as geographically non-discriminatory taxation, may drastically limit the scope for inter-regional variation in service levels within a given jurisdiction. As a result, there may be obvious gains to be derived from political decentralisation under a wide variety of circumstances.[14] This possibility is particularly evident, however, if we make the reasonable assumption that preferences tend to be much more homogeneous *within* given regions and localities than *between* them.[15] In this situation the differing preferences of different regions and localities can clearly be satisfied only under appropriately decentralised political decision-making. An optimal structure of multi-level government thus takes on a more 'federal' and less 'unitary' appearance.

A crucial assumption which we have so far retained is that the population is *completely immobile*. Relaxation of this assumption opens up interesting new possibilities. For example, in the very simple polar case of a regional or local public good, which is purely public only over a limited area, the same standard of service can be extended to additional persons at no extra cost. *Per capita* cost could therefore be further reduced by concentrating population through migration. Minimum *per capita* cost would require that the whole population be concentrated in a single jurisdiction. This case is probably of limited empirical significance, but it may have some validity for a service such as damage limitation through anti-missile defence. For overall efficiency, possible reductions in *per capita* cost of public goods achieved through population concentration must of course be balanced against possible increases in the cost of private goods production due to diminishing returns.[16]

As we have already seen, the extreme joint supply characteristic can readily be generalised to allow for congestion phenomena such that, beyond a point, the same standard of service can be supplied to additional persons in a given area only at some extra cost. Even here it is quite possible that *per capita* cost could be significantly reduced by increased population concentration. Beyond a point, however, the total cost of maintaining a given level of service may rise so steeply that *per capita* cost increases.[17] As density is increased, a new least-cost jurisdiction may be determined corresponding to a new and presumably somewhat higher optimal service level.

When public goods preferences vary widely (but incomes are similar), population mobility offers the further interesting possibility that an initial optimum may be improved by the regrouping of population in accordance with public goods preferences. Instead of having to consume a small volume of a given local public good in a jurisdiction dominated by low-demand people, a minority with high public goods demand may be able to move to another area dominated by high-demand people in which their preferences will clearly be better satisfied. It should be stressed that this point holds even under omniscient planning, where local public goods supply is initially Pareto-optimal in each jurisdiction with tax-prices calculated on strict marginal benefit principles.

The possible advantages are, however, greatly increased when the unrealistic assumption of omniscient planning is relaxed and the preference-revelation problems in a world of diverse preferences are explicitly recognised. Thus, because of preference-revelation problems, a low-demand person may find himself paying the same high tax rates as high-demand people for the large volume of public good supplied in a predominantly high-demand area. This inefficiency in initial fiscal arrangements can, however, be removed if our low-demand person can move to a low-demand, low-tax jurisdiction. More generally, when combined with a sufficient variety in the volume and mix of public goods available in different local jurisdictions, population mobility may significantly improve resource allocation as people 'vote on foot' by moving to jurisidictions in which their public goods preferences are most fully satisfied. As Tiebout first pointed out, population mobility thus offers a preference-revelation mechanism for local public goods which is not available for central public goods such as the Polaris submarine deterrent and applies only to a limited degree in the case of regional public goods for which the optimal number of jurisdictions is relatively small.[18]

When differences in income are allowed for, certain complications arise. High-income jurisdictions could generally be expected to offer a given standard of service at lower rates of tax. Low-income households would, of course, be attracted by these low tax rates. Various types of strategic behaviour can be expected as high-income enclaves attempt to limit the entry of 'undesirables', and low-income jurisdictions may find it necessary to depart from traditional tax principles of ability to pay and even from marginal benefit taxation in an attempt to retain high-income residents.[19] The efficiency of the Tiebout mechanism is in any case somewhat less than perfect, owing, for example, to limited population mobility and the existence of uncompensated spillovers associated with population movement.[20] On balance, however, the case for genuine decentralisation of political decision-making is clearly strengthened to the extent that the Tiebout mechanism is operative.[21]

Summarising the foregoing discussion, we see that when the concept of a public good is generalised to cover the broad spectrum of goods exhibiting varying but significant degrees of the crucial joint supply and non-exclusion characteristics, some degree of fiscal decentralisation is clearly required. Some goods, like national defence, approximate the concept of a central public good and should be provided by a one-branch agency or central government. Others may be regional public goods requiring a limited number of regional branches or governments for optimal provision. University education, highways and certain public health measures may be examples. Others again, like police and fire protection, are local public goods requiring a relatively very large number of local governments or agencies. Ideally, an even more elaborate structure might well be required with a different 'level' responsible for each relevant category of public good. The degree to which effective political decision-making power should be delegated to local units should depend upon the possible advantages to be derived in terms of preference revelation, which may be quite significant where taste and area heterogeneity is great. Where this is not the case, local units may simply be required to administer centralised decisions regarding the level of service provision.

IV. PUBLIC GOODS AND FISCAL CO-ORDINATION

The arguments of the preceding section suggest that efficiency in public goods supply may well require a considerable degree of genuine decentralisation of political decision-making powers to regional and local units. An important simplifying assumption underlying the discussion has, however, been that the benefits from public goods supply in a given jurisdiction do not extend into neighbouring jurisdictions. It remains to consider how the analysis is affected when this assumption is relaxed.[22]

The case for centralised provision would evidently be seriously undermined if we were to assume that, even though some benefits might be extended to neighbouring jurisdictions at little or no extra cost, impossibility of exclusion does not apply for non-residents. Even though non-exclusion applies for residents, exclusion is possible for non-residents and fees can be charged.

In general, however, it must be recognised that where it is very difficult, costly or inefficient to price-exclude households within a given locality, there will usually be some unchargeable spillover of service to the residents of other localities. Some part of the benefit may spill over directly, as in the case of pollution control or mosquito spraying; it may spill over through commuting or migration, as in the case of education, public health or road services; it may spill over through trade, as in the case of cost-reducing public intermediate goods. Some spillovers of benefit are therefore inevitable even with a system of optimal boundaries designed in accordance with the general principles discussed in the preceding section. The problem is, however, enormously more significant in the case of any actual system of multi-level government, with local and regional boundaries determined historically with little regard for economic considerations. Generalised non-exclusion problems, which lead us to predict the failure of decentralised market institutions, therefore remain to plague genuinely (and, *a fortiori*, non-optimally) decentralised political institutions.

Indeed, the existence and geographical scope of benefit spillovers, i.e. the non-exclusion characteristic, comes to replace *per capita* cost (i.e. joint supply) as the essential foundation of the case for centralised provision in the arguments of the preceding section.[23] In the case of a pure public good, for example, the benefits spill over without geographical limit, and decentralised political institutions may fail almost completely in large-number cases. If, however, exclusion applies and the benefits can be sold to non-residents, jointness alone provides no clear case for central provision.

By contrast, jointness or cost considerations emerge as directly relevant mainly for questions of production rather than provision in the strict sense. *Per capita* cost or jointness may, for example, justify a production unit serving a number of different jurisdictions. This is the point, first noted by Stigler and subsequently stressed by other writers, that 'economies of scale' are of only limited relevance to the design of optimal boundaries for public goods provision, at least if we abstract from various forms of organisational rigidity.[24] Jointness may, however, play an important indirect role, notably in extreme cases where cost considerations require a high degree of inter-regional uniformity in service standards, thus eliminating one major disadvantage of centralised provision.

The distorting effects of benefit spillovers can be quite subtle and complicated. Take, for example, the simple case of taste, income and area uniformity (and complete immobility), in which, as we saw in the preceding section, the same standard of local government service should clearly be provided throughout the country. Any spillovers in this case will be symmetrical, with spill-outs precisely matching spill-ins for any given jurisdiction. It is not true, however, as is sometimes suggested,[25] that such externalities necessarily cancel each other out leaving no net allocative distortion. Ignoring income effects, the spill-out will probably vary directly with own output, thus in effect creating a distorting substitution effect against local production. The receipt of an equivalent spill-in may not, however, create an offsetting substitution effect. In fact there will be no offset whatever if, as may well be the case, the amount of the spill-in is completely independent of own output. A suboptimal standard of service should therefore be expected.[26]

Further complications arise when the assumption of inter-area taste and income uniformity is relaxed and income effects are allowed for. Even retaining the assumption of symmetrical benefit spillover functions with the asymmetrical substitution effects assumed above, it becomes possible that total output and consumption of the local public good for the country as a whole may be *larger* than in the absence of spillovers – but still not Pareto-optimal.[27]

In any general analysis the assumption of symmetrical benefit spillover functions must clearly be abandoned. As a result it must be recognised that production in one local jurisdiction may benefit residents in another, but not vice versa. For example, because of prevailing winds, pollution control measures in A may benefit B's residents, but no reciprocal relationship may hold. Or – at least in the relevant ranges of production and consumption – education, public health or urban renewal measures in poverty-striken area C may greatly benefit residents of D, with only a weak reciprocal relationship for corresponding measures in D. In such cases, the distortion takes the form of a significant *relative* underexpansion of service provision in the area generating the larger spillover. By distorting the location of 'production', the effect of the spillover may be to cause a *larger volume of resources* to be devoted to the production of a *lower standard of service* over the country as a whole.[28]

A related problem which has been much discussed emerges in the Tiebout model of residential mobility, where high-income enclaves are able not merely to hive themselves off from a larger (city) unit, but may, by commuting, continue to receive the benefits of many city services as uncompensated spillovers. As a result the pattern of net spillovers may be highly asymmetrical between city and suburbs, with consequent underexpansion of city services and charges of suburban exploitation of the city.[29]

As with the market failure theorems of public goods analysis, the above discussion of the distortions to be expected under genuinely decentralised political institutions strictly applies only where large numbers of units (here local governments) are involved. Where, for example, what we have called 'regional' public goods are involved, the number of governments potentially concerned, at least under optimal decentralisation, is relatively small. Even in the case of local public goods, where the total number of units is much larger, the spillover benefits from local provision may be confined to a small number of contiguous units. In these small-number cases, if the spillover benefits are significant, the political units involved have an obvious incentive to get together and agree on some method of compensation for spillovers to avoid underprovision. The necessary degree of 'co-ordination' of the various area governments on a given 'level' can here be achieved through voluntary agreement.[30]

This is not, however, to suggest that the voluntaristic solution is entirely without problems. Even in the simplest conceivable case of a non-reciprocal spillover involving just two contiguous units, bargaining difficulties may obviously arise.[31] Problems of strategic behaviour are likely to be particularly severe in the case of spillovers which are both reciprocal and non-separable. Here the amount of the spill-in varies with the level of local provision, as may well be the case with education, and the equilibrium level of service for each local unit involved depends reciprocally upon the standard of service provided by the other units. Such small-number preference-revelation problems may possibly be reduced by the voluntary amalgamation of adjacent units.[32] Amalgamation may therefore be economically justified even though service provision over the amalgamated jurisdiction would tend in other respects to be more costly, as under an initially optimal system of boundaries determined in accordance with the analysis of the preceding section.

These voluntaristic procedures break down completely where the number of local units involved in a particular spillover is large. Large-number preference-revelation problems arise, as the benefits from a voluntary agreement embracing all parties, seen from the point of view of a single unit, come to depend less and less on own participation.[33] Some form of compulsion, such as the 'Pigovian' alternative of taxes and subsidies administered by a higher-level government or central agency, must therefore be considered. In an intergovernmental context, genuine large-number cases are likely to be significant only under a rigid and grossly non-optimal balkanised structure of multi-level government. A Pigovian solution might, however, also be considered in small-number cases, in view of the bargaining difficulties encountered under voluntaristic procedures.

As Pigou himself has warned, the tax–subsidy approach is likewise not without problems. Unless the relevant grants and taxes are appropriately designed and calculated, the system may do more harm than good.[34] Information problems arise, as can readily be seen by considering the information requirements for an ideal grant system.

The simplest case, already mentioned above, would seem to be that of a non-reciprocal spillover of service from one local government unit A to a neighbouring unit B and related to output by A. Assuming that no voluntary compensation agreement is possible, the distortion could be corrected if a higher level of government or centralised agency could arrange to pay a 'conditional matching grant' to local government A, related to output of the service, with a uniform 'matching' rate determined by the marginal collective benefit to B's citizens at the optimum level of output. In order to do this, the higher-level government must have sufficient knowledge of the cost function for the service, the spillover function, and the demand functions in A and B, to be able to determine the optimum level of output for the service and the marginal benefit to B at that level of output. Under genuinely decentralised political decision-making such information may not be at all readily available to a higher level of government. Small-number preference-revelation problems may arise as each local unit attempts to obtain a more favourable or less unfavourable grant arrangement.[35]

The problem is even more complicated in the case of reciprocal and non-separable spillovers, where, as we have seen, the equilibrium level of service for each local unit depends reciprocally upon the level of service provided by the other. In this situation there is in general no unique equilibrium under independent adjustment, and actual service levels will depend upon the strategies adopted by each unit. Design of an optimal grant structure here requires knowledge of local strategies in response to alternative grant policies, in addition to the relevant cost, spillover and demand functions.[36]

Where a number of local units are involved in a given spillover relationship, or where the number of spillover relationships is large, the information requirements are still more demanding, as the number of cost, spillover and demand functions which must be estimated is correspondingly greater. At best, therefore, only a very crude approximation to an ideally efficient grant scheme could possibly be expected.

It is interesting to notice that a conditional grant without 'matching' provisions is in general totally inadequate for this purpose. Except in very special cases of corner solutions, such a grant does not have the necessary stimulating substitution effect on service provision, but only an income effect. The effect of the grant is therefore purely redistributive and no different from that of a completely unconditional grant or one tied to some other local service generating no spillovers. It is true that a somewhat larger non-matching grant can generally be found which would have the same net stimulating effect on service provision as a matching grant of given revenue cost. The corrective substitution effect of the matching grant is, however, required to remove the disturbance to the optimum conditions represented by the divergence between marginal local benefit and marginal social benefit.[37]

Up to this point we have analysed the spillover problem under multi-level government on the assumption of genuinely decentralised political decision-making. As we saw in the preceding section, an alternative structure of decentralized provision can readily be imagined in which the local units are mere branches of a central agency, and are required to administer centralised decisions regarding the appropriate level of service provision for each unit. The use of centralised directives is, of course, a possible alternative to the voluntary agreements, amalgamations and the Pigovian grant system which we have just discussed. In this connection it is interesting to observe that the information requirements for an efficient system of uniform-rate conditional matching grants administered by a higher-level government are identical to those for an efficient system of centralised directives. In the simple case of a non-reciprocal spillover from one local government unit A to a neighbouring unit B, the design of an ideal grant requires the determination of the optimal level of output for the service in A in order to calculate the marginal spillover benefit to B at that level of output. But if the optimal level of service provision in A can be determined, a centralised directive could simply be issued to establish A's output at the optimal level. In the absence of constitutional rigidities, it would therefore seem pointless to bother with the refinements of a Pigovian grant system.[38]

Summarising the above discussion, we see that when spillovers are significant, as they may be even under optimal boundaries, some form of co-ordination of local units is required for optimal supply of local public goods. Such co-ordination may be possible on a purely voluntaristic basis through compensation or amalgamation agreements. Alternatively, a Pigovian system of corrective grants administered by a 'higher level of government' may be employed. A fourth and final possibility is a system of centralised directives. All these co-ordination devices involve costs which vary with the nature of the spillover and the number of local units involved. From an efficiency point of view the least costly approach should obviously be chosen, though the comparison may frequently be close and difficult.

In general, it seems clear that the efficiency case for genuine decentralisation of political decision-making in local or regional public goods supply is weakened by the existence of significant spillovers. It is not, however, completely demolished, since the benefits in terms of preference revelation for local public goods may well justify a combination of local decision-making and a voluntaristic compensation or Pigovian co-ordination device in preference to central provision. Only where there is considerable inter-area uniformity of demands for local public goods, or in special cases of extreme jointness where cost considerations either require or heavily favour a high degree of uniformity of consumption standards, do we find a clear case for a higher-level monopoly of effective political decision-making to internalise significant spillovers. In the more general case, optimal boundaries for political decision-making should be determined by balancing the advantages of a small unit in terms of preference revelation for local public goods against the advantages of a larger unit in terms of minimising spillovers and the consequent need for costly and inaccurate co-ordination devices.[39]

In order to justify a relatively simple three- or four-level structure of multi-level government on the basis of the factors so far considered, we should evidently have to assume a significant clustering in the spectrum of public goods in terms of the geographical scope of spillovers, preference homogeneities and jointness, suitably combined.[40] There seems, however, to be little justification for such an assumption. Indeed, even this assumption would not generally be sufficient, as a variety of single-purpose governments on a given level might in principle offer scope for a more detailed registration of voter preferences. Other factors, such as voter information costs, opportunities for log-rolling or political trading and administrative economies, may, however, help to justify something like the political conglomerates we observe in practice.[41]

V. PUBLIC GOODS AND FISCAL EQUALISATION

Grants to low-income regional or local governments have traditionally been justified in the literature mainly on grounds of equity. The best-known and most sophisticated approach is that of Buchanan, who attempts to show that a system of grants to low-income units can be derived from the fundamental horizontal equity principle that equals should be treated equally.[42] Buchanan begins by assuming that all governments at all levels treat equals equally *within their own jurisdictions*, both on the tax side and on the benefit side. He then proceeds to demonstrate that the fiscal residuum (benefits minus taxes) of individuals residing in low-income areas will be smaller than that of their equals in high-income areas, provided only that the budgets of the regional or local governments are redistributive. He concludes that unconditional grants to poor governments, administered by an appropriate higher-level government, may provide the best feasible means of reducing these inequalities. Efficiency considerations are not stressed, but the important point is made that, if the private-sector allocation of resources is initially ideal, the introduction of an effectively decentralised fiscal system provides an allocatively distorting incentive to factor flows out of low-income jurisdictions. Equalising grants would serve to reduce this incentive.[43]

Both the equity and efficiency aspects of Buchanan's analysis have been criticised. The well-known Scott–Buchanan debate focused, for example, on the treatment of private-sector allocation.[44] For our present purposes, however, we shall confine ourselves to the treatment of public-sector benefits. In his original formulation, total spending by each government is simply distributed over the relevant citizens in proportion to the assumed (equal) sharing basis, and the resulting money amount is taken as the measure of total individual benefit. In general, however, this method of benefit imputation has a clear rationale only in the case of welfare payments. In the case of public goods, such as health and education services, it becomes at best a mere 'cost imputation' and could not conceivably serve as a measure of individual benefits received.

Two of Buchanan's major propositions seem, however, to depend crucially on this simple approach to benefit imputation. The first is that an individual will be indifferent between two jurisdictions in which his fiscal residuum is the same even though the level of public service provided is quite different. The second, which is simply a special case of the first, is that if no redistribution is attempted and taxes are imposed on a strict benefit basis in proportion to benefits received, fiscal residua in different jurisdictions will be equal at zero. In both cases there is therefore no horizontal inequity and no distorting incentive to factor movement.[45]

In fact, as Buchanan himself points out in a subsequent paper, fiscal residua based on cost imputations must, in the case of public goods, be sharply distinguished from a true measure of taxpayer's surplus.[46] Equality of fiscal residua at zero, or at any other value, may conceal substantial differences in taxpayer's surplus. In any relevant welfare sense there may therefore be both horizontal inequities and incentives to factor movement where fiscal residua are equalised.[47] Except perhaps to the extent that public services take the form of welfare payments, no clear justification for fiscal equalisation in terms of 'residua' therefore emerges.

It might be thought that if the concept of the fiscal residuum was to be replaced by that of taxpayer's surplus, the original propositions might still hold. Public goods analysis suggests, however, that substantial modifications may be necessary. Thus, for example, it has become clear that benefit taxation can only be interpreted meaningfully in terms of an equality of *marginal* benefit and *marginal* taxation. Under strict benefit taxation by all governments, taxpayer's surplus would not therefore be equalised at zero or indeed at any other figure. The second proposition must therefore be completely abandoned.[48]

More fundamentally, however, public goods analysis casts some doubt on the basic proposition that the taxpayer's surplus of equals in different jurisdictions should be equalised. In particular, although this objective may well be appropriate from the point of view of equity, it is doubtful whether it can be justified from the point of view of efficiency.[49]

As in the case of the fiscal residuum, the taxpayer's surplus can generally be expected to be greater in high-income than in low-income jurisdictions. Even assuming a Pareto-optimal supply of local public goods with taxes based on strict marginalist benefit principles, it is still generally true that a high-income jurisdiction will tend to provide a higher level of service at somewhat lower rates of tax. If, Lindahl-like, we can ignore differences in tastes for public goods, the basic requirement is simply some positive elasticity of the marginal utility of income (or private good) schedule. As in Buchanan's original model, individuals in low-income areas would therefore have a fiscal incentive to move to high-income areas.

From the point of view of public goods supply, however, it is not at all obvious that such movement is necessarily inefficient. This is particularly evident in the simple polar case of a pure local public good where additional households can be provided with the same level of service at no extra cost. *Per capita* cost, and hence the tax rate in a high-income jurisdiction, could therefore be lowered as the result of an inflow of population from a low-income jurisdiction. Indeed, as we have already seen, minimum *per capita* cost of local public goods supply would here require that the whole population of the country be concentrated in a single local government area; though population immobility and considerations of efficiency in private goods production under diminishing returns no doubt rule this out as an overall allocative objective.[50]

The essential point, however, is that population movement produces spillovers on the cost side of public goods supply. People attracted to a high-income jurisdiction by the greater taxpayer's surplus take no account of the reduced cost of public goods supply and still lower tax rates for existing residents which their presence makes possible. If, therefore, we were to begin with an inter-jurisdictional distribution of population determined largely by considerations of efficiency in private goods supply, the efficient provision of local public goods may well require the preservation or even some widening of differentials in taxpayer's surplus between low- and high-income jurisdictions. Here there is no efficiency case for fiscal equalisation.

This conclusion is to some extent modified when the polar concept of a local or regional public good is generalised to allow for congestion phenomena. Beyond a point the addition of further residents, attracted by the higher taxpayer's surplus in a high-income jurisdiction, may cause *per capita* cost to rise. Migration may thus produce a spillover cost rather than a spillover benefit in the high-income area. The prospective migrant takes no account of the resulting increase in costs and taxes for existing residents, and migration may therefore tend to be excessive. If, say, for constitutional reasons, it is necessary to avoid formal fiscal or other barriers to internal migration, a fiscal equalisation grant might in principle be used to offset any distorting tendency. The aim of such a grant would be to narrow initial taxpayer's surplus differentials just sufficiently to compensate for the externality.[51]

Considerations of efficiency in the supply of local or regional public goods therefore suggest a possible case for some measure of fiscal equalisation between high- and low-income units. The relevant circumstances are, however, quite narrowly restricted, and the degree of equalisation justified on these grounds would fall far short of the original Buchanan conception of full equality of either fiscal residuum or taxpayer's surplus.

VI. PUBLIC GOODS AND OTHER FUNCTIONS

The discussion of the preceding sections has focused attention on the traditional and narrowly economic allocation branch problems which have been the central concern of modern public goods theory. The analysis can, however, be considerably extended by further generalisation of the public goods concept.

To begin with, it is possible to take account of some of the most important 'non-economic' factors which complicate the application of economic analysis to problems of multi-level government. For example, the previous discussion deliberately abstracted from troublesome problems of local or regional nationalism. Regions or localities with distinctive historical, ethnic, linguistic, religious or cultural background commonly show great concern with the preservation or enhancement of local or regional identity. In such cases 'group identity' can obviously be regarded as a local or regional public good in a generalised sense. Since a high degree of political autonomy may be essential to the preservation of group identity, decentralisation of political decision-making may legitimately be extended well beyond what might seem justified by narrowly economic considerations.[52]

It is also possible to extend the analysis into other branches of the well-known Musgrave trinity.[53] Following Baumol, economic stabilisation can be regarded as a generalised externality or public goods problem with an important spatial dimension. The anti-recession fiscal policies of one local unit, for example, would generally provide significant spillover benefits in the form of increased income and employment in neighbouring localities. The relevant multiplier (and induced investment effects) would be greater at the regional than at the local level, and greater again at the national level. Precisely analogous arguments hold for the corresponding anti-inflationary policies. Effective fiscal stabilisation policy is therefore out of the question at the local level, would at least require a very high degree of voluntary co-ordination at the regional level, and is evidently best performed by the central government. This is not, of course, to suggest that such policies should not take account of the uneven regional or local incidence of economic instability.

Even the redistribution function can to some degree be regarded as a generalised public goods problem. Middle- and upper-income individuals derive satisfaction from the relief of poverty, and charitable donations by one person therefore provide external benefits to others.[54] Under these circumstances the relief of poverty by redistributive fiscal measures in one locality may provide spillover benefits to better-off sections of the community across the country.[55] There is therefore a strong case here for assigning basic responsibility for the redistributive function to higher-level government. A similar argument can obviously be used to justify a programme of redistributive grants to low-income provinces and localities administered by higher levels of government. Much so-called 'regional policy' can also be justified in the same way. Where, however, the benefits of redistributive measures in a given locality are confined largely to middle- and upper-income residents of the same locality, redistribution takes on the characteristics of a local public good and lower-level provision may be justified.[56]

Fiscal harmonisation too is a generalised public goods problem. In the absence of some form of central co-ordination, including an appropriate assignment of the various tax types to the different levels of government, tax competition between different localities may cause serious misallocation of resources, both in the public sector and in the private sector. A cut in income-tax rates by one locality may inflict heavy external costs on other localities by attracting mobile capital or skilled labour; or, with mutually destructive retaliation, the result may be little change in private-sector allocation, but a massive starvation of the public sector. Central co-ordination of local and regional tax rates, and higher-level control of inter-regionally more potent tax sources such as the income taxes, find much of their justification here.

Some of the functions of multi-level government are admittedly relatively less amenable to public goods analysis than others. This is particularly true of those functions which lie in part outside the consumer-sovereignty tradition of modern public goods theory. The general redistributive function provides the most important example. In Musgrave's classic discussion the concept of a merit good is employed to epitomise these further problems.[57] In contrast to the public good, the central problem here is that, owing to ignorance or irrationality, individual preferences may be distorted and unacceptable. Some services, such as health and education or the control of additive drugs, may exhibit *both* public goods and merit goods characteristics. In the traditional literature on intergovernmental fiscal relations, strong merit goods overtones are frequently to be detected in arguments for specific grants-in-aid to lower levels of government. Although it is true that many alleged merit goods problems can be reformulated in terms of a generalised externality or public goods concept, not least in the field of intergovernmental fiscal relations, it may be doubted whether all such problems can be adequately explained in this way.[58]

The broader implications of the theory of public goods for the problems of multi-level government should be evident from the foregoing discussion. There are relatively few problems in the design of a fiscal constitution for multi-level government which cannot be significantly illuminated by the application of modern public goods analysis.

REFERENCES

1. See, in particular, R. A. Musgrave, *Theory of Public Finance* (New York: McGraw-Hill, 1959); P. A. Samuelson, 'The Pure Theory of Public Expenditure', *Review of Economics and Statistics* (1954); J. M. Buchanan, *The Demand and Supply of Public Goods* (Chicago: Rand McNally, 1968).

2. See, for example, C. M. Tiebout, 'A Pure Theory of Local Expenditures', *Journal of Political Economy* (1956), and 'An Economic Theory of Fiscal Decentralisation', in J. M. Buchanan (ed.), *Public Finances: Needs, Sources and Utilisation* (Princeton U.P., 1961); A. Williams, 'The Optimal Provision of Public Goods in a System of Local Government', *Journal of Political Economy* (1966); A. Breton, 'A Theory of Government Grants', *Canadian Journal of Economics and Political Science* (1965); J. M. Buchanan, 'Comment' on R. A. Musgrave, 'Approaches to a Fiscal Theory of Political Federalism', in *Public Finances: Needs, Sources and Utilisation*; J. M. Buchanan and R. E. Wagner, 'An Efficiency Basis for Federal Fiscal Equalisation', in *Universities–N.B.E.R. Conference on Economics of Public Output* (1968).

3. For a more detailed discussion of public goods characteristics, market failure problems and public provision, see J. G. Head, 'The Theory of Public Goods', *Rivista di Diritto Finanziario e Scienza delle Finanze* (1968).

4. For a general analysis of this aspect of the joint supply characteristic, see J. M. Buchanan, 'Joint Supply, Externality, and Optimality', *Economica* (1966).

5. For a general analysis of this dimension of joint supply, see J. M. Buchanan, 'An Economic Theory of Clubs', *Economica* (1965). The various dimensions of the relevant cost functions are nicely distinguished by C. S. Shoup, *Public Finance* (Chicago: Aldine, 1969) pp. 79–86.

6. See J. G. Head, 'Public Goods and Public Policy', *Public Finance* (1962).

7. Indeed, the standard conception of government units based on area should ideally be generalised to allow for the possibility of units based on economic ('functional'), racial, religious, linguistic and other characteristics. To simplify the discussion, we shall assume conventionally that the spatial dimension is in some sense more fundamental. It might, for example, be argued that, at least in some cases where other characteristics are of particular and independent significance, generalised public goods interaction (e.g. racial, religious or class prejudice) will tend to produce spatial groupings based on the relevant characteristic. In a more general analysis, however, the locational dimension of each public good would need to be supplemented by other dimensions in the design of an optimal structure of multi-level government.

8. See Buchanan, 'An Economic Theory of Clubs'.

9. See Samuelson, 'The Pure Theory of Public Expenditure'.

10. For a detailed analysis, see Tiebout, 'An Economic Theory of Fisca Decentralisation', in Buchanan (ed.), op. cit., pp. 82–7.

11. For a more detailed discussion, see ibid., pp. 87–90.

12. For the relevant optimality requirements, see Buchanan, 'Joint Supply, Externality, and Optimality'.

13. This point has recently been stressed by Hartle and Bird, who note that

what is involved here is the fundamental public finance distinction between public production and public provision. See D. G. Hartle and R. M. Bird, 'Criteria for the Design of Governmental Decision-Making Units', *Canadian Economics Association Conference* (1969). For the contrary view, see M. Olson, 'The Principle of "Fiscal Equivalence" ', *American Economic Review, Papers and Proceedings* (1969).

14. The advantages of decentralised political decision-making, based on the assumption of rigid inter-regional uniformity of service levels under centralised provision, are analysed by Y. Barzel, 'Two Propositions on the Optimum Level of Producing Collective Goods', *Public Choice* (1969).

15. This assumption is strongly supported by Hartle and Bird, in 'Criteria for the Design of Governmental Decision-Making Units'.

16. See Buchanan and Wagner, 'An Efficiency Basis for Federal Fiscal Equalisation'.

17. For a general discussion of the relevant cost relationships, see Shoup, *Public Finance*, pp. 84–6.

18. See Tiebout, 'A Pure Theory of Local Expenditures'. Also G. J. Stigler, 'The Tenable Range of Functions of Local Government', in Joint Economic Committee, *Federal Expenditure Policy for Economic Growth and Stability*, 1957.

19. For an interesting analysis of this possibility, see J. M. Buchanan, 'Principles of Urban Fiscal Strategy', *Public Choice* (1971).

20. On the latter, see J. M. Buchanan and C. J. Goetz, 'Efficiency Limits of Fiscal Mobility: An Assessment of the Tiebout Model', *Public Economics* (1972).

21. In principle, a higher-level government might create a sufficient variety of local 'branches' varying in the volume and mix of local public goods supplied. Constitutional and other rigidities and problems of preference relevation tend, however, to produce a considerable degree of uniformity in standards of service provision within any given jurisdiction.

22. It has also been assumed that the tax costs of public goods supplied in a given jurisdiction cannot be exported to neighbouring jurisdictions. This assumption too is very unrealistic, but will be retained for simplicity in the following discussion.

23. The crucial role of spillovers and the non-excludability characteristic in the case for centralised provision has recently been stressed by Olson (op. cit.) in his principle of 'fiscal equivalence'. See also G. Tullock, 'Federalism: Problems of Scale', *Public Choice* (1969).

24. See Stigler, op. cit., p. 218. See also C. M. Tiebout and D. B. Houston, 'Metropolitan Finance Reconsidered: Budget Functions and Multi-Level Governments', *Review of Economics and Statistics* (1962); and Tullock, 'Federalism: Problems of Scale'.

25. See, for example, Tiebout, 'An Economic Theory of Fiscal Decentralisation', in Buchanan (ed.), op. cit., pp. 91–2.

26. See B. A. Weisbrod, 'Comment' on Tiebout, ibid., pp. 131–2.

27. See Williams, 'The Optimal Provision of Public Goods in a System of Local Government'. Brainard and Dolbear have argued that overexpansion is possible in the Williams analysis only because his compensation scheme (to internalise the externality) would allow one local unit to be made worse off than under independent adjustment. This point was subsequently demonstrated rigorously for the case of a pure public good by Pauly. See W. C. Brainard and F. T. Dolbear, 'The Possibility of Oversupply of Local "Public" Goods: A Critical Note', *Journal of Political Economy* (1967); and M. V. Pauly, 'Optimality, "Public" Goods, and Local Governments: A General Theoretical Analysis', *Journal of*

Political Economy (1970). Especially in the more general case of asymmetrical spillovers, however, it could well be argued that independent adjustment equilibrium may represent an inequitable and unacceptable basis for compensation or negotiation. Williams's conception of 'local autonomy' may be an appealing and more acceptable alternative. If the public good can be inferior for at least one locality, the possibility arises in either framework that output and consumption may be larger, not only for the country as a whole, but also for each local unit. For a demonstration of this possibility in the Williams framework, see G. Brennan, 'The Optimal Provision of Public Goods: A Comment', *Journal of Political Economy* (1969).

28. See J. M. Buchanan and M. Z. Kafoglis, 'A Note on Public Goods Supply', *American Economic Review* (1963). The Buchanan–Kafoglis analysis is developed for the case of two persons, but applies equally to the case of two localities.

29. For a detailed analysis, see J. Rothenberg, 'Local Decentralisation and the Theory of Optimal Government', in *Universities–N.B.E.R. Conference on Economics of Public Output* (1968).

30. The possibility of voluntary agreement in small-number cases has been particularly stressed in the modern externality literature stemming from the classic discussion by Coase. See R. H. Coase, 'The Problem of Social Cost', *Journal of Law and Economics* (1960). The same arguments apply equally to spillovers between local government units.

31. For a formal analysis of some of these problems in a two-person setting, see O. A. Davis and A. B. Whinston, 'Some Notes on Equating Private and Social Cost', *Southern Economic Journal* (1965).

32. The special problem of reciprocal and non-separable externalities was first analysed by Davis and Whinston, who considered the case of two competitive firms related through their cost functions. They concluded that a merger of the two firms might offer the best solution. See O. A. Davis and A. B. Whinston, 'Externalities, Welfare, and the Theory of Games', *Journal of Political Economy* (1962).

33. This argument is familiar both from the public goods literature and the broader externality literature. See, for example, Musgrave, *Theory of Public Finance*, p. 80; and W. J. Baumol, *Welfare Economics and the Theory of the State* (Cambridge, Mass.: Harvard U.P., 1965) chap. 11.

34. See A. C. Pigou, *A Study in Public Finance* (London: Macmillan, 1929) p. 124.

35. If we depart from the standard Pigovian conception of a constant 'matching' rate, a somewhat simpler but still informationally extremely demanding solution would be to pay a conditional matching grant with the marginal matching rate equal to the spillover at each level of output. For this purpose, 'only' the spillover function must be determined.

36. For a detailed analysis of these problems in the analogous case of inter-firm externalities, see O. A. Davis and A. B. Whinston, 'On Externalities, Information and the Government-Assisted Invisible Hand', *Economica* (1966).

37. For a recent demonstration of these points in the analogous setting of interpersonal externality relationships, see M. V. Pauly 'Efficiency in the Provision of Consumption Subsidies', *Kyklos* (1970).

38. This argument is developed in relation to inter-firm externalities by Davis and Whinston, 'On Externalities, Information and the Government-Assisted Invisible Hand'. As we have seen in note 35 above, however, the information demands of the grant approach can be reduced by departing from the standard requirement of a uniform matching rate. The above argument therefore requires some modification, at least in the simpler cases of spillover interaction.

39. For an elegant formal synthesis of most of the relevant factors, see W. E. Oates, *Fiscal Federalism* (New York: Harcourt Brace Jovanovich, 1972) chap. 2.

40. Some such clustering is assumed, for example, by Breton, 'A Theory of Government Grants', p. 178.

41. See, for example, Tullock, 'Federalism: Problems of Scale'; Olson, 'The Principle of "Fiscal Equivalence"'; Hartle and Bird, 'Criteria for the Design of Governmental Decision-Making Units'.

42. See J. M. Buchanan, 'Federalism and Fiscal Equity', *American Economic Review* (1950).

43. Ibid., sect. III.

44. See J. M. Buchanan, 'Federal Grants and Resource Allocation', *Journal of Political Economy* (1952); A. D. Scott, 'Federal Grants and Resource Allocation', ibid.; and J. M. Buchanan, 'A Reply', ibid.

45. See Buchanan, 'Federalism and Fiscal Equity'.

46. See Buchanan, 'Comment' on Musgrave, 'Approaches to a Fiscal Theory of Political Federalism'.

47. See J. F. Graham, *Fiscal Adjustment and Economic Development* (Toronto, 1963) pp. 176–8; also A. D. Scott, 'The Economic Goals of Federal Finance', *Public Finance* (1964) pp. 254–5.

48. See Buchanan, 'Comment'.

49. See Buchanan and Wagner, 'An Efficiency Basis for Federal Fiscal Equalisation'.

50. Ibid., sect. II.

51. Ibid., sect. III.

52. For a detailed analysis, see Hartle and Bird, 'Criteria for the Design of Governmental Decision-Making Units'; also Olson, 'The Principle of "Fiscal Equivalence"'.

53. See Head, 'Public Goods and Public Policy', sect. 4.2.

54. See, for example, H. M. Hochman and J. D. Rodgers, 'Pareto-Optimal Redistribution', *American Economic Review* (1969).

55. This argument is reinforced by the further consideration that the better-off residents of the given locality may decide to enjoy their altruistic or other benefits at a safe fiscal distance by removing themselves or their capital to a less welfare-oriented locality.

56. This latter possibility has been explored in some detail by Pauly. See M. V. Pauly, 'Income Redistribution as a Local Public Good', *Public Choice Society Conference* (1972).

57. See Musgrave, *Theory of Public Finance*, pp. 13–14.

58. See J. G. Head, 'Merit Goods Revisited', *Finanzarchiv* (1969). For some discussion of merit goods problems in the context of multi-level government, see Tiebout and Houston, 'Metropolitan Finance Reconsidered: Budget Functions and Multi-Level Governments'. In the case of involuntary redistribution, for example, it is a familiar conclusion that central government provision is required, since high-income residents will otherwise relocate in more congenial fiscal surroundings. If some involuntary redistribution must be undertaken at the local level, the size of the optimal jurisdiction should be determined on the basis of some compromise between the advantages of a small unit in terms of preference revelation for local public goods, and the distributional advantages of a large unit which may serve to ensure the inclusion of a reasonable proportion of high-income residents. On this latter point, see Rothenberg, 'Local Decentralisation and the Theory of Optimal Government'.

3

On the Distinction between Direct and Indirect Taxation

ALAN R. PREST

I

HISTORICALLY, the distinction between direct and indirect taxation goes back a long way and has had many different meanings. In the definitive study of the subject to 1900, C. J. Bullock[1] found traces of the distinction as far back as the sixteenth century; he also isolated ten different senses in which various people had interpreted it. There have also been many attempts at synthesis over the years, with varying results: thus, around the turn of the century, C. F. Bastable,[2] after discussing various interpretations, settled for the idea that taxes paid by the people on whom they were levied should be classed as direct, whilst those shifted away to any degree should be indirect; whereas R. M. Haig concluded in 1934[3] that the distinction was colloquial rather than scientific and added 'students are more and more advised to avoid the use of these terms' – though in this he was far from being an innovator, H. Sidgwick having said much the same thing fifty years earlier.[4]

In modern times the conventions have hardened. For a variety of purposes – national accounts preparation, international comparisons of the tax-mix, and so on – a fairly standard pattern on the following lines has emerged:

Direct taxes	*Indirect taxes*
Personal income (including personal capital gains)	Import
Expenditure	Export
Corporate income (including corporate capital gains)	Excise
Social security (including payroll taxes)	Sales
Capital, death, inheritance, etc.	Property
Gifts	Stamp duties
	Licence duties
	Surpluses of public enterprises

Naturally, there are some glosses on this breakdown. Sometimes the distinction is paraphrased as one between income and outlay (rather than between direct and indirect) taxes; and taxes on capital and capital transfers, etc., may form a separate sub-compartment. But it does not seem unfair to say that a distinction on the lines above has often been endorsed in recent years both at official[5] and academic[6] levels. Furthermore, a parallel distinction has been made between the negative counterparts, in the form of subsidies and grants.

It seems worth while examining whether this modern form of the distinction between direct and indirect taxes can be justified and, if it cannot, what consequences follow. Before starting, one further point should be made. It can be argued that 'everybody' knows what is meant by the distinction; and so there is no danger of anyone misunderstanding statistical exercises embodying it. And I must hasten to add that I have used this classification myself on a number of occasions as a convenient means of grouping different taxes together.[7] However, it is one thing for a statement to be conventional and intelligible in general terms; it is an entirely different one for it to be precise and meaningful or highly relevant to economic problems. It is this latter belief or claim with which we are concerned in this paper.

We now examine the reasons found in the literature for distinguishing between taxes on direct/indirect lines. We shall look in turn at arguments about the general price level, relative prices, incomes distribution aspects and other miscellaneous contentions about administrative aspects and the like.

1. DIFFERENCES IN THE GENERAL PRICE LEVEL

It is sometimes argued that this is a (if not the) major distinction between the two tax groups.[8] It seems doubtful whether such a proposition can have generality. It clearly must depend on the assumptions made about the quantity of money and the velocity of circulation in the two alternative tax situations; and on the liability or non-liability of government purchases to indirect taxes. Although circumstances can be envisaged in which the general market price level would be higher in the indirect than in the direct tax case (e.g. if people expect prices to be higher in the indirect tax case, therefore seek for larger cash balances and the authorities respond to this demand by increasing the money supply; or if there are institutional reasons for thinking that the velocity of circulation may be higher in the case of business firms paying sales taxes than in that of individuals paying income taxes),[9] the multiplicity of possible cases set out in the well-known, but highly simplified, examples given by Musgrave[10] should suffice to warn one against the idea that there is any simple, universal distinction on these lines.

2. RELATIVE PRICES AND EFFICIENCY

It is sometimes alleged that the key to the distinction is the differing effects of direct and indirect taxes on relative prices.[11] It is easy enough to justify such an argument by pointing to the differential effects on prices of a universal poll tax and a highly selective sales tax, yielding the same revenue total. Whether the primary mechanism operates via product prices or factor rewards, the sales tax will have very different effects to the poll tax on relative product prices. But this is only one example, and it is not difficult to conjure up contrary ones. Suppose, for instance, we compare a uniform and universal *ad valorem* retail sales tax (or value-added tax) with an equal-yield highly progressive personal income tax. Whereas the former will do nothing of itself to alter relative prices of consumption goods, the latter may do so in a variety of ways, e.g. by altering the distribution of the labour force between industries with pleasant and unpleasant working conditions or by the reallocation of capital among unincorporated businesses in more and less risky activities. Similarly, if one gives any weight at all to the arguments about corporation taxes being passed forward, we than have a tax, normally classed as direct, which will have parallel effects to those usually attributed to selective excise or sales taxes.

If one concentrates on the relative prices of current and future consumption, there is a general presumption that a universal proportional income tax will increase the price of future, relatively to current consumption, compared to the situation with an expenditure tax.[12] But we also know that, in terms of their effects on the relative attractiveness of current consumption and saving (or investment), there is a general equivalence between the following:

Expenditure taxation.
Income taxation exempting profits, interest, etc.

Income taxation with instantaneous write-off of capital expenditure.
Value-added taxation, consumption variant.
Retail sales taxation.
Payroll taxation.

If these taxes are levied on a proportional and non-discriminatory basis, they may all be expected to leave the relative prices of current consumption and saving (or investment) unchanged.[13] Yet the standard international classification lumps together general and partial income taxation, expenditure taxation and payroll taxes in the direct taxes category and treats the others as indirect taxes, when the true distinction in this context is that between general income taxes and all the other taxes listed.

3. EFFECTS ON THE DISTRIBUTION OF INCOME

A distinction is often drawn between those (direct) taxes, the burden of which rests on the people on whom they are levied, and those (indirect) taxes, the burden of which is shifted to someone else.[14] Now it is clearly the case that if a differential income tax is imposed on a factor of production in completely inelastic supply to an industry, then this burden will stay put. And if we imagine a selective excise tax on a commodity with a perfectly elastic supply schedule, the tax will be shifted 100 per cent on to its consumers. But once again, these are particular examples which can readily be controverted. Nor does the picture change if we take a general income tax rather than a selective one. For reasons already mentioned – risk premia for capital, non-monetary rewards for labour – we may find shifts in relative prices in goods and factor markets which vitiate any simple-minded notions that income taxes stay put. More generally, there are three ways in which the distribution of real income may be affected by taxes: changes in relative pre-tax factor rewards, changes in relative tax deductions from factor rewards, and changes in relative prices in goods markets. It is far too naïve to think that income taxes only operate through the second mechanism and excise taxes only through the third. The more general presumption is that any tax – whether formally classed as direct or indirect – can operate through any or all of these mechanisms.[15]

A more subtle version of the shifting argument has been emphasised by Musgrave[16] – the proposition that it is the legislature's *intention* rather than actual recorded experience which is relevant. Thus, if the intention is that an income tax should stay put, this suffices to class it as direct, whether in fact it stays put or not; conversely if the intention is that a selective excise tax should be passed on to consumers. This is in fact an old argument going back (at least) to J. S. Mill; and it suffers from old difficulties. With a mixed bag of taxes introduced over a long historical period, it is not always easy to know what intentions were when taxes were originally introduced or tax rates raised. And presumably the intentions of the legislature tend to be based in any case on some knowledge or quasi-knowledge of what actually happens. So it must be questioned whether this version is really distinct from the standard one about shifting.

4. MISCELLANEOUS ARGUMENTS

There is a variety of other arguments advanced in favour of the common distinction. In our view, none of them really holds water; nevertheless, it is necessary to enumerate them.

(*a*) One is that different government agencies may be responsible for tax collection. This may well hold in some countries (the U.K. is an example where it is roughly true), but it clearly cannot have generality. There may be fewer than or more than two agencies in any one country; and the numbers and responsibilities of agencies can change over time.

(*b*) At first sight, the proposition that direct taxes are levied on income and indirect taxes on expenditure looks more persuasive. But one man's meat. . . . Given a circular flow of income between households, business firms, etc., this distinction can have very little meaning. In any case, it does not help one iota over the whole range of capital taxes, nor over an expenditure tax, nor head taxes.

(*c*) Another contention is that direct taxes are levied on individuals and indirect taxes on objects or transactions.[17] If the reference is to the basis of tax, we are back straight away to the preceding argument – that income and expenditure are simply two aspects of the same circular flow. If the reference is to the taxpayer, the distinction is meaningless; all taxes are alike in that they must be paid by individuals or incorporated bodies – they cannot be paid by inanimate objects. Finally, there is no need to dwell on the proposition that the effects of a tax are the same irrespective of whether payment is the legal responsibility of buyer or seller.[18]

(*d*) It is a double fallacy to say that indirect taxes can be avoided, but not direct taxes. There are many ways in which an *individual* can avoid either direct or indirect taxes, but for the *community* there is a total tax bill to be met, once the level of public expenditure and its intended inflationary impact are given, irrespective of the reactions of particular individuals.

(*e*) As is often the case, when economic arguments are weak, recourse is made to alleged psychological differences – in this case the proposition that taxpayers prefer and/or react differently to those taxes which are relatively obscure. It may be questioned whether they do; but in any case there is no single rule that the usual indirect taxes are more hidden or more obscure than the usual direct ones. The converse could plausibly be argued when there are substantial time-lags in the collection of income taxes or when, as is sometimes the case, the tax element in the final price of a commodity is plain for all to see.

(*f*) Finally, there are a number of arguments stemming from accounting or legal practices. Thus it may be said[19] that indirect taxes represent a business cost rather than a factor input; or that they are a legally required payment rather than a cost. We shall say more about propositions of this sort shortly.

II

What consequences follow if the standard distinction between direct and indirect taxes is abandoned? Questions would seem to arise about the following:

1. The validity of the factor cost concept of national income.
2. Comparisons – cross-sectional or historical – between ratios into which national income concepts enter (e.g. the tax/G.N.P. ratio or the investment/G.N.P. ratio).
3. The GATT rules about remission of indirect, but not direct, taxes on exports.
4. Alternative tax classifications.

Let us look at each of these in turn.

1. *The Factor Cost Concept of National Income*[20]

The standard presentation of national accounts, as exemplified in the U.K., gives us a total for the income side which is made to agree with that derived from the expenditure side by the device of deducting indirect taxes (net of subsidies) from the latter. We also find that the income side of the Personal Income account is equal to the income total in the main account *less* undistributed profits of companies and the trading surplus of public corporations *plus* transfer payments; and the expenditure side of this account involves the addition of personal consumption, personal saving and the element of direct taxation attributed to persons rather than to corporate bodies. How would these standard – one might almost say hallowed – computations be affected if the direct/indirect tax distinction were abandoned? As far as the main G.N.P. account is concerned, the most obvious answer is to adopt the current U.S. practice, i.e. instead of deducting net indirect taxes from the expenditure side, they should be added to the income side. The only other necessary change would be to show wages, salaries, profits, etc., as net of taxes levied on them; these taxes would then be added to net indirect taxes to give an overall total of taxation. Whether the Personal Income account needs any reconstruction is a matter for debate. The present form has the advantage of allowing the totality of personal taxes,[21] whether conventionally thought of as direct or indirect, to be shown on the outlay side of the account.[22] On the other hand, by entering one tax category as an element in consumers' expenditure and the other as the entirely separate item of taxes on income, credence is given to the idea that the distinction between them is meaningful. An alternative would be to convert the Personal Income account into a Disposable Income account excluding taxes on personal income from both sides. This has the great advantage of concentrating attention on the current resources people actually have at their disposal, and on a concept which many would think to be more useful than personal income for most purposes of economic analysis. It would also fit in with the incomes total in the proposed restructuring of the G.N.P. account. As for any incongruity in having a total of consumers' expenditure valued at market prices, whilst excluding personal income taxes, there seem to be two answers: first, this is a straightforward record of what individuals spend on their consumption requirements and so there is no ambiguity about it; second, the issue whether the expenditure total is greater than it would be in the absence of taxes on consumer goods takes one straight back to whether such taxes are shifted backwards or forwards. Suppose, for instance, the burden of such taxes fell entirely on corporate undistributed profits; one would then be dealing with personal income and expenditure totals which excluded all taxes on persons. Of course, taxes on consumer goods may not go to roost in that way; but in the present state of our ignorance it does not seem worth while worrying too much about any incongruity in putting disposable income and consumers' expenditure at market prices into the same table.[23]

Such would seem to be the main changes in the national income accounts as customarily presented. Their acceptability must depend on whether one attaches importance to the traditional concept of factor cost or not. This was the subject of a famous Anglo-American debate in the 1940s;[24] and to this day the relative prominence given to it in the U.K. and U.S. national accounts is very different. As far as *comparisons* of G.N.P. between years or between countries are concerned, it is difficult to see that factor cost totals can give us anything which market price totals cannot; indeed, they may be inferior.[25] It is noteworthy that Professor Hicks himself took the line in his 1948 article that more emphasis should be placed on the usefulness of a factor cost total for a single year than for comparative purposes – a somewhat different position to that taken in his 1940 article. For *single* year totals, the basic question is whether a total of incomes before deduction of income taxes tells us more than a total of incomes after such deductions have been made. It must be questioned whether this is really so. First, we must remember the arbitrariness of G.N.P. calculations for a single year; their usefulness must inevitably be very limited, whichever total is taken. Second, those who insist that single totals are significant and useful must be prepared to defend propositions such as that the conventional factor cost total is a 'true' representation of productive inputs, or a measure of the productive resources at a country's command, or the best measure of real factor inputs. One really must doubt whether this can be done.[26] Why is it not legitimate to argue that factor rewards, and the comparison between factor rewards (e.g. work income and property income), should be measured by what people receive net of taxes but gross of public transfers? The proposition that gross factor payments are a true cost but indirect taxes are not can easily be stood on its head; there may be a large element of rental payment in some of the former, and the latter, in the form of local taxes, may be the source of indispensable police or fire services without which production would be hamstrung. And if one is concentrating on entrepreneurs' decision-making processes, it is not difficult to imagine cases in which the appropriate cost measures are gross of indirect but net of direct taxes, rather than the other way around.[27]

Finally, one cannot escape the feeling that aggregates which correspond to actual payments – such as is broadly the case with the market price total – are more acceptable than those which may or may not do so, depending on whether or not personal income taxes are withheld by a firm from factor rewards. On all these grounds, there would at any rate be one person who would not be at all worried about the demise of the factor cost concept.

2. *Cross-Section or Historical Comparisons*

As this subject has recently been dealt with at some length in another context,[28] it is unnecessary to dilate on it here. There would seem to be two main consequences of the argments above. First, the total of national income at market prices and not the present factor cost total would have to be used for any such comparisons. There would seem to be no occasion for losing any sleep over this. We have argued elsewhere[29] that for comparisons of tax/national aggregate ratios the market price total has advantages over the factor cost one, even if the latter were accepted conceptually. And for comparing ratios of investment, consumption or exports to G.N.P., the market price concept would be the natural one to take. If the main interest is in a comparison of the ratio of incomes from work to incomes from property, the calculations can still readily be made on an ex-tax basis.

The second consequence is that we must regard comparisons of direct (or indirect) taxes/national aggregate ratios as inadmissible. But if our arguments above hold on the lack of any clear-cut distinction between the *modus operandi* and the effects of the two groups of taxes (as conventionally classified), this cannot be a great loss.

3. *GATT Rules*

The general principle here[30] is a twofold one: whereas sales and excise taxes levied on goods for sale inside a country can be applied to imports in just the same way as to home-produced goods, exports can be relieved of such taxes (i.e. the destination principle); but income taxes should be assessed on the origin principle, i.e. exports do not secure tax relief and imports do not attract tax. It is arguable whether such a distinction should be made, e.g. if it is thought that corporation taxes raise the domestic price level and/or that excise taxes and the like do not raise it. But there is no need to pursue these arguments at length here.[31] The essential point for our discussion is that the conventional portmanteau distinction between direct and indirect taxes is simply insufficient for the detailed application of such rules. We clearly need to have a much finer breakdown of taxes and specify, one by one, those which are and those which are not refundable on exports or chargeable on imports. There is no reason whatever to think that the application of detailed GATT rules would be the slightest bit more difficult if the conventional broad distinction between direct and indirect taxes were abandoned.

4. *Alternative Tax Classifications*

The last topic is whether there is any obvious alternative to the direct/indirect tax distinction. Professor Shoup has recently suggested[32] that for some purposes a line can be drawn between narrow-based and broad-based taxes. The idea would seem to be not so much a matter of either the exact basis or the exact effects of a tax, but rather of the method needed to analyse its effects. Thus, to take a specific example, if one has a low-rate duty on tobacco products, and if various conditions are satisfied – notably, factor reactions insufficiently large to shift supply schedules and consumer reactions insufficiently large to shift demand schedules – one can then analyse the effects of the tax within the framework of partial equilibrium analysis, deducing the effects on price and output of tobacco on the basis of given demand and supply conditions for it. In contrast, a uniform value-added tax raising a large amount of revenue relatively to G.N.P. can only be analysed on the basis of some specified macro-economic assumptions; alternatively, a set of differential sales taxes cannot be analysed by looking at each individual commodity and imagining that demand and supply conditions for it are not affected by changes in tax rates applying to other commodities. In other words, we need some form of general equilibrium analysis in either of the last two cases – in contradistinction to the partial equilibrium analysis which suffices in the tobacco example.

Where does this type of distinction get us? Some taxes fall fairly clearly into one category or the other: wide-ranging corporation taxes, payroll taxes, value added taxes and even some taxes on single items (e.g. widely used intermediate ones such as freight transport) can hardly be analysed by simple partial equilibrium techniques. On the other hand, subsidies often can. Nevertheless, there are obvious difficulties in trying to make too much of the distinction. Thus we might have an excise or sales tax covering only a few items of consumption expenditure, but among those few some which are partial substitutes for one another; or payroll taxes which exempt important categories of employees. It is easy to think up intermediate cases which do not fall with complete certainty into either category. One can invent various ground rules, such as saying that if a tax applies to more than 50 per cent of any of a defined list of bases (e.g. imports, consumption, payrolls, etc.), then it should be counted as a broad-based tax. But this is clearly only a rough-and-ready solution without any analytical justification.

So although one might claim that a distinction on these lines could avoid some of the direct/indirect difficulties (e.g. we should classify both employers' social security contributions and selective employment tax in the U.K. as broad-based taxes; whereas the national accounts treatment is to put the former in the direct and the latter in the indirect tax box), it would not seem sufficiently sharp to justify adoption as a general method of classification. But perhaps one need not worry too much. Professor Shoup's *Public Finance* is 652 pages long, but he manages perfectly well without (as far as I can see) mentioning the direct/indirect distinction once, and without insisting that the broad-based/narrow-based distinction is capable of application right across the board.

REFERENCES

1. C. J. Bullock, 'Direct and Indirect Taxes in Economic Literature', *Political Science Quarterly* (1898), reprinted in his *Economic Essays* (Cambridge, Mass.: Harvard U.P., 1936).

2. C. F. Bastable, *Public Finance*, 3rd ed. (London: Macmillan, 1907) p. 345.

3. R. M. Haig, 'Taxation', in *Encyclopaedia of the Social Sciences*, vol. XIV (London: Macmillan, 1934).

4. 'The common classification of taxes as Direct and Indirect appears to be liable to mislead the student by ignoring the complexity and difficulty of determining the incidence of taxation.' H. Sidgwick, *Principles of Political Economy*, 1st ed. (London: Macmillan, 1883) p. 567.

5. Thus the U.N. *Yearbook of National Accounts*, vol. I (New York, 1968) p. xxviii, defines indirect taxes as 'taxes on goods and services which are charge-

able to business expenditure and taxes on the possession or use of goods and services by households. The main categories are import, export and excise duties, local rates, entertainment duties, betting taxes, sales taxes, business licences, stamp duties and motor vehicles. Profits of state monopolies should also be included. Real estate and land taxes are treated as indirect taxes unless they are considered merely as administrative devices for the collection of income taxes.'

6. Cf. the well-known contribution by Lady Hicks, 'The terminology of Tax Analysis', *Economic Journal* (Mar 1946).

7. See also J. F. Due, 'Introduction: The Issues', in Brookings Institution and National Bureau of Economic Research, *The Role of Direct and Indirect Taxes in the Federal Revenue System* (Princeton U.P., 1964) p. 3: 'Little is to be gained by seeking to establish definitions of direct and indirect taxes. Instead, we shall simply interpret the term "direct tax" as referring to personal and corporate income taxes and death taxes and "indirect tax" as referring to levies upon the production or sale of commodities.'

8. Cf. W. Beckerman, *Introduction to National Income Analysis* (London: Weidenfeld & Nicolson, 1968) pp. 34–5. See also B. Hansen, *Fiscal Policy in Seven Countries* (Paris: O.E.C.D., 1969) p. 29.

9. Cf. A. Morag, *On Taxes and Inflation* (New York: Random House, 1965) chap. 2.

10. R. A. Musgrave, *Theory of Public Finance* (New York: McGraw-Hill, 1959) p. 366; see also C. E. McLure, Jr, 'Tax Incidence, Macroeconomic Policy and Absolute Prices', *Quarterly Journal of Economics* (May 1970).

11. 'The distinction between direct and indirect taxation is made for analytical reasons, the object being to separate those taxes which directly affect relative prices from those which do not'. Richard Stone, Appendix to *Measurement of National Income and Contruction of Social Accounts*, (Geneva: United Nations, 1947) p. 31.

12. For some qualifications to these propositions, see A. R. Prest, 'The Expenditure Tax and Saving', *Economic Journal* (Sept 1959).

13. For the detailed argument see Carl S. Shoup, *Public Finance* (Chicago: Aldine, 1969) esp. chaps. 9 and 16. In particular, the proposition about the *ex ante* equivalence of the payroll tax to the rest is due to Professor Shoup (though it should be noted that in this case there is a near equivalence, rather than an exact one, to the other taxes listed).

14. For instance, the *Oxford Dictionary* defines an indirect tax as 'Not levied directly upon the persons on whom it ultimately falls, but charged in some other way especially upon the production or importation of articles of use or consumption, the price of which is thereby augumented to the consumer, who thus pays the tax in the form of increased price'. *New English Dictionary* (Oxford, 1901) vol. v, part ii. And in the article by E. R. Rolph on 'Taxation' in the *International Encyclopaedia of the Social Sciences* (New York: Macmillan and Free Press, 1968) vol. xv, it is argued that this is the common interpretation of the distinction, e.g. ibid., p. 522: 'A direct tax in this usage refers to one in which the legal taxpayer cannot shift any of the tax liability to other people, such as customers or suppliers.'

15. See A. R. Prest, 'Statistical Calculations of Tax Burdens', *Economica* (Aug 1955), and 'The Budget and Interpersonal Distribution', *Public Finance*, parts I and II (1968).

16. Musgrave, *Theory of Public Finance*, p. 230, and *Fiscal Systems* (New Haven: Yale U.P., 1969) p. 173.

17. Cf. Musgrave, *Fiscal Systems*, p. 173. There would seem to be a change in Musgrave's position between the publication of *Theory of Public Finance* in

1959 and *Fiscal Systems* in 1969. In the former the distinction is entirely in terms of shifting intentions; in the latter, although shifting intentions are mentioned (along with other possible bases for differentiation), the main emphasis is on the objects/individuals distinction.

18. A distinction on the lines of direct taxes being paid by individuals and indirect taxes being paid by incorporated bodies is not very fruitful. In the U.K., local rates are paid by many individuals and corporation tax is only paid by companies; yet the former is conventionally classed as indirect and the latter as direct. This line of argument could also lead to the conclusion that a retail sales tax incorporated in prices and one collected from purchasers on a coupon basis are two different animals.

19. R. and G. Stone, *National Income and Expenditure*, 5th ed. (London: Bowes & Bowes, 1969) p. 20: '. . . [indirect taxes] must be excluded from domestic income because they represent a business cost which does not remunerate any input into the productive system'.

20. We shall use the terms 'national income' and 'G.N.P.' interchangeably here; and we shall not concern ourselves with the distinction between G.N.P. and G.D.P.

21. Leaving aside such questions as the (in my view, unjustified) omission of capital taxes and of capital gains (and taxes thereon) from the Personal Income account. See A. R. Prest 'Government Revenue, the National Income and all that" to be published in R. M. Bird and J. Head (eds), *Modern Fiscal Issues* (Toronto: Toronto University Press).

22. This is not universal practice, e.g. in the U.S.A. social insurance contributions are shown as a negative item on the income side rather than a positive item on the outlay side.

23. The imposition of taxes on consumers' expenditure could affect the disposable income total if, for instance, such tax revenues were used to increase transfers to persons.

24. Cf. J. R. Hicks, 'Valuation of Social Income', *Economica* (May 1940); S. Kuznets, 'On the Valuation of Social Income: Reflections on Professor Hicks' article', ibid. (Feb. and May 1948); J. R. Hicks, 'The Valuation of the Social Income: A Comment on Professor Kuznets' Reflections', ibid. (Aug. 1948).

25. See Musgrave, *Theory of Public Finance*, chap. 9; also Prest, 'Government Revenue, the National Income and all that'.

26. Cf. E. R. Rolph, *The Theory of Fiscal Economics* (Berkeley and Los Angeles: California U.P., 1954) pp. 66 ff.

27. e.g. a company may have to decide whether to concentrate more production at plant A than at plant B. The relevant cost totals would be net of corporation tax but gross of any petrol duty involved in road transport costs.

28. See Prest, 'Government Revenue, the National Income and all that'.

29. Ibid.

30. *GATT Basic Instruments and Selected Documents*, 9th supplement (Geneva, 1961) p. 186.

31. It might be noted that the often reiterated argument that, given fixed exchange rates, a country raising its revenue from sales taxes and the like is, *ceteris paribus*, likely to be in a better balance of payments position than one raising its revenue from income taxes (by virtue of the possibility of remitting the former, but not the latter, on exports, and, *mutatis mutandis*, on imports) depends critically on the assumption about how far the domestic market price level will change if a country switches from one tax system to the other.

32. Shoup, *Public Finance*, esp. chap. 1.

Part Two
FISCAL POLICY AND DEVELOPMENT FINANCE

4

The Contribution of Finance to Industrial Development: The Nigerian Experience

ENOCH A. ANYANWU

I. INTRODUCTION

ALTHOUGH the discussion in this paper concentrates on the role of finance in stimulating industrial development in Nigeria, it should be noted that the other factors of production are as important as finance in promoting industrial development. All the factors of production are complementary in promoting and fostering industrial progress. What makes financial supply appear to be the crux of the development problem is its role in creating investment, which is a many-sided actor on the economic scene.

Entrepreneurship, for example, is a very important factor affecting industrial development when it comes to the question of making investment decisions which are crucial to industrial development. Nigeria is well endowed with active entrepreneurs of all calibres, including those who take decisions and operate under conditions of risk and uncertainty as well as the imitating entrepreneurs. The detailed studies of the transport and bakery industries in Nigeria undertaken by Hawkins and Kilby respectively have emphasised the spontaneous entrepreneurship of many Nigerians, and such findings contrast with the situation in other underdeveloped countries where most people clamour for the Civil Service or nationalised industries job.[1]

Hawkins remarked that one of the important features of the road transport industry is that it is very largely in African hands. It represents the most important example of the emergence of local enterprise in Nigeria and is thus of great significance for the future development of the country. The ability to produce a class of entrepreneurs who are more than traders is a requirement of any society before economic growth can become a continuous process. Kilby also noted that one aspect of his study of the bread industry which has a broad significance was the factual evidence pertaining to African entrepreneurial performance. Of the many bottlenecks inhibiting the development of African economies, none, he said, is narrower than the short supply of effective entrepreneurs. He identified the dominant favourable characteristics exhibited by Nigerian entrepreneurial performance with keen perception of, and response to, economic opportunity, willingness to adapt to changing market conditions, and marked competitive ability.

The strong testimony given by these non-Nigerians to the entrepreneurial skill of the Nigerians has been one of the important factors fostering industrial development in Nigeria, because it has contributed to the successful attraction of external and internal finance for industrial investment. There has been a steady flow of external finance into Nigeria because the external investors have confidence in the managerial ability of the Nigerians – an ability that ensures that the rate of return on the capital invested will be realised. In both the large and small enterprises the functions of the modern entrepreneurial organisation, involving the undertaking of risk and the handling of economic uncertainty, planning and innovation, co-ordination, administration and control, and routine supervision, were in full operation in Nigeria. Thus while we concentrate in the rest of this paper on discussing the role of finance in fostering Nigeria's industrial development, it should be borne in mind also that there were other factors whose contribution to this development was as crucial as that of finance.

II. THE GROWTH OF INDUSTRIAL DEVELOPMENT

Nigeria's industrial development accelerated in the 1950s and 1960s at a very fast rate, particularly during the ten-year period 1955–65. For example, as of late 1961 the Federal Ministry of Commerce and Industry listed about 700 industrial plants employing ten or more people;[2] although the statistics for the number of industrial plants before 1950 are not available, it is obvious that the number would not be more than 200. One support for this estimate is based on the analysis made from the 292 selected industrial establishments shown below, which shows that over 90 per cent were built after 1950. Of the 292 industrial projects considered, 259 were in operation at the end of 1965, while 33 were either under proposal or construction. Of the industrial establishments in operation, 60 were located in the

Federal Territory (Lagos), 57 were located in the Northern Region, 60 in the Eastern Region, 62 in the Western Region and 20 in the Mid-Western Region; and of those under construction, 4 were sited in the Federal Territory, 11 in the Northern, 8 in the Eastern, 6 in the Western and 4 in the Mid-Western Regions (see Table 1).

Table 1
Location of Selected Industrial Establishments at End of 1965

Project	*Federal*	*Northern*	*Eastern*	*Western*	*Mid-Western*	*Total*
In operation	60	57	60	62	20	259
Under construction or proposal	4	11	8	6	4	33
Total	64	68	68	68	24	292

Capital investment in these industrial projects ranged from amounts as low as £10,000 for the boat-building yard in the Northern Region, timber processing in the Western Region and doughnut bakery products in Lagos, to the £8 million petroleum refinery in the Western Region.[3] On the other hand, the number of employees ranged from 10 in the Onitsha market abattoir and 20 in Nigerian Ropes Ltd, Apapa, to 2,800 in Kaduna Textiles Ltd and furthermore to 3,200 in African Timber and Plywood (Nigeria) Ltd, Sapele. It is regretted that the figures of capital investment and employment for all the industrial projects could not be obtained owing to the difficulty of getting them. Table 2 shows those industries whose amount of capital investment and numbers in employment could be obtained.

Of the 259 industrial projects in operation by the end of 1965, the number whose capital investment data were available was 167, with a total capital investment of £85·66 million, thus giving the average investment of £513,000 per project. From Table 2 we see that the average investment per enterprise in the Northern (£613,000) and Eastern (£625,000) Regions exceeded the national average by approximately 20 and 22 per cent respectively, while in the Federal Territory, Western and Mid-Western Regions the average investment per enterprise was lower than the national average. With regard to the industries under construction the position was quite distinct in three respects. Firstly, the national average investment per industry, at £1,731,000, was more than three times as large as that of the average for industries already in operation. Secondly, the average

Table 2

Industries whose Capital Investment and Employment were Known

Region	*Capital investment*			*Employment*		
	No. of industrial establishments	*Total amount* (£m.)	*Average per establishment* (£'000)	*No. of industrial establishments*	*Total employment*	*Average employment per establishment*
1. *Industries in operation*						
Federal	29	9·50	328	50	6,770	135
Northern	41	25·14	613	46	11,750	260
Eastern	46	28·75	625	50	10,580	220
Western	41	19·86	484	51	8,980	180
Mid-Western	10	2·41	241	18	6,780	380
Total	167	85·66	513	215	44,860	209
2. *Industries under construction*						
Federal	2	0·70	350	n.a.	n.a.	–
Northern	5	12·82	2,564	3	1,900	630
Eastern	5	10·01	2,001	3	3,600	1,200
Western	5	2·33	466	2	270	135
Mid-Western	4	10·50	2,625	1	60	60
Total	21	36·36	1,731	9	5,830	648

n.a. = not available.

investment per industry in the Mid-Western Region exceeded the national average, whereas it was below the national average in the case of industries in operation. Thirdly, the average investment per industry in the Mid-Western, Northern and Eastern Regions exceeded £2 million as compared with under £630,000 for the Northern and Eastern Regions, and under £250,000 for the Mid-Western Region, in the case of industries already in operation. These three distinct features suggest a strong tendency towards large-scale investment in industries after the mid-1960s as compared with the period before. This tendency towards large-scale investment in industrial enterprises marked a very important development in the financing of industrial development and in the acquisition of experience in management.

The employment data shown in Table 2 tend to exhibit a trend similar to that of capital investment. The average employment per industry in the Mid-Western, Northern and Eastern Regions exceeded the national average. Since the average size of investment per industry in the Northern and Eastern Regions was larger than in the Western Region and in the Federal Territory, it would not be surprising that the average number of employees per industry in the former was larger than in the latter. The main reason why the average employment per industry in the Mid-Western Region exceeded the national average was because of the large number (3,200) employed in African Timber and Plywood (Nigeria) Ltd, Sapele; this large figure had the effect of swelling the Mid-Western Region's total number of employees.

Judging from capital investment and employment per industry in Nigeria, the industrial projects in that country are of considerably small scale when compared with the corresponding sizes in developed countries. This, of course, lends support to one of those characteristics which distinguish the developing countries from the developed ones, namely, that production is often carried out under conditions of small-scale operation in the former groups of countries but under conditions of large scale in the latter. In order to gain an impression of the strong tendency for capital investment and employment in Nigerian industrial enterprises to concentrate around figures of very low ranges, Table 3 has been constructed to show the frequencies.

It is interesting to note from this table that the frequency distribution of capital investment sizes in each region except the Northern is fairly symmetrical, with the largest concentration around the range £100,000 and under £500,000. In the case of the Northern Region the

Table 3

Frequencies of Capital Investment and Employment Grouping

Capital investment (£)	*Federal Territory*	*Northern Region*	*Eastern Region*	*Western Region*	*Mid-Western Region*
0 and under 50,000	6	13	11	8	1
50,000 and under 100,000	3	4	11	7	4
100,000 and under 500,000	13	11	13	18	4
500,000 and under 1 million	4	4	3	3	–
1 million and under 5 million	3	8	7	4	1
5 million but not over 8 million	–	1	1	1	–
Employment					
0 and under 500	48	42	43	47	14
500 and under 1,000	2	1	6	2	2
1,000 and under 1,500	–	2	–	1	1
1,500 and under 2,000	–	–	1	–	–
2,000 and under 2,500	–	–	–	1	–
2,500 and under 3,000	–	1	–	–	–
3,000 and under 3,500	–	–	–	–	1

largest concentration of the frequencies occurs around the range 0 and under £50,000, thus being highly positively skewed to the left. On the part of employment, the largest concentration of the frequencies of employment size occurs around the range 0 and under 500, thus making the frequency distribution in this case highly positively skewed to the left. The frequencies falling under the range 0 and under 500 account for about 90 per cent of all frequencies for the regions, leaving only 10 per cent for all the other class intervals from 500 to under 3,500, thus showing the preponderance of the number of employees in all industrial projects falling within the range 0 and under 500. The frequency distributions of both capital investment and employment for all regions combined are shown in Fig. 4.1.

The reasons for the concentration of the frequencies of capital investment and employment size around very low class intervals – 0 to 500,000 and 0 to under 500 respectively – are quite clear. Firstly, it is largely due to the problem of availability of finance for large-scale industrial establishments. Unlike the situation in the developed countries, the Nigerian indigenous investors are people with little capital, and owing to lack of confidence and mistrust of one another they are unable to pool their small resources so as to form large industrial concerns capable of attracting large-scale investment, as is the case in most developed countries. Secondly, although the external investors are comparatively wealthier and are in a better position to raise and invest considerable sums of money in Nigeria, they are often cautious and hesitant about investing large sums in industrial projects, particularly during the early period of industrialisation, owing to the absence of several essential factors (e.g. well-developed infrastructure, expanding internal market, sufficient power and water supply, availability of skilled industrial labour, etc.) whose existence is a prerequisite for large-scale investment. Thus, while the mining and petroleum industry is an attractive sector for large-scale foreign investment, the industrial sector – especially during the early stages – is not.

It was due to the above two reasons that capital investments in Nigerian projects concentrated around the range £0–500,000, with 76 per cent of the frequency distribution falling within that range, while for employment the concentration was around the range 0–500 employees despite the fact that most of those industrial projects already in operation were oriented towards labour-intensiveness. Nigeria is not unique in this regard; the history of economic development reminds us that during the early stages of industrial growth of the present-day industrialised nations, the sizes of their capital investments and employment were relatively as small as those of Nigeria today.

III. FINANCING THE INDUSTRIAL PROJECTS

The industrial projects discussed in the previous section were financed by both internal and external investors. The domestic financing could be divided into two aspects, namely, (1) Government and other public authority financing, and (2) private financing (including individuals, financial institutions and companies). Similarly, the foreign financing could be divided into (1) loans, grants and direct investment from foreign governments and other public authorities, and (2) loans and equity investment from foreign private individuals and companies, including financial and non-financial institutions. Here loans are defined as comprising hard loans (on conventional terms) and soft loans (on lenient terms) repayable in the receiving country's currency. These various aspects of financing Nigeria's industrial development are discussed below.

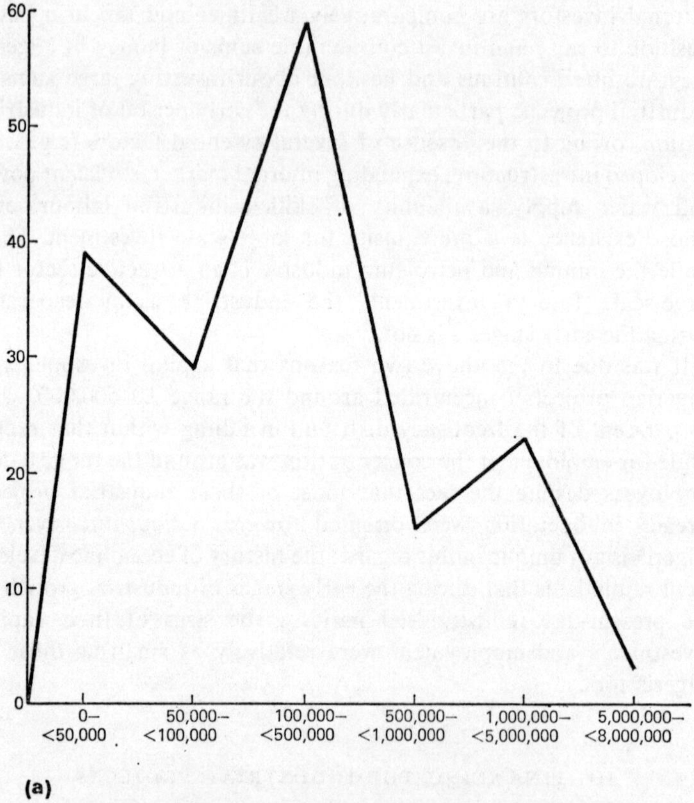

Fig. 4.1. Frequency distribution of capital investment and employment by size: (*a*) capital investment; (*b*) employment

1. *Domestic Financing: The Government and the Public Authorities*

The majority of the industrial projects selected for discussion were financed directly and indirectly by the Federal and Regional Governments or by their agencies – the Development Corporations. Writing in 1938, Professor Frankel noted that public listed capital in Nigeria formed 46 per cent of the total capital invested in Nigeria between 1928 and 1934;[4] but by 1965 the proportion must have risen considerably because of the large effort by the public sector in promoting the industrialisation of the country.

The sources of capital for the Government and the other public authorities for financing these industrial projects were revenues from

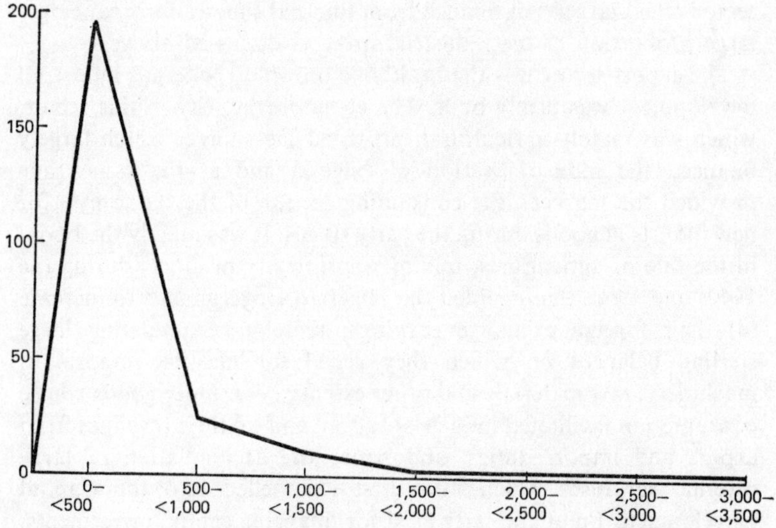

(b)

import and export duties, grants from the Marketing Boards, plus loans and grants from foreign governments and loans from domestic sources. The industries financed by the public sector ranged from those processing agricultural products (e.g. rubber, timber, oilseeds, etc.) to those manufacturing cement and assembling motor vehicles. In the Eastern Region, for example, out of the selected 60 industrial projects in operation, 12 were owned 100 per cent by the Government and its agencies, 11 were owned by Nigerian private interests, about 25 were owned by foreign interests (individuals and companies) and 12 were owned jointly by Nigerian private interests, foreign interests and the Regional Government. It is, however, necessary to distinguish between ownership and financing of the industries. For example, whereas the Eastern Regional Government owned about 12 of the 60 industrial projects, the money with which they were financed could have come partly from grants and loans from foreign governments and partly from loans from domestic sources. But certainly not less than 70 per cent of the investments made by the Federal and Regional Governments were financed by revenues from import and export duties, grants from Marketing Boards and loans raised from the domestic money and capital markets. In other words, the public sector relied largely on finance from internal sources for financing a large proportion of the industrial projects discussed above.

The export sector was the backbone on which Nigeria's industrial development was firmly built. The economic activity in this sector, which was mainly agricultural, provided the sources which largely financed the industrialisation of Nigeria and at the same time provided the market – the consuming section of the economy – for new industrial goods during the early stages. It was mainly the boom in the sale of agricultural, mining and forestry products during the 1940s and 1950s that enabled the Nigerian Governments to increase (*a*) their foreign exchange earnings, thereby accumulating large sterling balances on which they relied for massive imports of machinery, raw materials and other essential consumer goods whose consumption facilitated industrialisation, and (*b*) their revenues from export and import duties, and hence the accumulation of large revenue surpluses which were first channelled into the Capital Development Fund and later used for financing capital investments. Moreover, the same export boom enabled the Marketing Boards to accumulate large surpluses from their marketing operations, and these surpluses were handed over to the Regional Governments and their agencies (the Development Corporations) in the form of grants and loans for financing various industrial projects. It was therefore largely on the backs of the Nigerian farmers that industrial development in Nigeria was built in the early stages.

Nigeria's sterling balances in the U.K. – which were predominantly working balances in the hands of private banks and normal reserves held by the Currency Board and Crown Agents for the Federal and Regional Governments – stood at £263 million in March 1955. These balances originated partly from the proceeds of the sale of Nigeria's export crops under the long-term contract purchased by the U.K. Government, and partly from the reserves of the Marketing Boards and the budget surpluses of the Federal and Regional Governments which were deposited in the U.K. Table 4 shows that Nigerian official holdings of the sterling balances on 31 March 1955 totalled £180·1 million, of which the Federal, Regional and local Governments held 41 per cent, the Marketing Boards held about the same, and the other official bodies, e.g. Development Corporations, held 18 per cent. But it is interesting to note that by 30 April 1965 the total sterling balances stood at only £73·9 million, of which the official holding was only £16·4 million.

Table 4
The Run-down of Nigeria's Sterling Balances
(£million)

Holders	*31 Mar 1955*	*31 Dec 1957*	*31 Dec 1958*	*31 Dec 1961*	*30 June 1963*	*30 Apr 1965*
Federal Government	47·3	56·0	50·6	27·1	22·2	1·59
Regional Governments	23·2	33·8	31·0	19·5	7·1	4·80
Local government bodies	3·1	3·5	3·5	3·9	3·9	*
Development Boards and Regional Development Corporations	13·0	8·0	6·1	1·3	0·6	*
Marketing Boards	74·0	40·3	32·0	0·4	5·7	1·72
Other semi-official[a]	19·5	11·3	7·2	9·4	5·3	8·30*
Total official	180·1	152·9	130·4	61·6	44·8	16·41
West African Currency Board[b]	54·0	77·0	70·0	6·8	–	–
Central Bank assets (overseas)[c]	–	–	–	75·7	61·8	56·10
Commercial banks (net balances due from abroad)[d]	24·3	8·8	10·6	6·1	0·9	0·60
Post Office Savings Bank	4·7	4·4	–	1·6	–	–
Total official and banking	263·1	243·1	211·0	151·8	107·5	73·90

Source: Federal Office of Statistics, *Digest of Statistics*; Central Bank of Nigeria, *Economic and Financial Review*.

Notes:

(*a*) Comprises L.E.D.B.; Coal, Railway and Electricity Corporations; W.A.A.C. (Nigeria) Ltd; Ports Authority; University College and Hospital, Ibadan; WAIFOR, etc.

(*b*) Backing for the currency in circulation. After the establishment of the Central Bank the sum is equivalent to the estimated West African Currency Board currency that is still in circulation.

(*c*) Includes gold held in Nigeria and dollar securities.

(*d*) Includes the value of holdings of U.K. Treasury bills and other Government securities in the U.K. by Nigerian banks.

* In 1965 'other semi-official' consisted of local governments, development and other statutory corporations, and the universities.

The quick run-down of the reserves held by the official bodies, from £180 million in 1955 to only £16·4 million in April 1965, gives an indication of how these savings had been quickly used up for financing both industrial and non-industrial projects.

Between the financial years 1946/7 and 1958/9 the Federal Government budget surpluses (which constituted one of the important sources of the sterling balances) amounted to £47 million as compared with £19 million for the Regional Governments between 1952/3 and 1955/6, and it was these surpluses which helped in financing industrial development.

The revenue from import and export duties levied from 1951/2 to 1960/1 amounted to £452 million, about 64 per cent of the total Government revenues collected by the central Government during that period. As the level of public current expenditure was running well below that of current revenues, the Federal and Regional Governments were thus able to accumulate the large budget surpluses discussed above. In addition, the trading surpluses accumulated by the Marketing Boards between 1939–40 and 1960–1 amounted to about £158 million, and a large proportion of these surpluses was made available to the Regional Governments and the Development Corporations for financing development projects.

Another source through which the public sector acquired the funds for financing industrial development was by borrowing from the domestic money and capital markets. This source will be discussed in Section V.

2. *Domestic Financing: The Private Sector*

Owing to the low level of private domestic saving, the main burden of financing industrial development had to be borne by the public sector. Consumer expenditure was a high proportion, about 85 per cent, of the G.N.P., and this was responsible for the low contribution of private domestic financing to industrial development in the Federation. To erect an industrial enterprise one needs not only fixed capital equipment but also liquid capital, and in this respect the setting-up of an industrial project differs from trading. In Nigeria, for example, a trader uses more liquid capital, and even though the quantity of capital may be large, it is largely in the form of liquid capital; on the other hand a Nigerian industrialist needs both fixed capital and working capital. This is one of the handicaps affecting the growth of industrial establishments that are wholly financed, controlled and managed by Nigerians. Owing to the low level of income, private domestic savings are low and the tendency is to move into the field of trading which requires little or no fixed capital equipment compared with industrial enterprise. Perhaps one way of overcoming this handicap is for more Nigerians to pool their scarce resources and form limited-liability companies capable of financing large-scale enterprises, but various social and political handicaps prevent the successful formation of such companies, contrary to the situation in the developed countries.

However, despite these obstacles to the growth of industrial enterprises financed, controlled and managed by the indigenous private sector, some limited success has been made in this respect. We noted above that of the 60 industrial establishments in operation in the Eastern Region, 11 were completely owned and financed by the indigenous private sector; similar figures in the other regions were: Northern Region, about 4 out of the 57 operating; Western Region, about 9 out of 62; Federal Territory, 2 out of 60; and Mid-Western Region, 3 out of 20. In the Eastern Region, for example, there were such prominent industrial entrepreneurs as J. D. Okeke & Brothers, who established the saw-milling industry in Port Harcourt, employing 25 workers with a capital investment of £35,000; they also set up a timber-processing plant at Enugu employing 500 people. Another indigenous industrialist from the Eastern Region was Mr Ugochukwu, who set up Ugochukwu Tyres Ltd at Onitsha with a capital investment of £40,000 and employing about 50 people. Next was Mr Okwuba, who set up the Okwuba Commercial Syndicate at Onitsha, employing 23 people and producing sandals.

Perhaps two of the most successful indigenous industrialists were Messrs J. A. Odutola and T. A. Odutola, all of the Western Region. The former successfully set up four industrial projects (two in the Western Region, one in the Eastern Region and one elsewhere in the Federation). His industrial projects in the Western Region were J. A. Odutola Plastic Foam Company Ltd, producing polyurethane foam, and Odutola Tyre Retreading Company Ltd, Ibadan, with a capital investment of £75,000 (which was the second largest capital investment by an indigenous Nigerian). The project in the Eastern Region was Odutola Tyre Retreading Company Ltd, Aba, with a capital investment of £50,000. Altogether his capital investments in the last two projects amounted to £125,000, which by Nigerian standards was a substantial contribution to industrial financing by one individual.

Another successful industrialist, with the same surname but completely unrelated, was Mr. T. O. Odutola, who also financed three tyre retreading and production factories, one in each of the three main Regions, at Ibadan in the Western Region, Onitsha in the Eastern Region and Kano in the Northern Region. These three industrial establishments, with a total capital investment of over £150,000, were owned 100 per cent by him, and offered employment to over 300 people who worked three shifts in 1960–61. Total output of tyres from the three plants was about 52,000. It is seen, therefore, that of the selected 259 industrial establishments in operation by 1965, no fewer than 30 were wholly financed, controlled and managed by Nigerian private investors, excluding those which were jointly financed and managed by them and other investors. The success of most of these indegenous industrialists was due to their concentration on the production of some products rather than dispersing their entrepreneurial efforts, which caused the failure of most of the Nigerian bread bakers.

The bread industry contains a large number of vigorous indigenous entrepreneurs who entirely dominate the industry to the complete exclusion of foreign industrialists. In this regard the study of the Nigerian bread industry by Peter Kilby shows how the growth of the industry in Nigeria bears undoubted witness to the entrepreneurial ability, foresight, innovation and managerial capacity of the Nigerians.[5] In no other industry is production carried out in so many small units as in the bread industry: investment in the industry ranges from an amount as low as £30 for rented spaces, an oven, a sack of flour and a few simple implements, to £300,000 for a fully mechanised modern bakery. But it was not so much the large number of small units that was of importance as the great entrepreneurial ability which the Nigerians showed that led to the emergence and growth of this industry as a modern industry.

During Kilby's interviews and investigations he came across a large number of industrialists in the bakery industry who showed varying degrees of both success and failure in certain respects. The most typical of these was Edward Adebanjo Idowu, who resigned his lucrative and secure Civil Service post as a first-class clerk in 1941 to establish a small soft-drink bottling plant. In addition, he experimented in making stout from local Guinea corn and established a contracting service in electrical wiring and plumbing. In 1948 he added a simple hand-baking operation to his enterprises. With £1,862 of his own and £981 from two relative partners he purchased an imported dough-brake, one second-hand van, bread pans and the materials to build ovens, and a four-room building in Ibadan. After assembling the bakery he inaugurated the tightly controlled production regime. Furthermore, he engaged in engineering activities and constructed and sold large numbers of cassava graters, groundnut decorticators, palm-kernal crackers, palm-fruit crushers, yam-flour hammer mills and poultry batteries.

In 1961 he improvised a device for waxing bread wrappers, but by far his greatest and most profitable adaptive innovation was his imitation of the imported dough-brake, which he first produced in 1954. Having not yet forgotten his brewing experiments earlier on, and being attracted by company reports to the stockholders of the country's only beer producer indicating an annual return on investment of nearly 100 per cent, he became determined to be Nigeria's first indigenous brewer. After setting up a pilot brewery operation, he launched at the same time a vigorous campaign to secure a loan from the Western Region Finance Corporation and registered his product in the non-excise category of 'native liquor'. In 1960 he was granted a loan of £5,150, followed several months later by the Federal Board of Customs and Excise decision that his stout was liable to excise duty. Although he got 'Sports Stout' in full production it was only for less than a year, and it came to a halt owing to the burden of the retroactive excise duty, the pressure from the only established expatriate brewery firm to its distributors not to handle 'Sports Stout' and, finally, the poor reception given to his product by consumers. In 1962, still heavily in debt, Idowu initiated on a substantial scale the production of writing chalk. His problems were the same as he started with in baking: low quality and lack of an adequate market.[6]

The story of Idowu's industrial adventures at producing a variety of products is typical of that of several other Nigerians. This provides a case of both industrial success and failure. Firstly, there was the readiness to take up new ventures even at the risk of losing relatively well-paid and secure jobs in the Civil Service. Secondly, there was the tendency to be involved in more than one entrepreneurial activity at a time, which was one of the main causes not only of his failure but also that of many other Nigerians. Kilby discovered that the less educated the bakers were, the greater was their tendency to concentrate solely on one enterprise,[7] but unfortunately Idowu was of the educated class and hence found it difficult to concentrate on one enterprise. Thirdly, the manner in which he financed his industrial undertakings was typical of that of many other Nigerians; namely, he combined personal savings with loans from relatives and partners plus loans from the Development Corporations. Fourthly, the causes of Idowu's failure were also typical of those of other Nigerians: he failed to develop marketing channels and to improve the quality of his product; to these can be added the dispersion of entrepreneurial effort caused by being involved in too many undertakings, all at the expense of effective specialisation in any single enterprise. Fifthly, there was the element of vulnerability of the local businessman to foreign competitors as a result of the latter's greater technical competence and financial strength. These handicaps led to a low level of productivity which constituted a peril to the business of the indigenous investor.

A vast majority of the successful bakers fell into the production-oriented entrepreneurs, each of whom mixed his own ingredients, experimented periodically with his product and spent considerable time in the bakery every day supervising production. On the other hand, very few of these production-oriented entrepreneurs showed any marked initiative or dynamism in the sphere of marketing.

If we extend Kilby's conclusion on the Nigerian bakers to all the other classes of entrepreneurs, we can visualise a situation in which the majority of Nigerian industrialists are identified with possessing a keen perception of and response to economic opportunity, willingness to adapt to changing market conditions and marked competitive ability. All these business qualities helped, at least indirectly, in attracting capital for industrial investment.

3. *External Financing: The Public and Private Sectors*

These two aspects of external financing (by both the public and private sectors) will be discussed together in this subsection.

We noted above that the majority of the industrial projects selected for discussion were financed directly and indirectly by Nigeria's public sector, and putting together Nigeria's public sector and private sector it can be estimated that these two sectors between them financed not less than 60 per cent of industrial projects, thus leaving about 40 per cent which were financed externally by both public and private sources. The foreign private sector played a more dynamic part than the foreign public sector in financing industrial development. The foreign private sector included important limited-liability companies such as the U.A.C., John Holt and the Nigerian Tobacco Company, as well as individuals and partnerships. Most of the large- and medium-scale industries, such as oil refining, cement milling, steel milling, steel re-rolling, flour milling, textiles, brewing, pharmaceuticals, phonograph records, assorted raw-material processing and assembly operations of various types, were either wholly financed from external sources or jointly financed by domestic and foreign sources.

Private foreign investment played a very important role in supplementing domestic funds. Professor Frankel noted that the largest part of foreign private capital investment in Nigeria up to 1910 was through the activities of the trading companies, whose gradual amalgamation into the present large concerns, among which the United Africa Company (U.A.C.) stands pre-eminent, has been so characteristic a gesture of economic development in Nigeria in particular, and West Africa in general.[8] He estimated that the U.A.C.'s investment by 1910 was not less than £25 million, and in 1961 it stood at £48·5 million for Unilever Ltd.[9] It is indeed very difficult to estimate the total amount of foreign capital investment in Nigeria, particularly the proportion that went into industrial development. This difficulty is due to poor and inadequate statistical data.

Of all the countries from which foreign capital flowed into Nigeria, Britain was by far the most important. It can be estimated that between 60 and 65 per cent of the foreign private investment in the industrial projects in operation at the end of 1965 came from Britain. The perponderance of the amount of overseas capital coming from Britain was due largely to the strong trade and political links between the two countries. For example, between 1959 and 1961 the U.A.C., a subsidiary of the Unilever Group, earmarked on average 45 per cent of the year's capital expenditure in Nigeria to manufacturing.[10] Most of the investments in the mining industry, the export sector (agricultural), internal trade and distribution services, as well as in manufacturing industry, were financed by British investors. Despite the familiar difficulties of tracing out the ownership of internationally traded securities, we see no reason to suppose that the percentage of industrial finance supplied by British investors was less than 65 per cent of total foreign capital inflow.

The flow of foreign finance from the U.S.A. into Nigeria for industrial development was comparatively negligible. Sokolski noted that at the end of 1960 the value of American direct investment in all of West African manufacturing, excluding smelting, was approximately $1 million. On the other hand, U.S. investment in Nigeria in 1957 was $15 million and in 1959 $16 million, while investment in fixed assets reached £15 million ($42 million) in 1962.[11] Although the level of U.S. investment in both Nigeria and West Africa in general was absolutely low, the pattern of allocation of investment between manufacturing activities and tertiary services is of great interest. A much greater attention was shown in investment in non-manufacturing activities. Compare, for example, the $1 million American direct investment in all West African manufacturing, excluding smelting, at the end of 1960 with $10·5 million in non-manufacturing activities in the same area ten years earlier, thus suggesting that the preponderance of U.S. investment was made in distribution facilities or petroleum companies. Following this same pattern of paying greater attention to non-manufacturing activities, one would expect little increase in fixed investment assets in manufacturing by U.S. private companies after 1962.

The attitude of U.S. investors to investment in manufacturing in Nigeria is not unique to Nigeria; rather it follows the line of American policy on investment in general between the developed rich countries and the less developed poor ones. V.K.R.V. Rao, the Indian economist, once quoted a brilliant young American economist as saying that 'the most serious obstacle to American investment in poor countries is poverty itself. . . . Our industrial capitalist is most easily attracted to developing countries, not to those still stagnant.' Furthermore, that same American economist added that American overseas investments in manufacturing are largest in countries where incomes are high, and the ranking of countries having American investment in *manufacturing* parallels their income *per capita*. The same fact was also observed and commented upon by a young English economist, who, when making a study of American overseas investment and European economic integration, found that on the whole there is a close relationship between the amount of American capital invested in the various European countries and the value of their G.N.P.[12] Rao also discovered that during the nine years between 1950 and 1958, when American private investment overseas rose by $15·3 billion, the share of manufacturers in this increase was \$4·7 billion; but the part that went to Africa, Asia and Australia (and Australia must have claimed the largest share) was only \$518 million, or less than a seventh of the total increase in investment in manufacturing.[13] The finance for some of the industrial establishments came from Italy, West Germany, Sweden, Norway, the Netherlands, Switzerland, Lebanon, India, Canada and Japan. The inflow of funds from those countries increased tremendously between 1955 and 1965, during which period the share of investment by British investors declined although it still remained comparatively high.

Capital inflow from foreign governments continued and was as important as the inflow of foreign private investment. Whereas the supply of U.S. private investment in manufacturing activities was very scarce, the U.S. government was more sympathetic to appeals for industrial development. For example, during the 1962–8 Development Plan the U.S. Government committed itself to giving Nigeria \$225 million as compared with \$25 million (loan) by West Germany, \$25·2 million by Italy, \$8·4 million by Israel, \$3·4 million by the Netherlands and \$14 million by the U.K.

4. *The Economic Advantages and Burden of External Financing*

The inflow of external finance undoubtedly facilitated the expansion of Nigeria's industrial activity and thus enabled the industrial sector to contribute more to the G.N.P.[14] The growth of the industrial sector would lead to the diversification of the economy and at the same time facilitate the expansion and diversification of employment opportunities, and the improvement of the balance of payments (depending on the value and size of the import content of the inputs), as well as increasing the supply of useful by-products. The participation of foreign finance in Nigeria's industrial development programme in the form of both equity and loans was important and essential to the promotion of industrialisation. All the recently industralised countries, with the notable exception of the Soviet Union and Japan, relied heavily on foreign loans and investments during the crucial early period of their industrial growth. This was particularly true of the U.S.A. and Canada. The rapid increase in Nigeria's industrial projects between 1955 and 1965 involved the superimposition of a heavy programme, and this, of course, led to a shortage of foreign exchange which, if not relieved by the inflow of foreign finance, would in turn have led to the drastic curtailment of consumer goods imports.

Foreign financial participation, which took the form of foreign exchange, therefore had the beneficial effect of directly relieving the foreign exchange shortage. At the same time it indirectly operates in an anti-inflationary manner by permitting more of the existing foreign exchange resources to be used to bring in consumer goods to lessen the pressure on prices. These fundamental advantages are unique to foreign financial participation, and they are of such significance that they alone may make possible accelerated investment while maintaining economic stability.[15] Another great advantage of foreign financial participation in Nigeria's industrial development programme was the important part it played in bringing in technical and managerial skills which usually are just as likely to be the limiting factor in industrial development as a shortage of capital. A large percentage of foreign investment was usually tied in with technical assistance, largely because foreign investors were generally unwilling to risk their capital unless there was a sufficient supply of technical know-how guaranteeing against loss through mismanagement.

On the other hand, foreign financial participation brings with it an economic burden. It automatically plunges a country into external debt, and the heavier the inflow without any corresponding level of repayments, the greater will be the economic burden. In any economy like that of Nigeria, which is dependent on the export of primary commodities for the accumulation of foreign exchange, the burden is greatest when there are considerable price fluctuations in world markets. When this happens, an increased proportion of the curtailed income has to be remitted abroad in payment of the debt, and this would place a relatively increased burden on the country's immediately available resources.

Although, as we have argued above, the industrial enterprises in which foreign finance has been invested are meant to be earning foreign exchange, their earnings would depend on their productivity and the competitiveness of their products in the world market. Also, the payment of the equity shares to investors would depend on the earnings of the enterprises; if in periods of depression these earnings are reduced, the payment of dividends on the capital is *pro tanto* reduced also. With regard to fixed-interest-bearing debt, however, the debt charges remain whether the capital is yielding a corresponding return or not. The greater the proportion of the equity investment in total investment, the smaller will be the fraction of the investment involving contractual payments for debt service. In other words, the economic burden of external investment is comparatively lighter, the greater the proportion of the equity investment, because then the remittances to be made abroad for dividends vary in amount with the prosperity or adversity of the projects. In this regard Professor Frankel regarded Malaya as being fortunate in the sense that the bulk of the capital she received from abroad (mostly from Britain) took the form of equity investment. He then argued that when, as a consequence of adversity, exports dwindled to a very small amount, the same circumstances reduced almost to vanishing point the sum to be remitted abroad in payment of dividends on externally owned capital.[16]

Not all the receiving countries are as fortunate as Malaya, and certainly Nigeria is among the unfortunate ones because a substantial proportion of investment in the industrial projects was of the fixed-interest-bearing type. Some of the industrial projects sponsored by the Regional Development Corporations have been financed out of loans, some of which were hard loans. In such cases the economic burden of external financing is very great, especially during the early period when most of the industrial projects are producing well below capacity, management efficiency is poor and productivity very low. Under such circumstances the earnings of the industries will be low and not enough to pay the debt charges abroad.

These, I think, were the circumstances which led to Ghana's accumulation of over £200 million in external debt between 1955 and 1966.[17] Foreign capital investment, which formed a large proportion of this huge external debt, was in the form of fixed-interest-bearing loans used in financing some projects for which proper feasibility studies were not undertaken. In Nigeria also there were many such projects which were not economically sound and for which proper feasibility studies were not carried out. One difference between the situation in Ghana and that in Nigeria was that the latter's export economy was much more diversified than Ghana's, with the result that when the price of cocoa (the mainstay of Ghana's export economy) dropped heavily and fluctuated between 1955 and 1965, Nigeria's export economy was sustained by the export earnings from crude petroleum. The second difference between the two countries was that the rate at which the Nkrumah regime pursued the industrialisation of the Ghanaian economy was considerably faster than that at which the Balewa regime pursued the industrialisation of Nigerian economy, with the result that when the difficulties arising from the payment of external debt charges emerged, they proved to be more crippling generally to the Ghanaian economy than to the Nigerian economy.

Apart from the direct economic burden of external debt charges, there is also the indirect burden. During periods of depression a debtor country exports a greater volume of her products in order to obtain the same absolute monetary return. We may use the same example taken by Professor Frankel to illustrate this. For the year ending June 1935, Australia's exports realised £88 million in sterling, out of which about one-third was required for interest payment. But six years before, her exports were valued at nearly £140 million sterling and only one-fifth of that sum was required to meet interest payment on external debt. What is more, the volume of goods which Australia had to export to meet her interest charges in 1935 was roughly as much as in 1928/9.[18] By exporting considerably more in order to earn foreign exchange with which to pay external debt charges, a debtor country precipitates the worsening of the terms of trade against itself and thereby lowers its purchasing power. Consequently the difficulties of meeting the increased fixed interest burden contracted during the earlier stages are, in a period of depression, intensified by the decline in customs revenues owing to the lower volume and value of imports. This is followed by budget deficits which lead to the reduction of public expenditure, and the repercussions might spread on to affect employment, income and the lowering of living standards, depending on how large is (*a*) the export sector in relation to the whole economy, and (*b*) the external debt in relation to export earnings.

IV. SOME SPECIFIC FACTORS THAT FACILITATED FINANCING

There were three prominent factors which, among other things, played a very important role in encouraging and facilitating the financing of Nigeria's industrial development. These factors were (1) the existence of a good road transport system, (2) the Government's policy of fostering and promoting industrialisation, and (3) the existence of a promising domestic money and capital market. The role played by each of these factors is briefly discussed below.

1. *Good Road Transport System*

Although the rapid development of the infrastructure in general (namely road, railway and sea transport, power and water supply, health and sanitation, education and housing) in the Federation since the Second World War has played a very important part in Nigeria's industrial development, road transport has played a more spectacular role than any other aspect of the infrastructure. Road transport is closely related to the industrial projects discussed above, and the entrepreneurial performance of Nigeria's indigenous businessmen was fully identified with the rapid growth of this particular transport system. The road transport industry of Nigeria is composed of small firms owned and operated by Nigerians. The significance of road transport lies in the fact that, unlike traditional agriculture and trading, it is an industry that requires the use and operation of fixed capital equipment.[19]

The most significant thing about Nigerian road transport is that it is very largely in African hands. It represents the most important example of the emergence of local enterprise in Nigeria and is thus of great significance for the future development of the country. The ability to produce a class of entrepreneurs who are more than traders is a requirement of any society before economic growth can become a continuous process. The rapid expansion of Nigeria's road transport industry can be seen from the following statistics. The stock of commercial vehicles at the beginning of the year rose from 7,300 in 1950 to 16,900 in 1956 (an average increase of 22 per cent per annum), the annual gross addition to the stock of vehicles rose from 2,900 in 1950 to 7,340 in 1950, while the net addition to stock rose from 400 in 1951 to 3,200 in 1956.

Table 5 shows the distribution of commerically owned vehicles according to various age groups of the vehicles. From this table it will be seen that in all regions the majority of vehicles were under five years old, and for the country as a whole 86 per cent fell into this category. This shows how the road transport industry tried to modernise its equipment. By 1964 the number of commercial vehicles registered (i.e. gross addition during the year) stood at 6,320, excluding the Southern Cameroons. This decline in registration compared with 7,340 in 1956 was only due to the breakaway of the Southern Cameroons from the Federation. The increase in the number of vehicles was also accompanied by a tremendous increase

Table 5
Percentage of Commercially Owned Vehicles in Various Age Groups at the Beginning of 1955

Age in years	*Lagos (Fed. Terr.)*	*Western Region*	*Northern Region*	*Eastern Region*	*Nigeria*
Under 1 year	29	30	25	34	29
1 year and under 2	24	27	19	31	25
2 years and under 3	17	19	16	18	17
3 years and under 4	9	9	8	6	8
4 years and under 5	10	6	8	5	7
5 years and under 6	4	3	6	2	4
6 years and under 7	3	2	5	1	3
7 years and under 8	1	1	3	*	1
8 years and over	3	3	10	2	5
Total	100	100	100	100	100

* Less than 1 per cent.

Source: Hawkins, *Road Transport in Nigeria*, p. 20.

in road mileage, both tarred and untarred. Tarred road mileage increased from 2,688 in 1956 to 7,500 in 1963, while untarred mileage rose from 32,580 to 41,920 during the same period.[20]

The growth in the road transport industry had a great impact on industrial development. In the first place, it led to the lowering of transport costs and hence facilitated increased internal demand for manufactured products through the lowering of prices. Secondly, it brought the markets in the villages, districts and provinces closer to the urban centres where the industrial plants are located. In other words, it facilitated the integration of the markets into a national economy. Thirdly, the expansion of the road transport services stimulated the expansion of primary production for both the export and domestic markets. It made previously inaccessible areas accessible, and also assisted in the prompt evacuation of produce from the place of production to other centres, and the bringing back in return of local produce and imported goods from other centres. In short, it assisted specialisation in production, thus resulting in the realisation of comparative cost advantage. Finally, the road transport industry has played a very important role in producing that class of Nigerian entrepreneurs whose skill and performance lie not merely in the ability to trade, but in the capacity to invest profitably in fixed capital.

2. *Fiscal Incentives and Other Official Measures*

The industrial projects selected for discussion came into existence largely between 1955 and 1965, with the exception of about a dozen which were established before 1955. In other words, over 95 per cent of these industries have been in existence for about only nineteen years or less, and hence fall within the category of what is usually termed 'infant industries'. It is the practice all over the industrial world to protect infant industries, despite the weight of the argument against such a practice.

In 1958 the Federal Government published a White Paper[21] in which it briefly explained the role it was going to play in promoting industrial development in Nigeria. The White Paper listed the following ways by which the Federal Government could assist industrial development. Firstly, by providing a framework of law which is suited to industry – not only in the cases of regulating companies and banking, providing protection of patents and trade marks and against bankruptcy, but over a wider field which includes land tenure and the labour code. Secondly, by arranging for the provision of public utilities such as roads, railways, ports, water supplies and electric power which businesses cannot economically provide for themselves. Thirdly, by taking positive steps to attract capital and industrial know-how through the employment of the appropriate fiscal system. Fourthly, by making a direct contribution by way of advisory services and the provision of capital from public funds so that enterprise is not stultified by lack of means or capital wasted by lack of expertise.

The Regional Governments strengthened the determination of the Federal Government to promote industrial development by publishing similar White Papers setting out the role they themselves would play. For example, with regard to the last item – the contribution of expertise and capital – we have noted above how the Federal and Regional Governments financed a large number of industrial projects jointly with other investors. In addition, the Joint Planning Committee and the National Economic Council were set up not only to co-ordinate on a national level the projects of all the Governments of the Federation, but also to offer advice and services to external investors seeking information relating to incentives offered to industrialists, the location and siting of industries, etc.

Of the four measures listed in the White Paper which the Federal

Government pursued in order to promote industrial development, the one most relevant to our study is the third – the building-up of a suitable fiscal system. Before the 1958 White Paper various sorts of fiscal incentives had been granted. For instance, in 1952 the Income Tax (Amendment) Ordinance was passed which gave generous 'initial allowances' as well as 'annual allowances' to both public and private companies, thus permitting them to write off from profits, for the purpose of computing taxable income, a large amount of their capital investment in fixed assets during the early years of trading. This enabled the companies to amortise their capital quickly and to build up liquid reserves at an early date, thereby making further investment easier. In 1957 an amendment to this Ordinance included capital expenditure on clearing and planting land within the scope of these allowances, thus encouraging investment in plantations.

In the same year of 1952 the Aid to Pioneer Industries Ordinance was passed, its functions being to provide relief from company tax for a period varying from two to five years to public limited companies.[22] In the light of the I.B.R.D.'s comments that the Aid to Pioneer Industries Ordinance, 1952, did not offer as many inducements and for as long periods of exemption as the laws of other countries, the Industrial Development (Income Tax Relief) Ordinance was passed in 1958,[23] its intention being to provide a simpler procedure, more generous benefits and less onerous qualifying conditions for relief from company tax. The I.B.R.D.'s comments also prompted the passing of the Industrial Development (Import Duties Relief) Ordinance, 1957, which authorised the repayment of part or all of any duty paid on imported raw, semi-processed or processed materials, including components or reagents, used in the manufacture or processing of goods or in the provision of services. The Ordinance also authorised the granting of concessions wherever it could be shown that without such benefits the prospective industry would be unable to provide goods or services. Duty concessions might also be granted on imported capital goods, while repayment might be made in respect of duty paid on fixed plant for manufacturing or processing or on materials imported for the construction of such plant or installation.

The steps taken above to promote industrial development were supplemented by the Federal Government's readiness to consider the imposition of protective import duties where full relief from duties on materials was insufficient. But these protective measures would be granted only in those cases where the local industry would be able eventually to compete with imported goods without protection; yet no indication was given as to how to determine that such a stage had been reached. However, the inclusion of such a provision implied that any request for the imposition of protective duties would not only have to demonstrate the need for such assistance, but would normally also have to show that the need would one day cease.[24] In 1956 the Federal Government instructed all the Purchasing Departments of the Governments of the Federation to place orders with local manufacturers, provided the quality and price of their goods were competitive with comparable imported products. Thus, by promoting this 'buy made in Nigeria campaign', a considerable measure of assistance was afforded to local industries in their struggle to get over their industrial teething problems.

Also in 1956 the Federal and Regional Goverments issued a joint statement aimed at encouraging the inflow of overseas capital and skills in every form of industrial enterprise, and support was given to the principle of partnership between overseas and indigenous capital and skilled personnel. The statement emphasised that there would be no rigid insistence on local participation, although the Federal and Regional Governments or their agencies might wish to share in the financing of certain large enterprises (e.g. refineries) which had a special significance to the public. This statement was made in order to reduce the disinclination of foreign capital and technical skills to enter Nigeria on a scale sufficient to satisfy the country's requirements.

In addition to the granting of the various fiscal incentives discussed above, the Federal Government also set up several advisory and other auxilliary services which aimed at assisting, facilitating and promoting industrial growth. One of these was the Industrial Advisory Group set up in 1956 within the Federal Ministry of Commerce and Industry in accordance with the International Bank mission's recommendation. The functions of the Group were fourfold:

(*a*) to examine in detail problems of establishing individual industries;
(*b*) to persuade entrepreneurs and investors, both indigenous and expatriate, to undertake such enterprises;

(*c*) to advise upon Federal Government participation in industrial projects; and

(*d*) to advise on legislation and administrative measures.

The third aspect of the measures taken by the Federal Government to promote industrial development was the granting of investment aids to local and foreign entrepreneurs. For example, the Federal Loans Board, which was established in 1956, provided loans for projects designed to further industrial development both in the Federal territory of Lagos and, under certain conditions, throughout the Federation. An amount of £300,000 was earmarked for this purpose. The investigation of all loan applications was carried out by the Federal Department of Commerce and Industry, and every endeavour was made to ensure that the projects to which loans were made were not only profitable in themselves, but also contributed to the general economic development of the area. By the end of 1957 over a hundred applications had been received and loans amounting to over £80,000 had been approved.[25]

All these tax incentives and measures had the effect of facilitating the financing of industrial development by local and external investors, and also of protecting the newly established industrial projects from severe foreign competition. The successful effects of these measures can be seen in the rapid increase in the number of industrial enterprises after 1955. Most of the industrial projects were set up after that year. However, not all economists favour giving industries artificial protection, while some argue that in underdeveloped countries it is an essential policy to be pursued if industrial development is to become a reality. By restricting the imports of those commodities which are produced by the infant industries, domestic demand was thereby created for the domestic output. Professor Hirschman, for instance, does not oppose import restriction provided it is applied to the import of a particular product (and not to all products) so that the protection afforded to that industry can facilitate the enlargement of the domestic market for its product, thereby inducing further investment in the setting-up of an import-substitute industry.[26] In a slow-moving economy Professor Hirschman would therefore be willing to favour protection as a means of helping those industries which are on or near the threshold, provided protection is given to one industry at a time. The ideal thing would be to start with an autonomous investment in an industry which is capable of generating induced investment in both directions on its suppliers and on its customers (e.g. a large steel mill). Such a type of industrial development policy is in accordance with the unbalanced-growth approach whose main advantage for an underdeveloped country is that the amount of savings available is not outstripped by the number of autonomous investments chosen at a time.

On the other hand, those who believe in pushing ahead on all aspects of industrial development at the same time – i.e. the protagonists of the balanced-growth approach – favour the application of quantitative restrictions on a large number of imports because this offers the most important and flexible instrument of control over the foreign exchange accounts of the developing economy. Although this approach would lead to a considerable amount of inflationary pressure, they argue that in the course of time such an inflation will be self-destroying when the forced investment dramatically expands the national output and the infant economy gets over the hump.

We noted above that one of the basic conditions for the successful industrialisation of the Nigerian economy, or that of any other developing economy, was the availability of a sufficient supply of good management, effective labour, an efficient and developed transport network and a sufficient supply of finance from both internal and external sources. In order to employ these conditions effectively to promote industrial development, protective tariffs are needed so that the economy can withstand competition from foreign countries at higher stages of economic development. In addition to imposing protective tariffs Nigeria has also encouraged development by 'direct methods', such as the acceptance of technical assistance and foreign capital.

Apart from granting protection and attracting the supply of technical assistance and capital to all the industries in the Federation, it was also the role of the Federal Government to consider the special problem of protecting indigenous entrepreneurs to enable them to promote the growth of local manufacturing. In this respect the Regional and Federal Goverments not only granted the indigenous entrepreneurs development loans, but also imposed restrictions on entry by foreigners in some industries such as bread. It was indeed essential to offer the indigenous entrepreneurs this special protection, because most of them operated with very small capital and also lacked experience in efficient management and effective supervision.

The local businessmen are generally vulnerable to foreign competition because their foreign counterparts possess greater technical competence and financial strength. In addition, the latter do not suffer from the handicap of inefficient management which the local businessmen suffer from.

3. *The Domestic Money and Capital Market*

We have noted from our discussion above that one of the greatest problems in Nigeria's industrial development was the availability of finance for sound industrial projects, and also that the financing of the projects so far operating had come from various sources, both external and internal. Without the existence of money and capital markets, both within and outside the Federation, the raising of the various categories of investment capital for financing industrial enterprises would have been impossible. It is therefore our intention in this last part of our study to survey the role played by the domestic money and capital market in raising the finance for the country's industrial development.

The first important step to promote the growth of a money and capital market in Nigeria was taken in 1958 when the Federal Minister of Commerce and Industry appointed a Committee to advise on ways and means of fostering a share market in Nigeria.[27] The Committee examined not only the steps whereby a stock exchange could be brought into being as an institution, but also considered all the means whereby the buying and selling of stocks and shares could be facilitated. The Committee tackled their problem under three headings, namely:

(*a*) the functions of a share market;
(*b*) the conditions under which a share market can grow; and
(*c*) ways in which the growth of a share market can be encouraged in Nigeria.

A share market is a place where anybody can go to buy or sell shares of public limited-liability companies. Before 1958 there was no such facility for the purchase or sale of shares, and those who had Nigerian shares or Government stocks found it extremely difficult to sell them, which was annoying to those who preferred cash to holding entitlement to dividends or interest on their capital. Hence the significance of the establishment of a share market in Nigeria lay in the fact that it encouraged the public to lend money to the Government by subscription to the public issue of Government stock. Secondly, it encouraged the public again to purchase the shares and stocks of public limited-liability companies. In other words, it enabled the Governments and the limited-liability companies to harness the people's savings for the development of Nigerian industry. The investors were now reasonably assured of the existence of a market where they could convert their shares into hard cash whenever they chose to do so.

The creation of the Central Bank of the Federation in 1959 not only facilitated the development of the share market, but also resulted in the birth of the money market. Public confidence in shareholding as an investment is essential, and the creation of the Lagos Stock Exchange helped to sustain this confidence. It is the responsibility of the Central Bank to create and maintain conditions of such confidence.

Another landmark in the establishment of a money and capital market was reached in 1959 when the Treasury Bills Ordinance was passed, its purpose being to make provision for the Federal Minister of Finance to authorise the Central Bank to issue Treasury bills to the extent that the amount outstanding at any one time should not exceed 10 per cent of the estimated revenue of the Federal Government during the year then current. For example, in 1960/1 the estimated revenue of the Federal Government was of the order of £95 million, so that the amount of the Federal Government's Treasury bills outstanding during that year would not be more than £9·5 million.

Relying on the strength of the Treasury Bills Ordinance, the Central Bank undertook to raise the sum of £2 million for the Federal Government in May 1959 in the following order:

400,000 5% Federation of Nigeria Development Stock 1964;
600,000 5½% Federation of Nigeria Development Stock 1969;
1 million 6% Federation of Nigeria Development Stock 1979.

The warm response to the Federation of Nigeria Development Loan, which resulted in the oversubscription of all the stocks, was a reflection of the significance attached to the existence of the Lagos Stock Exchange. The response came not only from institutional sources but also from the private sector to the order of £100,000; this was most encouraging, especially in circumstances in which the general public had not yet been accustomed to that type of investment. The existence of the Lagos Stock Exchange solved the question of marketability and also provided the assurance that the stocks (or shares) could be converted into cash if and when necessary. Before the issue of the Development Stock in May 1959, the Nigerian Cement Company Ltd had offered 174,898 shares of £1 each at par four months previously. This was the first public issue of company shares, and it was made by one of the cement companies established in the Eastern Region.

In both the private and public sectors there was an increasing interest in the growth of a money and capital market in Nigeria. The public subscriptions served as a means of attracting Nigerian capital participation in development. For the Governments of the Federation particularly, the growth of the market enabled them to attract the savings of the public for development purposes, and gratitude for the efficient service of the Central Bank within so short a time after its establishment.

The activities in the money and capital market of the Federation of Nigeria broadened significantly after 1959. For instance, from January to December 1962 about 21 Treasury bill issues were recorded, and the Treasury bill rediscount operations in 1961 totalled £14·3 million, declining slightly to £12·3 million in 1962, but rising again to £13·4 million in 1963. On the capital market side, the Central Bank had, by the end of 1962, succeeded in floating the Second and Third Development Loan Stocks amounting to £10 million and £7 million respectively, in addition to the £2 million raised under the First Development Loan Stock. The Second Development Loan Stock was floated in March 1961, the Third in February 1962. These were quickly followed by the flotation of the Federation of Nigeria Fourth Development Loan of £15 million in February 1963; this was the largest internal loan so far floated in the country. The number of transactions in the Lagos Stock Exchange, which only completed its first full year of operation in June 1962, rose from 334 in 1961 (second half of the year) to 711 in 1963, of which 415 were on industrial shares and debentures and 296 on Government stocks; during the same period the value of transactions rose from £76,000 in 1961 (second half of the year) to £5·2 million in 1963, of which £4·9 million was in Government stocks and £0·3 million in industrial stocks and shares.

The Treasury bill issues in 1965 totalled 52 as compared with 21 in

1962, while the amount outstanding stood at £42 million on 23 December 1965 as against £24 million on the same date in 1962. The number of transactions in the Lagos Stock Exchange increased from 711 in 1963 to 985 in 1964, but the most encouraging development in this respect was the spectacular increase in the value of the transactions in industrial stocks and shares in 1964. Of a total value of £7 million for the transactions in both industrial and Government stocks, the share of the former was £1·1 million (16 per cent) compared with £0·3 million (less than 6 per cent) in 1963. This was an indication of a strong trend towards public demand for industrial stocks and shares which encouraged more public companies to seek quotation for their securities on the Stock Exchange. In other words, it was evidence that the Nigerian public was becoming accustomed to investing in stocks and shares.

On the other hand, as the volume of transactions in Treasury bill issues and the floating of Development Loan Stocks increased, the public debt of the Federation Governments increased also. For example, the total public debt of the Federal Government[28] on 30 June 1961 was £74·33 million, of which internal loans amounted to £37 million and external loans £37·33 million; by 30 September 1965 the total debt had increased $2\frac{1}{3}$ times to £170·14 million, of which £119·7 million was internal and only £50 million external. Compared with 1961 the internal loan portfolio had more than tripled itself four years later, while loans from external sources increased by only one-third. Since a substantial proportion of these loans was spent on financing industrial projects by the Federal and Regional Governments, the availability of such an increasingly large sum of finance from internal sources indicated the large extent to which Nigeria could rely on its internal sources for financing its industrial development. Although the problem of the economic burden of public debt, which we have discussed earlier, also increased along with the increase in debt, the adverse repercussions would be proportionately less because of the preponderance of loans from internal sources.

From our discussion above we can now form an impression of Nigeria's rapidly developing money and capital market, which played a very significant role in facilitating the financing of that country's industrial development. The remarkable growth in the activities of the market could be attributed to three important factors, namely:

(*a*) the increasing financial requirements of the Governments of the Federation for economic development;
(*b*) the efforts of the industrial companies to obtain private participation by Nigerians in company ownership; and
(*c*) the Central Bank's continued efforts to widen opportunities for local investment of funds.

V. CONCLUSIONS

In concluding this paper we wish to reconsider three issues. The first is the crucial role of finance in industrial development in relation to the other factors of production; the second is the need to pay as much attention to industrial development as to agricultural development; and the third is the importance of creating that investment atmosphere essential for attracting the external capital inflow necessary for facilitating Nigeria's industrial development.

First, financial accumulation has often been regarded as the crux of the development problem in a developing country such as Nigeria because of its effects and impact on all the other factors of production. While it is important to note that all the factors of production are complementary in promoting industrialisation, it is also important to note that a sufficient supply of finance is essential for transforming all the other factors of production into conditions suitable for their use in the production process. For example, although there is a sufficient supply of land in Nigeria, part of it cannot be transformed into industrial estates and sites suitable for industrial establishment until a sufficient supply of finance is available to facilitate the transformation. The existence of industrial estates such as the trans-Amadi Industrial Layout and the Ikeja Industrial Estate no doubt played an important role in attracting industries into Nigeria; but without the availability of finance it would have been impossible to transform the original acres of land into these industrial estates that we see today, provided with amenities such as roads, storm-water drains, railroad sidings, electricity and water supply. Thus it is this crucial role which finance performs in transforming other factors of production into conditions suitable for absorption in the industrial production process via investment creation that tends to make it appear to be the crux of the development problem.

Second, although industrialisation provides the major means

whereby more diversification can be introduced into an underdeveloped economy, and also helps to bring greater stability to an economy largely dependent on primary exports and hence highly vulnerable to fluctuations in the world market, yet it does not provide the cure for all the ills of economic development. This implies that as much attention has to be paid to the expansion of agricultural production as is paid to the promotion of industrialisation, because basically it is only by raising agricultural production that the necessary conditions for industrialisation can be created. Thus while great emphasis is being placed on the contribution of finance to industrial development, similar emphasis should also be placed on the contribution of finance to agricultural production.

Third, while it has been argued above that in Nigeria the domestic financial contribution to the nation's industrial development programme was substantial, the large external capital inflow which also assisted industrial expansion cannot be overlooked. Today no underdeveloped country can industrialise fairly extensively without some financial contribution from abroad, which can be supplied in various forms. While it is desirable that various forms of fiscal incentives should be granted to foreign investors in order to attract a large inflow of foreign capital and industrial know-how, it is also essential to combine these fiscal incentives with other non-fiscal measures in order to obtain the maximum external capital inflow. Foreign investors need to know not only that the necessary incentives exist in the host country, but also that the necessary measures exist for protection of their capital investment. In other words, the creation of incentives to stimulate private investment must go side by side with the provision of guarantees to protect these private investments. It is sometimes not realised that early threats of nationalisation of foreign firms in many developing countries, which are just about to embark on fairly extensive industrialisation programmes, constitute a big handicap to external capital inflows. This handicap limits not only the size of the financial contribution to industrial development but also the capacity of capital to transform the other factors of production into conditions suitable for their participation in the industrial development process.

REFERENCES

1. E. K. Hawkins, *Road Transport in Nigeria: A Study of African Enterprise* (Oxford U.P., 1958); P. Kilby, *African Enterprise: The Nigerian Bread Industry* (Stanford: Hoover Institution Studies, 1965).

2. Federal Ministry of Commerce and Industry, *Industrial Directory* (Lagos, 1962).

3. The analysis of industrial establishments into regions does not imply that all establishments in each region were financed from the resources of that region alone. For example, the ordnance factory in the Northern Region was wholly financed by the Federal Government, while the petroleum refinery in the Eastern Region was partly financed by all the Federation Governments and partly by Shell–B.P. However, it is in the case of educational institutions, hospitals, dam projects, etc., that there are more cases of Federal financing in other regions.

4. S. H. Frankel, *Capital Investment in Africa* (Oxford U.P., 1938) p. 179.

5. Kilby, *African Enterprise*, p. 42.

6. Ibid., pp. 88–9.

7. Ibid., p. 89.

8. Frankel, *Capital Investment in Africa*, p. 162.

9. *The Economist* (London), 29 Apr. 1961, p. 479.

10. *U.A.C. Statistical and Economic Review*, no. 28, p. 52.

11. A. Sokolski, *The Establishment of Manufacturing in Nigeria* (New York: Praeger, 1965) p. 197.

12. V.K.R.V. Rao, *Essays in Economic Development* (London: Asia Publishing House, 1964) p. 262.

13. Ibid.

14. In 1957 the industrial sector contributed less than 5 per cent to the G.D.P., as compared with about 30 per cent in India and 20–33 per cent in Egypt.

15. M. D. Bryce, *Industrial Development* (New York: McGraw-Hill, 1960) p. 179.

16. Frankel, *Capital Investment in Africa*, p. 188.

17. *The Times* (London), 10 July 1970.

18. Frankel, *Capital Investment in Africa*, p. 188.

19. See Hawkins, *Road Transport in Nigeria*, for a detailed account of Nigeria's transport business.

20. Federal Office of Statistics, *Annual Abstract of Statistics* (Lagos, 1965) pp. 52–3.

21. Federation of Nigeria, Sessional Paper No. 3 (1958).

22. A pioneer industry was defined as one which either was not at present being carried on in Nigeria or was not established on a scale suitable to the economic development of Nigeria. See Sessional Paper No. 3 (1958) p. 4.

23. Federation of Nigeria, Ordinance No. 8 (1958).

24. It is difficult to define when an industry ceases to be an infant. This is a general problem for which no general solution has been found.

25. Federation of Nigeria, Sessional Paper No. 3 (1958) p. 9.

26. A. O. Hirschman, *The Strategy of Economy Development* (New Haven: Yale U.P., 1958) p. 121.

27. Federation of Nigeria, *Report of the Committee Appointed to Advise on Ways and Means of Fostering a Share Market in Nigeria* (Lagos: Federal Government Printer, 1958).

28. The Federal Government public debt was the same as the public debt of the entire Federation. In fact, a substantial proportion of the loans was floated for on-lending to the Regional Governments and the statutory corporations.

5

Some Aspects of Domestic Financing of Central Government Expenditure: The Case of Kenya

NIZAR JETHA*

THE public sector plays an important role in the Kenyan economy. It accounts for 25 per cent of the total G.D.P. and 35 per cent of the total gross fixed capital formation. The central Government forms the major segment of the public sector. The central Government's contributions to the total G.D.P. and gross fixed capital formation amount to 11 per cent and 16 per cent respectively, or in other words, the central Government is responsible for about 45 per cent of both the public sector's contribution to the G.D.P. and gross fixed capital formation. These statistics, however, fail to convey adequately the importance of the central Government *vis-à-vis* the other public (the public sector excluding the central Government) and private sectors, since significant proportions of the expenditures incurred by the latter, and in particular the capital outlays, are financed by the central Government.[1] The central Government expenditure as a proportion of G.D.P., which is in the region of 25 per cent, brings out more clearly the fact that the Government is in a position to influence the economy significantly through its expenditure and financing decisions. This paper will be concerned only with the financing of expenditures.

There will be two further limitations on the scope of this paper. External sources of finance will not be discussed, and the discussion of domestic financing will be confined to the two major sources of finance – taxation and domestic borrowing. These limitations are, however, not as restrictive as they seem at first sight. For one thing, the domestic sources of finance account for over 90 per cent of total revenue, as will be seen from Table 1.[2] For another, taxation and

* The author is indebted to Professor John Due and Nurali Peera for helpful comments. Thanks are also due to Mahesh Gheewala of the Treasury and Tito Birech-Kuruna of the Central Bank for their assistance. The author alone is responsible for the errors.

Table 1
Economic Analysis of Central Government Accounts, 1963–4 to 1968–9
(K£ million)

Recurrent revenue	*1963–4*	*1964–5*	*1965–6*	*1966–7*	*1967–8*	*1968–9*
Taxation	37·10	42·27	43·93	52·97	58·77	64·80
Income from property	0·92	1·04	1·06	1·33	1·37	1·47
Interest, dividends and profits	1·59	2·00	1·73	2·41	2·73	4·77
Transfers:	12·18	11·21	8·02	4·88	4·27	2·34
Domestic	(2·86)	(1·70)	(3·29)	(1·54)	(2·41)	(1·38)
Rest of the world	(9·32)	(9·51)	(4·73)	(3·34)	(1·86)	(0·96)
Sales of goods and services	3·91	4·47	4·86	5·32	6·54	7·03
Reimbursement of expenditure	1·25	1·18	0·84	1·58	1·95	1·92
Total	56·95	60·16	60·44	68·50	75·64	82·33
Capital revenue						
Recurrent surplus or deficit	+0·63	+3·27	−0·29	+3·71	+6·12	+7·11
New borrowing:	10·74	11·73	11·44	15·66	16·11	15·39
External	(10·74)	(10·70)	(9·43)	(7·84)	(7·83)	(7·10)
Internal	(–)	(1·03)	(2·01)	(7·82)	(8·28)	(8·29)
Loan repayments from other sectors	0·48	0·86	1·16	1·19	3·56	3·98
Capital grants:	0·64	0·27	0·43	0·16	0·05	–
Domestic	(–)	(0·04)	(0·06)	(0·03)	(0·01)	–
Rest of the world	(0·64)	(0·23)	(0·37)	(0·13)	(0·04)	–
Total	12·50	16·13	12·74	20·75	25·85	26·49

Recurrent expenditure						
Expenditure on goods and services	29·33	34·75	37·53	41·75	44·01	47·52
Subsidies	0·41	0·28	0·78	0·62	2·47	2·81
Interest:	4·05	4·41	4·73	5·25	5·40	5·98
External debt	(2·94)	(3·26)	(3·46)	(3·74)	(3·54)	(3·58)
Internal debt	(1·11)	(1·14)	(1·27)	(1·51)	(1·86)	(2·40)
Other transfers:	22·53	17·45	17·69	17·16	17·64	18·91
Domestic	(16·58)	(13·96)	(13·72)	(13·76)	(14·80)	(17·80)
Rest of the world	(5·95)	(3·49)	(3·97)	(3·40)	(2·84)	(1·11)
Surplus (+) or deficit (−) on recurrent account	+0·63	+3·27	−0·29	+3·71	+6·12	+7·11
Total	56·95	60·16	60·44	68·50	75·64	82·33
Capital expenditure						
Gross capital formation	3·15	4·23	6·43	10·01	14·38	16·60
Investment in government enterprises	–	–	0·05	0·30	0·52	0·33
Loans to other sectors	6·38	6·08	5·63	6·31	6·84	9·84
Loan repayments to other sectors:	2·27	3·13	4·68	3·47	2·72	2·98
External debt	(1·75)	(1·79)	(2·86)	(2·84)	(1·85)	(1·67)
Internal debt	(0·01)	(0·84)	(1·30)	(0·09)	(0·09)	(0·57)
Sinking fund	(0·51)	(0·51)	(0·51)	(0·55)	(0·78)	(0·74)
Net surplus(+) or deficit (−)	+0·70	+2·49	−4·04	+0·65	+1·39	−3·26
Total	12·50	16·13	12·74	20·75	25·85	26·49

Sources: *Statistical Abstract* (1969); Statistics Division, Ministry of Economic Planning and Development (S.D., M.E.P.D.).

domestic borrowing (excluding short-term borrowing) are responsible for over 70 per cent of the total revenue.

Kenya provides an outstanding example of a country that has, since independence, succeeded in increasing substantially the reliance placed on local sources in financing recurrent and development expenditures. The share of domestic finance in total revenue has grown from 70 per cent in 1963–4 to 90 per cent in 1968–9. The bulk of the increase in domestic sources has come from taxation and domestic borrowing.

Sections I–III will be devoted to a discussion of tax effort since independence, and current problems and future prospects concerning taxation. The subsequent section will deal with domestic borrowing from similar viewpoints. Finally, a brief concluding section will discuss the possibilities of using the Government's financial operations, including taxation and debt policies, for stabilisation purposes.

I. TAXATION POLICY

The country's tax performance since independence has been quite impressive. From 1963–4 to 1968–9, total tax revenues grew at the rate of 11 per cent per annum, raising the ratio of tax revenues to G.D.P. (at factor cost) from 11 per cent to 15 per cent. Direct taxation (the major component of which is income tax) grew at the rate of 12 per cent per annum. The annual rates of increase for import and excise duties were 10 per cent and 14 per cent respectively. Excise duties have grown at a higher rate than income tax and import duties. Finally, despite a high rate of growth for direct taxation, indirect taxation accounts for over 60 per cent of the total tax revenue (Table 2).

The relatively low level of taxation in the pre-independence period has facilitated increased taxation in the last few years. However, faced with the necessity of raising tax revenues rapidly to meet the recurrent costs of ambitious development plans as well as to create budget surpluses to finance capital expenditures, the Government has not paid sufficient attention to equity considerations in its tax policy. Kenya, like other developing countries, experiences a severe shortage of tax personnel, and particularly that needed for the purposes of income and capital taxation; consequently, tax revenues might have increased at a lower rate if greater emphasis had been attached to equity considerations. A conflict between equity and

Table 2
Central Government Tax Revenues, 1963–4 and 1968–9
(K£'000)

Direct taxes	*1963–4*	*1968–9*
Income tax	13,231	23,611
Export duties	170	351
Estate duties	152	308
Total direct taxation	13,553	24,270
Indirect taxes		
Import duties	13,694	21,830
Excise duties	6,019	11,793
Stamp duties	780	911
Petrol and diesel tax	1,070	1,789
Licences under the Traffic Act	699	1,278
Second-hand motor vehicles purchase tax	199	215
Motor drivers' licences	63	96
Entertainment tax	62	77
Betting and pools taxes	100	130
Other (mainly licences)	712	898
Total indirect taxation	23,398	39,017
Total direct and indirect taxation*	36,951	63,287

* The totals differ slightly from those shown in Table 1 because the revenue from central Government personal tax in 1963–4 and the revenue derived by the central Government from the G.P.T. transferred to it by Nairobi and Mombasa in 1968–9 have been excluded from this table for reasons of comparability (see note 6).
Note: Airport tax was introduced in June 1970; it is expected to yield K£130,000 in 1970–1.
Sources: *Statistical Abstract* (1969) and S.D., M.E.P.D.

administrative costs is inevitable. But in a country with rapidly growing revenue requirements and a serious deficiency of skilled manpower, the problem assumes a rather acute form. It is hoped that as administrative resources improve, more attention will be given to the redistributive function of taxation policy. Tax proposals will be discussed with particular reference to equity considerations. Only those features of the tax structure that are relevant for the purposes of the discussion will be described.[3]

1. *Income Taxation*

The introduction of pay-as-you-earn (PAYE) arrangements for the collection of income tax from employees, lower personal allowances (and in particular the married allowance), and elimination of

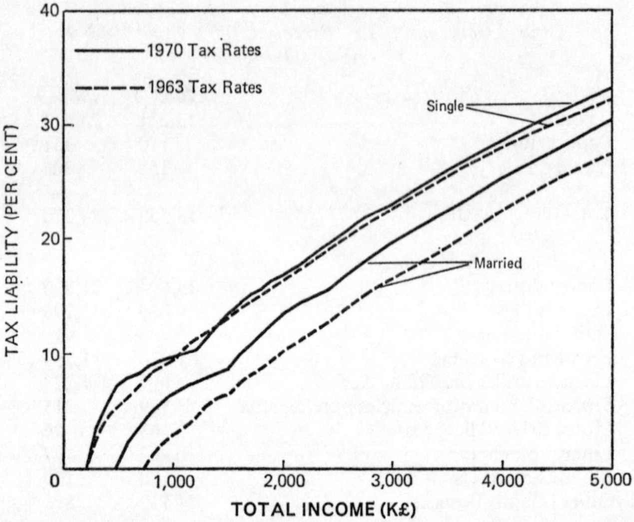

Fig. 5.1. Effective Rates of Tax for Single and Married Persons, 1963 and 1970

averaging provisions and passage, education and dependant allowances, have greatly improved the coverage of income tax in recent years. The single and married allowances have declined from K£225 and K£700 in 1963 to K£216 and K£480 respectively.[4] In 1963 a child allowance was granted for up to four children, and the allowance varied from K£75–250 according to the age of the child. The allowance continues to be given for four children, but it is now fixed at K£120 per child. The nominal tax rates have changed only very slightly since 1963. Currently, income tax at the rate of Shs. 2/50 in the £ is levied on all chargeable income; in addition, surtax, whose rates range from Shs. 3/– to Shs. 13/– in the £, is levied on chargeable income in excess of K£1,000. The effective tax rates applicable to single and married persons in 1963 and 1970 are illustrated in Fig. 5.1.

The numbers of taxpayers are as follows: over 200,000 employees, 16,500 individuals (one-man firms and partnerships), 600 clubs and trusts and 3,900 companies. The PAYE and lower personal allowances have significantly increased both the number of employees subject to tax and the employees' chargeable income. In the year of income 1964, when PAYE had not been in operation and the married allowance was K£600, only 37,000 employees were subject to tax, as against the present figure of about 200,000. The total chargeable income of employees has risen from K£31 million in 1964 to K£45 million in 1968–9. The number of other taxpayers has not changed much. Despite recent progress towards a more broadly-based income tax, the scope of the tax continues to be rather narrow. Only 2 per cent of the population is subject to the tax, and the aggregate income[5] assessed to tax amounts to less than 50 per cent of the monetary G.D.P.

2. *Personal Allowances*

The size of the personal allowances is a major reason for the restricted scope of the income tax. At present, single persons, married persons and married persons with four children are liable to income tax only if their incomes are five, ten and twenty-five times greater respectively than the *per capita* G.D.P. (of about K£40). Clearly, the income-tax net cannot be cast very widely when personal allowances are so large in relation to the *per capita* income. Far-reaching changes in the magnitude and structure of personal allowances will be needed if income tax is to be set on a course that would lead to a significantly enlarged coverage.

Administrative capacity imposes a severe constraint on the extent to which personal allowances can be reduced. It is very doubtful whether it would be administratively practicable to reach incomes that are less than five times the *per capita* G.D.P. (i.e. about K£200) through an income tax in the foreseeable future. This being the case, substantial differentiation in the treatment of single persons, married persons without children and married persons with children will inevitably restrict the income-tax base by excluding persons with incomes of more than, say, ten to fifteen times the *per capita* G.D.P. from its scope. To put it differently, given that it is administratively impracticable to tax incomes of less than about five times the *per capita* G.D.P., married and child allowances must be small in relation to the single allowance if the scope of the tax base is to be broadened significantly. This may be achieved by reducing the differentiation in the tax treatment of taxpayers of differing circumstances and/or by narrowing the criteria used for the purposes of differentiation.

There may be a case for the retention of a degree of differentiation in the treatment of single and married persons on administrative as well as equity grounds. However, if the maximum amount of allowances that may be claimed by a taxpayer is to be realistic in relation to the *per capita* G.D.P., then there would be very little room for differentiating between married persons with different family sizes. It may therefore be asked if child allowances should be retained at all. On equity grounds, the case for the continuance of these allowances is not clear-cut. In a country where the extended family is prevalent and family ties are strong, child allowances cannot take proper account of the burden imposed on a taxpayer by his obligations towards persons financially dependent on him. This may be seen as an argument for the substitution of dependant allowances for child allowances, but experience has shown that dependant allowances are open to widespread abuse. The administrative case for the abolition of child allowances is very strong indeed. A considerable amount of time has to be devoted to determine if the child allowances claimed by taxpayers are due to them. A major reason for this is that a taxpayer is entitled to claim a child allowance not only for his own child, a stepchild or a legally adopted child, but also for a child 'who is in taxpayer's custody by virtue of any custom of the community to which he belongs'. Given the diversity of customs in the country, the operation of these provisions is bound to be time-consuming and arbitrary.

3. *The Relationship between Income Tax and Graduated Personal Tax*

The graduated personal tax (G.P.T.) is a tax on income, but it is less sophisticated than the income tax. It was introduced to provide an independent source of revenue to local authorities.[6] The rates of tax range from Shs. 48/– for incomes between K£48 and K£96 to Shs. 600/– for incomes in excess of K£600. Since income tax and G.P.T. are the two major direct taxes, it is desirable that they should neatly dovetail into one another to give a progressive direct tax structure. This is not the case at present for some taxpayers over a certain range of income. Lower personal allowances under income tax will ensure that the tax liability for income tax and G.P.T. combined is progressive at each income for all taxpayers.

For married persons with children, the combined income tax and G.P.T. liability is regressive over certain ranges of income, the regressive portion being directly related to the number of children for whom child allowances are claimed. The nature of the problem is best brought out by discussing the extreme case – that of married persons with four children. It will be seen from Fig. 5.2 that in this case the direct tax structure is regressive from about K£700 to K£1,200.

The reason for the above feature is not far to seek. The maximum rate of G.P.T. is payable at an income of just above K£600; thereafter, the amount of G.P.T. payable does not vary with income, and consequently the liability to G.P.T. as a percentage of income declines. Thus if income tax and G.P.T. together are to give a progressive direct tax structure, income tax should become payable before the G.P.T. at the maximum rate is due. However, for married persons with four children the liability to income tax starts only when income exceeds K£960. Lower personal allowances for married persons (married and/or child allowances) will therefore eliminate the regressive segment.

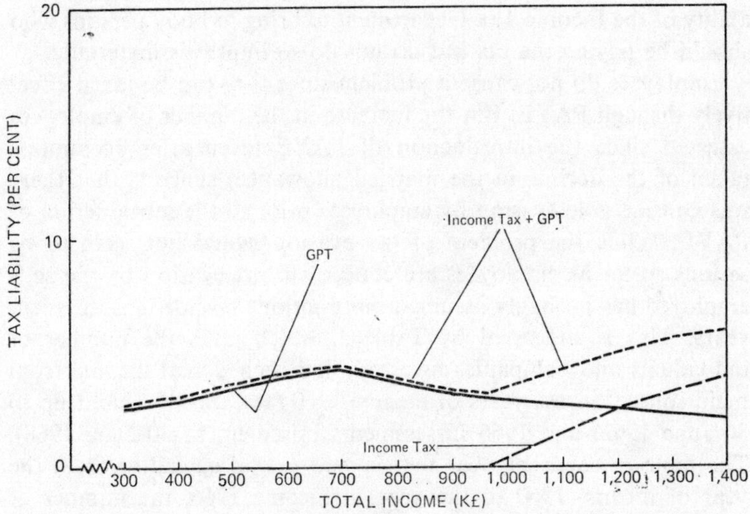

Fig. 5.2. Income Tax Payable, G.P.T. Payable and Income Tax plus G.P.T. Payable (Married Person with Four Children)

Alternatively, the defect in the direct tax structure can be rectified by changing the structure of G.P.T. The introduction of a few additional tax rates at the upper end of the G.P.T. scale will eliminate the regressive segment. Since personal allowances are not available for G.P.T., this proposal will also increase the tax liability of married persons as a percentage of that of a single person (from the income at which higher rates become applicable). The major disadvantage of using G.P.T. to correct the defect is that additional G.P.T. rates would greatly complicate the already difficult task of assessing the tax in county councils.

4. *The Problem of Tax Evasion*

It was mentioned that administrative considerations will need to be borne in mind in determining future personal allowances. This point requires elaboration. Lower personal allowances will increase the number of persons liable to income tax (and surtax). The most difficult problem that will arise will therefore be in connection with the detection of persons who do not pay income tax at present but will come into the tax net with lower personal allowances. There is a great deal of tax evasion at present; consequently, lower personal allowances will aggravate the problem of tax evasion unless the ability of the Income Tax Department to bring to book persons who should be paying the tax but do not do so improves materially.

Employees do not cause a problem since they can be taxed effectively through PAYE. But the increase in the number of employees assessed since the introduction of PAYE (even after account is taken of the decline in the married allowance) suggests that there was considerable evasion by employees prior to the introduction of PAYE. While the problem of tax evasion would not seem to be serious so far as employees are concerned, tax evasion by the self-employed has probably assumed more serious proportions in recent years. This is suggested by Table 3, which gives the number of individuals and companies assessed, and their actual income from main source[7] in the years of income 1960 (assessments raised up to 30 June 1962) and 1966 (assessments raised up to 30 June 1968). The table reveals that over the six-year period extending from the year of income 1960 to the year of income 1966, the number of individuals assessed increased by only 698 (from 15,733 to 16,431). The agricultural and commercial sectors need a specific mention. The decline in the number of taxpayers (individuals and companies) in the agricultural sector from 2,704 to 1,386, and in the assessed income from K£6·38 million to K£4.94 million, would seem to be primarily due to the land settlement programme and lower profitability. However, the taxation of the more prosperous African farmers in the large-farm areas has been causing serious problems owing to an absence of proper accounting records; this factor has undoubtedly contributed to the decline in the number of taxpayers and the magni-

Table 3

Individuals and Companies (including Clubs and Trusts): Number of Taxpayers and Actual Income from Main Source, 1960 and 1966

	Year of income 1960						*Year of income 1966*					
	Individuals		*Companies*		*Total*		*Individuals*		*Companies*		*Total*	
	No. of tax-payers	*Actual income from main source* (K£'000)	*No. of tax-payers*	*Actual income from main source* (K£'000)	*No. of tax-payers*	*Actual income from main source* (K£'000)	*No. of tax-payers*	*Actual income from main source* (K£'000)	*No. of tax-payers*	*Actual income from main source* (K£'000)	*No. of tax-payers*	*Actual income from main source* (K£'000)
Agriculture	2,103	2,101	601	4,279	2,704	6,380	768	1,131	618	3,813	1,386	4,944
Mining	34	23	11	548	45	571	34	44	10	474	44	518
Manufacture	469	523	241	5,397	710	5,920	386	624	422	15,473	808	16,097
Construction	387	451	92	709	479	1,160	179	330	85	703	264	1,033
Electricity, water, etc.	23	25	7	574	30	599	16	29	8	1,362	24	1,391
Wholesale and retail trade	5,023	5,099	793	3,968	5,816	9,066	5,713	8,968	1,131	8,557	6,844	17,525
Finance	74	54	303	1,950	377	2,004	55	87	254	2,947	309	3,034
Real estate	639	635	345	762	984	1,397	331	274	385	802	716	1,076
Transport, communications, etc.	244	235	60	622	304	857	513	397	105	1,859	618	2,256
Services	1,397	2,356	323	769	1,720	3,125	885	2,192	345	1,397	1,230	3,589
Other	5,340	2,665	451	654	5,791	3,319	7,551	3,446	549	613	8,100	4,059
Total	15,733	14,167	3,227	20,231	18,960	34,398	16,431	17,522	3,912	38,000	20,343	55,522

Source: East African Income Tax Department *Reports* for 1961–2 and 1967–8.

tude of assessed income. Equally formidable problems are being encountered in the taxation of African traders, but these problems are not reflected in the tax statistics of the commercial sector because the Africanisation of that sector had not proceeded far over the period under consideration. With the growing numbers of large farms coming into African ownership, and the rapidly increasing importance of Africans in retail and wholesale trade, the problem of tax evasion may become more intractable.

There are no quick or easy solutions to the problem of tax evasion by the self-employed. Apart from the recruitment of more and better-trained tax personnel, the most promising solutions would seem to be the establishment of additional income-tax offices[8] and a greater flow of information from sources such as public credit agencies, public trading corporations, marketing boards and exchange control to the tax authorities. These measures will only be successful if they are accompanied by proper guidance from the Government to the tax authorities on the treatment of tax defaulters. How severely should the Income Tax Department deal with, for example, African farmers and traders who are suspected of making substantial incomes but who, for one reason or the other, do not keep records? The Department cannot handle such issues satisfactorily unless it knows the degree of strictness in the treatment of tax offenders that would be politically acceptable.[9]

II. OTHER DIRECT TAXATION AND CAPITAL TAXATION PROBLEMS

This section will deal very briefly with the relevance of tax incentives for savings under income tax in developing countries such as Kenya, and with taxation of capital.

1. *Tax Incentives for Savings*

Three types of savings receive a preferential treatment. These are savings to provide for old age (pension funds,[10] annuity contracts and provident funds), life assurance and housing for owner-occupation.

Any concession for saving under income tax incorporates an element of inequity in the income-tax structure, since two persons with equal incomes will then pay the same amount in taxes only if they happen to save equal amounts and hold their savings in the same form. There is, however, a presumption that tax concessions for savings encourage increased savings. It may therefore be contended that the price in terms of reduced equity is worth paying. This contention would seem to possess a greater degree of validity where income tax is broadly based and the bulk of the population is assessed for income tax (and can consequently claim tax concessions) than in a country like Kenya where only 2 per cent of the population is assessed for income tax. Given the country's narrow coverage of income tax, it is clear that the benefits of tax concessions accrue primarily to the rich, which is not the case in developed countries with broadly-based income taxes. Further, in developing countries with greater disparities in the distribution of incomes and a lower importance of revenue from income tax in relation to total tax revenues than in developed countries, it is inappropriate to blunt the edge of income tax as a weapon for securing a more equitable distribution of incomes by allowing tax concessions for savings.[11]

The relief for owner-occupied housing takes the form of an exemption of its imputed income.[12] Such income must be taxed, for its exemption gives rise to serious inequities in the tax structure. The seriousness of the matter is due to the following reasons: first, housing expenditure accounts for a large proportion of income; second, both the likelihood of a person living in his own house and the cost of the house will vary directly with income; and finally, house property represents a major application of wealth in developing countries, where, for this reason, the case for taxing the imputed income would seem to be stronger than in developed countries.

2. *Taxation of Capital*

Kenya levies an estate duty but capital gains are not taxable. Estate duty is imposed on the estates of persons dying either domiciled in Kenya or possessing immovable property in Kenya. Any disposition made by the deceased over three years immediately preceding his death is exempt.

Opportunity for tax avoidence available through gifts *inter vivos* makes the estate duty inadequate as an effective weapon for reducing the concentration of wealth. Two alternative methods of tackling the problem will be discussed. First, all gifts could be made taxable at the full estate duty rates. All gifts made would be aggregated to determine the amount of estate duty, but credit would be given for duty paid in respect of all previous gifts. Similarly, on the death of the deceased, all gifts made during his lifetime would be aggregated with the value of the estate at the time of death for the determination of the amount of duty payable, but credit would be given for duty paid in respect of all gifts. Alternatively, the estate duty could be replaced by a progressive tax on inheritances and gifts received throughout a lifetime.

It is suggested that a capital gains tax should be introduced on all *realised* capital gains in respect of real estate and equities. The proposed scope of the tax will ensure that the bulk of the capital gains are caught in the tax net.

Something needs to be said about the proposed inclusion of agricultural real property within the scope of the tax because it may prove to be controversial. An important argument against the inclusion of agricultural land within the scope of a capital gains tax is that this might affect the land consolidation and registration programme adversely. A major problem with this programme is maintaining the tax registry up to date after title deeds have been registered. A capital gains tax would make it more difficult to keep the register up to date since farmers might not get sales recorded on the land register in order to evade the tax liability. A possible solution would be to make capital gains on land subject to tax only if the value of the holding exceeds some minimum figure, perhaps K£1,000. This will effectively confine the tax to the country's 3,000 large-scale farms (farms of over 20 acres).

III. INDIRECT TAXATION

The treatment of indirect taxation will be as selective as that of direct taxation. The absence of any discussion of a sales tax will probably be the most conspicuous omission. It does not, however, seem necessary to discuss a sales tax separately, because analytically the type of sales tax that would seem to be appropriate in Kenya – a sales tax collected from importers and manufacturers – is no different from changing the rates of import duties and changing the scope and rates of excise duties. There is bound to be some pressure from Uganda and Tanzania, both of whom levy sales taxes, on Kenya to introduce the tax, for the problems of inter-state smuggling might assume serious proportions if Kenya did not follow suit. It would therefore be very surprising if a sales tax is not introduced in Kenya in the near future. The major advantage of a sales tax in Kenya would be its contribution to a degree of flexibility in the pursuit of an indirect tax policy within the framework of broadly similar rates of import and excise duties in the East African Community.[13]

Table 4

Import Duty, Excise Duty and Diesel and Petrol Tax Collections by Major Commodities, 1963 and 1969

(K£'000)

	1963		1969	
Foodstuffs		2,363		3,903
Import duties		911		1,055
Excise duties:		1,452		2,848
Sugar	1,452		2,819	
Biscuits	–		29	
Beverages and tobacco		6,243		10,131
Import duties		1,558		1,348
Excise duties:		4,685		8,783
Beer	2,154		4,334	
Cigarettes, cigars and tobacco	2,433		3,792	
Spirits	98		223	
Mineral waters	–		434	
*Basic Materials**		52		679
Fuels		4,863		8,554
Import duties		3,787		6,765
Petrol and diesel tax		1,076		1,789
Chemicals		460		1,327
Import duties		460		671
Excise duties:		–		656
Soap	–		494	
Paints and distemper	–		162	
Textiles		3,324		4,564
Import duties		3,324		4,128
Excise duties:		–		436
Woven fabrics	–		436	
*Semi-manufactures**		796		1,553
*Metals**		396		796
*Transport equipment**		1,501		3,627
*Machinery**		540		1,215
Miscellaneous manufactured articles		1,436		2,179
Import duties		1,414		1,988
Excise duties:		22		191
Matches	22		191	
*Miscellaneous commodities and transactions**		440		682
Total		22,414		39,210

* Only import duties are levied.

Note: The totals in this table and in Table 2 are not directly comparable because the former are on a calendar-year basis and the latter on a financial-year basis.

Source: *Annual Abstract* (1969); *Economic Survey* (1970).

1. *Recent Trends*

Table 4 indicates the structure and recent trends in indirect taxation (defined in the table as import duties, excise duties and petrol and diesel tax). It will be seen that about 80 per cent of the indirect tax revenue comes from beverages and tobacco, fuels, textiles, food and transport equipment. Of these five commodity groups, the growth rate of revenue from transport equipment of 15·8 per cent per annum is the highest. The revenues from textiles, beverages and tobacco, food and fuels grew at rates ranging from 5·4 to 9·8 per cent per annum. It should also be noticed that the greater proportion of the revenue from foodstuffs and beverages and tobacco is derived from excise duties.

About 60 per cent of the import duty revenue is derived from fuels, textiles and transport equipment. The sluggish growth in revenue from textiles and the decline in revenue from beverages and tobacco are due to import substitution. The negligible rate of growth of revenue from food is to be explained by import substitution and the replacement of foreign sugar by Ugandan sugar. The increase in revenue from machinery is primarily due to the rapid growth of machinery imports.

Turning to excises, the feature that stands out in relief is the considerable extension in the coverage of exicse taxation in recent years. In 1963 commodities other than beer, cigarettes and sugar accounted for only 3 per cent of the total excise revenue; their contribution has now risen to 16 per cent. The main reason for this is that certain excise duties, particularly those on mineral waters, soap and woven fabrics, introduced after 1963 are now making a growing contribution to revenues.

2. *Taxation of Consumer Goods and Services*

The difficulty of constructing an indirect tax structure that is progressive over a wide range of income and particularly at high incomes is perhaps the most important problem in the sphere of indirect taxation. The tendency of the marginal propensity to consume to decline as income increases, and the frequent exclusion of major services from the scope of indirect taxes, are important causes of this. For Kenya, empirical data on income elasticities are available only for low and middle income groups.[14] Sketchy though it is, the evidence illustrates the difficulty of devising a progressive indirect tax structure by showing that the range of expenditures for which income elasticity at high incomes is likely to exceed unity is limited. The limitations of using income elasticities for assessing the distributional implications of indirect taxes are well known and need not be discussed here.

The income elasticities of major excisable commodities are discussed first. The elasticity of demand for tobacco and beverages (mainly cigarettes and beer) is high for both low and middle groups (1·12 and 1·11 respectively). However, evidence from other countries suggests that the elasticity is unlikely to exceed unity at higher incomes. The elasticity of sugar is high at low incomes (the elasticity of 1·06 suggests that sugar is a 'luxury' at low incomes), but rather low (0·28) at middle incomes. Clearly, at higher incomes the income elasticity of demand may be expected to be relatively inelastic. The elasticity for clothing (which may be assumed to coincide with the excisable commodity woven fabrics) is much higher at middle incomes (1·64) than at low incomes (0·89). It is therefore possible that the elasticity for this commodity is high over a wide range of income. No evidence exists for wine and spirits, but elasticities for these commodities may also be expected to be high over a wide range of income. The elasticity for soap would seem to be unitary at low incomes (the elasticity for the group whose largest component is soap is 1·09), but will almost certainly be lower at middle and high incomes. Finally, the elasticity for mineral waters is to be expected to be low at high incomes; at middle incomes, the elasticity for the group that includes tea, coffee and mineral waters is only 0·29.

Although the evidence in connection with housing, durable consumer goods and services is even more incomplete than for excisable commodities, these categories of expenditure may be expected to have high elasticities over a wide range of income, on the basis of experience in other countries. For housing, the elasticities at low and middle incomes are 2·34 and 1·08 respectively. Housing at low incomes was defined as the expenditure on housing materials and paid labour for housing construction and repair; this may account for the unusually high elasticity. As for durable consumer goods, the elasticity at low incomes for a category comprising furniture, bedding, utensils and equipment is 0·99. At middle incomes the elasticity for furniture and household utensils is 1·95. The elasticity for services (transportation, medical expenses and other services in equal parts) at low incomes is 1·08. At middle incomes the elasticities for meals taken away from home, health (medical expenses and personal toilet items) and recreation (entertainment, books, stationery, magazines and records), the three relevant categories of expenditure, are 0·82, 1·20 and 1·26 respectively.

On the basis of the above discussion, high rates of tax on housing, durable consumer goods and services would seem to be justifiable. As far as indirect taxation on housing is concerned, it is proposed that improvements should be brought within the scope of property rating. At present municipalities levy rates only on site values and not on the value of the whole property. The extension of rating to improvements will widen the municipalities' tax base, a highly desirable result in view of the demand for urban services. As for durable consumer goods (excluding motor vehicles which will be discussed separately), most of the durable consumer goods bear the general 'catch-all' rate of 30 per cent and the highest rate does not exceed 50 per cent; a greater differentiation of rates between durable consumer goods and other goods would be desirable.[15]

Motor-vehicle taxes are making a significant contribution to revenues.[16] The structure of motor-vehicle taxation, however, leaves much to be desired. The import duties on motor vehicles are in the range of $33\frac{1}{3}$ – 80 per cent, varying with the cubic capacity of the engine. The minimum rate of tax is rather low in relation to rates on non-luxury goods, while the maximum rate is not sufficiently high to have a significant effect on imports of very expensive cars. Second, the annual licence fees are based wholly on the tare weight of the vehicles and do not take adequate account of the ability to pay (as reflected in the cost of the vehicle) and the differing costs imposed by vehicles on society by way of wear and tear of roads. Finally, the current indirect tax rates (import duties and petrol and diesel consumption tax combined) on petrol are much higher than on diesel, the object of the differential rates being to give a measure of relief to the agricultural sector, which is an important user of diesel fuel. However, since the annual licence fees are equal for all vehicles, the concession results in a lower burden of taxation on the owners of diesel vehicles relatively to the owners of other vehicles.

The exclusion of most services from tax is a prominent feature of Kenya's indirect tax structure. Entertainment tax, betting and pools taxes and airport tax are the only service taxes that are levied. As will be seen from Table 2, their yield is negligible. It is desirable that the scope of service taxes be extended. A tax on foreign travel and a tax on hotel accommodation and meals taken at hotels and restaurants would seem to be particularly relevant. A tax on foreign travel may have the side benefit of discouraging foreign travel by Kenya residents, whose expenditure on foreign travel currently equals one-half of the country's gross earnings from foreign travel. A tax on services provided by hotels and restaurants should bring substantial revenue, for these services form a very significant proportion of the total receipts of service establishments for goods and services. According to the Survey of Services (1966), of the total receipts of all service establishments of K£24·24 million, K£11·21 million or just under one-half of the total accrued to hotels and restaurants. A tax at a moderate rate is unlikely to discourage tourism.

There will undoubtedly be additional revenue opportunities in respect of domestic[17] as well as imported goods. Further, the revenue opportunities will change in line with the changes in the structure of the economy. Import substitution will, as in the past, call for an increased reliance on taxes on local production and bring automatic increases in yields of income and corporation taxes on the manufacturing sector.[18] As far as the immediate future is concerned, consideration will have to be given to the imposition of internal taxes on commodities such as articles of clothing, footwear, household utensils, canned foods, tyres and tubes, and furniture, whose domestic production now accounts for a substantial proportion of total consumption. Some of these commodities may have low elasticities, and equity considerations will therefore need to be carefully weighted against revenue requirements.

3. *Taxation of Capital Goods*

Most capital goods are admitted into the country free of import duty. This will be seen from Table 5, where import duties are classified by three end-uses of imports, viz. intermediate consumption, capital formation and final consumption. The table should be interpreted with care since the distinction between the end-uses is bound to be somewhat arbitrary. The table does, however, give a broad indication of the relative importance of import duties from the three end-uses. It will be noticed that in 1968, of the total import duty revenue of K£23·23 million, the revenue from capital goods accounted for only K£1·74 million. The bulk of the import duty revenue from capital goods came from vehicles used for commercial purposes.

Table 5
Allocation of Import Duties by End-Use of Imports, 1968
(K£'000)

	*Total**	*Intermediate consumption*	*Capital formation*	*Final consumption*
Agriculture, forestry, hunting and fishing	192	129	–	63
Mining and quarrying	28	28	–	–
Food, beverages and tobacco	2,585	773	–	1,812
Textiles and clothing	5,644	2,788	30	2,826
Leather and footwear	194	14	–	180
Wood, cork and furniture	176	100	34	42
Paper and printing	596	535	–	61
Chemicals and rubber	1,266	756	–	510
Petroleum and coal products	6,071	4,480	–	1,591
Building materials, pottery and glass	269	178	1	89
Basic metal industries	354	354	–	–
Metal manufactures	500	231	21	247
Machinery	991	285	370	335
Transport equipment	2,976	1,125	1,230	621
Miscellaneous manufacturing	805	175	54	576
Services	21	20	–	1
Unallocable	561	–	–	561
Total*	23,228	11,971	1,741	9,516

* Figures may not add to totals because of rounding.

Notes:

1. All goods which loose their identity in the production process have been treated as intermediate goods. Thus, estimated imported food consumed at hotels has been treated as an input in the production of hotel services, and goods which form elements of buildings and construction works have also been treated as intermediate goods.
2. All spare parts have been treated as intermediate goods.
3. Small implements and hand tools which are normally written off within a year have been treated as intermediate goods.
4. All goods consumed by households, durable as well as non-durable, have been treated as 'final consumption'.

Source: S.D., M.E.P.D.

It is worth asking if the present exemption of capital goods from import duties should be permitted to continue. Two cogent arguments can be put forward against the present practice. First, it may be argued that the exemption of capital goods from import duties, together with the investment allowance[19] under income tax, encourages the substitution of capital for labour in the productive process and is therefore undesirable in a labour-surplus economy.

Second, it may be argued that the export of funds through over-invoicing in respect of capital goods imports is not penalised, since over-invoicing cannot result in a higher amount of duty where a good enters duty-free.[20] In fact there is considerable incentive for over-invoicing, since it results in the availability of increased depreciation allowances and, in the case of machinery for manufacturing, a higher investment allowance as well.

The arguments for the retention of the present arrangements would, on balance, seem to be stronger. The major arguments are as follows. First, import duties on capital goods, other things being equal, may adversely affect the overall rate of investment. Second, import duties at moderate rates are unlikely to have a perceptible effect on over-invoicing (the reason being that the penalty will not increase *pari passu* with the rate of import duty because higher import duties will give rise to higher depreciation, and in some cases investment allowances), whereas duties at high rates, while they might significantly curb over-invoicing, will increase the chances of the overall rate of investment being adversely affected. There is no doubt that the problem of over-invoicing is best tackled through administrative means. Third, the administrative problem of exempting exports from the import duty paid on machinery used in their production will become unnecessarily cumbersome. Last but not least, goods which are not intended to bear taxation will be taxed fortuitously.

Nevertheless, if it is thought that capital should be made relatively more expensive to labour, then a more general solution such as the devaluation of the K£ might be more appropriate. The pros and cons of action through import duties on capital goods and a change in the external value of the currency are beyond the scope of this paper. It is worth noting, however, that the latter solution will also change the relative factor prices facing the public sector, which accounts for a sizeable proportion of capital formation but is exempt from the payment of import duties.

4. *Taxation of Inputs*

Table 5 shows that import duty revenue from intermediate goods accounted for K£11·97 million in 1968. The relative importance of revenue from intermediate goods is due more to the importance of these goods in the import structure than to high tax rates, for most intermediate goods either enter duty-free or are taxed at lower rates than the final consumer goods.

There are a number of primarily non-revenue reasons for taxing inputs. Many inputs will also be taxed solely for revenue purposes. This is to be expected in a country where excise duties have a narrow coverage. However, when a sales tax is introduced, a much wider range of domestically produced goods is likely to become subject to tax, and the need for relying on taxes on inputs for revenue considerations will be less. The revenue duties on inputs should therefore be reviewed when a sales tax is introduced. There are some advantages in confining revenue duties to final products where non-revenue considerations for taxing inputs are not involved: the possibilities of 'tax pyramiding' are reduced, the assessment of the degree of effective protection given to various products becomes easier, and the relief of exports from taxes is simpler administratively. However, since the duties on textiles, petroleum and transport equipment account for about 70 per cent of the total revenue from intermediate consumption, the scope for modifying revenue duties on inputs is rather small.

5. *A Digression on Agricultural Taxation*

The agricultural sector is the recipient of almost all open subsidies (as distinct from hidden subsidies resulting from, *inter alia*, the provision of services at a price below the cost) granted by the Government.[21] This is therefore a convenient place for a word or two on agricultural taxation.

The present system of taxation as it impinges on the agricultural sector is highly unsatisfactory. The problem of taxing farmers through the income tax have already been discussed above. The prevalence of under-assessments has virtually transformed the G.P.T., the other major direct tax, into a poll tax in rural areas.[22] There is considerable scope for an improvement in the operation of both these taxes on agricultural producers, but past experience does not hold out hope for a marked improvement.

A possible solution may be the abolition of G.P.T. on farmers and the introduction of broadly-based export taxation[23] and land rating. Moderate rates of export duties on a wide range of exports would be preferable to high rates of duties confined to one or two major exports. Farmers who pay income and corporation taxes might be permitted to deduct export duties paid from the former, because otherwise those estates with proper accounting records will be taxed more harshly than the others. This proposal would only make sense in the context of a realistic exchange-rate policy. Land rating may have adverse effects on the land consolidation and registration programme at this stage. Nevertheless, its introduction in districts where land registration has been completed deserves careful consideration. The G.P.T. could continue in its present form on the employed, and a separate tax levied on the non-agricultural enterprises in rural areas.

IV. DOMESTIC BORROWING

This section will be concerned with domestic borrowing. Both long-term and short-term borrowing will be discussed. The line between long-term and short-term borrowing is obviously blurred, since even a long-term security will become a short-term security as it nears its maturity date. Nevertheless, it will be convenient to regard borrowing through Government stocks and the National Social Security Fund (N.S.S.F.) and Post Office Savings Bank (P.O.S.B.) as long-term borrowing, and that through Treasury bills, the Cereals and Sugar Finance Corporation and tax reserve certificates as short-term borrowing.

1. *Long-term Borrowing*

Total public debt, excluding short-term Government borrowing, increased from K£86·11 million to K£142·42 million, or by 65 per cent, from 1964 to 1969. Over the same period the domestic debt increased from K£17·09 million to K£47·81 million, or by 180 per cent. As a result, the ratio of domestic debt to total debt has risen from 21 per cent to 34 per cent. Nearly all of the growth in domestic debt is accounted for by market borrowing through Government stocks.

(*a*) *Government stocks.* New long-term domestic borrowing, which was nil in 1963–4, has increased continuously and amounted to over K£8 million in 1968–9 (see Table 1). This dramatic improvement in the marketability of Government debt must be attributed primarily to the extension of exchange control against the Sterling Area outside the Scheduled Territories (Kenya, Uganda and Tanzania) in June 1965 and the introduction of the N.S.S.F., a compulsory savings scheme. The introduction of exchange control has contributed significantly to the increased supply of domestic funds by staunching

Table 6
Holders of Kenya Government Local Stock Issues (Nominal Values)
(K£'000)

Holders	*Dec 1963*	*Dec 1969*
Central Government	3,351	9,912
Local Government	763	1,078
East African Community institutions	870	891
Other public sector	495	474
Central Bank of Kenya*	3,707	3,510
Post Office Savings Bank	950	2,114
Commercial banks	1,635	6,184
National Social Security Fund	–	17,417
Insurance companies	2,012	4,879
Other companies	983	2,455
Private	320	780
Non-resident holders:		
Other East African	401	352
Other Sterling Area	1,497	1,723
Non-Sterling Area	106	42
Total	17,090	51,811

* The 1963 figure refers to the holdings of the East African Currency Board.
Source: Central Bank of Kenya, *Economic and Financial Review*, II 3 (Jan–Mar 1970).

the outflow of capital motivated primarily by political considerations. The balance of payments statistics reveal that private long-term capital (including net errors and omissions which can be taken to reflect unrecorded private capital transfers), which recorded a net outflow of K£20 million in 1964, had turned into a net inflow of K£17·2 million by 1968.

The role of the N.S.S.F. as well as other factors in the development of the market for Government stocks is best brought out by an analysis of the recent changes in the holdings of the Government stocks of various public and private entities. The relevant data are displayed in Table 6.[24] It will be seen that the holdings of the public sector (excluding the central Government, N.S.S.F. and P.O.S.B.) have remained virtually constant. The central Government's holdings of its own stocks have increased substantially and should continue to rise in line with the growth of sinking funds and pension funds. Part of the increase in the holdings over the period under consideration has come from the switching of some pension funds held in sterling securities to the Central Bank in return for an equivalent amount of domestic stocks. It should be noted that the Government has not yet borrowed from the Central Bank through stocks; the Central Bank's current holdings were derived by it from the East African Currency Board.

The N.S.S.F. and P.O.S.B., the major public institutions for tapping private savings, have increased their holdings to a considerable extent. The N.S.S.F., which holds about one-third of the total Government stocks outstanding, has in fact emerged as the most important holder. The increase in the holdings of the P.O.S.B. is due not to the growth in its deposit liabilities but to a switching of sterling securities to the Central Bank in exchange for domestic Government securities. There was considerable scope for switching because under the colonial legislation the P.O.S.B. was not permitted to invest more than one-third of its resources in Kenya Government securities. Those aspects of the operations of the N.S.S.F. and P.O.S.B. that are germane to the present discussion will be explored in detail later.

A sizeable increase is also discernible in the holdings of institutional investors – commercial banks and insurance companies. The bulk of the increase in the commercial banks' holdings has occurred since 1968 and is to be explained by a section in the Banking Act, 1968, which requires all banks incorporated outside Kenya to keep within Kenya at all times, and out of their funds, a capital assigned to their Kenya branches amounting to at least 5 per cent of their total local deposit liabilities. The relative importance of Government stocks in the asset structure of commerical banks in the future will depend, *inter alia*, on the role they are expected to play in the financing of Government expenditure. In the past, the Government has not encouraged commercial banks to invest in its stock issues; indeed, on some recent occasions it has discouraged them from so doing by not accepting their applications for stocks. A possible explanation is that, given the ease with which the Government has been able to raise finance from other sources, it has not found it necessary to pursue a policy that would have affected the banks' ability to lend to the private sector. The Government's attitude may change if it experiences difficulties in raising sufficient long-term finance from other sources. At the end of 1969 commercial banks' 'investments' (mainly Government stocks) amounted to less than 6 per cent of their deposit liabilities, a ratio far below that found in other countries.

One reason for the growth of insurance companies' holdings is the Government's policy of requiring these institutions to cover their local liabilities with local assets. This policy was strengthened by the introduction of exchange control, which restricted the transfer abroad of premiums in respect of life assurance.[25] The local assets of insurance companies have not grown rapidly in recent years, partly because of the emigration of non-citizens and partly because the growth in the number of life policies has been accompanied by a decline in the average sum assured (per policy). A reason for the latter factor is that life insurance, whose use as a savings medium was confined mainly to non-Africans until very recently, is now attracting substantial African savings. The increasing African interest in life assurance, together with the fact that even the surface of the vast African market has not yet been scratched, suggests considerable possibilities for the future growth of savings through this medium. Insurance companies may therefore be expected to provide a rapidly growing market for Government stocks.

Although the holdings of companies and the rest of the private sector (individuals and non-corporate bodies) have doubled over the period, they remained small in absolute magnitudes. The unattractiveness of the Government stock for the individual is probably due to a peculiarity of the local money market. The differential between interest payable on deposits held with building societies and hire-purchase finance companies for one to two years and the gross redemption yields of Government stocks is rather small. A further and more important reason for the small individual holdings may be that blue chips yield at least as much as Government stocks, in addition to holding out considerable prospects for capital gains. Therefore, unless the structure of yields changes significantly or individuals' preference for Government stocks becomes stronger, individuals' holdings cannot be expected to gain much relative importance.

Finally, the increase in the holdings of non-residents has been confined to the holdings in the Sterling Area outside the Scheduled Territories. The greater part of it probably reflects the increase of investment in stock from emigrants' funds blocked under the exchange control. The blocked funds may be expected to rise steadily for some years to come.[26]

The growth in the supply of domestic funds has been accompanied by changes in the cost of borrowing and the maturity structure of the Government debt. The gross redemption yields on stocks have declined substantially since the introduction of exchange control,[27] and the maturity structure has been changing in favour of the relatively longer-dated stocks.[28] The latter tendency is to be explained primarily by the nature of the N.S.S.F.'s demand for Government stocks.

(*b*) *National Social Security Fund.* The N.S.S.F. was established in August 1966. It is a provident fund requiring equal contributions from employees and employers. The contributions vary with the employees' incomes until the maximum contribution is reached. At present all employers of five or more employees, and their male employees, contribute to the Fund. It is intended to bring all employees, both male and female, within the scope of the Fund shortly. By the end of 1968, even though the registration of employers with fewer than five employees was not complete, over 470,000 employees had been registered. At that date the contributions amounted to K£5·47 million.[29]

The benefits payable to a contributing employee depend on his contributions, on the employer's contributions made in his respect and on the accrued interest. The benefits take the following forms: an old-age benefit, a survivors' benefit for contributors' families, an invalidity benefit where a contributor is permanently incapacitated, and an emigration benefit when a contributor leaves the country. Additionally, all contributing employees will receive free in-patient treatment in all Government hospitals when the necessary legislation is passed.

The Fund is empowered to hold its resources in a wide range of investments, but, as is to be expected, the bulk of its resources are invested in Government stocks. At the end of 1968, out of the total investments of K£12·30 million, investment in Goverment stocks amounted to K£11·31 million, the remainder being equally distributed between Nairobi City Council stocks and equities. Of the amount held in Government stocks, K£1·32 million was in medium-term stocks and K£10·98 million in long-term stocks.

There is a presumption that the N.S.S.F. has enhanced the flow of personal savings. Any comment on the effect of the N.S.S.F. on business savings would be highly speculative. It is possible for the contributions from the high-income employees to have left their overall savings unchanged. Similarly, savings of the members of private provident funds who were contributing at least as much as required under the N.S.S.F. have probably not increased on the introduction of the Fund, since contributions to the private provident funds were revised downwards. However, it is highly probable that part of the contributions of the low-income employees who did not belong to private provident funds, and those who contributed to such funds at lower rates than required for the N.S.S.F., represent additional savings. There were strong demands from trade unions for a pay-out of private provident funds on the establishment of the N.S.S.F., but the Government has resisted the pressure so far. Thus, the establishment of the Fund did not lead to a dissaving of the past savings accumulated through private provident funds.

Widening of the membership of the Fund and rising incomes should result in a rapid increase in contributions. Provided that the benefits are closely related to the contributions and accrued interest, the investible surplus should continue to furnish a growing source of long-term finance for the Government.

(*c*) *Post Office Savings Bank*. The P.O.S.B. provides deposit facilities to the public, and invests the proceeds in Government securities. The Bank's deposit liabilities in the last few years have remained almost unchanged at K£5 million. The Bank's deposits were much higher in the late 1950s, but it has not recovered from heavy net withdrawals, which reflected a massive capital outflow from Kenya as a consequence of political uncertainties, that took place in the early 1960s. In the light of this recent experience, it is difficult to be optimistic about the future growth of the Bank's deposits. Despite its disappointing performance, the Bank must be regarded as a major institution for initiating persons in low-income groups into the savings habit. This is clear from the fact that new accounts with the Bank have been increasing at the rate of 35,000 per annum, and the total number of accounts has grown from 450,557 in 1963 to 581,226 in 1968.

The Bank pays a tax-free interest of 3 per cent on deposits. The present policy of exempting interest paid on savings accounts from income tax is inconsistent with the Bank's objective of catering primarily for the small investor, since persons in low-income groups will not be liable to income tax anyway. But the adoption of a higher rate of interest and making it taxable at a time when total deposits are not increasing could result in reduced deposits if investors with high marginal rates of tax close their accounts. This will in turn significantly raise the already high cost per transaction. The

Table 7

*Short-term Borrowing by the Government, 1963–4 to 1968–9**

(K£'000)

Year from 1 July to 30 June	*Joint Consolidated Fund*	*Cereals and Sugar Finance Corporation*	*Treasury bills*	*Central Bank of Kenya*	*Other*	*Total*
1963–4	3,822	13,437	–	–	78	17,337
1964–5	2,153	12,778	–	–	129	15,060
1965–6	1,052	13,029	3,000	–	2,274	19,355
1966–7	895	9,140	–	–	1,708	11,743
1967–8	–	12,643	–	–	1,439	14,082
1968–9	–	15,022	8,000	850	3	23,875

* Excluding tax reserve certificates.

Note: Normally sums borrowed are repaid in the same financial year. In the financial year 1968–9, however, borrowing exceeded repayments by K£5·68 million, primarily because Treasury bills amounting to only K£3 million were redeemed during the year.

Source: *Exchequer Accounts*, 1963–4 to 1968–9.

deposit held per account is about K£10. This relatively high average masks a great deal of variation, because the amounts held in the majority of accounts are less than K£2. In 1968 the total number of transactions and the total administrative costs amounted to 851,785 and K£95,189 respectively; this suggests that the cost per transaction is in the region of Shs. 2/–. The current policy should therefore be reviewed only when the deposits held primarily for tax considerations decline in importance.

2. *Short-term Borrowing*

Details of the gross short-term borrowing (excluding tax reserve certificates) utilised by the Government in each financial year from 1963–4 to 1968–9 are set out in Table 7. A number of features stand out. First, the Cereals and Sugar Finance Corporation is the most important source of short-term funds. Second, Treasury bills, issued for the first time in 1965–6 and discontinued in the same financial year, made a second appearance in 1968–9.[30] Third, borrowing from Joint Consolidated Fund (Crown Agents) declined continuously from independence until 1967–8, when it disappeared completely. Lastly, borrowing from the Central Bank by way of a short-term advance was resorted to for the first time in 1968–9. The three major sources of short-term funds for the Government – Treasury bills, the Cereals and Sugar Finance Corporation and tax reserve certificates – are now discussed briefly.

(*a*) *Treasury bills.* The salient features of Treasury bills from their introduction at the end of March 1969 to March 1970 have been summarised in Table 8. One interesting feature is that the demand for Treasury bills by the banking system, which holds virtually all the bills, has been very strong.[31] It will be seen that the amount of tender for every issue has greatly exceeded the amount offered. Another noteworthy feature is that the average rate of discount on allotted bills has declined with every successive issue. The reliance placed on this source of finance will no doubt depend on the overall requirements of monetary policy as well as on the Government's financial needs.

(*b*) *Cereals and Sugar Finance Corporation.* The Cereals and Sugar Finance Corporation provides deposit facilities to the public. The rates of interest for deposits requiring fourteen days', three months' and six months' notice are 3½, 4 and 4½ per cent per annum respec-

Table 8

Treasury Bills, 24 March 1969 to 31 March 1970

Date of issue	*Amount offered* (K£'000)	*Tenure*	*Total amount of tender* (K£'000)	*Amount allotted* (K£'000)	*Amount redeemed* (K£'000)	*Amount out-standing* (K£'000)	*Average annual rate of discount of allotted bills* (%)
24 Mar 1969	1,000	30 days	1,865	1,000	Nil	1,000	4·2193
	1,000	60 days	1,860	1,000	Nil	1,000	4·2504
	1,000	91 days	2,515	1,000	Nil	1,000	4·2500
Total	3,000	–	6,240	3,000	Nil	3,000	
22 Apr 1969	1,000	91 days	2,935	1,000	1,000	3,000	4·0862
23 May 1969	2,000	91 days	4,980	2,000	1,000	4,000	3·9806
23 June 1969	2,000	91 days	4,000	2,000	1,000	5,000	3·9508
23 July 1969	1,000	91 days	4,575	1,000	1,000	5,000	3·9006
22 Aug 1969	2,000	91 days	5,130	2,000	2,000	5,000	3·7201
22 Sep 1969	2,000	91 days	5,270	2,000	2,000	5,000	3·7038
22 Oct 1969	1,000	91 days	5,010	1,000	1,000	5,000	3·6906
21 Nov 1969	2,000	91 days	6,750	2,000	2,000	5,000	3·6888
22 Dec 1969	–	–	–	–	2,000	3,000	–
22 Jan 1970	1,000	91 days	4,250	1,000	1,000	3,000	3·6149
23 Feb 1970	–	–	–	–	2,000	1,000	–
31 Mar 1970	–	–	–	–	–	1,000	–

Source: Central Bank of Kenya, *Economic and Financial Review*, II 3 (Jan-Mar 1970).

tively. The minimum level of deposit is K£5,000. The bulk of the deposits came from the public sector (Government Departments, semi-governmental bodies, local authorities), but deposits from insurance companies and other private-sector institutions are also important. The Corporation provides finance to the Government and Government agents for the purchase of sugar from overseas, maize and wheat and for the provision of short-term credit to cereals farmers; it deposits its surplus funds with the Government.

The Corporation has been very successful in attracting short-term funds; the Corporation's deposits have increased from K£4·87 million in 1963 to K£7·98 million in 1969. Even this does not give a complete picture of the Corporation's success, for in every year from 1963–4 to 1966–7 the Corporation had on occasions refused to accept further deposits. In 1967–8, however, the Corporation found itself short of cash and discounted bills amounting to K£1 million with the Central Bank, as well as raising a short-term loan of K£3·21 million from the Treasury.

Over one-half of the Corporation's deposits are repayable at fourteen days' and three months' notice.[32] Given this, and the comparability of the Corporation's interest rates with the rates of discount on Treasury bills, a high degree of substitutability may be expected to emerge between deposits with the Corporation and Treasury bills. As far as the commercial banks are concerned, however, there is a significant difference between Treasury bills on the one hand and deposits held with the Corporation on the other, the reason being that the former are liquid assets for banking purposes whereas the latter are not.

(*c*) *Tax reserve certificates.* Tax reserve certificates may be used to discharge the liability to income tax, surtax and corporation tax, provided they have been held for more than three months. The rate of interest, which is tax-free, is 4 per cent per annum, and the maximum period for which a certificate may be held is three years. The certificates have never been very popular in Kenya. The amount of certificates outstanding as at 30 June 1969 was K£3·17 million.

3. *Financing of Planned Development Expenditure*

The central Government's development expenditure in Kenya's latest Development Plan has been projected at K£180 million for the five-year period 1969–70 to 1973–4. The division of the total financial requirements between internal and external sources is to be K£85 million and K£95 million respectively. The following financing pattern has been tentatively forecast for domestic funds: (1) surplus on recurrent budget, K£20 million; (2) borrowing from the N.S.S.F., K£30 million; (3) other local borrowing (excluding Treasury bills and borrowing from the Central Bank), K£10 million; (4) borrowing from the Central Bank and Treasury bills, K£25 million.[33] The Plan stresses that the actual pattern of financing will be decided 'on a yearly basis and adapted to the overall monetary and financial situation at the time the budget is under preparation'. Broadly speaking, the internal financing targets would seem to be attainable on the basis of the past experience and taxation and borrowing possibilities discussed above.

The reliance to be placed on budget surpluses is quite modest. As will be seen from Table 1, budget surpluses contributed about K£20 million (at current prices) in the preceding five years, from 1964–5 to 1968–9. The borrowing of K£30 million from the N.S.S.F. over the Plan period is realistic, since the Fund should have a minimum surplus of K£6 million per annum. The target for borrowing of K£10 million from entities other than the N.S.S.F. is not as unambitious as it seems, given that, of the total local debt outstanding as at 30 June 1969, K£13·3 million will mature over the Plan period (and will therefore have to be converted) and that local authorities might have to raise substantial funds from the market. Borrowing from the Central Bank and through Treasury bills is expected to account for 30 per cent of the total domestic finance; whether this relatively high proportion is realistic or not will depend on the conditions prevailing over the Plan period.

There were signs, when the Plan was being prepared, that the economy, which had been growing at an impressive rate of 6·4 per cent per annum between 1964 and 1968 (in constant prices), was slowing down. This has probably influenced the relatively low emphasis on budget surpluses and the relatively high reliance on borrowing from the Central Bank and Treasury bills. Instruments available for stabilisation purposes form the subject of the next section.

V. FINANCIAL POLICY FOR STABILISATION

Kenya's growth rate of 6·3 per cent per annum over the period 1964 to 1969 cannot be regarded as unsatisfactory if compared with growth rates in other countries, both developing and developed, over the same period. The G.D.P. grew at the rate of only 5·6 per cent in 1969, but a higher rate of progress is expected in 1970. The trend with respect to private capital formation has been less satisfactory. Gross fixed capital formation undertaken by the private sector, which grew at an impressive rate of 15·2 per cent per annum from 1964 to 1967, declined by 3 per cent in 1968 and showed a growth of only 7·6 per cent in 1969. Consumer prices have been remarkably stable, rising at the rate of only 2·3 per cent per annum over the period of 1964–9 (see Table 9).

The monetary scene has undergone a radical transformation from 1966. The current account of the balance of payments, which was in substantial surplus in 1964, began to show large deficits from 1966. This change has been accompanied by growing inflows of long-term capital. Complete details of the foreign exchange reserves are not available prior to the establishment of the Central Bank, but these have grown from K£42 million in 1966 to K£65 million in 1969.[34] The foreign exchange reserves in 1969 equalled 50 per cent of the imports for that year. A net debit on current and long-term capital accounts and a decline in the external assets in 1967 were exceptional, being induced by the devaluation of the £ sterling.

The deposit liabilities of the banking system have soared in recent years, particularly after the introduction of exchange control. It will be seen that the deposits held with commercial banks have grown from K£65 million in 1964 to K£113 million in 1969. The banks have preferred to use additional deposits to increase their liquid assets rather than to extend credit. Lending by banks (loans, advances and bills discounted), which grew from K£55 million in 1964 to K£68 million in 1967, remained almost constant from 1967 to 1969; as a result, the advances (including loans and bills discounted)/deposits ratio fell from 84 per cent to 62 per cent between 1964 and 1969. Over the same period, the cash and liquidity ratios rose from 4·7 and 10·0 per cent to 24·3 and 29·9 per cent respectively.[35] A liquidity ratio of around 30 per cent may not seem very high, but it is certainly very high in relation to the liquidity ratios maintained by the banks in the past, and to the minimum ratio required by the Central Bank. The liquidity ratios of the banking system from 1950 to 1954 rarely fell below 50 per cent, and fluctuated around the rate of 20–30 per cent from 1955 to 1959. However, from 1960 to 1968 the liquidity ratios varied from 10 to 20 per cent, and were at times less than 10

Table 9

Leading Economic and Financial Indicators, 1964–9

	1964	*1965*	*1966*	*1967*	*1968*	*1969**
National income (1964 prices) (K£ m.)						
G.D.P. at factor cost	331·4	331·1	381·2	396·1	425·6	449·5
Gross fixed capital formation:	45·1	45·5	56·8	76·3	77·9	82·0
(1) Public	11·1	11·6	17·8	24·2	27·5	27·9
(2) Private	34·0	33·9	39·0	52·1	50·4	54·2
Consumption:	293·9	301·6	336·5	347·8	380·2	n.a.
(1) Public	49·9	55·7	60·9	66·1	70·0	n.a.
(2) Private	244·0	245·9	275·6	281·7	310·2	n.a.
Balance of payments (total net credits) (K£m.)						
Current account	17·5	0·2	Dr. 6·6	Dr. 21·5	Dr. 14·1	Dr. 7·7
Long-term capital movements	Dr. 15·6	8·1	14·7	16·1	16·1	24·6
Total current account and long-term capital movements	1·9	8·3	8·1	Dr. 5·4	2·0	16·9
Monetary institutions and accounts with I.M.F.	3·4	Dr. 1·8	Dr. 10·5	5·8	Dr. 11·3	Dr. 23.2
Short-term capital movements	Dr. 0·3	Dr. 0·6	Dr. 2·0	Dr. 4·8	1·1	–
Total monetary and short-term capital movements	3·1	Dr. 2·4	Dr. 12·5	1·0	Dr. 10·2	Dr. 23·2
Balancing item	Dr. 5·1	Dr. 5·9	Cr. 4·4	Cr. 4·4	Cr. 8·2	Cr. 6·3
Foreign exchange reserves (December) (K£m.)	n.a.	n.a.	42·1	31·6	43·3	65·1
Commercial banking (December)						
Total deposits (K£m.)	65·0	69·6	77·4	85·0	95·1	112·9
Total advances (K£ m.)	54·6	57·6	55·5	68·0	66·8	70·0
Advances/deposits ratio (%)	84·0	82·7	71·7	80·0	70·2	62·0
Cash ratio (%)	4·7	4·1	5·6	9·4	15·1	24·3
Liquidity ratio (%)	10·0	11·5	16·8	7·8	17·9	29·9
Consumer prices (July 1964 = 100)						
Wage-earners' index (December)	100·6	107·2	109·7	111·8	112·7	112·6
Middle income index (December)	101·0	102·4	106·7	109·6	110·4	111·6

* The 1969 figures for national income and balance of payments are estimates.

Source: *Statistical Abstract* (1969); *Economic Survey* (1970); S.D., M.E.P.D.

per cent. The minimum ratio that the banks have been required to maintain for the first time from December 1969 is $12\frac{1}{2}$ per cent.

The economic and financial milieu prevailing in the economy in the latter part of the period under consideration would not seem to have been adequately taken into account by the Government in the formulation of its financial policy. When the banking system was inundated with liquidity and external assets were increasing at a rapid pace, reflecting that the economy was capable of higher growth rates than were being achieved, the Government ran large recurrent surpluses (K£6·12 million in 1967–8 and K£7·11 million in 1968–9; as shown in Table 1) and increased its cash balances with the banking system (which stood at an already comfortable level of K£8·36 million as at 30 June 1967) by K£0·84 million in 1967–8 and K£1·90 million in 1968–9 (see Table 10). A more expansionary financial policy would have been appropriate.

There are indications that the implications of growing liquidity and external assets have now been understood.[36] The budget proposals for 1970–1 provide for an increase in the recurrent and development expenditures of about 17 per cent. Tax rates have been increased only slightly; increased taxation and measures requiring taxpayers to discharge their tax liability sooner will bring an additional revenue of K£1·3 million. The proposals provide for development expenditures of K£38 million, or an increase of about K£8 million over the likely out-turn of development expenditure in the preceding year. The financing of the development expenditure is to be as follows: external finance, K£14 million; domestic loans and advances, K£16·5 million; transfer from the recurrent account, K£6 million; other domestic sources, K£1·5 million. Domestic advances refer to deficit financing (borrowing from the Central Bank). It was stated in the budget speech that an advance of K£5 million has been obtained from the Central Bank for the Development Exchequer, and more advances would be arranged for 'in the coming years if the situation so allows'. The size of the recurrent surplus would seem to be rather high in the context of some of the past tendencies – underestimation of tax yields and the failure of the development expenditure to grow at the planned rate due to administrative factors. Nevertheless, the latest budget constitutes a stride in the right direction. It is to be hoped that it marks a departure from the relatively passive budgetary policies of the past.

The problem of stimulating an economy is almost universally more

Table 10
Financing of Government Deficit and Disposal of Government Surplus, 1967–8 and 1968–9
(K£'000)

	1967–8	*1968–9*
(1) Exchequer Account, surplus (+) or deficit (−) (excluding net tax reserve certificates and other short-term borrowing)	+436	−101
(2) Net tax reserve certificates, increase (+) or decrease (−)	+721	−90
(3) Net short-term borrowing, increase (+) or decrease (−)	-	+5,680*
(4) Exchequer Account, surplus (+) or deficit (−) ((1) + (2) + (3))	+1,157	5,489
(5) Change in Paymaster-General's balance at the Central Bank, increase (+) or decrease (−)	+438	−3,615
(6) Change in Government deposits at the Central Bank, increase (+) or decrease (−) ((4) + (5))	+1,595	+1,874
(7) Change in Government deposits with commercial banks, increase (+) or decrease (−)	−753	+22
(8) Change in Government deposits with the banking system, increase (+) or decrease (−) ((6) + (7))	+842	+1,896
(9) Change in commercial bank advances to Government, increase (+) or decrease (−)	+11	+33
(10) Change in net government deposits, increase (+) or decrease (−) ((8) + (9))	+853	+1,929

* Treasury Bills, K£5 m; Cereals and Sugar Finance Corporation, K£677,000; other, K£3,000.
Source: Central Bank of Kenya, *Economic and Financial Review*, II 1 (July–Sep 1969).

difficult than the problem of restraining an economy. For this reason, and because of the topical nature of the problem, the remainder of the paper will discuss some of the financial measures available for stimulating the economy and their limitations. The measures to be discussed include possibilities of increasing government expenditure, scope for downward adjustments in tax rates, financing of budgetary deficits through borrowing from the Central Bank and Treasury bills, and means for raising the level of bank lending to the private sector.

Increased public expenditure may be expected to have an expansionary effect in a situation of high liquidity, regardless of the manner in which it is financed. Even in the balanced budget case, where additional expenditures are financed by additional taxes, the effect will be somewhat expansionary since in a situation of high liquidity the marginal propensity to spend on consumption and investment (in the private sector) is likely to fall short of unity.

Further, since net income is assumed to increase, there is no reason why judicious tax increases should depress the level of investment. But it may be too much to expect a government that does not have the administrative capacity to implement its development plans fully to undertake large short-term variations in its expenditures. Nevertheless, the situation is not completely hopeless. First, Plan priorities may be modified in favour of projects for which administrative constraints are not serious. In the past, one reason for the high shortfalls of development expenditures has been the severe administrative problems of implementing projects that had been accorded high priority. Second, the tight reins that have been placed on the recurrent budget may have to be relaxed somewhat. There are reasons to believe that strict control over the growth of the recurrent budget, which has at times been maintained by indiscriminate pruning of recurrent estimates, has hampered the implementation of some planned projects. However, the result of a relaxation may be some loss of financial control, since projects that have not been adequately prepared may be given the 'go ahead'. Third, public bodies that have the capacity to increase expenditures may be encouraged to do so by the provision of loans and opportunities for borrowing from the market. The administrative capacity of the municipalities is particularly relevant here. Last but not least, capital transfers to public financial institutions for the provision of loans to the private sector for the purposes of agricultural, commercial, industrial and housing developments may be increased. It will be seen from Table 1 (against the item entitled 'Loans to other sectors') that such transfers are of considerable importance in the capital budget. The only problem associated with this measure is that the repayments record has been appalling in the past.

The economy may require a greater stimulus than can be achieved through a balanced budget expansion. In that event, increased expenditure will have to be accompanied by an unchanged or a lower overall tax rate depending on the level of deficit that is called for. Membership of the East African Community restricts Kenya's ability to vary tax rates. The scope for varying the rates of customs and excise duties is very limited since the efficient working of the East African Common Market is dependent on the uniformity of these taxes in Kenya, Uganda and Tanzania. Freedom of action with respect to company taxation (corporation tax) is also limited for the same reason. Further, a reduction in the rate of corporation tax is unlikely to bring forth additional investment by foreign companies because their tax liability would not decline, given the provisions of the double taxation agreements. There is greater flexibility in connection with income tax. An increase in the magnitude of personal allowances will be highly inconsistent with the long-term desirability of extending the coverage of income tax. However, this objection would not apply to reductions in the nominal rates of income tax and surtax. The other major fees and taxes whose rates may be varied are graduated personal tax, school fees, petrol and diesel tax and motor-vehicle licence fees. The difficulty with the first two of these is that, once reduced, they will not be easy to raise again owing to political factors. A sales tax, when introduced, will of course provide a major economic regulator.

The two major means for financing a budgetary deficit are borrowing from the central Bank and through Treasury bills. It is important to point out that in the present circumstances the expansionary effects of a given amount of expenditure financed by borrowing from the Central Bank or through Treasury bills would be equivalent. The reasons for this are that almost all Treasury bills are held by the banks, and given their very high cash ratios, the banks will finance additional Treasury bill holdings by running down their cash (which will leave their liquidity ratios unchanged) rather than by reducing their lending to the private sector. In view of this equivalence between Central Bank borrowing and Treasury bills, it is surprising that the Government has been replacing Treasury bills by borrowing from the Central Bank. It will be seen from Table 8 that Treasury bills outstanding fell from K£5 million in November 1969 to K£1 million in March 1970, and it has already been mentioned that an advance of K£5 million from the Central Bank was announced in the budget introduced in June 1970. The practice of paying interest on the banks' deposits with the Central Bank was also stopped recently. The intention may be to force the commercial banks to lend to the private sector by reducing the flow of earning assets emanating from the public sector. The reaction of banks to a lower profitability resulting from the unavailability of interest-bearing deposits at the Central Bank and Treasury bills is difficult to predict on the basis of *a priori* reasoning.

The failure of bank lending to the private sector to grow from 1967[37] would seem to be due to a slackening in the pace of development and the banks' reluctance to lend to the new African businessmen who are taking over from non-citizens. There are four possible measures that the Government can take to rectify the situation. First, pressure could be exerted on the banks to increase their lending to Africans. Second, the minimum rate of interest on bank loans and advances, which stands at 7 per cent per annum, could be reduced. If necessary, this measure could be accompanied by reductions in the rates of interest payable on savings deposits, which earn 3 per cent per annum at present, and time deposits, interest payable on which varies from 3 to 4·5 per cent per annum. Third, the Government could transfer its surplus cash balances from the Central Bank to the National Bank of Kenya Ltd, a bank wholly owned by the Government. This will increase the liquidity base of the National Bank of Kenya Ltd, one of whose major objectives is to lend to African businessmen. A recently announced decision of the Government to acquire equity participation in the local subsidiary of the National and Grindlays Bank Ltd will extend the Government's ability to control the level of bank lending. Finally, the Government could borrow from the banking system through Government stocks, Treasury bills or the Cereals and Sugar Finance Corporation and transfer the proceeds to the National Bank of Kenya Ltd or public development finance institutions for re-lending to the private sector.

This completes the brief survey of the instruments in the Government's economic armoury for stabilisation purposes. While some important individual measures are subject to limitations, the complete inventory affords considerable scope for the pursuit of a stabilisation policy.

REFERENCES

1. For the nature of the transfers to the private sector and a description of the institutions through which the Government channels capital funds to the private sector, see 'Public Sector Financial Institutions in Kenya', *Economic and Financial Review* (Central Bank of Kenya) II 2 (Oct.–Dec. 1969) 9–14.

2. The contribution of external finance is much greater if technical assistance is taken into account. It is estimated that Kenya received technical assistance amounting to K£6.7 million in 1967–8. See H. W. Singer and A. C. Doss, 'Technical Assistance to Kenya: Some Thoughts on Flows and Programming', *Eastern Africa Economic Review*, I 1 (June 1969) 17–27.

3. For a comprehensive description of Kenya's tax structure, see my 'Central Government Taxes in Kenya', *Bulletin for International Fiscal Documentation*, XXIV 4 (Apr. 1970) 141–51.

4. 20 Kenya shillings = 1 Kenya pound (K£) = U.S. $2.80.

5. The following concepts of income are used in the annual reports of the East African Income Tax Department: (1) aggregate income = total income of taxpayers prior to certain deductions and allowances. (2) actual income = aggregate income *minus* deductions for interest paid, losses, deficits brought forward, retirement benefit payments and alimony. (3) chargeable income = actual income *minus* single, married, child and non-resident allowances.

6. Up to 1963 a personal tax was levied by the central Government. G.P.T. was introduced in 1964 as local government tax. From 1967–8 Nairobi and Mombasa, the country's two largest municipalities, have been required to transfer one-half of their G.P.T. collections to the central Government. In 1970 the central Government took over the responsibility for primary education, health and roads, and G.P.T. from county councils. Thus, G.P.T. is now a local government tax in municipalities but a central Government tax in county councils. For the evolution and initial structure of G.P.T., see my 'Low-Income Taxation in Kenya', *British Tax Review* (July–Aug. 1966) 251–67.

7. The concept of 'income from main source' needs some explanation. It includes only the income from the source from which the taxpayer derives the bulk of his income. Thus, if an agricultural producer has rent and pension income, such income would be excluded from the concept of income from main source, which will include only the producer's agricultural income.

8. At present the Income Tax Department has offices only in Nairobi, Mombasa, Nakuru and Kisumu. At some stage it will certainly be necessary to have a tax office in every district.

9. The East African Income Tax Department is a 'common' institution run by the East African Community for the benefit of the three partner states. A separate Income Tax Department for Kenya would bring some advantages. The flow of information from various public bodies to the tax authorities should improve as the Income Tax Department would be in a better position to maintain close contact with other Government Departments. Further, more effective action on tax avoidance might be possible if the Income Tax Department had to implement the political will of only one Government. It will be very surprising if the political attitudes of three different Governments on the problem of tax evasion coincide.

10. Details of contributions made by companies to pension funds are not available. It is known, however, that employees and individuals claim deductions in respect of retirement provisions amounting to about K£600,000.

11. One feature of the tax structure can only be discussed properly in the context of company taxation but is too important to go completely unmentioned.

Companies are taxed through a corporation tax levied on total profits. Dividends are subject to surtax but not income tax. There would not seem to be any rationale for the exemption of dividends from income tax, given the wide acceptance of the view that companies and their shareholders are separate tax entities. The imposition of income tax on dividends will produce substantial revenue. Complete details of the level of dividend income for recent years are not available, but the dividend income (excluding dividends paid by one company to another) in the year of income 1964 exceeded K£4 million.

12. Imputed income of owner-occupied housing was taxable up to 1960. In that year the aggregate income assessed from this source amounted to K£930,000. However, there is no doubt that in most cases the imputed income assessed was substantially below the market rents. According to the national income statistics, the imputed income of owner-occupiers (in the monetary sector) amounted to £K3.5 million in 1967. About 30 per cent of the taxpayers were assessed on the imputed income when such benefit was taxable. This figure has been quoted in the *Report of the East African Commission of Inquiry on Income Tax, 1956–57* (Nairobi, 1957) p. 151.

13. The divergence in Uganda's revenue requirements from those of Tanzania and Kenya, together with these two countries' unwillingness to agree to substantial increases in customs and excise duties and income tax, was a reason for the introduction of a sales tax in Uganda in 1968 See John F. Due, 'The Uganda Sales Tax on Importation and Manufacture', *Eastern Africa Economic Review*, I 1 (June 1969) 1–16.

14. For data on income elasticities at low incomes, see *Economic Survey of Central Province*, 1963–64 (Nairobi, 1968), and B. F. Massell, 'Consistent Estimation of Expenditure Elasticities from Cross-Section Data on Households Producing Partly for Subsistence' (mimeographed, 1968). Data on income elasticities at middle incomes will be found in *The Pattern of Income, Expenditure and Consumption of African Middle-Income Workers in Nairobi, July 1963* (Nairobi, 1964), and B. F. Massell and J. Heyer, 'Household Expenditure in Nairobi: A Statistical Analysis of Consumer Behaviour', *Economic Development and Cultural Change*, XVII 2 (Jan. 1969) 212–34.

15. Imports of durable consumer goods are not as important in the import structure as is often supposed. In 1968, out of total imports of K£127 million, imports of refrigerators, washing machines, radio and television sets, watches, cameras, gramophones and record players, tape-recorders and dictating machines amounted to only K£1 million.

16. Their contribution in 1968 was as follows:

	(K£'000)
Licences under the Traffic Ordinance	1,214
Second-hand motor vehicles purchase tax	202
Motor drivers' licences	86
Import duties on motor vehicles and parts	3,277
Import duties on petrol and diesel	5,477
Petrol and diesel consumption tax	1,563
Total	11,819

It should be noted that the figure of K£11·8 million exaggerates the contribution of road vehicles to revenues, since part of the import and consumption taxes on diesel is borne by industrial machinery, particularly in the agricultural sector. However, the diesel consumption of non-road users is not known.

17. Most excise duties are levied on a specific basis. When a sales tax is introduced, the opportunity should be taken to transform all excise duties into *ad valorem* duties.

18. As will be seen from Table 3, actual income from main source assessed in the manufacturing sector increased from K£5·9 million in 1960 to K£16·1 million in 1966.

19. New machinery for the manufacture of goods or materials and new machinery installed in hotels qualify for an investment allowance of 20 per cent, in addition to the normal depreciation allowances.

20. Over-invoicing in respect of machinery is more difficult to detect than for other goods because every piece of machinery is unique in some ways and will often be imported directly by the manufacturer, whereas there will be more than one importer for most other goods.

21. Of the total subsidies of K£2·81 million in 1968–9, agriculture received K£2·76 million (in the form of a fertiliser subsidy and subsidies for wheat and maize exports).

22. The 1968 G.P.T. statistics for rural areas (county councils) are as follows:

Annual tax liability (Shs.)	*Number of taxpayers*
48	610,053
72	47,116
108	17,295
156	10,422
240	3,914
360	1,718
480	892
600	5,689
	697,099

See *Development Plan, 1970–74* (Nairobi, 1969) p. 67.

23. Export duties are levied on coffee and sisal, but no duty is collected from sisal because its current price is lower than the minimum price at which the duty becomes payable.

24. See 'An Analysis of the Kenya Government Local Funded Debt', *Economic and Financial Review* (Central Bank of Kenya), I 3 (Apr–June 1969) 7–8.

25. After the institution of exchange control, all new life insurance policies issued to residents can only be written in an East African currency, and premiums in respect of these policies cannot normally be transferred outside the Scheduled Territories. More recently, the amount of reinsurance that can be placed overseas in respect of non-life insurance has been restricted, and when the State Reinsurance Corporation commences its operations, all insurance companies will be required to reinsure a part of their business with the Corporation.

26. Emigrants can transfer overseas K£2,500 initially and K£1,000 per year thereafter for five years. All remaining funds are credited to a blocked account. Balances on blocked accounts may be used for the purchase in Kenya of specified securities issued by the Kenya Government or by local authorities and officially quoted in Kenya. The redemption proceeds of these securities, which must have a life of not less than five years at the time of acquisition, are transferable.

27. See 'Recent Trends in the Kenya Government's Local Funded Debt', *Economic and Financial Review* (Central Bank of Kenya), II 1 (July–Sep. 1969)

9–10. Note that the monthly gross redemption yields of short-term, medium-term and long-term stocks to which the article refers are unweighted averages (i.e. redemption yields of individual securities are aggregated and divided by the number of stocks). Weighted averages (the amounts of each stock outstanding being the weights) are needed for a proper assessment of the cost of Government borrowing.

28. The maturity structure of Kenya stocks* in 1968 and 1969 was as follows:

	Outstanding at 30 June 1968		*Outstanding at 30 June 1969*	
	(K£'000)	(%)	(K£'000)	(%)
Short-term[a]	11,711	33·7	12,300	25·7
Medium-term[b]	12,961	37·3	17,320	36·2
Long-term[c]	10,100	29·0	18,191	38·1
Total	34,772	100·0	47,811	100·0

* Excluding Treasury bills.

[a] Under 5 years; [b] 5 to 15 years; [c] over 15 years.

29. The statistics concerning registrations, contributions and benefits are as follows:

Year	*Employers registered* (*as at Dec*)	*Employees registered* (*as at Dec*)	*Contributions* (K£ m)	*Benefits* (K£ m)
1966	3,564	252,107	1·17	–
1967	17,918	379,582	4·56	0·02
1968	19,376	473,570	5·45	0·13

See *Reports* of the National Social Security Fund for 1966, 1967 and 1968.

30. The whole issue of Treasury bills in 1965–6 was held by the East African Currency Board.

31. The commercial banks accounted for 97 per cent of the amounts tendered for the first issue. See 'Treasury Bills', *Economic and Financial Review* (Central Bank of Kenya), I 2 (Jan–Mar 1969) 8–10.

32. The position as at 30 June 1969 was as follows:

	(K£ m)
Deposits repayable at 14 days' notice	2·90
Deposits repayable at 3 months' notice	1·31
Deposits repayable at 6 months' notice	3·77
	7·98

33. See *Development Plan, 1970–74*, pp. 162–5.

34. In March 1970 the reserves stood at K£74·7 million.

35. Cash is defined as Kenya notes and coins and balances with the Central Bank. Liquid assets are defined as cash, net balances with domestic banks, net balances with foreign banks denominated in convertible currencies, and Treasury bills. Strictly, the liability to foreign banks in respect of amounts borrowed for a period of ninety days or more is to be excluded from the definition of liquid assets. This has not been done in the computations given in Table 9 because the necessary data have not been published by the Central Bank.

36. In his budget proposals for 1970–1 introduced on 17 June 1970, the Minister

for Finance stated that 'it has become increasingly clear to me that the economy is not at full stretch; not all the resources available are being used. We have been running a very substantial balance of payments surplus and the liquidity of the banking system has risen sharply. I am convinced these two trends are not unconnected.'

37. According to the latest figures, bank loans, advances and bills discounted grew from K£70 million in December 1969 to K£80 million in March 1970. Most of the increase was, however, accounted for by advances to the public sector.

6

Patterns of Government Capital Formation in the Economic Development of Japan, 1878–1967

TETSUYA NOSSE

THE process of economic development is normally accompanied by changes in the size and pattern of government capital formation. This paper attempts to delineate some of the theoretical relationships involved, making use of empirical data on the behaviour of government capital formation in Japan for a ninety-year period, from 1878 to 1967. During this period the Japanese economy followed a typical course of development, so that a time series analysis of this economy for these years throws up behavioural relationships similar to those encountered in cross-sectional analyses of several advanced countries.

This paper is principally concerned with the investigation of three major issues:

(1) the stages of economic development and their empirical generalisation;
(2) the changing role of government capital formation; and
(3) the changing pattern of the public investment structure.

In the first case an empirical study is made of the more strategic developmental variables with a view to determining their relative importance in Japan's economic development. The findings in this area are used as a test of Professor Rostow's 'stages of growth' hypothesis [20]. Second, the study of the changing role of government capital formation consists of an analysis of changes in the size and structure of government investment, and hence the government capital stock, at every stage of its development. This part of the investigation centres around the examination of socio-economic factors which have determined the direction of public-sector participation, as well as their behaviour in relation to the growth and development process. The analysis continued in the second part of the paper could therefore be considered a test of the 'Hirschman process' [10]. Finally, the changing pattern of public investment by type is looked at from two angles: (*a*) the time profile of the public investment structure by type, and (*b*) the changing 'capacity' of the government capital stock over time.

The following symbols and terms are used throughout this paper:

Y = Gross National Product
N = population
$Y_{\bar{p}}$ = G.N.P. of non-primary industries
Y_p = G.N.P. of primary industries
C = private and public consumption
G = public expenditure, i.e. expenditures out of ordinary government budget, extraordinary budget, government enterprises and public enterprises of national and local authorities
I = private capital formation
I_g = government (or public) capital formation
K = private capital stock
K_g = government (or public) capital stock
L = working population
α = share of profits to private sector
α_g = share of profits to public sector
β = share of wages and salaries.

All figures were estimated in real terms using G.N.P. deflators (base 1934–6) and official data listed in references [32]–[40].

I. THE STAGES AND GENERALISATION OF ECONOMIC DEVELOPMENT

There exists a wealth of studies highlighting the relationships between the development process and its more strategic causal factors. This is also evident in the case of the Japanese economy. In this section an attempt is made to analyse these significant relationships in empirical terms and analagously to devise suitable criteria for distinguishing the various subperiods of development since 1878.

It is well established that the various stages of economic development are normally accompanied by changes in *per capita* G.N.P. Therefore, using *per capita* G.N.P. (Y/N) as an index of economic development, we test its relationship with three other possible indices: the Hoffman ratio (I/C), the non-primary G.N.P. ratio ($Y_{\bar{p}}/Y_p$), and the total investment/G.N.P. ratio (I/Y). The relationships between *per capita* G.N.P. and the other three indices were investigated by means of a regression analysis of data for the period 1878–1967. Upon examination of the scatter diagrams and long-run values (see Appendix I), double log functions were employed. The results obtained are summarized below (T-values in parentheses under the coefficients).

$$\log(I/C) = \underset{(28{\cdot}678)}{-\ 2{\cdot}6591} + \underset{(21{\cdot}329)}{0{\cdot}8954} \log(Y/N) + \underset{(11{\cdot}455)}{0{\cdot}3466}\, Q$$

$$R^2 = 0{\cdot}9401,\ d = 1{\cdot}4956$$

$$\text{where } Q \begin{cases} = 1 \text{ (1940–51, during the war)} \\ = 0 \text{ (1886–1967, except the above period),} \end{cases}$$

$$\log(Y_{\bar{p}}/Y_p) = \underset{(14{\cdot}821)}{-\ 1{\cdot}0255} + \underset{(22{\cdot}246)}{0{\cdot}7121} \log(Y/N) + \underset{(1{\cdot}4882)}{0{\cdot}0396}\, Q$$

$$R^2 = 0{\cdot}9210,\ d = 1{\cdot}2724,$$

$$\text{where } Q \begin{cases} = 1 \text{ (1940–51)} \\ = 0 \text{ (1878–1967, except the above period),} \end{cases}$$

$$(I + I_g)/Y = \underset{(5{\cdot}7378)}{0{\cdot}0705} + \underset{(12{\cdot}505)}{0{\cdot}6387} \times 10^{-3}\,(Y/N) + \underset{(7{\cdot}5307)}{0{\cdot}1457}\, Q$$

$$R^2 = 0{\cdot}8379,\ d = 1{\cdot}4180,$$

$$\text{where } Q \begin{cases} = 1 \text{ (1940–51)} \\ = 0 \text{ (1886–1967, except the above period).} \end{cases}$$

As can be seen, there were highly significant correlations between *per capita* G.N.P. (Y/N) and the Hoffman ratio (I/C), the non-primary G.N.P. ratio ($Y_{\bar{p}}/Y_p$) and the total investment ratio (I/Y) for the period under consideration. The results were confirmed using both linear and semi-logarithmic functions. We further broke up the entire period into various subperiods in which different sets of forces appeared to determine the size of government capital formation. In this context, socio-economic factors such as institutional and political problems, wars, openness, etc., were taken into account. These considerations led us to believe that it is reasonable to divide the period after 1878 into four stages with seven subperiods, as follows:

I. The period of public-sector dominance and the establishment of infrastructure:
   (*a*) 1878–95. From the foundation of the Meiji Government to the Sino-Japanese War.
   (*b*) 1896–1905. End of the Sino-Japanese War to the Russo-Japanese War.

II. Multiple government activities along with urbanisation and industrialisation:
   (*c*) 1906–11. Displacement after the Russo-Japanese War.
   (*d*) 1912–31. Establishment of superstructure and the promotion of public works in the boom after the First World War.

III. (*e*) 1932–45. The Pacific War.

IV. The period after the Second World War:
   (*f*) 1946–59. Recovery and reconstruction.
   (*g*) 1960–7. Selective policies supporting economic growth.

The above divisions approximate very closely to the categories made by Rostow for the Japanese economy, i.e. the preconditions before 1880; the 'take-off' between 1880 and 1900; and maturity after 1900.

Tables 1 and 2, showing the average values of the symbols of economic development, tend to confirm the basis of subdivision into discrete periods.

Table 1

Changing Values of the Symbols of Economic Development

Period, subperiod and years	*Per capita G.N.P. (at average 1934–6 prices)* (Y/N)	*Hoffman ratio* (I/C)	*Non-primary G.N.P. ratio* ($Y_{\bar{p}}/Y_p$)	*Total Investment ratio* ($(I + I_g)/Y$)
I (*a*) 1878–95	60·1	0·103	1·80	0·095
(*b*) 1896–1905	87·7	0·119	2·13	0·111
II (*c*) 1906–11	108·0	0·139	2·36	0·135
(*d*) 1912–31	155·4	0·187	3·45	0·159
III (*e*) 1932–45	215·6	0·378	4·92	0·292
IV (*f*) 1946–59	214·8	0·425	4·33	0·299
(*g*) 1960–7	538·9	0·631	8·29	0·403

It can be seen from Tables 1 and 2 that:

(*a*) The private investment ratio (I/Y) increases throughout all periods.
(*b*) The share of government investment in government expenditure (I_g/G) is stable.
(*c*) The share of government expenditure (G/Y) rose in the long run, while remaining fairly constant in the post-war period. This was due to the rapid growth of (Y/N).
(*d*) The share of government investment to private investment (I_g/I) is less stable, reflecting the impact of public investment in generating new capacity.

Table 2

Regression Estimates of Various Ratios as a Function of Per Capita G.N.P. (Y/N) in the Form

$y = a_0 + a_1 \log (Y/N)$

Period	*y*	*Regression coefficient (l)*	*T-value of l*	*R*	*d*
All periods (1879–1967, except 1943–6)	G/Y	0·3899	6·0444	0·6770	0·3444
	I_g/Y	0·0957	6·4841	0·7030	0·6342
	I/Y	0·2530	10·1920	0·8427	0·5444
	I_g/G	0·0211	0·7607	0·1007	0·6628
Before World War II (1879–1942)	G/Y	0·6657	9·2140	0·8545	0·6903
	I_g/Y	0·1618	8·2158	0·8259	1·0056
	I/Y	0·1485	6·7239	0·7667	1·0942
	I_g/G	0·0393	0·8851	0·0839	0·6815
After World War II (1947–67)	G/Y	−0·1924	2·0713	0·4976	1·3202
	I_g/Y	0·0173	0·7797	0·2020	1·0540
	I/Y	0·1440	3·3313	0·7088	1·0699
	I_g/G	1·4137	1·9037	0·4559	1·3425

Accordingly, the ratio of government capital formation to G.N.P. tended to increase as the economy developed, although the increasing rate can be interpreted from the relationship between (G/Y) and (I/Y), thereby suggesting that there may be some 'complementarity' between public investment and private investment.

The regression estimate testing the correlation between (I_g/Y) and (G/Y) is as follows:

$$(I_g/Y) = \underset{(1{\cdot}1056)}{0{\cdot}0078} + \underset{(10{\cdot}968)}{0{\cdot}2046}\,(G/Y)$$

$$R = 0{\cdot}8599,\ d = 0{\cdot}9492$$

(with values during World War II (1942–45) excluded).

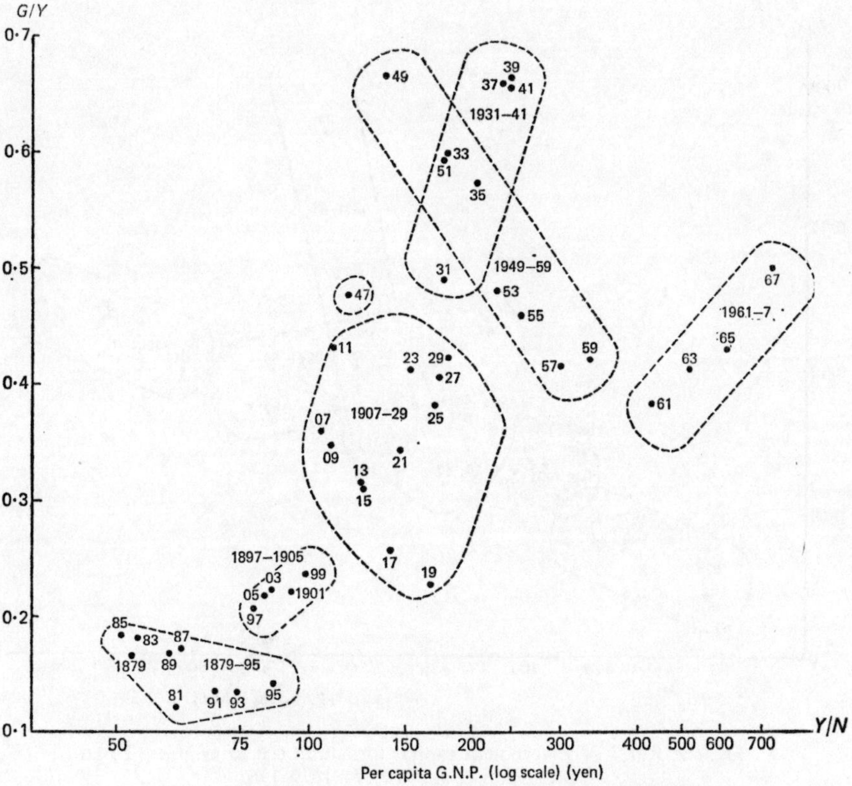

Fig. 6.1. Share of government expenditure in G.N.P., 1879–1967

Based on the above considerations, our next concern was to ascertain how these factors were determined during the long-run process of development since 1878. Figs. 6.1 and 6.2 show the differences in the share of government expenditure in G.N.P. and the ratio of government investment to G.N.P. respectively by means of scatter diagrams in which values are grouped according to the periods of classification.

In Table 3 various average ratios in terms of the selected periods are presented.

As has been previously shown, the government expenditure/G.N.P. ratio was highly correlated with the government investment ratio, both moving in sympathy with economic development, prob-

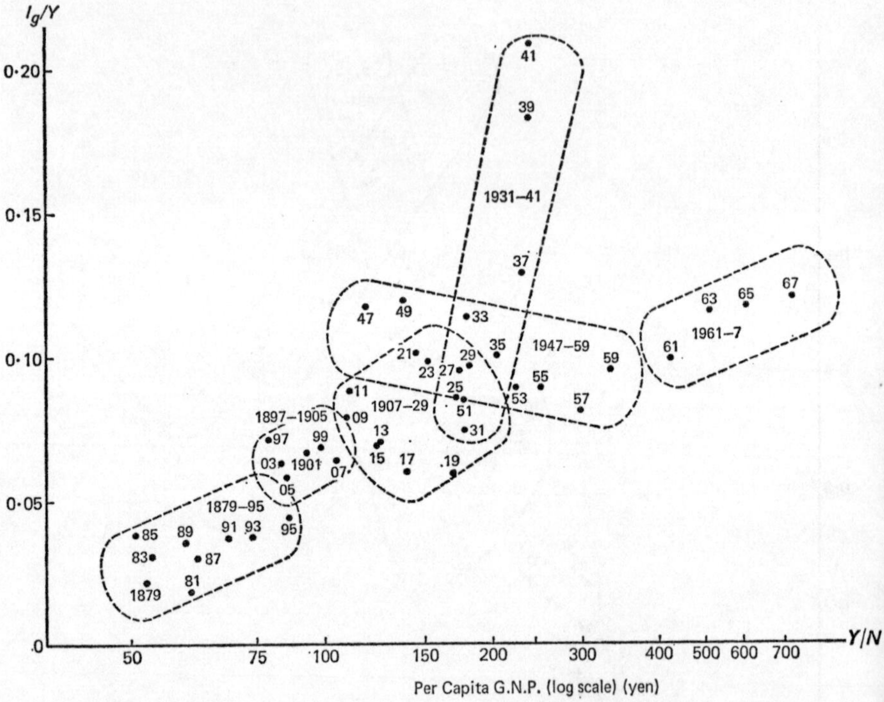

Fig. 6.2. Ratio of government capital formation (I_g) to G.N.P. (Y) and per capita G.N.P. (Y/N), 1879–1967

ably on account of the impact of active public-sector policies which were carried out on a continuous basis. The above argument notwithstanding, periodical differences were also observed. These differences could be explained in terms of two sets of factors. First, every period was characterised by a displacement effect which showed up through the shock of socio-political factors (wars, dramatic changes of policy, etc.). Second, the government investment ratio was observed to have a ten-year cycle with the peak occurring in approximately the middle of each period. Such peaks could be explained by the impact of policy in relation to economic needs. The conclusion, therefore, emerges that there may be a cyclical process of 'complementarity' and 'substitutability' between government capital formation and private capital formation in each ten year cycle, with noticeable long-run changes in the former relative to the latter.

The above findings emerge in a clearer light when reference is made to certain historical facts. Because of data limitations, our quantifications begin with the year 1878 when the 'precondition' stage had almost ended. However, the basic policy begun during the period 1868–77 (the Meiji Restoration) was followed through in successive government activities in the post-1878 period. With the establishment of the Meiji Government, Japan's basic economic policy was centred around the building-up of the stock of social overhead capital and the establishment of three 'breakthrough' industries – steel and iron (1869), railways (1870) and cotton (1869) – all of which were publicly funded and owned. This was followed by the provision of other forms of infrastructure, such as education (1872), communications (1873) and public works (1873), as well as other support for transportation and commuter facilities. During this 'precondition' stage the government investment ratio relative to *per capita* G.N.P. was relatively high owing to the high level of government capital formation.

During the next period (1878–95) the government capital (except railways) previously established was sold off very cheaply to the new elite industrialists, thereby providing the 'big push' which has for long played a key role in the developmental process. This highlights the point about the substitutability between private investment and government capital formation previously mentioned. This investment process in terms of private investment tended to decrease the government investment/G.N.P. ratio.

Next comes the displacement effect created by the Sino-Japanese War (1894–5). Because of the expanded infrastructure, the government investment/G.N.P. ratio shows a considerable increase. In 1897 a big steel company – Yahata – and several government banks were publicly created. Redevelopment of railways, mining, telephone services, tobacco and military industries was also supported by the expanded scale of public debt policy.

We now turn to Period II, which witnessed the movement of the economy towards 'maturity'. First, the period 1906–11 saw the highest displacement effect which occurred immediately after the Russo-Japanese War (1904–5). In 1911 the government expenditure ratio showed a 99 per cent increase over its 1905 level while the government investment ratio rose by 40 per cent. Of some significance

Table 3

Various Ratios Concerned with Government Investment

Period, sab-period and years	*Government expenditure ratio* (G/Y)	*Government investment ratio* (I_g/G)	*Government investment ratio to G.N.P.* (I_g/Y)	*Government investment/private investment* (I_g/I)	*Government capital/private capital* (K_g/K)
I (a) 1878–95	0·141	0·213	0·033	0·855	0·531
(b) 1896–1905	0·220	0·298	0·066	1·541	1·411
II (c) 1906–11	0·379	0·203	0·077	1·326	1·328
(d) 1912–31	0·356	0·233	0·082	1·089	1·076
III (e) 1932–45	0·630	0·224	0·153	1·223	1·215
IV (f) 1946–59	0·502	0·193	0·095	0·471	0·477
(g) 1960–7	0·433	0·263	0·114	0·393	0·382

Note: In estimating capital stocks for both the private and public sectors the P.I. method was employed, the average service life of stocks was assumed to be five years, and real values were computed using a 1934–5 average base price. The assumption that the average life of capital stock is five years is based on the following four reasons:

1. The capital stock in our case includes equipment and reserves, so that the average service life is shorter than that of fixed assets.

2. While it is impossible to give an exact categorisation of the concept of average life, five years' service on average is approximately equal to that statutorily defined as average.

3. The average capital/output ratio (K/Y) was estimated to be 3·393 for the period 1906–67, which is reasonable. In estimating the capital stock the following formula was used:

$$\frac{(\dot{K} + K_g)}{(K + K_g)} = \frac{(I + I_g)}{Y} \cdot \frac{Y}{K + K_g}.$$

The long-run average growth rate of capital stock estimated on the basis of our compiled data was approximately equal to the long-run growth rate of G.N.P. in the form

$$\frac{\dot{Y}}{Y} \text{ and } \frac{(K \dot{+} K_g)}{(K + K_g)}.$$

The results are summarised:

Period	$\dot{Y}/Y$	$\frac{(K \dot{+} K_g)}{(K + K_g)}$
Before World War II (1906–37)	0·044	0·054
After World War II (1949–67)	0·107	0·106
All the period (1906–67)	0·063	0·070

during this period was the nationalisation of the railways under the National Railway Act (1905). Some of the key industries (iron and steel, wool and cotton, mining and munitions) were also put under public management (1906), while the Fourth Plan for irrigation and water was carried out in 1910.

During the later stage of this period (1912–31) we see a further expansion of externality-intensive public-sector capital assets, financed by the ample supply of funds made available during the loan following World War I. Public works in the form of ports and roads (1915) and railways (1917) were expanding apace, and the burden of education was centralised. Interestingly enough, during the depression of 1931 a policy of road construction was used as a means of solving the unemployment problem.

The above trends were maintained during the Pacific War period (Period III, 1932–45), but during this era government capital formation was concentrated on military expenditure. The result was that by 1940 – the time Rostow depicted for the attainment of maturity – both the government expenditure and investment ratios reached their highest levels.

Post-war public investment policy falls into two distinct periods. During the first period (1946–59) the government investment plan was aimed at reconstruction and provision of some basic utilities, while in the second period beginning in 1960 investment policy was directed towards compensatory and discretionary capital formation in order to maintain an appropriate relationship with private investment, which expanded enormously with the rapid growth of the private sector. The first investment period (1946–9), aimed at reconstruction, was typified by selective government investment designed to replace basic overheads damaged during the war. Once this first investment objective was achieved, the government became responsible for the 'optimum investment' plan (1950–4). This was typified by compensatory finance aimed at stabilising the flexibility of private investment which arose out of the Korean War. In contrast to this positive policy, the later period was characterised by a plan for 'basic works' (1955–9) which included the provision of such things as electricity, railways, ports and roads. The programme of basic works, in conjunction with the investment boom, was intended to assure the economic bases for the activities of the private sector. On account of the various factors mentioned above, the government investment and expenditure ratios reached their highest level with the bulk of the investment being financed through the newly created government financial infrastructure (the Recovery Fund, the extraordinary budget, the Export–Import Bank and other financial institutions). It should be noted, however, that during the post-war period the greater part of the investment portfolio took the form of private investment, in contrast to the pre-war situation.

From 1960 onwards government capital formation was multifaceted, with policy being directed to both capacity building and redistribution. The major emphasis was placed on housing, the levelling-up of low productivity in small and backward industries, and similar policies aimed at securing a stable civilian life which in term was intended to lend support to labour-force supply and contribute to technical progress. Thus by 1963 we see a second high level of government investment supported by a public debt policy specifically introduced for its financing, and corresponding to Japan's new age of 'high mass-consumption'.

In summary, there seems to be a very close connection between government capital formation and private capital formation in Japan. Within this context, the following specific points are worthy of note:

(*a*) The government investment ratio has ten-year cycles owing to its changing role (with complementarity and substitutability with private investment).

(*b*) Over the longer run, however, the government investment ratio tended to decline because of the development of private investment.

(*c*) Government investment reaches a peak in each distinct period owing to the displacement effect of government expenditure, but determined more or less by economic needs.

(*d*) In cyclical terms, government investment and hence government capital assets tended in the longer run to show a close relationship with the relevant private-sector variables.

(*e*) The role of public investment in the pre-war period was different from that in the post-war years.

The findings are supported by quantitative evidence. In Figs. 6.3 and 6.4 we show the long-run relationship between government and private capital formation as well as capital stocks in both sectors.

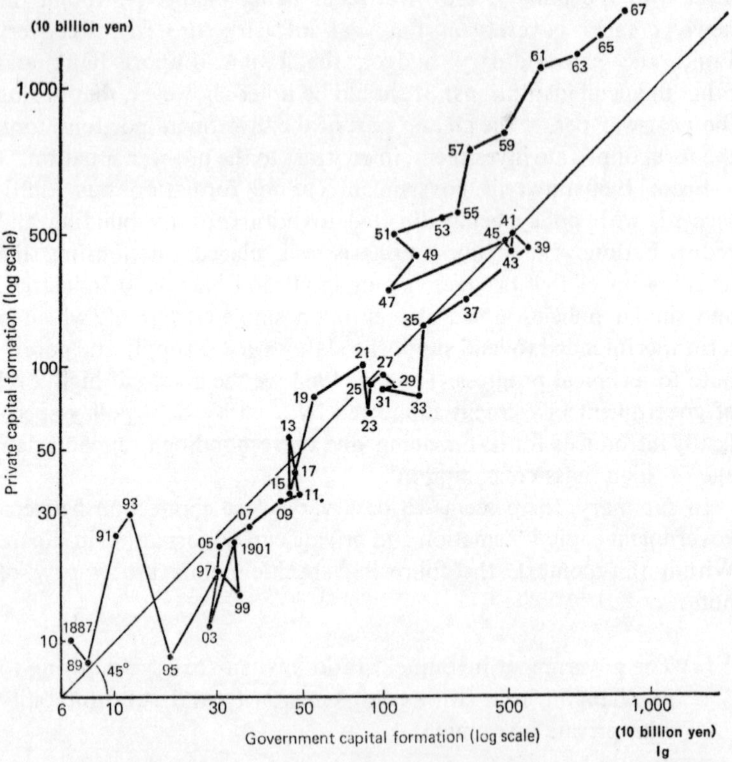

Fig. 6.3. Relationship between private capital formation and government capital formation, 1887–1967

The data clearly reveal a Hirschman type of development for both types of investment. It should also be noted that when international comparisons are made, Japan's government investment has played a stronger leading role, though this role changes cyclically within five distinct time periods (1887–95, 1897–1911, 1913–23, 1925–45 and 1947–67).

In order to test the relationship between public and private investment behaviour, we tried the following regression analysis. The results run as follows:
In the form $\log I = a_0 + a_1 \log I_g$, and standard deviations in the parentheses:

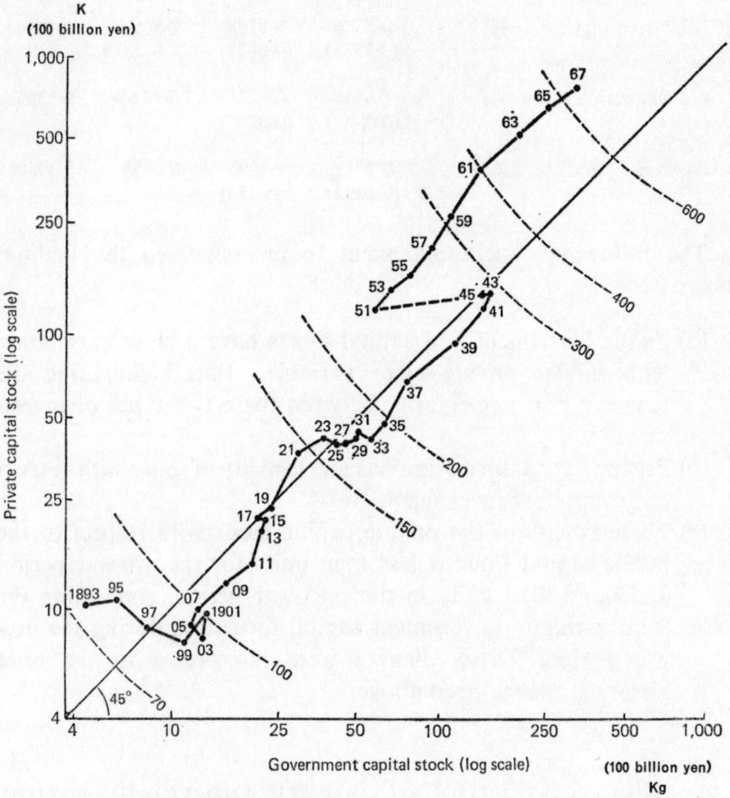

Fig. 6.4. Relationship between private capital stock and government capital stock, with the scale of per capita G.N.P., 1893–1967

	a_0	a_1	R^2	σ
All the period (1877–1967)	−0·4035 (0·1569)	1·1159 (0·0530)	0·8579	0·8343
Pre-war period (1877–1944)	0·2092 (0·1530)	0·9024 (0·0553)	0·8233	1·3682
Post-war period (1947–67)	0·2083 (0·2625)	1·0459 (0·0768)	0·8979	2·1254

In the form $\log K = b_0 + b_1 \log K_g$, and standard deviations in the parentheses:

	b_0	b_1	R^2	d
All the period (1903–67)	0·5586 (0·2571)	0·9188 (0·0628)	0·8694	0·1766
Pre-war period (1903–44)	1·6446 (0·0867)	0·6236 (0·0220)	0·9744	0·3259
Post-war period (1945–67)	−0·2712 (0·1392)	1·1396 (0·0316)	0·9923	2·0949

The following conclusions seem to emerge from the findings noted above:

(*a*) Public investment and capital assets have a close correlation with similar private-sector variables, thus highlighting the long-run complementarity between these two types of investment.[1]

(*b*) Private capital formation has an elasticity of unity with respect to government investment.

(*c*) The elasticity of the private capital stock with respect to the public capital stock is less than unity for the pre-war period and more than unity in the post-war period, confirming the leading role of government capital formation during the pre-war period. These changes were interpreted in the brief historical sketch given above.

II. THE CONTRIBUTION TO GROWTH AND THE GESTATION PERIOD OF GOVERNMENT INVESTMENT

In this section we show how public investment has contributed to economic growth in the time profile and how long is the gestation period of government investment. In order to clarify these issues, we employ the Cobb–Douglas production function of the type

$$Y(t) = A(t)\, K_g(t)^{\alpha_g(t)}\, K(t)^{\alpha(t)}\, L(t)^{\beta(t)} \tag{1}$$

where we assume

$$\alpha_g(t) + \alpha(t) + \beta(t) = 1.$$

Further, we assume that the rate of return is equal for both capital stocks in public and private sectors, so that

$$\alpha_g(t)\,/\,\alpha(t) = K_g(t)\,/\,K(t)$$

and hence

$$\alpha_g(t) = (1 - \beta(t)) \left(1 + \frac{K(t)}{K_g(t)}\right)^{-1} \tag{2}$$

where $\beta(t)$ can be estimated from the data in the form (wages and salaries)/(G.N.P.).

In addition, since

$$\frac{\dot{Y}(t)}{Y(t)} = \frac{\dot{A}(t)}{A(t)} + \alpha_g(t)\frac{\dot{K}_g(t)}{K_g(t)} + \alpha(t)\frac{\dot{K}(t)}{K(t)} + \beta(t)\frac{\dot{L}(t)}{L(t)},$$

the contribution of government capital stocks to growth of G.N.P. is measured in the form

$$\frac{\alpha_g(t)\,\dot{K}_g(t)\,/\,K_g(t)}{\dot{Y}(t)\,/\,Y(t)} \tag{3}$$

and that to increase in productivity of labour is estimated in the form

$$\alpha_g(t)\,\frac{\dfrac{\dot{K}_g(t)}{K_g(t)} - \dfrac{\dot{L}(t)}{L(t)}}{\dfrac{\dot{Y}(t)}{Y(t)} - \dfrac{\dot{L}(t)}{L(t)}}. \tag{4}$$

The contribution of the increase in government capital stock to the increase in *per capita* G.N.P. is also measured in the form[2]

$$\frac{\alpha_g \dfrac{L}{N}\dfrac{\dot{K}_g}{K_g}}{\left(\dfrac{\dot{Y}}{Y} - \dfrac{\dot{N}}{N}\right)}. \tag{5}$$

1. The estimated values required for the computation in (3), (4) and (5) are listed in Appendix II below. (We assume the same average value of 0·6166 for β in the pre-war period.) The share of government profits (α_g) and the rate of increase in government capital stock are generally greater in the pre-war period than in the post-war period, so that these affect the contribution ratios. It can be seen also that the share of wages and salaries as well as that of government profits is fairly stable, so that the contribution depends mainly on the growth rate of government capital stock ($\dot{K}_g/K_g$) in relation to that of the private capital stock ($\dot{K}/K$) and the labour force ($\dot{L}/L$). We may summarise the cyclical pattern of these ratios by period in Table 4.

Table 4

Various Growth Rates

Period, subperiod and years	*Gross National Product* ($\dot{Y}/Y$)	*Government capital stock* ($\dot{K}_g/K_g$)	*Private capital stock* ($\dot{K}/K$)	*Working population* ($\dot{L}/L$)	*Population* ($\dot{N}/N$)
II (c) 1906–11	0·053	0·098	0·017	0·0044	0·0113
(d) 1912–31	0·038	0·061	0·043	0·0071	0·0137
III (e) 1932–7	0·057	0·073	0·043	0·0109	0·0129
IV (f) 1949–59	0·117	0·099	0·110	0·0218	0·0134
(g) 1960–2	0·108	0·103	0·115	0·0130	0·0091

Note that, on the other hand, the estimated average values of the share of profits (government and private) and wages and salaries make the following production functions in the form (1) above as

$$Y(t) = A(t)\, K_g(t)^{0\cdot137}\, K(t)^{0\cdot177}\, L(t)^{0\cdot686} \quad \text{for all periods,}$$

$$Y(t) = A(t)\, K_g(t)^{0\cdot155}\, K(t)^{0\cdot228}\, L(t)^{0\cdot617} \quad \text{for pre-war periods,}$$

and

$$Y(t) = A(t)\, K_g(t)^{0\cdot095}\, K(t)^{0\cdot184}\, L(t)^{0\cdot721} \quad \text{for the post-war period.}$$

2. In line with this approach, we tried first to ascertain the relative differences in the contribution of government capital formation in the pre-and post-war periods, and second to observe its periodical pattern. The results concerned with the first problem are summarised in Table 5. The average values shown above have been substituted in the forms (3) and (4) in this case, and the contribution of the growth rates of private capital stock, labour force and technical progress are shown for reference.

It is clear from this result that, while both public and private capital stocks make equal contributions, the degree of contribution of the former declines during the more developed stage of the post-

Table 5

Contribution of the Increases in Factors of Production to the Growth of G.N.P. ($\dot{Y}/Y$) and the Increase in Productivity of Labour ($\dot{Y}/L$)

Period	*by/to*	($\dot{Y}/Y$)	($\dot{Y}/L$)
All the period (1906–67)	$\dot{K}_g/K_g$	*0·1714*	*0·1788*
	$\dot{K}/K$	0·1683	0·1673
	$\dot{L}/L$	0·1190	–
	$\dot{A}/A$	0·5413	0·6558
Pre-war period (1906–36)	$\dot{K}_g/K_g$	*0·2477*	*0·2649*
	$\dot{K}/K$	0·1977	0·1919
	$\dot{L}/L$	0·0977	–
	$\dot{A}/A$	0·4568	0·5405
Post-war period (1949–62)	$\dot{K}_g/K_g$	*0·0889*	*0·0874*
	$\dot{K}/K$	0·1907	0·1920
	$\dot{L}/L$	0·1346	–
	$\dot{A}/A$	0·5860	0·7207

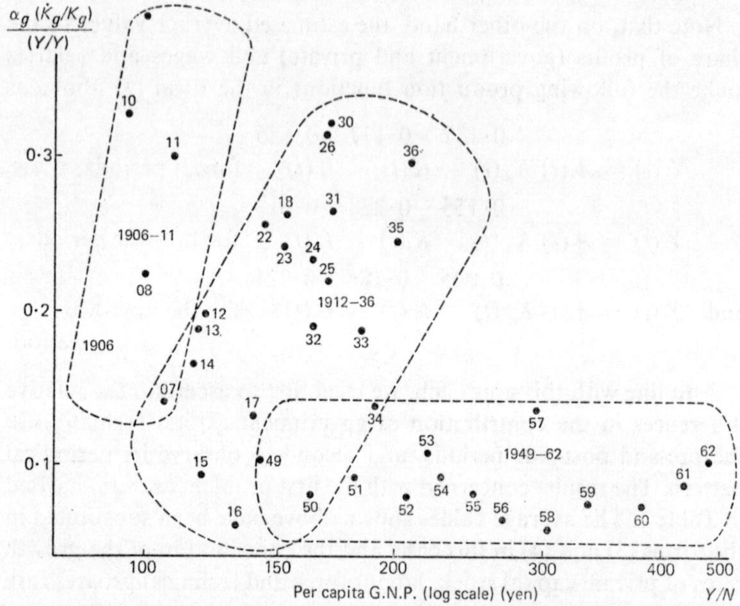

Fig. 6.5. Contribution of the growth of government capital stock ($\dot{K}_g/K_g$) to the growth of G.N.P. ($\dot{Y}/Y$), 1906–62

war period, when the preconditional and leading role of government investment had lost its effect.

3. Finally, we observe the cyclical pattern of the contribution of government capital stock to growth. First, as the data compiled in Appendix II indicate, there seems to be a *seven-year lag* between high government investment and the contribution of public capital stock to growth. While high government capital formation means an increase in government capital stock, it takes some years for the capital/input ratio to decline as the result of the full capacity effects on output. We may therefore say that public investment has a seven-year gestation period, with the cycle taking place in the short run during the process of economic growth. Second, the long-run contribution of public investment to growth could be divided into three phases. In the early stage the contribution is high while G.N.P. grows slowly, while in the later stage the opposite is true. In the intermediate stage we find a high contribution corresponding to a high growth rate of G.N.P. This tends to explain the long gestation period of government capital stock in the early stage having full

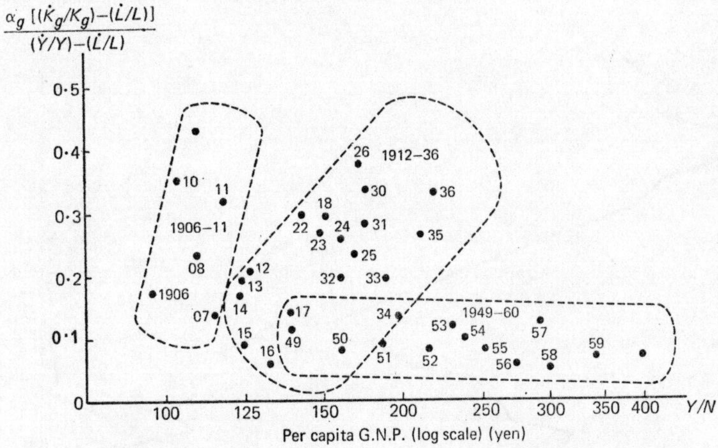

Fig. 6.6. Contribution of the growth of government capital stock/labour ratio $\left(\frac{\dot{K}_g}{K_g} - \frac{\dot{L}}{L}\right)$ to the increasing ratio of the productivity of labour $\left(\frac{\dot{Y}}{Y} - \frac{\dot{L}}{L}\right)$, 1906–60

effects on capacity in the later stages when it becomes substitutable with the private capital stock. This tendency is shown in Figs. 6.5, 6.6.

III. THE CHANGING PATTERNS OF PUBLIC INVESTMENT

So far we have analysed the general pattern and the contribution of government capital formation in the long-run economic development process. Let us finally look at the changing patterns of public investment by type during different periods. Our main interest lies in ascertaining (1) the time profile of public investment structure by type, and (2) the structure of capacity-building public assets by type.

1. In order to see first the changing time profile of government capital formation by type, we take (as above) the government investment/G.N.P. ratio, which is classified by type. Denoting I_{gi} as government investment to the type of capital i, the ratio of which to G.N.P. is

$$\frac{I_{gi}}{Y} = \frac{I_{gi}}{I_g} \cdot \frac{I_g}{Y} = \frac{I_{gi}}{I_g} \cdot \frac{I_g}{G} \cdot \frac{G}{Y}$$

then this ratio depends on the government investment/G.N.P. ratio (and hence, if its share in government expenditure is stable as stated above, on the government expenditure/G.N.P. ratio) and on the

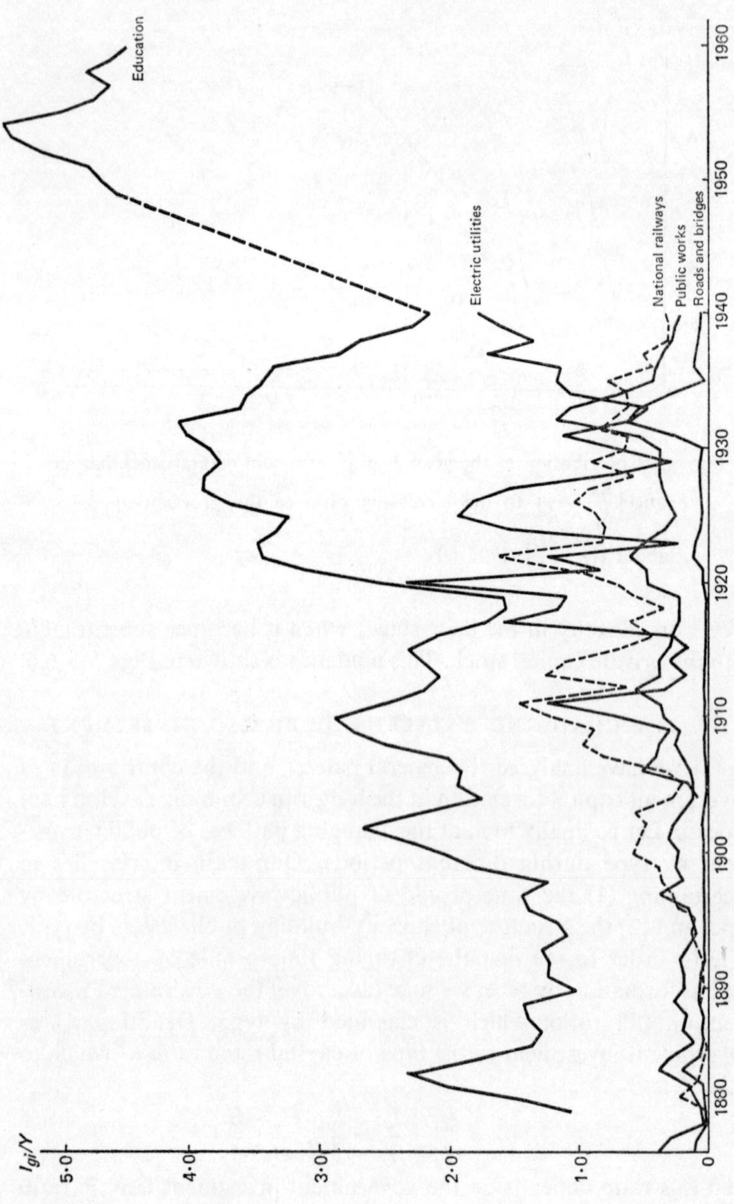

Fig. 6.7. Share of government capital expenditure by types, 1878–1960

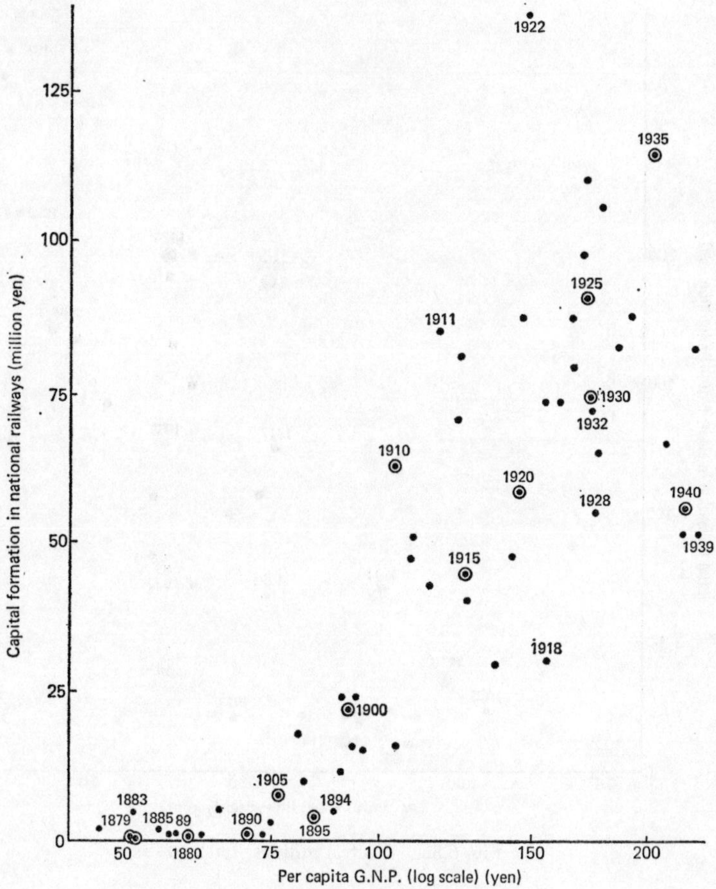

Fig. 6.8A. National railways, 1879–1940

weight of investment to a specific type of capital. It is then noted that this weight can be determined either by the replacement period of an asset or by socio-political factors such as wars and institutional changes. We check this in Fig. 6.7 in which, owing to the limitation of original data, the investment/G.N.P. ratios in education, public works, roads and bridges, national railways and electric utilities are shown separately. Furthermore, we also add Figs. 6.8A to 6.8E to show the changes in real values of public capital formation corresponding to the growth of *per capita* G.N.P.

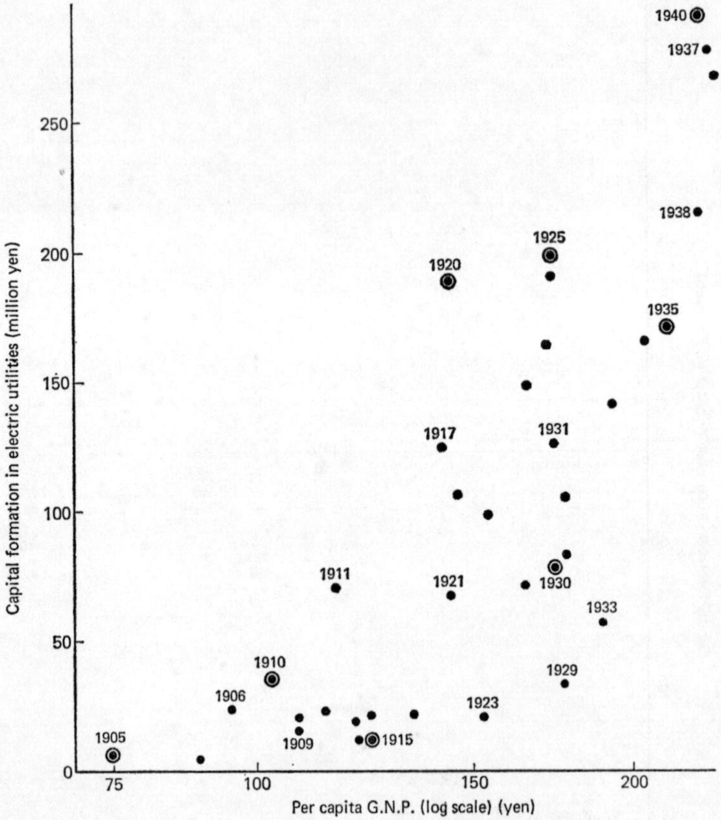

Fig. 6.8B. Electric utilities, 1904–40

From these diagrams and our compiled data in Appendix III, the following generalisations about the time profile of government capital formation may be suggested.

First, economic development (the increase in *per capita* G.N.P.) has a strong relationship with any type of public capital formation; the relationship seems to be technical in nature. We observe that the formation of social overheads starts with education, followed by public works, roads and bridges, national railways and electric utilities. Therefore, the weight in the investment profile changes periodically because of their replacement periods and technical requirements.

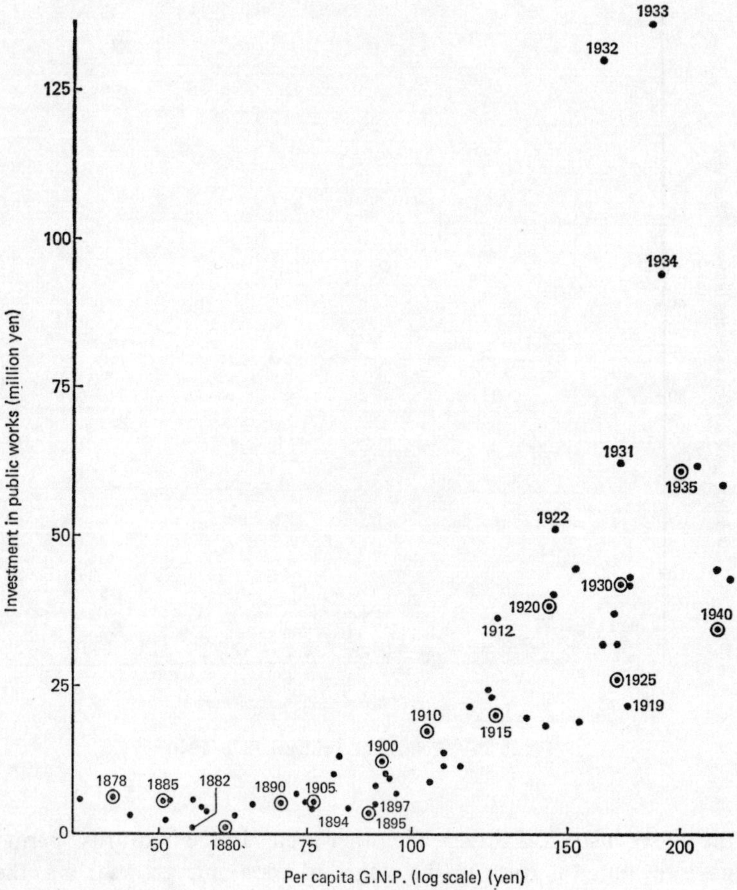

Fig. 6.8c. Public works, 1878–1940

Second, there seems to be some *ten-year cycles* in each type of public investment. As shown previously, this cycle is determined by the government investment ratio, the replacement period socio-political factors. Generally, the high levels of capital formation in 1910–11 and 1921–2 can be interpreted as the effects of the high levels of government expenditure, while those of 1931–2 are explained as the policy for unemployment in the Great Depression. The mild amplitude in the 'take-off' period is due to the preconditional accumulation of capital stocks of every type. In addition, as stated in

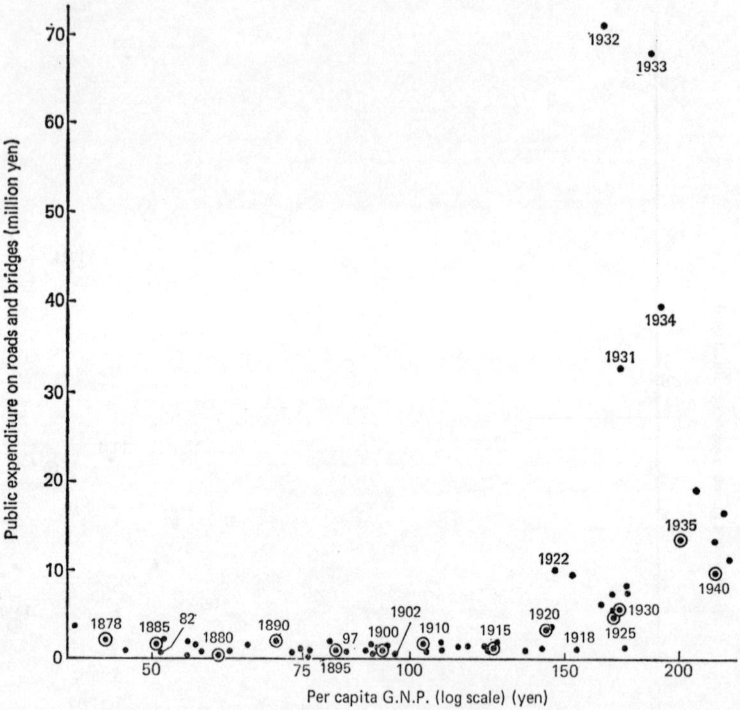

Fig. 6.8D. Roads and bridges, 1878–1940

the above historical survey, the other cycles in the 'maturity' period have meaningful roles in the stages of economic growth; e.g. the nationalisation of railways in 1905, the River and Water Act in 1897, the sharp increase in educational costs in 1902, etc.

Third, starting with education, we can see some *five-year lags* shift in the weight to the next public works, roads and bridges, and national railways, with further five-year lags shift in the weight to electric utilities. These lags have been accelerated to make long-run ten-year cycles with expanding amplitudes.

These observations suggest that (*a*) there is some order in the formation of social overheads which may be maintained cyclically in the process of economic development, and (*b*) the replacement period of general overhead capital with vintage seems to be approximately equal to ten years.

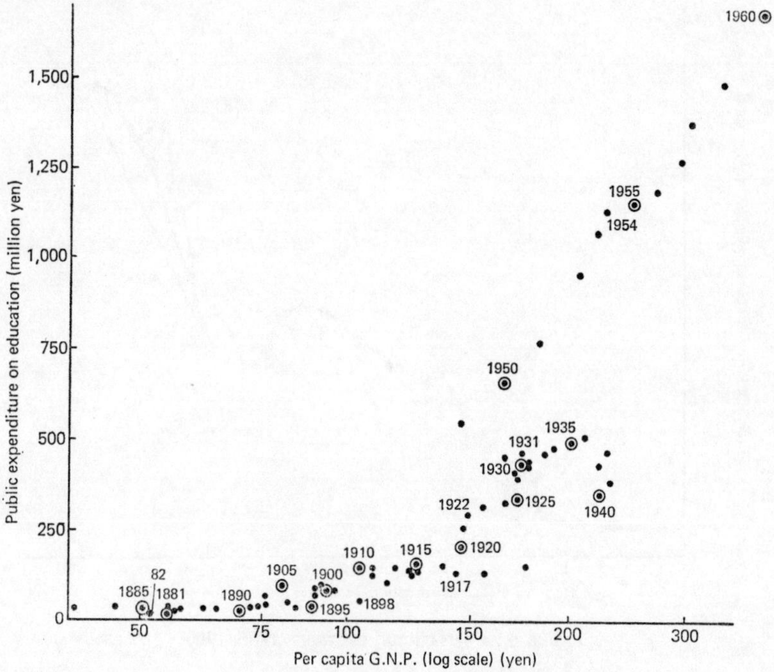

Fig. 6.8E. Education, 1881–1960

The above discussions suggest the cyclical patterns of government capital formation involving internal changes in structural composition of social overheads in the stages of economic development. We have nevertheless to find a generalisation to fit the long-run pattern of behaviour of social overheads and capacity.

To look at this 'social overheads and capacity' trend, we present Figs. 6.9A to 6.9D, where the long-run relationship between capital stocks and capacity is plotted according to the type of social overhead.

Two interesting facts can be observed from the above analysis. First, starting with the initial setting of external capital, the process of public capital formation have proceeded in more or less step-to-step discrete jumps, probably owing to the lumpiness of public investment in social overheads. Second, capacity showed an increasing trend generally in relation to continuous unit increase in the stock of social overheads. An explanation is provided below along with Fig. 6.10.

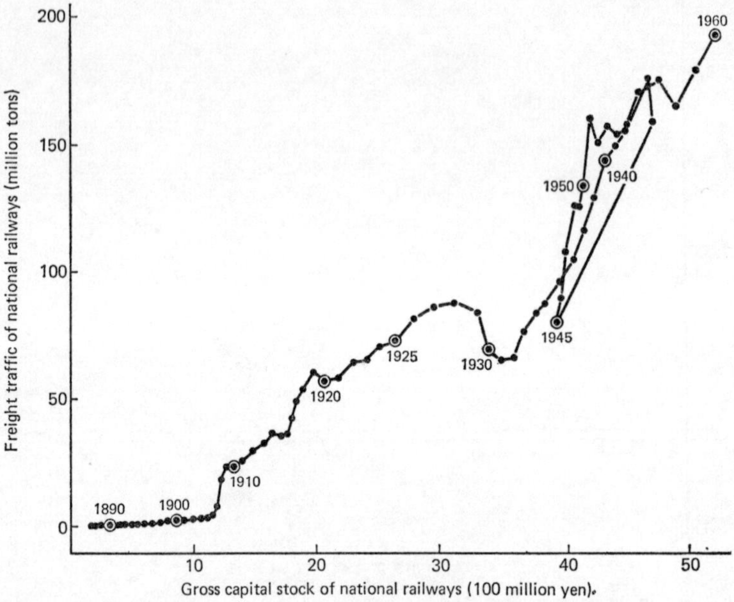

Fig. 6.9A. National railways, 1886–1960

In Fig. 6.10 the stocks of social overheads are measured in the horizontal axis and their capacity in the vertical axis. If technical progress is continuous in the sense that it does not depend on the volume of capital stocks but is embodied in other factors, the capacity function will shift from F_1 to F_2 and so on continuously. We therefore have a potential trend of capacity growth path of $P_1P_2P_3$. (Note, however, that the path may be tracing a step-to-step process if technical progress is of a vintage type with the capitals. For simplicity, however, we postulate the continuous capacity increase.) On the other hand, because of the lumpiness of government investment in social overheads, the actual capacity will not generally coincide with the physical potential capacity. Therefore, when the capital stock is Ok_1, there is a 'deficit capacity' of c_1c_1' ($= A_1B_1$). And the public authority needs to install a large scale of capital formation of the amount k_1k_2 to make a gross stock of Ok_2. Then at point P_1, where potential and actual capacities can coincide, the deficit capacity may be solved. However, we have an 'excess capacity' of $c_1'c_2$ ($= A_2C_1$), which, with technical progress, can satisfy the actual demand up to

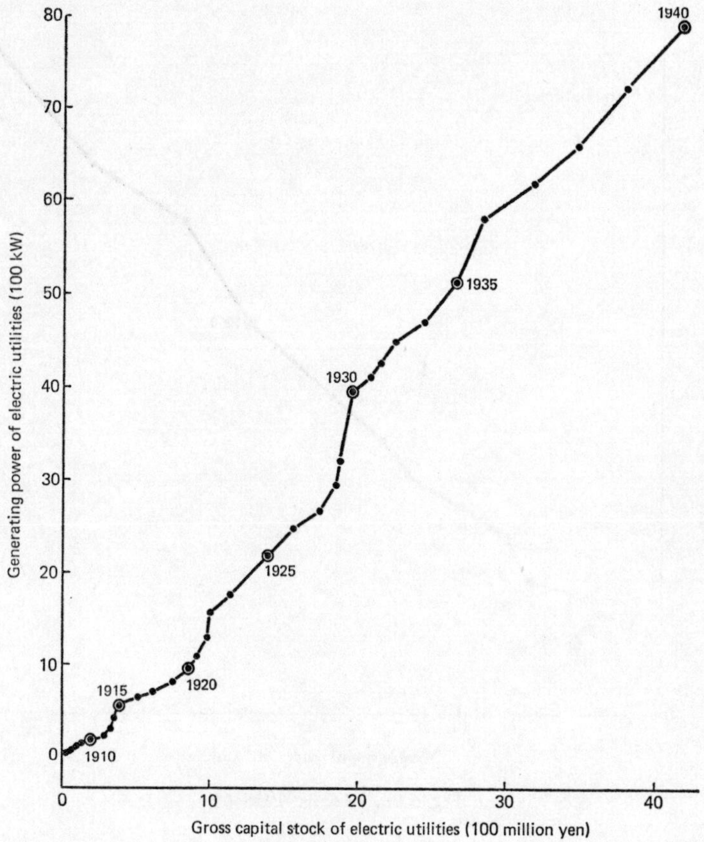

Fig. 6.9B. Electric utilities, 1903–40

the point A_2. In viewing this, we can see that the volume k_1k_1' is 'required investment' while $k_1'k_2$ is 'preconditional investment' in social overheads. Thus, again, a new capital formation of k_2k_3 (or possibly a new type with vintage) must be required to solve the new deficit capacity of A_2B_2, and then a new excess capacity A_3C_2 will be effective up to the point A_3, and so on.

This generalisation is of course specific to the special type of public capital; the process is determined not only by technical needs but also on socio-political factors, as analysed previously. We can see, however, a long-run time profile of government capital formation

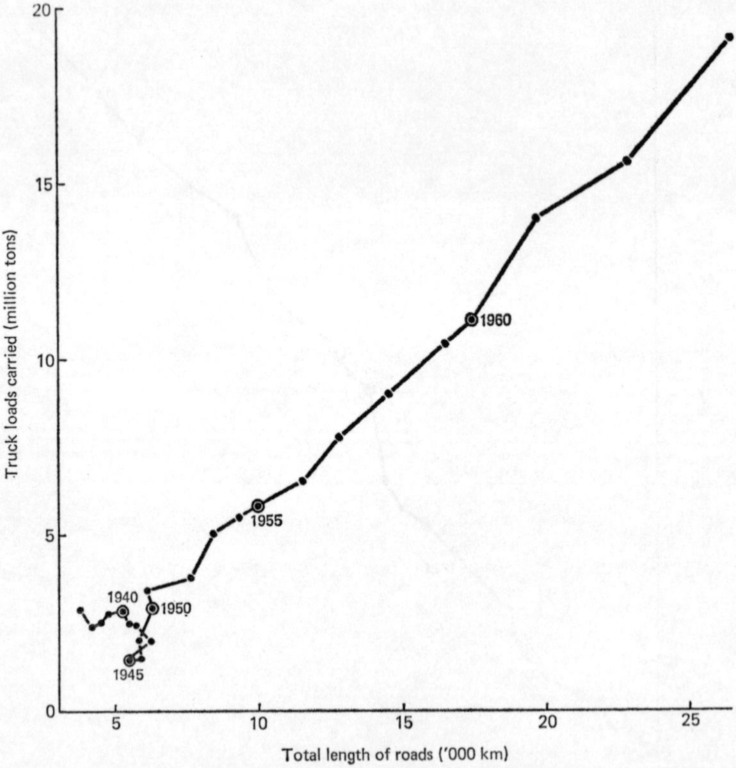

Fig. 6.9c. Roads, 1936–63

through piecing together the above process by type of capital according to the stages of economic development.

IV. CONCLUDING REMARKS

The arguments contained in this paper were built around three main investigations: (1) the general empirical survey of government capital formation in the economic development of Japan since 1878; (2) its changing role; and (3) its pattern by type of social overhead. Our thesis may now be briefly summarised.

First, taking *per capita* G.N.P. as the index of economic development, public investment has a more or less definite time profile, in

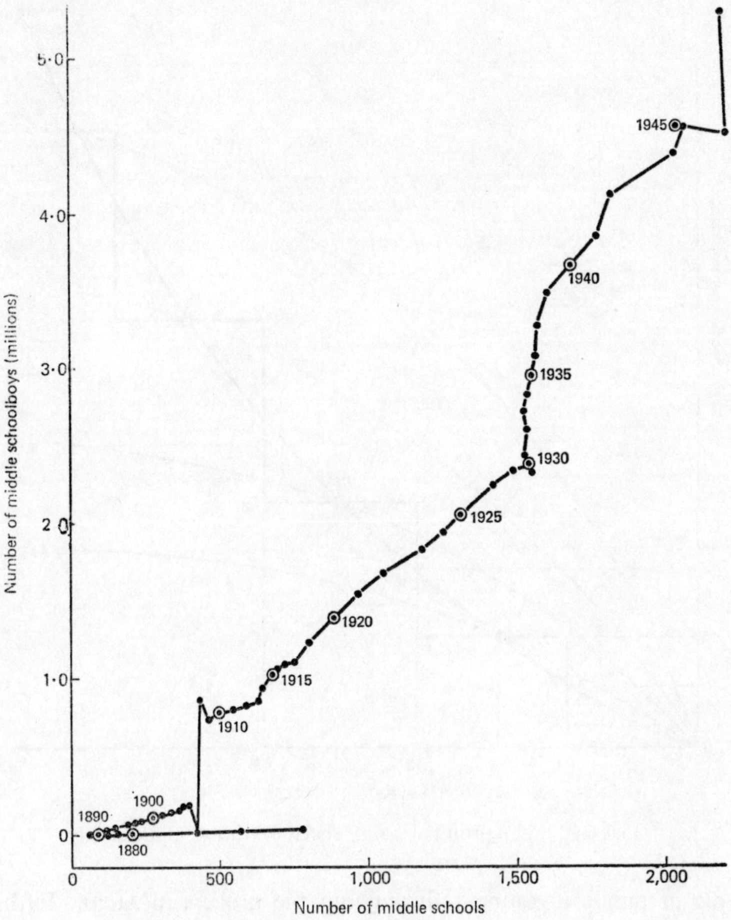

Fig. 6.9D. Education (middle schools), 1878–1947

which it has a strong relationship with private investment partly owing to technical need and partly for socio-political reasons. Second, the government investment ratio is determined periodically by the government expenditure ratio and has some ten-year cycles, involving, however, a normal pattern of ten-year cycles of each type of social overhead capital. Third, these cycles make a long-run trend or pattern in the stages of 'take-off' to 'maturity' and to 'high mass-consumption' periods. Fourth, we have observed the leading

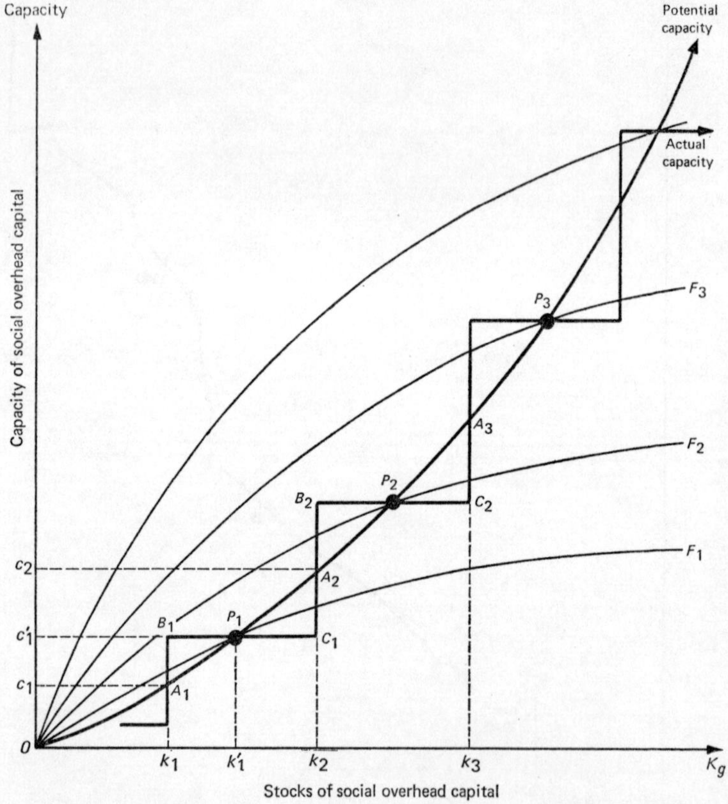

Fig. 6.10. Long-run pattern of social overheads and capacity

role of public investment throughout the process in Japan. Fifth, each type of capital has an increasing capacity in the long run owing to technical progress which has a step-to-step improvement caused by the lumpiness of the instalments of capital.

In an attempt to reach more significant results, a cross-section analysis for different countries may be needed. Further analysis may also be required to clarify the feature of capacity-building effects of government capital, e.g. by setting up partial models to test them. These problems might be solved using the approach which has been tentatively applied in this paper.

NOTES

1. For reference, the dependence of private fixed capital formation (I_f) upon disposal profits (P_d) and public investment (I) in the post-war period (1950–63) appeared as

$$I_f = \underset{(0{\cdot}377)}{2{\cdot}347\, P_d} + \underset{(0{\cdot}446)}{0{\cdot}311\, I_{g,-2}} - \underset{(125{\cdot}5)}{48{\cdot}69}$$

$$R^2 = 0{\cdot}973,\ d = 1{\cdot}936.$$

2. This is explained as follows: Since $\frac{Y}{N} = \frac{Y}{L} \cdot \frac{L}{N}$,

$$\left(\frac{\dot{Y}}{N}\right) = \left(\frac{L}{N}\right)\left(\frac{\dot{Y}}{L}\right) + \left(\frac{Y}{L}\right)\left(\frac{\dot{L}}{N}\right)$$

$$= \frac{L}{N}\left(\alpha\frac{\dot{K}}{K} + \alpha_g\frac{\dot{K}_g}{K_g} + \beta\frac{\dot{L}}{L} + \frac{\dot{A}}{A} - \frac{\dot{L}}{L}\right) + \frac{Y}{L}\left(\frac{\dot{L}}{L} - \frac{\dot{N}}{N}\right)$$

$$= \alpha\frac{L}{N}\frac{\dot{K}}{K} + \alpha_g\frac{L}{N}\frac{\dot{K}_g}{K_g} + \left(\beta\frac{L}{N} + \frac{Y}{L} - \frac{L}{N}\right)\frac{\dot{L}}{L} - \frac{Y}{L}\frac{\dot{N}}{N}$$

and therefore we can compute the ratio of contribution of $(\dot{K}_g/K_g)$ to $(\dot{Y}/N)$ as shown above in (5).

REFERENCES

English

[1] Andic, S., and Veverka, J., 'The Growth of Government Expenditure in Germany since the Unification', *Finanzarchiv*, N.F., XXXIII (1963–4).

[2] Balopoulos, E. T., 'Measuring the Effects of the Budget on Aggregate Demand and/or Balance of Payments', in A. T. Peacock (ed.), *Quantitative Analysis in Public Finance* (New York: Praeger, 1969).

[3] Bonin, J. M., Finch, B. W., and Waters, B., 'Alternative Tests of the "Displacement Effect" Hypothesis', *Public Finance*, XXIV 3 (1969).

[4] Copeland, M. A., *Trends in Government Financing* (Princeton U.P., 1961).

[5] Emi, K., *Government Fiscal Activity and Economic Growth in Japan, 1868–1960* (Tokyo: Kinokuniya, 1963).

[6] Fabricant, S., *The Trend of Government Activity in the United States since 1900* (New York: N.B.E.R., 1952).

[7] Gupta, S. P., 'Public Expenditure and Economic Growth: A Time-Series Analysis', *Public Finance*, XXII 4 (1967).

[8] Hicks, U. K., *British Public Finances: Their Structure and Development, 1880–1952* (Oxford U.P., 1954).

[9] ——, *Development Finance: Planning and Control* (Oxford U.P., 1965).

[10] Hirschman, A. O., *The Strategy of Economic Development* (New Haven: Yale U.P., 1958).

[11] Kindleberger, C. P., *Economic Development*, 2nd ed. (New York: McGraw-Hill, 1965).

[12] Lotz, J. R., 'Some Economic Effects of Increasing Public Expenditures: An Empirical Study of Selected Developed Countries', *Public Finance*, XXIV 4 (1969).

[13] ——, 'Measuring the Effects of Fiscal Policy in Developing Countries', *Finanzarchiv*, N.F., XXIX 2 (1970).

[14] Michas, N. A., 'Variations in the Level of Provincial–Municipal Expenditures in Canada: An Econometric Analysis', *Public Finance*, XXIV 4 (1969).

[15] Musgrave, R. A., *Fiscal Systems* (New Haven and London: Yale U.P., 1969).

[16] Peacock, A. T., and Wiseman, J., *The Growth of Public Expenditure in the United Kingdom* (Oxford U.P., 1961).

[17] ——, and ——, 'Measuring the Efficiency of Government Expenditure', in A. R. Prest (ed.), *Public Sector Economics* (Manchester U.P., 1968).

[18] Reddy, K. N., 'Growth of Government Expenditure and National Income in India: 1872–1966', *Public Finance*, XXV 1 (1970).

[19] Rosovsky, H., *Capital Formation in Japan, 1868–1940* (New York: The Free Press, 1960).

[20] Rostow, W. W., *The Stages of Economic Growth* (Cambridge U.P., 1960).

[21] Selowsky, M., 'On the Measurement of Education's Contribution to Growth', *Quarterly Journal of Economics*, LXXXIII 3 (Aug 1969).

[22] Simpson, D., 'Investment, Employment, and Government Expenditures in the Highlands, 1951–60', *Scottish Journal of Political Economy*, IV 3 (Nov. 1963).

[23] Veverka, J., 'The Growth of Government Expenditure in the United Kingdom since 1970', *Scottish Journal of Political Economy*, X 1 (Feb 1969).

Japanese

[24] Fugita, T., *Nippon Shihonshugi to Zaisei* [*Japanese Capitalism and Public Finance*] (Jitsugyo-no-Nippon, 1959).

[25] Hijikata, S., *Nihon Zaisei no Hatten* [*Development of Japanese Public Finances*] (Tonan Shobo, 1943).

[26] Kimura, M. (ed.), *Zaisei: Nihon Keizai no Bunseki* [*Public Finances: Analysis of the Japanese Eocnomy*] (Shunjū-sha, 1960).

[27] Maeda, K., *Kōkyō Tōshi Ron* [*Public Investment Analysis*] (Tōyōkeizai Shinpō, 1964).

[28] Sato, S., *Nihon Zaesei no Kōzō to Tokuchō* [*Structure and Character of the Japanese Public Finances*] (Tōyōkeizai Shinpō, 1966).

[29] Suzuki, T., *Gendai Nippon Zaisei-shi* [*Modern History of the Japanese Public Finances*] (Tokyo U.P., 1952).

[30] ——, (ed.), *Nippon no Zaisei: Kozō to Kinō* [*Japanese Public Finances: Structure and Functions*] (Shisei-dō, 1961).

[31] Takeuchi, Y. (ed.), *Nippon no Shakai-shihon* [*Social Overhead Capital in Japan*] (Kashima-shuppan, 1967).

Official

[32] *Meiji Ikō Honpō Syuyō Keizai Tōkei* [*Hundred-Year Statistics of the Japanese Economy*] (Bank of Japan, 1966).

[33] Emi, K., and Shionoya, Y., *Zaisei Shishutsu* [*Government Expenditure: Estimates of Long-term Economic Statistics of Japan since 1868*] (Tōyōkeizai Shinpō, 1966).

[34] Ohkawa, K. (ed.), *Shihon Stock* [*Capital Stock*], in the same series (1966).

[35] Minami, R., *Tetsudō to Denryoku* [*Railways and Electric Utilities*], in the same series (1965).

[36] Ministry of Finance, *Meiji Zenki Zaisei Keizai Shiryō Shusei* [*Survey of Fiscal Activity in the Early Meiji Era*] 21 vols. (Kaizō-sha, 1931–5).
[37] ——, *Meiji-Taishō Zaisei Shi* [*History of Public Finance in the Meiji and Taishō Eras*], 20 vols. (Keizai-orai Sha, 1955–8).
[38] ——, *Shōwa Zaisei Shi* [*History of Public Finance in the Shōwa Era*], 18 vols. (Tōyō Keizei Shinpō, 1954–65).
[39] ——, *Zaisei Tōkei* [*Annual Report of Public Revenues and Expenditures*], *1952–69*.
[40] ——, *Nippon no Zaisei* [*Annual Abstract of Japanese Public Finance*], *1953–70* (Tōyōkeizai Shinpō).

Appendix I

Various Ratios in the Economic Development Process: Two-Year Averages for 1878–1967

Period, subperiod and year			Per capita G.N.P. (at average 1934–6 prices) (Y/N)	Hoffman ratio ($I + I_g/C$)	Non-primary ratio ($Y_{\bar{p}}/Y_p$)	Total investment ratio ($I + I_g/Y$)	Government expenditure ratio (G/Y)	Government investment ratio (I_g/G)	Government investment ratio to G.N.P. (I_g/Y)	Government investment/private investment (I_g/I)	Government capital/private capital (K_g/K)
			Symbols of economic development				*Various ratios*				
I	(a)	1879	47·7	–	1·57	–	0·165	0·133	0·022	–	–
		1881	57·3	–	1·52	–	0·121	0·149	0·018	–	–
		1883	48·7	–	1·71	–	0·181	0·170	0·031	–	–
		1885	45·5	–	1·87	–	0·183	0·211	0·039	–	–
		1887	58·9	0·084	1·88	0·074	0·171	0·174	0·030	0·679	–
		1889	56·0	0·079	2·18	0·073	0·168	0·212	0·036	0·952	–
		1891	67·2	0·099	1·69	0·125	0·135	0·272	0·037	0·414	–
		1893	73·7	0·129	1·91	0·133	0·134	0·279	0·037	0·390	0·473
		1895	86·2	0·125	1·88	0·068	0·140	0·314	0·044	1·841	0·590
	(b)	1897	79·1	0·112	2·08	0·125	0·206	0·346	0·071	1·330	0·967
		1899	98·5	0·113	2·03	0·103	0·236	0·290	0·069	2·009	1·522
		1901	92·6	0·135	2·17	0·122	0·220	0·302	0·067	1·200	1·446
		1903	85·3	0·117	2·15	0·087	0·222	0·261	0·058	2·021	1·694
		1905	83·1	0·116	2·21	0·118	0·217	0·290	0·063	1·145	1·424
	(c)	1907	104·8	0·122	2·26	0·116	0·359	0·180	0·064	1·229	1·272
		1909	108·9	0·141	2·32	0·139	0·348	0·226	0·079	1·302	1·311
		1911	110·3	0·154	2·51	0·149	0·431	0·204	0·088	1·446	1·401

	(d)	1913	124·8	0·170	2·34	0·154	0·311	0·224	0·070	0·833	1·200
		1915	124·1	0·167	2·88	0·119	0·315	0·219	0·070	1·367	1·101
		1917	139·9	0·147	3·02	0·111	0·257	0·233	0·060	1·170	1·045
		1919	168·1	0·138	2·69	0·140	0·226	0·262	0·059	0·727	1·063
		1921	145·5	0·186	3·04	0·217	0·343	0·294	0·101	0·873	0·836
		1923	151·7	0·224	3·58	0·173	0·413	0·238	0·098	1·314	0·914
		1925	170·8	0·224	3·43	0·168	0·382	0·224	0·086	1·035	1·084
		1927	173·2	0·204	3·94	0·180	0·406	0·234	0·095	1·116	1·142
		1929	180·1	0·204	4·07	0·170	0·422	0·228	0·096	1·304	1·190
		1931	176·1	0·206	5·46	0·158	0·489	0·173	0·085	1·154	1·185
III	(e)	1933	178·7	0·202	4·59	0·176	0·596	0·190	0·114	1·816	1·386
		1935	202·7	0·216	5·04	0·199	0·573	0·174	0·100	1·015	1·331
		1937	225·2	0·255	4·73	0·237	0·659	0·195	0·129	1·187	1·160
		1939	232·5	0·364	4·46	0·366	0·664	0·315	0·209	1·328	1·262
		1941	231·2	0·500	4·55	0·363	0·656	0·279	0·183	1·014	1·181
		1943	223·4	0·560	5·46	0·337	–	0·193	0·183	1·185	1·108
		1945	215·2	0·546	5·64	0·363	–	–	–	1·013	1·074
IV	(f)	1947	117·8	0·447	2·70	0·325	0·477	0·246	0·117	0·566	0·479
		1949	137·4	0·516	3·39	0·341	0·666	0·179	0·120	0·540	0·549
		1951	176·4	0·465	3·90	0·271	0·593	0·125	0·074	0·375	0·478
		1953	219·4	0·391	4·59	0·267	0·480	0·185	0·089	0·499	0·463
		1955	243·3	0·352	4·48	0·248	0·459	0·193	0·089	0·555	0·493
		1957	285·5	0·379	5·33	0·311	0·416	0·194	0·081	0·351	0·458
		1959	323·5	0·426	5·91	0·328	0·421	0·226	0·095	0·408	0·417
	(g)	1961	415·4	0·537	7·12	0·404	0·384	0·258	0·099	0·325	0·360
		1963	488·0	0·634	8·11	0·406	0·414	0·280	0·116	0·399	0·369
		1965	567·8	0·683	8·92	0·396	0·431	0·273	0·118	0·422	0·382
		1967	684·3	0·668	8·99	0·405	0·502	0·240	0·121	0·424	0·417

Appendix II

Economic Growth and Government Capital Formation

Period, subperiod and year		Various growth rates: Gross national product ($\dot{Y}/Y$)	Government capital stock ($\dot{K}_g/K_g$)	Private capital stock ($\dot{K}/K$)	Working population ($\dot{L}/L$)	Population ($\dot{N}/N$)	Contribution of the increase in government capital stock to various growth rates: Contribution to the growth of G.N.P. $\frac{\alpha_g(\dot{K}_g/K_g)}{\dot{Y}/Y}$	Contribution to the increase in productivity of labour $\alpha_g\left(\frac{\dot{K}_g}{\bar{K}_g}-\frac{\dot{L}}{L}\right)/\left(\frac{\dot{Y}}{Y}-\frac{\dot{L}}{L}\right)$	Contribution to the increase in per capita G.N.P. $\alpha_g\left(\frac{L}{N}\frac{\dot{K}_g}{K_g}\right)/\left(\frac{\dot{Y}}{Y}-\frac{\dot{N}}{N}\right)$	Reference: Share of government profits (α_g)	Share of wages and salaries (β)
II (c)	1906	0·060	0·099	0·015	0·0053	0·0090	0·177	0·184	0·114	0·108	–
	1907	0·083	0·100	0·014	0·0051	0·0080	0·141	0·143	0·085	0·117	–
	1908	0·058	0·101	0·008	0·0044	0·0116	0·223	0·231	0·151	0·127	–
	1909	0·036	0·105	0·012	0·0041	0·0123	0·392	0·425	0·320	0·133	–
	1910	0·042	0·096	0·020	0·0038	0·0130	0·327	0·345	0·253	0·142	–
	1911	0·041	0·084	0·037	0·0035	0·0136	0·310	0·315	0·238	9·146	–
(d)	1912	0·055	0·073	0·036	0·0029	0·0145	0·198	0·201	0·141	0·149	–
	1913	0·048	0·061	0·040	0·0027	0·0144	0·188	0·191	0·139	0·147	–
	1914	0·041	0·046	0·038	0·0023	0·0143	0·167	0·168	0·131	0·149	–
	1915	0·063	0·039	0·031	0·0018	0·0137	0·093	0·091	0·060	0·151	–
	1916	0·092	0·037	0·025	0·0015	0·0141	0·060	0·059	0·035	0·149	–
	1917	0·049	0·043	0·042	0·0012	0·0119	0·132	0·131	0·086	0·152	–
	1918	0·032	0·054	0·061	0·0055	0·0112	0·263	0·285	0·197	0·155	–
	1919	0·025	0·071	0·063	0·0035	0·0054	–	–	–	0·149	–
	1920	0·016	0·081	0·071	0·0085	0·0169	–	–	–	0·148	–
	1921	0·005	0·085	0·066	0·0100	0·0126	–	–	–	0·153	–
	1922	0·051	0·084	0·059	0·0116	0·0127	0·256	0·285	0·165	0·157	–
	1923	0·050	0·076	0·044	0·0085	0·0127	0·242	0·258	0·156	0·161	–

		1924	0·047	0·068	0·042	0·0084	0·0131	0·233	0·249	0·155	0·160	–
		1925	0·046	0·062	0·042	0·0084	0·0146	0·218	0·231	0·153	0·162	–
		1926	0·030	0·058	0·042	0·0083	0·0168	0·314	0·371	0·332	0·165	–
		1927	0·018	0·059	0·037	0·0082	0·0151	–	–	–	0·165	–
		1928	0·018	0·057	0·033	0·0081	0·0152	–	–	–	0·169	–
		1929	0·009	0·053	0·031	0·0023	0·0137	–	–	–	0·170	–
		1930	0·028	0·055	0·024	0·0019	0·0156	0·322	0·333	0·329	0·167	0·621
		1931	0·035	0·058	0·026	0·0044	0·0147	0·265	0·280	0·204	0·158	0·645
III	(e)	1932	0·052	0·058	0·029	0·0096	0·0157	0·189	0·195	0·120	0·168	0·631
		1933	0·059	0·061	0·037	0·0119	0·0151	0·187	0·189	0·111	0·178	0·618
		1934	0·083	0·064	0·040	0·0127	0·0131	0·138	0·131	0·074	0·181	0·613
		1935	0·056	0·071	0·042	0·0134	0·0138	0·244	0·261	0·147	0·192	0·590
		1936	0·055	0·086	0·048	0·0113	0·0122	0·297	0·325	0·168	0·189	0·598
		1937	0·034	0·095	0·061	0·0064	0·0076	–	–	–	–	–
		–	–	–	–	–	–	–	–	–	–	–
		–	–	–	–	–	–	–	–	–	–	–
		–	–	–	–	–	–	–	–	–	–	–
IV	(f)	1949	0·145	0·166	0·114	0·0261	0·0221	0·104	0·107	0·055	0·091	0·744
		1950	0·135	0·124	0·158	0·0214	0·0174	0·081	0·080	0·040	0·088	0·722
		1951	0·118	0·118	0·145	0·0249	0·0161	0·092	0·092	0·046	0·093	0·715
		1952	0·105	0·099	0·129	0·0184	0·0150	0·079	0·078	0·041	0·084	0·743
		1953	0·094	0·117	0·099	0·0265	0·0137	0·107	0·116	0·057	0·086	0·737
		1954	0·081	0·093	0·094	0·0278	0·0145	0·092	0·099	0·051	0·081	0·753
		1955	0·075	0·071	0·086	0·0266	0·0118	0·082	0·079	0·045	0·086	0·743
		1956	0·090	0·064	0·080	0·0190	0·0100	0·064	0·057	0·034	0·091	0·720
		1957	0·101	0·078	0·097	0·0184	0·0084	0·135	0·126	0·070	0·177	0·718
		1958	0·120	0·077	0·101	0·0161	0·0092	0·057	0·053	0·029	0·082	0·736
		1959	0·106	0·085	0·109	0·0149	0·0095	0·074	0·071	0·038	0·093	0·700
	(g)	1960	0·117	0·089	0·102	0·0123	0·0084	0·073	0·070	0·037	0·095	0·681
		1961	0·114	0·109	0·121	0·0130	0·0093	0·087	0·087	0·046	0·092	0·684
		1962	0·093	0·110	0·123	0·0136	0·0095	0·102	0·105	0·055	0·086	0·703

Appendix III

Share of Government Investment by Types to G.N.P. (%)

Period, sub-period and year			*National railways*	*Electric utilities*	*Public works*	*Roads and bridges*	*Education*
I	(a)	1878	–	–	0·393	0·114	–
		1879	0·002	–	0·303	0·089	–
		1880	0·029	–	0·046	0·006	–
		1881	0·016	–	0·059	0·006	1·055
		1882	0·232	–	0·129	0·028	1·476
		1883	0·095	–	0·180	0·039	2·043
		1884	–	–	0·390	0·219	2·343
		1885	0·014	–	0·290	0·070	1·755
		1886	0·030	–	0·123	0·033	1·363
		1887	0·050	–	0·208	0·046	1·294
		1888	0·046	–	0·176	0·028	1·406
		1889	0·075	–	0·258	0·078	1·433
		1890	0·033	–	0·193	0·065	1·025
		1891	0·183	–	0·191	0·053	1·244
		1892	0·029	–	0·226	0·021	1·226
		1893	0·091	–	0·173	0·026	1·284
		1894	0·128	–	0·092	0·018	1·094
		1895	0·110	–	0·124	0·019	1·166
	(b)	1896	0·231	–	0·158	0·020	1·397
		1897	0·271	–	0·381	0·024	1·443
		1898	0·357	–	0·194	0·020	1·235
		1899	0·386	–	0·249	0·024	1·807
		1900	0·580	–	0·232	0·031	2·027
		1901	0·534	–	0·297	0·027	2·300
		1902	0·491	–	0·275	0·046	2·680
		1903	0·580	–	0·199	0·036	2·250
		1904	0·276	0·092	0·117	0·013	1·744
		1905	0·209	0·151	0·129	0·004	1·943
II	(c)	1906	0·332	0·522	0·150	0·009	1·914
		1907	0·790	0·408	0·213	0·024	2·011
		1908	0·970	0·373	0·261	0·032	2·495
		1909	0·889	0·287	0·219	0·019	2·758
		1910	1·226	0·707	0·342	0·031	2·902
		1911	1·466	1·263	0·369	0·024	2·508
	(d)	1912	0·629	0·332	0·573	0·029	2·202
		1913	1·281	0·168	0·368	0·018	2·078
		1914	1·104	0·295	0·378	0·020	2·209
		1915	0·671	0·164	0·303	0·019	2·323
		1916	0·404	0·294	0·269	0·012	2·116
		1917	0·614	1·595	0·234	0·015	1·720
		1918	0·351	1·156	0·219	0·013	1·562
		1919	0·557	1·094	0·221	0·014	1·572
		1920	0·719	2·339	0·474	0·042	2·512
		1921	1·061	0·822	0·488	0·043	3·089

Appendix III—*Continued*

Period, sub-period and year		*National railways*	*Electric utilities*	*Public works*	*Roads and bridges*	*Education*
	1922	1·628	1·254	0·606	0·121	3·454
	1923	0·816	0·226	0·497	0·106	3·491
	1924	0·804	1·527	0·325	0·063	3·331
	1925	0·874	1·940	0·250	0·047	3·241
	1926	1·050	1·843	0·303	0·053	3·729
	1927	0·923	1·563	0·349	0·069	3·911
	1928	0·578	0·723	0·375	0·074	3·897
	1929	0·930	0·293	0·375	0·068	3·787
	1930	0·653	0·717	0·372	0·049	3·858
	1931	0·628	1·123	0·545	0·285	4·028
III (e)	1932	0·790	0·674	1·178	0·646	4·120
	1933	0·646	0·461	1·065	0·537	3·619
	1934	0·655	1·081	0·705	0·297	3·564
	1935	0·797	1·176	0·427	0·034	3·443
	1936	0·437	1·147	0·410	0·127	3·371
	1937	0·501	1·720	0·359	0·102	3·862
	1938	0·319	1·363	0·275	0·083	2·682
	1939	0·304	1·623	0·256	0·068	2·288
	1940	0·339	1·804	0·211	0·060	2·164

Appendix IV

References for Compilations

Period, sub-period and year			*G.N.P. Deflator* (average 1934–6 = 100)	*Per capita G.N.P.* (at the base average 1934–6 = 100)
I	(a)	1878	25·2	44·0
		1879	32·6	51·4
		1880	36·5	59·7
		1881	40·1	54·8
		1882	37·5	51·0
		1883	33·0	46·4
		1884	32·1	40·4
		1885	32·0	50·7
		1886	28·7	61·6
		1887	30·4	56·2
		1888	30·3	57·1
		1889	31·9	54·9
		1890	33·6	69·9
		1891	32·2	64·6
		1892	30·5	72·9
		1893	30·8	74·4
		1894	31·9	88·6
		1895	35·1	83·8
	(b)	1896	38·5	76·2
		1897	42·9	81·9
		1898	46·3	104·4
		1899	44·0	92·6
		1900	49·5	93·3
		1901	51·8	91·9
		1902	53·0	80·4
		1903	55·1	90·1
		1904	56·4	90·2
		1905	62·2	76·0
II	(c)	1906	59·9	95·5
		1907	57·4	114·0
		1908	59·9	108·9
		1909	57·4	108·8
		1910	57·6	103·8
		1911	61·5	116·8
	(d)	1912	65·1	126·0
		1913	66·9	123·7
		1914	61·8	122·8
		1915	58·7	125·4
		1916	61·5	136·7
		1917	80·0	143·2
		1918	106·6	156·8
		1919	137·7	179·4
		1920	147·4	145·0
		1921	133·4	146·0
		1922	131·5	148·1

Period, sub-period and year			*G.N.P. deflator*	*Per capita G.N.P.*
		1923	130·8	155·3
		1924	131·6	167·5
		1925	131·3	174·1
		1926	125·0	173·8
		1927	123·0	172·7
		1928	118·5	180·0
		1929	116·2	180·3
		1930	103·5	176·0
		1931	91·2	176·4
III	(e)	1932	93·1	167·1
		1933	96·8	190·2
		1934	*97·8*	196·5
		1935	*99·9*	208·7
		1936	*102·3*	216·8
		1937	112·9	233·5
		1938	123·5	228·2
		1939	150	236·8
		1940	189	228·3
		1941	212	234·0
		1942	254	227·7
		1943	299	219·3
		1944	361	211·9
		1945	–	–
IV	(f)	1946	4,090	116·4
		1947	10,410	119·1
		1948	18,760	130·7
		1949	23,240	144·0
		1950	24,490	166·0
		1951	28,099	186·7
		1952	28,498	213·3
		1953	30,609	225·4
		1954	32,160	232·3
		1955	32,160	254·2
		1956	33,138	273·5
		1957	34,589	297·4
		1958	34,190	306·5
		1959	34,951	340·4
	(g)	1960	36,220	392·2
		1961	33,106	438·5
		1962	39,846	467·5
		1963	42,166	508·3
		1964	43,180	555·9
		1965	45,647	579·6
		1966	47,424	644·5
		1967	49,345	723·6

7
Enlarging the Economic Base for Domestic Savings

TARLOK SINGH

THE pressure to mobilise domestic savings has led many underdeveloped economies to resort to tax policies and other measures which have in turn inhibited the growth of genuine savings. Three features are to be generally observed: continuous increase in indirect taxation with greater burdens falling on the consumption and disposable income of the ordinary citizen; somewhat undiscriminating exploitation of the small sector represented by urban and industrial activity; and upward movements in prices to the serious detriment of the poorer sections and of those with relatively fixed incomes. It cannot be said of any post-war plan of economic development that measures for harnessing domestic savings have been related adequately to economic policy as a whole.

I

In the earlier phases of planning for economic development, there was perhaps excessive emphasis on the shortage of capital resources and of foreign exchange. This led to preoccupation with investment in physical stock and with external assistance in its various forms. Over the past decade one country after another has come to perceive that the principal sources of rapid growth and development are to be found within its own structure of production, institutions, technology and ways of adaptation and functioning. The role of social development and of human resources is also being acknowledged more fully, if still superficially. Internal and external factors alike have highlighted self-reliance and change from within as leading principles in the strategy for economic development, with the contribution of external sources being, for large countries at any rate, essential enough and yet ancillary to the total process. These insights have come from the actual experience of wrestling with the growing and increasingly complex economic, social and political problems of development. They indicate that a much more central place should be given in planning and economic policy to steps to enable each national community and its various regional and social components to save to the limits of their true potential.

There are marked differences in the rates at which different underdeveloped countries are able to save. Those among them which have more or less socialist economies are generally credited with high rates of savings. This may well be correct, but is to be explained even more in terms of the institutional techniques available for mobilising savings than of changes in the scale and character of production. In the 1960s a few small and favourably situated countries, mainly with dynamic, private economies and considerable inflows of external resources, have succeeded in developing impressive export sectors. Primarily for this reason, they have been able to achieve both high rates of growth and high rates of savings. However, in the great majority of underdeveloped countries and especially in those which began with extremely low rates of savings, such increase in domestic savings as has taken place cannot be described as sufficiently significant or dependable. There are several countries which can be cited in this group.[1]

India's case is fairly illustrative of this situation. At the commencement of planned development, in 1950–1, her rate of domestic savings was placed at 5·5 per cent of the national income. For about fifteen years a modest increase was realised, domestic savings rising to about 7 per cent in 1955–6, 8.5 per cent in 1960–1, and 11 per cent in 1965–6. As plans and current economic problems interacted upon one another, several types of imbalance also developed within the economic system. For a period these remained subdued, but from around 1963 they came more and more into the open. A series of adverse economic developments reduced the rate of domestic savings to 8 per cent in 1967–8, followed by a small increase to 8·8 per cent in 1968–9.

II

Statistics such as these have to be taken with extreme caution, not only in comparing countries, but also in assessing the performance of any individual economy. There are difficult problems of measurement which have yet to be resolved. The assumption that in an under-

India: Gross and Net Domestic Saving in 1960–1 and 1965–6
(at current prices, in million rupees)

	Gross saving				*Net saving*			
	Amount		*Per cent*		*Amount*		*Per cent*	
	1960–1	*1965–6*	*1960–1*	*1965–6*	*1960–1*	*1965–6*	*1960–1*	*1965–6*
Household sector	12,130	25,190	63·2	68·1	7,510	18,110	63·4	72·9
Financial assets	4,570	9,540	23·8	25·8	4,570	9,540	38·6	38·4
Physical assets	7,560	15,650	39·4	42·3	2,940	8,570	24·8	34·5
Private corporate sector	2,760	3,950	14·4	10·7	1,170	1,050	9·9	4·2
Public sector	4,310	7,850	22·4	21·2	3,160	5,700	26·7	22·9
Total	19,200	36,990	100·0	100·0	11,840	24,860	100·0	100·0

developed economy all savings may be thought of as a 'pool', which is related to the entire national product in some more or less defined manner and may be readily drawn upon either by the public or the private sector, is scarcely borne out by the facts. Nor can 'private' investment, as distinguished from 'public' investment, be regarded as a homogeneous concept. When we go beyond aggregate rates of savings to the three main streams, which are commonly referred to as government savings, corporate savings and household savings, we confront a number of problems which are only now beginning to be explored.

In the table below, which is drawn from a recent study in India, data on gross and net savings are presented for two years, 1960–1 and 1965–6.[2] From the standpoint of internal resources which can be harnessed for development through fiscal policies and financial institutions, savings which may occur in the form of physical assets can scarcely be reckoned along with savings in the form of financial assets. However we may arrive at their value, they do not form a stream of resources which can be tapped without a number of institutional and other conditions being met. In attempting to estimate the size of individual components of the national savings aggregate, the study referred to above did not seek the causes of various changes from year to year or over the period of investigation. To this extent it remained incomplete and its findings cannot be utilised directly for economic policy. One conclusion, however, remains beyond doubt. It is in the household sector that much the larger part of saving occurs. Therefore, the household sector presents not only the task of mobilising the available savings but, what is even more basic, the larger task of creating and strengthening the conditions for steady expansion of the total potential for savings. This calls for an analysis of the nature and operations of the household sector and for a strategy for linking it up organically with the more rapidly growing public and corporate sectors of the economy, thereby also enlarging the productive resources of the entire economy.

III

In pointing to the need for a more fundamental approach to the future shape of the household sector, it should be stressed that, in consequence of development already undertaken, the *capacity* to save now available within an economy such as India's has grown appreciably. There are several reasons why this capacity is not being reflected adequately in the volume of saving which has actually materialised. In mentioning some of these reasons, we begin to appreciate the need for a much wider approach to economic policy. In most underdeveloped countries, increasing non-development expenditures, including defence, have considerably lowered the feasible scale of economic and social investment. Rising prices have led to erosion in the value of past and current savings as well as to the diversion of resources to real estate, trading and speculative activity. The choice of investments has been frequently faulty and, in particular, there has been failure to secure the necessary balance between short-term and long-term investments, so that in each phase the economy could generate the resources required to sustain the next phase. The management of public enterprises has been far from satisfactory, and up to the present the returns on public investment as a whole have been small. Finally, there have been serious failures in economic management at the national level and in putting the available productive capacities to effective use. Nor have all the changes which were feasible within the existing tax structure and its administration been undertaken so far. The tax system remains poorly adapted to the existing scheme of income, wealth and resource distribution and to the changes which are now taking place in these respects, as a result of growth, diversification and technological developments within the economy. In many countries the traditional dichotomy between agricultural and non-agricultural incomes has persisted, though it has long been a survival of earlier notions on the nature of land and of returns derived from it.

IV

The aspects to which attention has been drawn above serve to emphasise that, for realising the existing savings potential, besides measures commonly embodied in plans of development there has to be a much more comprehensive outlook on taxation, prices and incomes, on credit, interest rates and the financial structure, on ways of gathering up small savings directly and through social security funds, and on possibilities of developing new systems of self-generating finance in industry, transport, housing and other sectors of the economy. But, even as such measures may be pursued, we come face to face with a greater difficulty, namely, that in most underdeveloped economies, savings are currently being drawn only from a relatively small part of the economy. Though expanding gradually, both in urban and in rural areas, the economic base remains extraordinarily slender. In India, for instance, studies undertaken by the National Council of Applied Economic Research showed that, of the urban households investigated, 46 per cent dissaved, 15 per cent neither saved nor dissaved, and about 39 per cent showed positive savings. The savings of the top 14 per cent of urban households with incomes of Rs. 3,000 or more per annum were equivalent to the entire amount of urban saving. In the rural household sector the net savings of the lower 60 per cent were found to be negative. The top 1 per cent of rural households accounted for 59 per cent of the net savings in the rural household sector.[3]

What these and other similar investigations suggest is that within the national economy, and more especially in the rural sector, far too many of the existing economic units are operating at the margin or on a deficit basis. Therefore, the essential question is how to increase rapidly the proportion of economic units engaged in agriculture and small industry and even in transport and trade which can function efficiently and have the capacity to generate their own resources for future growth. It is in this respect that the great majority of functioning economic units are marked out most sharply from public and corporate enterprises when these are run even with a fair degree of efficiency. Marginal and deficit units tend to pull the entire economy downwards, and workers and self-employed persons associated with them benefit but little from the growth of the economy and its modern infrastructures. This weakness at the very foundation of the economic system affects the nature and volume of the employment that is generated and the extent to which the benefits of growth can reach out to different regions and to different sections of the community. In turn it has a direct impact on the rate of savings and the rate of growth. Over a short period, development concentrated in a comparatively small segment of a national economy may seem to yield striking results by way of growth and savings, but the central problem is to find, within each given situation, the appropriate means by which development can spread out and be realised in depth and as a continuing, cumulative process. The crucial line of advance, then, has to be to try to reshape the economy so that, without disrupting current production, each economic unit, especially within the presently unorganised sector, begins to operate at a profit and receives increasing support from the modern financial and industrial sectors. To the extent that the modern sector is able to fulfil this function, it serves an expanding area of economic activity, draws increased savings into the financial system and stimulates new potentials. In other words, the effort to build up a more unified or integrated economy, in which the present distance between the organised and unorganised sectors is steadily reduced and the bulk of the labour force is involved in productive work at rising levels of efficiency, becomes the key to the generation of adequate domestic savings and, equally, to the attainment of other related objectives, notably growth, employment, equitable distribution and balanced social development.

It would be beyond the scope of this paper to spell out in detail the specific measures required for the reconstruction of agriculture and other unorganised activities within the economy. The roots of low rates of domestic savings are to be found ultimately in the low productivity of agriculture and much other activity, in widespread unemployment and underemployment and the poor use of human resources, and in the rapid growth of population. The raising of levels of living and of productivity for the mass of the people, providing work and education for all, achieving substantial self-reliance in food, capital formation and foreign exchange, have to be dealt with as facets of the same common task. In most under-developed countries only a small part of the population, of the economy and of the resources inherent in it have yet been brought into play. Economic growth and development have proceeded within altogether too narrow a focus. Agriculture, industry, transport and energy alike have looked to limited areas of demand: to public investment, to the growth of the organised sector, to the better-off sections of the population, to cities and towns. The dimensions of the problem of domestic savings begin to emerge fully only when we consider how closely it is related to changes in the economic and technological relationships which subsist between the more and the less organised segments of economic activity and to policies aimed at the rebuilding of economic units at the very base of the economy.

REFERENCES

1. United Nations, *World Economic Survey, 1965*, part I: *The Financing of Economic Development*, pp. 13–42; and World Bank, *Annual Report for 1970*, pp. 53–6.

2. Government of India, Department of Statistics, Central Statistical Organisation, *Estimates of Saving in India, 1960–61 to 1965–66* (1969) pp. 13, 19.
3. National Council of Applied Economic Research, *All-India Rural Household Survey: Saving, Income and Investment*, II (1965) 94–100; and *Urban Income and Saving* (1962) pp. 74–81.

Part Three
FEDERAL FINANCE

8
Federal–State Financial Relations in Malaya*

CLIVE T. EDWARDS

MALAYA, while sharing many of the features of recently formed federations such as Nigeria and the West Indies, is distinct in that the division of the country into separate states is not based on any major form of racial diversity or geographic insularity. The potential for racial conflict between the politically dominant Malays and the economically dominant Chinese is prevalent within almost all the eleven states. Consequently, more attention is devoted to preserving nation-wide communal interests rather than specific state interests.

The communal division of the population largely explains the high degree of centralisation of government power in Malaya. The Malays, although politically dominant in each of the eleven states, realise that it is easier to retain indefinite control over one central government than over eleven separate state governments. In addition, they recognise that, with central control over a wide range of policies, the redistribution of income from the richer to the poorer, more backward and predominantly Malay states is possible. These highly pronounced unitary forces prompt one to ask why a federal rather than a unitary form of government was adopted. An answer to this question can be found in the origins of the present federal system.

Before the Second World War, Malaya was divided into three

* The Malay Peninsula has experienced several political changes since 1960. The mainland states, which were grouped together in 1948 to form the Federation of Malaya, joined Singapore, Sabah (North Borneo) and Sarawak to form Malaysia in 1963. At this juncture, the terminology for the mainland states was changed from Federation of Malaya to States of Malaysia in order to distinguish this part of Malaysia from Singapore, Sabah and Sarawak. Subsequently Singapore left the Malaysian Federation. Following Singapore's departure, the mainland states were renamed West Malaysia, and Sabah and Sarawak were jointly referred to as representing East Malaysia. This paper is concerned with the problem of federal–state financial relations in West Malaysia. For ease of exposition, the terminology for the mainland states has been abbreviated from West Malaysia to Malaya. This paper is reprinted from the author's book *Public Finance in Malaya and Singapore* (Canberra: A.N.U. Press, 1970).

parts: the Federated Malay States, the several unfederated Malay States, and the Straits Settlements. The treaty which brought the Federated Malay States together in 1893 was brief; apart from emphasising the precarious nature of small areas existing on their own and the need for such small areas to combine for common benefit, little else was mentioned. The treaty did not even define the respective functions of the Federal and state governments. A Federal Council was created in 1909 and legislative (but non-executive) power was transferred from the states to this body. With the rapid development of the rubber and tin industries in the Federated Malay States, it became increasingly necessary for the Federal Council to undertake expenditure on an inter-state basis and, as a result, there was a steady transfer of executive power from the States to the central authority after 1909. Expenditure was concentrated on infrastructure developments designed to assist the expansion of the rubber and tin industries; the direct needs of the majority of inhabitants in the states were overlooked. Twenty years later, stringent central control had practically eliminated any display of initiative on the part of the states. At the request of the rulers, an attempt was made to define federal and state functions in 1927 and, in consequence, a number of federal departments were transferred back to the states. But financial control remained at the centre, block grants being made to each state to meet budget deficits. Within the limits of their financial resources, the states were free to allocate expenditure as they wished and, in the ensuing years, increased attention was paid to local problems previously neglected.

The unfederated states of Kelantan, Kedah, Perlis and Trengganu were brought under British protection in 1909 and a series of agreements were signed by which British advisers were appointed to each state. A British adviser was appointed to Johore in 1914. In each territory, legislative and executive authority rested with the state government. The unfederated Malay States did not support a closer association with the Federated Malay States; they had observed the reduction in legislative and executive power of the separate Federated Malay States and preferred to preserve the degree of independence they had attained.

The Straits Settlements of Singapore, Penang (including Province Wellesley) and Malacca, which were united to form a Crown Colony in 1866, were governed from Singapore by a governor and a nominated executive and legislative council.

I. POST-WAR DEVELOPMENTS

1. *Malayan Union Agreement, 1946*

On resuming power after the Second World War, the British Military Administration sought to integrate the many separate political units. Under the pre-war governmental structure, similar enactments would have been required in at least six legislatures if uniform legislation were to be achieved throughout Malaya. The British recognised that unless this governmental structure were reformed, progress in the direction of self-government would be hampered. To achieve an integrated Malaya, the British encouraged the Malay sultans to transfer their sovereignty to the British Crown. A Malayan Union was then created by the British on 1 April 1946, embracing the former Federated and unfederated Malay States and the Settlements of Penang and Malacca. Singapore remained a separate Crown Colony, but this decision was not 'to preclude or prejudice in any way the fusion of Singapore and the Malayan Union in a wider Union at a later date should it be considered that such a course were desirable'.[1]

Under the provisions of the Malayan Union Agreement, the states could make laws on subjects declared by the Governor to be of a purely local nature or on legislative matters delegated to them by the Union legislature, but any such law could be altered or repealed by the Union legislature and would be declared void if repugnant to Union legislation. In effect, the Union Agreement sought to convert the states into local authorities on the British pattern.

The life of the Malayan Union was short. Opposition from Malays grew rapidly after the proposals had been accepted by the British Parliament early in 1946. The aim of the Union – progress towards self-government – was favoured by the states and an integration of the separate political units was not a matter of dispute. But the Malays objected to the manner in which the changes were implemented; there was not, in their words, the 'degree of local consultation to which they considered themselves entitled'.[2] The Malays found the changes objectionable on two other grounds. First, the citizenship provisions, which effectively created a communally egalitarian society, brought into prominence fears of non-Malay political domination. Second, the Malays objected to the complete loss of the pre-war powers of the Malay rulers, contending that the individuality of the states would be lost in the larger body within which the states were to be merged. The British were forced to allay

Malay anxiety and, on 1 February 1948, a federal constitution was substituted. The new agreement contained provisions very similar to the Union Agreement, but it was acceptable to the Malays because the citizenship clauses protected their pre-war preferential position and because the agreement indicated that the individuality of the states would be recognised. The British did not object to the revisions, for the new constitution still offered prospects for a high degree of cohesion and a basis for common loyalty.

Malaya, then, differs from many other federations in that the basis of potential conflict within the country – communal problems – cuts across any type of territorial division. This was the primary reason for the adoption of a centralised form of government. The strength of allegiance of residents to particular states, nurtured during the long period of divided rule, largely explains why a federal system was adopted in preference to the British unitary suggestion.

2. *Federation of Malaya Agreement, 1948*

The constitutional division of power between the Federal and state governments under the Federation of Malaya Agreement made explicit the financial implication of the Malayan Union Agreement. The preamble proclaimed that the major purpose was to form a federation 'with a strong central government'.[3] The list of matters over which the Federal Government had power to legislate was extremely wide, covering indeed all major fields of government activity. The states were given residual legislative powers. Executive power, however, was divided between the two tiers of government in order to give weight to the second objective of the agreement: the principle of maintaining the individuality of the states.

State revenue heads were specifically detailed in the agreement and included certain excise taxes (for example, toddy), revenue from lands, mines and forests, specified licence fees, entertainment duties, and charges for goods and services supplied by the states (for example, water). All items not mentioned were to be federal revenue heads. These included the main sources of tax revenue – trade and income taxes. Considerable debate occurred over whether excise and sales taxation should be federal or state revenue heads, but the Financial Secretary considered that the imposition of different taxes on articles sold throughout Malaya would be unwise, and the matter was left to be reconsidered at a later date.

The agreement recognised that the expenditure to which the states were committed would exceed their revenue. Thus provision was made for block grants to be made by the Federal Government to balance state budgets. The states spend 31 per cent of public funds in 1950 but collected only 13 per cent of total revenue raised in Malaya: they were dependent on outright grants from the Federal Government for 55 per cent of their revenue. While state revenue showed little growth potential, state expenditure, concentrated mainly in the field of community services, showed high growth potential. Thus not only was there a substantial excess of state expenditure over revenue, but it was inevitable that, with the passage of time, the extent of imbalance would increase.

In exchange for block grants, the Federal Government was given extensive powers of control over state budgets. Estimates of revenue and expenditure, for example, had to be submitted to the Federal Government for approval. Further, it was provided that any excess of state revenue (including federal grants) over expenditure at the end of each financial year would revert to the Federal Government.

3. *Defects of the 1948 Financial Provisions*

The success of a federal system depends on an acceptable division of resources and functions between the centre and the states so that efficiency in the use of scarce resources is encouraged and extreme inequity in the treatment of individuals in different states is avoided. Given the heavy dependence of the states on federal grants, it is necessary to consider the effects of the principles which have governed their allocation.

Under the 1948 Federation of Malaya Agreement, state deficits were met by lump-sum grants determined annually. The Agreement did not prescribe any method by which such grants were to be determined. Inevitably, annual wrangling occurred and, because the Federal Government was an interested party, the total allocation depended heavily on the Federal Government's financial position and prospects. Although such grants were made in an arbitrary manner without any recognition of definite allocative principles, the size of grants to the several states during the period 1948–55 was related to population. Nevertheless, there were several anomalies: Kelantan, with 9 per cent of the population, received less than 5 per cent of the total grant allocation in this period, a fact which illustrates the importance attached to the bargaining power of the individual states. If the intention had been to distribute federal funds according to population, this should perhaps have been made explicit.

This undefined form of federal assistance gave rise to three major problems. First, the states were encouraged to widen rather than narrow the gap between expenditure and revenue. The states reasoned that the greater the deficiency, the better were their prospects of maintaining (if not increasing) their respective shares in the total federal handout. Outright grants did not foster any sense of financial responsibility on the part of state governments; inefficiency as well as efficiency in the use of funds could secure large grants. In addition, because the benefit of any net savings on state account accrued to the Federal Government, the state governments were encouraged to spend at the end of each financial year in excess of their immediate needs. This factor strengthened the tendency to spend on questionable projects. Second, the allocative system did not give any incentive to states to exploit their own sources of revenue. In fact, the states found it easier and more rewarding (both politically and economically) to concentrate their efforts on attempting to obtain larger federal grants than on attempting to collect their own revenue; there were no changes in state tax rates between 1948 and 1954, and revenue collection arrears increased in each year after 1948. Third, despite extensive powers of review, the Federal Government found it difficult to control state expenditure. The allocation of expenditure between economic services (a joint federal–state responsibility) and community services (a state responsibility) was the result of acrimonious political bargaining rather than of national economic evaluation. The grant system militated against the careful allocation of scarce resources within the public sector. Moreover, because of uncertainty as to the future level of grants, the system discounted long-term outlays.

4. *Attempts towards Solution*

(*a*) *1955 proposals*. Following a disparaging report on federal–state financial relations by the 1954 International Bank for Reconstruction and Development (I.B.R.D.) mission to Malaya,[4] a committee was set up late in 1954 to review the allocation of revenue between the centre and the states under the 1948 Federation Agreement. The Committee accepted most of the recommendations of the I.B.R.D. mission. The suggested adjustments were designed to establish an allocative system which would increase that part of state revenue (defined to include grants) accruing directly to the state governments independently of any action on the part of the Federal Government. The proposed system was based on fixed principles to avoid the annual wrangling which had been a characteristic feature of previous federal–state financial relations. The Committee also sought to define state expenditure responsibilities more precisely so as to establish a closer relationship between the limited sources of state revenue and those fields of expenditure which were the legislative responsibility of the states. Thus, the principle of financial autonomy for the states was adopted to supplement the principle of partnership under a strong central government embodied in the 1948 Agreement.

The Committee recognised that national emergencies and problems of economic growth, economic fluctuation and income redistribution were essentially Federal Government responsibilities and that, if the Federal Government were to cope with these problems, it must have full control over the major sources of tax revenue. In this respect, the Committee endorsed the provisions of the 1948 Agreement. State revenues were to be those identifiable with and collected within the state and for which no national policy considerations were likely to arise. The Committee expressed an interest in extending the list of declared state revenue heads, but rejected such a move, arguing that 'the field was too limited in scope and the practical difficulties too great'.[5] Hence, to deal with the fundamental problem of imbalance between state expenditure and declared revenue, reliance had to be placed on reallocating functional responsibilities between the Federal and state governments and on federal grants.

In respect of federal–state functional responsibilities, the Committee sought to clarify the intention of the 1948 Agreement. The Committee considered that state expenditure on education, medical, health, drainage, irrigation and new village services should be financed completely by specific federal grants. These expenditures were considered to be of national importance, and it was concluded that the Federal Government should be responsible for ensuring adequate and uniform standards throughout Malaya. Thus the Committee sought to emphasise to the states that, while they had full executive power in these fields, their policy-making power was subordinate to that of the Federal Government. Having given the Federal Government responsibility for financing a large part of state expenditure, the next problem was to devise a sound and equitable means of bridging the remaining state budgetary gap. To this end, two forms of assistance were proposed: general grants to all states and special grants to particular states.

There are two principles unpon which grants may be based: derivation and need. Under the derivation principle, states receive grants in proportion to federal tax collections from their citizens. This principle favours relatively wealthy states but it is not easily applied, for the taxes collected within a state are not necessarily borne by the residents of that state. As pointed out by J. R. Hicks, 'derivation can easily become enmeshed in tax metaphysics'.[6]

The second principle, that of need, may be interpreted in two ways: national interest or state need. The benefit of grants made for activities which are recognised to be in the national interest may accrue unevenly among states. The objective of such grants is not to even up development among the states, but to undertake projects considered to be of value to the nation as a whole. It is conceivable that grants made on this basis may widen the discrepancy between advanced and backward states. Grants based on state need are deliberately designed to achieve a high degree of equality among states in the provision of certain services. However, where backward states are politically influential (as in Malaya), the line of demarcation between national interest and state need becomes blurred; the politically dominant Malays, for instance, interpret equality among states in the provision of government sevices as being in the national interest.

Grants based on the derivation or need principle may assume the form either of conditional or unconditional grants. Conditional grants enable the Federal Government to exercise a measure of control over the direction of state expenditure. Matching provisions (whereby the state is required to make a contribution before advantage can be taken of federal assistance) may be incorporated in an endeavour to stimulate local initiative. Matching provisions, however, discriminate among states; wealthier states can raise revenue more easily than poorer states and are therefore able to take greater advantage of such grants. The degree of discrimination may be reduced by graduating matching provisions inversely with the relative wealth of states. Unconditional grants are designed to enhance the degree of state autonomy.

In suggesting a basis for federal – state grants in Malaya, the Committee recognised the two main principles – derivation and need – and the two main forms of grant – conditional and unconditional.

The Committee realised that it was impossible to determine with any accuracy the origin by state of most sources of federal tax revenue. But the Committee had already decided not to add to the independent sources of state revenue. Sensing a need to pacify the wealthy states, the Committee decided that the petrol duty should be shared by the Federal and state governments (in a 70:30 ratio), and that the state governments' share should be allocated in the same proportion as duty was raised in the areas covered by the respective governments. Since petrol distribution was undertaken by two companies only, problems of administration were considered to be minimal. No conditions were attached to the grant.

Grants based on the needs principle assumed three forms. First, as discussed above, it was considered to be in the national interest that expenditure on education, medical, health, drainage, irrigation and new village services should be financed by specific federal grants. The decision to eschew matching provisions for these grants illustrates how conscious the Committee was of the need to assist backward states. In contrast, the I.B.R.D. mission had suggested that the Federal and state governments should share the cost of educational, medical and health services.

Second, it was considered necessary to ensure that each state had sufficient finance to permit it to provide minimal standards for services over which the states exercised full legislative power. For this purpose, the Committee recommended an unconditional *per capita* grant (equal to M$16) calculated on the basis of the adult population of each state. The object of this grant was to promote the balanced development of state functions while preserving a degree of state budgetary autonomy. The rate could be varied marginally from year to year, and was to be determined by the High Commissioner after consulting Federal and state governments. The Committee did not specify any principles for determining the *per capita* grant.

Third, the Committee recognised that some states lagged behind others in economic and social development. It therefore recommended that supplementary, unconditional assistance be given to these states (Kelantan, Trengganu, Perlis and Pahang) to enable them to raise the standard of public services other than those financed completely by federal grants. In the case of each state, the amount of assistance was to be equal to 25 per cent of the *per capita* grant. It is interesting to note that the Committee did not specify why it considered that the need for grants by certain states should be greater than the need of other states; it evidently realised that attempts to measure relative need by reference to criteria such as relative poverty and/or relative sparsity of population would raise a host of contentious and complicated side issues; the more densely populated but richer western states could make a case for assistance because of relatively greater traffic congestion problems, for example.

To assist states in their adjustment to the new system, a transitional grant was given to those states which would otherwise face serious financial embarrassment. The purpose of this grant was to ease the impact on the states of requisite downward expenditure adjustments. It was provided that such grants would be reduced progressively each year.

The Committee's proposals, brought into effect on 1 January 1956, provided the states with revenue of a stable and continuing nature.[7] The striking feature of the proposals was the emphasis given to the need to even out differences in the standard of public services among states. The Committee refrained from placing emphasis on forms of assistance which would have permitted the more advanced states to gain most; no attempt was made to increase the independent sources of state revenue, grants based on the derivation principle accounted for only 22 per cent of the recommended level of federal–state grants, and no matching provisions were attached to any of the grants. The proposals reflected the prevailing political climate. Because of weaker round-table bargaining strength, backward states had not gained relative to advanced states under the financial provisions of the 1948 Agreement. In the field of community services, for example, the disparity in the level of development among the various states had steadily widened. The Malays were conscious of the need to raise the standard of public services in backward, predominantly Malay, states, and progress towards self-government had enhanced the political power of the Malays. The Committee translated Malay feelings into concrete proposals.

Apart from expenditure heads financed by specific federal grants, the states were no longer obliged to submit annual estimates to the Federable Government for approval. The new arrangements were designed to enhance state autonomy, initiative and financial responsibility; a decision as to whether a particular service should or should not be expanded was to be made without reference to the Federal Government. Further, the states were no longer required to remit any excess of state revenue over expenditure to the Federal

Government, a serious obstacle to forward planning thereby being removed.

The 1955 provisions, then, relieved the states of the problem of bargaining with the centre for grants, and the contentious issue of revenue allocation was placed on a semi-scientific basis. But, following implementation of the Committee's proposals, it quickly became apparent that the two main deficiencies of the 1948 Agreement remained. First, the policy-making powers of the state governments in the field of community services continued to be greater than implied in the constitutional provisions; the Federal Goverment still had 'to pay the piper for tunes called by the States'.[8] Second, the Federal Government continued to finance state deficits with the result that the states looked to the Federal Government for assistance as a matter of course; this arrangement did not give the states any incentive to exercise economy in the allocation of scarce funds.

(*b*) *1957 proposals*. Following the U.K. decision to grant independence to Malaya, a Constitutional Commission was formed and its report, published in February 1957, reconsidered federal–state financial relations.[9] The Commission opposed any extension of state tax powers, arguing that such a trend would cause a wasteful duplication of staff and 'would almost certainly hamper the conduct of business on a national scale and retard the development of unity in the nation'.[10] It was readily perceived that heavy dependence would have to be placed on grants unless the functional responsibilities of the two tiers of government were rearranged. It was in this latter sphere that the Commission made a significant contribution. It considered that, wherever possible, legislative and executive power should go hand in hand. To achieve this objective, the Commission recommended that expenditure on educational, medical and health services should become federal responsibilities. There was no objection from the state governments to this recommendation.

The rearrangement of functional responsibilities reduced but did not eliminate state budgetary problems; grants were still an important feature of federal–state financial relations. The Commission summarily dismissed tax-sharing arrangements. Reading between the lines of the 1954 Committee Report, it assumed (incorrectly) that the petrol duty allocation was designed to finance state road-maintenance expenditure. On investigation, it was discovered that there was no close relationship between the cost to the states of maintaining their roads on the one hand, and the amount of petrol sold and thus the amount of petrol revenue raised in the states on the other. The Commission therefore concluded that it was undesirable in principle to allocate to the states the proceeds of any particular tax – a confusion of the essence of the two allocative principles, derivation and need. The 1954 Committee Report indicated that the petrol duty allocation was based on the principle of derivation, not need. It would be purely coincidental if grants based on each principle turned out to be identical. The Commission's task would have been eased if reference had been made in the 1954 Committee Report to its progenitor, a report to the Nigerian Government on revenue allocation.[11] This report clearly delineates the main allocative principles, a crucial step which the 1954 Malayan Committee Report unfortunately overlooked.

In place of tax sharing, the Commission advocated an unconditional grant based on state road mileage. The Commission did, however, recommend that 10 per cent of the export duty on tin should be returned to the states in which tin was produced (notably Perak and Selangor); reimbursement was considered to be partial compensation for the permanent loss of a valuable state asset, and it was thought to provide the states with an incentive to promote the development of tin mining.

In considering the *per capita* grant, the Commission indicated that it could not understand why no account was taken of children; population statistics by state were just as comprehensive for children as for adults. The answer, however, is not difficult to discover. Because of a paucity of population statistics in Nigeria (particularly acute in the case of children), the authors of the Nigerian report favoured a *per capita* grant based on the adult male population. Apart from minor adjustments, the 1954 Malayan Committee transcribed the Nigerian report. The 1957 Constitutional Commission rectified this anomaly; the base of the *per capita* grant was extended to include children and the value of the grant was lowered, but the Commission declined to state principles for the determination of the grant, despite a pungent attack on the 1954 Committee for its failure to do so.

The Commission favoured the abolition of the development grant, for the states were not expected, let alone encouraged, to spend the grant on capital items. In order to encourage the states to undertake capital development projects, power was given to the Federal Government to make discretionary, conditional grants (or loans). Provision was made for special grants to meet extraordinary emergency requirements, and a state Reserve Fund was established to assist states which faced difficulties in balancing their budgets.

Under its terms of reference, the Commission was obliged to recommend machinery for consultation between the Federal and state governments. The Commission favoured a consultative organisation (termed the National Finance Council – N.F.C.) consisting of the Prime Minister, one other federal minister, and the Chief Secretary of each state. 'We do not think', the Commission reported, 'that it would be right, or indeed practicable, to give any executive functions to the body which we recommend . . . or to allow its powers to affect or diminish the ultimate responsibilities of the Federation and the States within their respective spheres.'[12]

The Federal Government was required to consult the N.F.C. when calculating state grants, assigning part of the federal taxes to the states, drawing up annual federal–state loan requirements, and undertaking national development projects. The N.F.C. was required to meet annually (if not more regularly) to consider issues of interest to both the Federal and state governments.

The Commission's suggestions on finance were written into the Federal Constitution of 1957. The decision in 1962 to remit to producing states a share of the federal export duty collected on iron ore has been the only change since then.

By readjusting federal–state functional responsibilities and by giving the Federal Government power (within reasonable limits) to embark on any development or conservation scheme declared to be in the national interest, even where the scheme involved direct interference with state rights, the Commission Report strengthened the unitary features of the Malayan Federation. In the allocation of funds, increased emphasis was placed on state needs. General grants based on fixed indicies (population and road mileage) were given to all states; such grants favoured backward states relatively more than advanced states. By strengthening unitary features, grants-in-aid were effectively transformed into a discretionary federal responsibility; in contrast to the 1954 Committee Report, the Commission refused to impose any specific ties on the Federal Government in respect of these grants. The restraints on the power of the Federal Government to redistribute income among states are indeed few.

II. THE WAY AHEAD

The attempts to devise a workable system of revenue allocation have met with limited success. Bargaining, particularly for allocations apart from the *per capita* and road grants, continues to be an integral feature of federal–state financial relations, and the Federal Government has been very lenient in its treatment of deficit states. Increased loan advances from the Federal Government since 1960 have added to the dependence of the states on federal handouts, and have had two side effects: they have enabled the states to ignore the revenue potential of their own tax heads, and they have weakened incentives for economy.

There is no simple answer to the problem of revenue allocation in a federation, but in searching for improvements, two principles – efficiency in the allocation of scarce resources and the desire to avoid unnecessary inequity in the treatment of individuals – should be borne in mind.

State revenue has increased slowly since 1950, but there is considerable scope for expansion in respect of the major sources of state revenue, particularly land taxation (including betterment charges). Federal grants can be manipulated to encourage the states to explore the revenue potential of their own tax heads, and it is recommended that this be done. To this end, two suggestions appear appropriate. First, an attempt should be made to estimate the land tax (including betterment charge) potential of each state and, for this purpose, the N.F.C. should invite the judgement of an independent, impartial committee consisting, for example, of land-tax experts from the World Bank and/or the U.K. Because land tax is the major potential source of state revenue, it alone would serve as an adequate measure of state tax effort. Second, the *per capita* and road-maintenance grants to each state should be reduced (in stages) by the extent that a state's land-tax potential exceeds its land-tax effort. In this way, a 100 per cent premium would be granted to encourage the states to explore their land-tax and betterment charge potential.

The object of this latter proposal would be circumvented if the Federal Government were to continue to give additional assistance to permit states to balance their budgets. Three supplementary suggestions should therefore be made. First, development grants should be tied specifically to capital expenditure on development projects; it should be made clear to the states that associated recurrent expenditure should be financed from betterment charges and from general state revenue. Second, special assistance should be given to states to enable them to raise public service standards or to balance budgets, provided that their land-tax effort is satisfactory and that they have avoided extravagant expenditures. This provision is incorporated in recognition of the fact that, assuming the same tax rates, the potential land-tax yield of some states would be less than that of others; fiscal capacity differs markedly among states. Finally, states which manage to balance their budgets without fully exploiting their land-tax effort (and without, therefore, receiving their full *per capita* and road grants) should be expected to provide a matching contribution to federal grants made for development purposes.

The proposals have several advantages over existing arrangements. First, the proposals endeavour to increase the independent revenues – and thus the autonomy – of the state governments. The states would be encouraged to rely more on their own resources, and the total amount of revenue raised in Malaya would be increased. Second, by restricting the conditions for development grants, the states would have an incentive to work out where capital funds are to be spent in advance, and to assess their ability to service such capital projects. Third, the Federal Government could still use its discretion in helping poorer states in the interests of the Federation as a whole; it has the means to iron out national inequalities as it sees fit. The proposals would reduce the reliance of the states on the Federal Government as the easiest way of obtaining additional finance and, by clarifying allocative criteria, federal grants would be made on a more objective basis. Finally, the proposals do not restrict the Federal Government in determining the amount of grants to be made to states. It is recognised that the Federal Government should have ultimate responsibility for deciding how to deal with the financial situation from time to time. The N.F.C. would continue to be the body through which the Federal and state governments would discuss grant allocations.

This paper has been reprinted because it draws heavily on the contribution of both Sir John and Lady Hicks to the problems of federal–state financial relations. In particular, a sizeable reference has been made to the excellent report on the economics of federal–

state financial relations with specific reference to Nigeria, which was essentially written by Sir John and Lady Hicks. The author has expressed his high regard for this Nigerian Report and for the Jamaican Report on Taxation. Lady Hicks was the driving force behind both.

REFERENCES

1. *Malayan Union and Singapore: Statement of Policy on Future Constitution*, Cmd 6724 (London: H.M.S.O., 1946) p. 3.

2. *Constitutional Proposals for Malaya* (Kuala Lumpur: Government Press, 1946) p. 6.

3. *Federation of Malaya Agreement, 1948* (Kuala Lumpur: Government Press, 1948) p. 2.

4. International Bank for Reconstruction and Development, *The Economic Development of Malaya* (Baltimore: Johns Hopkins Press, 1955) pp. 222 ff.

5. *Report of the Committee Appointed to Review the Financial Provisions of the Federation of Malaya Agreement, 1948* (Kuala Lumpur: Government Press, 1955) p. 3.

6. J. R. Hicks, 'The Nature and Basis of Economic Growth', in U. K. Hicks *et al.*, *Federalism and Economic Growth in Underdeveloped Countries* (London: Allen & Unwin, 1961) p. 73.

7. The legislation, however, scaled down the grant for each adult person from M$16 to M$12.

8. I.B.R.D., *The Economic Development of Malaya*, p. 224.

9. Colonial Office, *Report of the Federation of Malaya Constitutional Commission, 1957* (London, H.M.S.O., 1957).

10. Ibid., p. 9.

11. *Report of the Commission on Revenue Allocation* (Lagos: Government Printer, 1951). Both Sir John and Lady Hicks were members of this Commission. In a later discussion, Lady Hicks pointed out to me that the Chairman of the 1954 Malayan Committee was also a member of the 1951 Nigerian Commission.

12. Colonial Office, *Report*, p. 63.

9

Federal Finance in Underdeveloped Countries*

K. V. S. SASTRI

I. THE SPREAD OF THE FEDERAL IDEA

FEDERALISM continues to flourish in the face of repeated pessimistic forecasts by political scientists. Harold J. Laski declared in 1939: 'I infer in a word that the epoch of federalism is over.'[1] A more guarded statement was made by Professor Sir Kenneth Wheare in 1946 that, under the irresistible pressures of economic crises and wars, the federal principle was doomed to be modified, and perhaps modified in particular cases to the point of extinction.[2] Curiously enough, however, soon after, in 1953, Professor Max Beloff was able reassuringly to report that the idea was resurgent and enjoyed 'a widespread popularity such as it had never known before'.[3] The explanation for the darker prophecies lies in the rigidity and the weakness revealed in the working of traditional federalism, while the new lease of life has been derived from the adaptability inherent in that mode of polity and its essentially protean character.

In the aftermath of the Second World War, colonialism was dissolved. Thus, in the case of the British Empire, imperial bonds between unequal partners were transmuted into equal Commonwealth ties between quondam dependencies and Great Britain. The emergence of free and viable political units out of the ex-dependencies was generally made possible only through the agency of federalism. As it was the doctrines of freedom and equality which had shattered the imperial bonds, so they also naturally enough continued to hold sway over statesmen's deliberations for new constitutional forms; and federalism, with its characteristic capacity to admit any

* This paper was written while the author was visiting the Department of Economics at the University of Wisconsin during 1969–70; and thanks are due, among my colleagues at that university, to Professors Martin H. David and Eugene Smolensky for helpful comments. I have had the usual encouragement from my teacher, Lady Hicks. If, in spite of all this help, errors are still present in this piece. I claim sole proprietary right to them.

possible blend of the two apparently conflicting ideals of national unity and regional independence over the wide intermediate range between sovereignty and multifarious singleness at one end of the scale and unification and integral oneness at the other, furnished the compromise formula for political union. The desire to hang together to avoid the hazard of hanging separately (to use the classic words of Benjamin Franklin), and the mutually opposed feelings of separateness deriving from past history and present aspirations on the one hand, and of the commonness of interests induced by economic logic and political exigencies on the other, are amicably accommodated in a federal polity alone. That the idea has proved practicable in all the six continents of the world, separated by widely differing cultures, epochs, economies, histories and societies, is a tribute to its malleability, pragmatic potential and capacity to preserve diversity in unity and unity in diversity.

The federal form of government thus comprises a set of entities exhibiting variations within very broad limits; and it is the choice of the common characteristics of the small number of 'classical' federations (the chronologically later among which borrowed from the earlier constitutions) for defining the federal principle that has misled political scientists into incautious speculations that federalism was tending to wither away. Traditional federalism as illustrated by the early experience of the U.S.A. during the heyday of narrowly circumscribed governmental activities has been subsequently transformed into co-operative federalism; and the new federations in the underdeveloped countries have had the advantage of starting from the vital current form instead of from the dead historical.

In the following account, intergovernmental fiscal arrangements in the 'new' federations, namely India, Pakistan, Malaysia, the West Indies, Nigeria, and Rhodesia and Nyasaland, will be considered. Such, indeed, has been the pace of political developments that some of these federations have either been dissolved or undergone major constitutional changes: and of all those only India continues to work its original constitution. The West Indies Federation, as also the Federation of Rhodesia and Nyasaland, has disintegrated, and their study is of purely historical interest at the time of writing. Pakistan has passed through some constitutional crises, but the federation itself continues even though in a truncated form thanks to the emergence of the Sovereign Republic of Bangladesh out of the erstwhile province of East Bengal. As for Malaysia, Singapore has separated from the federation. These facts must be borne in mind while reading this account. The justification for referring to federations which are now defunct lies in the importance and interest of the arrangements devised in them.

II. THE PROBLEMS OF FEDERAL FINANCE

This paper proposes to deal with the problem of financing federal government – a problem complicated by the interplay of political and economic factors.

It is inherent in the nature of federal union that the federating units should enjoy legislative independence; and this necessarily implies some degree of financial independence. The 'classical' definition of 'dual' federalism, indeed, calls for financial independence coextensive with legislative; according to that doctrine, the regional governments must possess the power to raise finances adequate (or almost adequate) to their expenditure commitments – a principle of federal finance familiarly known as that of financial independence and responsibility. This is undoubtedly the logical deduction from the legal definition of 'dual' federalism, and would be the ideal for that type of federation. However, it must be observed that the principle may well be impracticable and undesirable, even if feasible. This is because the tax and non-tax heads allotted to any layer of government must be such as can best be administered by it without weakening the efficiency of a national fiscal policy designed for ensuring growth with stability, protection of the balance of payments, and effecting an accepted degree of alleviation of distributional inequalities in personal incomes – the administrative imperative that the tax heads allotted to a layer of government must be suitable to its functional responsibilities.

Suitability is a much more urgent principle of federal finance than independence, as is revealed by a review of financial arrangements in federations, old as well as new. That the practical principle of efficiency in tax administration should take precedence over a political ideal like regional independence would appeal to all who rejoice at the triumph of practical politics over doubtful idealism.[4] Efficiency is here to be understood in relation to the intergovernmental division of functional responsibilities. Since this is the era of national planning for economic development and equal economic opportunities, the responsibilities of national governments in federations are more than ever, and so too are the functions of regional governments which are acknowledgedly the best agents for administering the social services.

The economic functions of the national government which include defence require that it control tax powers capable of yielding more revenue than its normal peace-time expenditure commitments necessitate, while the regional governments are normally saddled with heavier expenditure commitments than can be supported by the sources of revenue which they are best fitted to administer. This is the crux of the federal problem: the national government has most of the money and the regional governments have most of the problems, and all this makes nonsense of the principle of financial independence. Since fiscal control of national economic ends cannot be impaired, while moneys needed for financing public expenditures could be obtained by any layer of government through a mechanism of simple intergovernmental financial transfers, and since the national government must be endowed with powers commensurate with its overwhelming national commitments, the national government has generally become a financial provider for the regional and (through them) the local governments in federations. Inter-regional differences in incomes and fiscal capacities make the problem even more complex.

To give concreteness to the above proposition, a quick review of the main revenue sources of governments is necessary. (1) Customs duties must be a national concern because of their obvious impact on import policy and the balance of payments, and (2) export duties fall in the same category. (3) Since excises admit of manipulation for influencing the *effective* level of customs duties and hence the state of the balance of payments, they are best handled by the national government. (4) Corporate taxation impinges on the economic climate for investment, and its federalisation is necessitated by the objectives of ensuring 'a nationally integrated policy towards private investment, both domestic and foreign', 'a minimum of inter-regional uniformity of rates so as to prevent investment from being forced into wrong locational patterns', and 'a well-articulated fiscal policy for keeping the national economy on an even keel of steady progress'.[5] (5) The same objectives also call for the federalisation of the personal income tax; but it might be objected to this that it would be sufficient if the national government levies the tax on the higher income brackets. However, Canadian and Australian experience in connection with the Second World War threw up the weakness inherent in federal–state concurrency in the field of personal income taxation; and further, inter-regional inequalities are best tackled under an arrangement which yields the national government substantial revenue sources which it must, in any case, normally possess commensurately with its overriding commitments in emergencies. The sophisticated and expensive expertise needed for administering the personal income tax can perhaps be furnished in an underdeveloped country only by the national government; so that if the tax is not made a wholly federal subject, the national government itself may in almost all cases have to administer the states' taxes for them, and the same results could be obtained (with the added advantage of achieving a financially strong national government) by allocation to the states of a part of the tax proceeds on the basis of an agreed formula.

It is thus that whatever arguments might be advanced in favour of concurrent jurisdiction in the field of personal income taxation in advanced countries (and they are not convincing) have little relevance in the context of the underdeveloped. With the unique exception of the U.S.A., with its vast wealth of resources, none of the older federations has had a happy experience with federal–state concurrent personal income taxation. Also, problems of double taxation are best avoided and simplicity achieved in the tax by making it an exclusively federal subject. Lady Hicks has rightly observed that the taxes of the lower-layer governments must be capable of yielding steady (non-fluctuating) revenues, must be easy to assess and collect, and must preferably have an unequivocally localised base so as to avoid jurisdictional disputes.[6] All the arguments may be said to point to the federalisation of the personal income tax. Sir Jeremy Raisman does not seem to have taken all these considerations into account when, for Nigeria, he allocated the whole of the personal income tax to the regional governments subject to the qualification that, in the event of a defence emergency, the national government could assume it strictly for the duration of the emergency.[7] (6) As Lady Hicks has said, sales taxation by the regional governments would engender 'confusion to business of a multiplicity of tax formulae', thus causing hindrance to inter-state trade. 'On this account the national government might decide to restrict the autonomy of sales taxes fairly drastically, while still recognising their value.' It is for this reason that she suggests a tax on value-added as a good source of revenue for the regional governments.[8] The most elastic and lucrative revenue sources have, thus, inevitably to be monopolised by the national government, necessitating federal financial transfers to the regional governments on a large scale.

The problems of federal finance are best discussed under certain convenient heads.

1. There are the initial issues of forming a federal union through either 'aggregation' or 'disaggregation'.[9] Establishment of a common tariff seems much easier in a federation formed through a process of 'disaggregation' than in one achieved through 'aggregation', as is evidenced by a contrast of the Indian case with that of the West Indies.[10] This is because, before federation, the regions might each have relied to a varying extent on customs duties for revenues as well as for fostering economic development. One of the most interesting cases is that of Jamaica which, prior to federation, had leaned heavily on customs duties. While freedom of inter-state commerce would strengthen the forces of industrial agglomeration, adversely hitting the backward regions, the loss of revenue from customs duties (which in conditions of economic backwardness are generally bound to be one of the mainstays of public finances) is generally bound to be substantial; moreoevr, the incidence of that loss may be unequally distributed among the several regions. Compensation for the loss is not simple to arrange, as was proved in the case of Jamaica. Indeed, compensation is only a first tentative step; and, sooner or later, the regions may realise that the main consideration is that federal financial transfers should be sufficient to ensure budgetary equilibrium at a 'normal' level, rather than that compensation for a specific revenue loss should continue under that label.[11] This is well illustrated by Australian experience in respect of the federalisation of both customs and excises and later of the income tax. The Braddon clause was given only a limited lease of life, while the income-tax reimbursement grants were replaced by the Financial Assistance Grants – a significant change of nomenclature. Such a change in the regional governments' approach would then show appreciation of the fact that it is the total financial transfers rather than the relative magnitudes of their individual components that are really significant.[12] Compensation seems rather impossible as a general basis for federal financial transfers.[13]

2. Financial imbalance of regional governments is complicated by its unequal inter-regional impact. Unequal endowments of

natural resources among the several regions, and differential inter-regional impact of federal policy, are two very important factors that require inter-regional differentiation of federal financial transfers in order to stem the process of widening inter-regional economic inequalities.[14] To tackle this problem it is essential to arm the national government with adequate financial powers in excess of its normal peace-time expenditure requirements. The feasible degree of inter-regional redistribution through federal financial transfers depends upon the range of inter-regional inequalities, the degree of national consciousness and unity, and the relative magnitude of the problem. Other things being equal, (*a*) the greater the range of inequality, the greater the probability of federal financial transfers being oriented to a given degree of inter-regional distribution; (*b*) the greater the sense of national oneness (or the stronger the 'aggregative' forces), the greater the chances of such redistribution; and finally (*c*) the smaller the size of the problem (the less the finances needed) relative to federal revenue and the G.N.P., the greater the possibility of its solution within the context of national growth targets. Federal bonds are bound to be severely strained by a pace of inter-regional redistribution that is either so intolerably slow as to make no apparent dent in the problem, or so intolerably fast as to threaten to kill the goose that lays the golden egg (by lowering the rate of growth of the G.N.P.).

3. The problem of financial imbalance is dynamic and calls for flexibility and adaptability of the financial provisions of the constitution. A rigid specification of the quanta of federal financial transfers, on the assumption that a *permanent* solution is possible, would be unduly to simplify the problem. At the time of forming the federal union, in more than one federation, it has been hoped that there was a long-term tendency for federal financial transfers to wither away.[15] But experience has shown that this is merely an example of wishful thinking. To cope with the changing situation, there must be provision for review of the arrangements; and the question is whether regular periodic review would prove sufficient, or if continuous review is required. Other questions concern the machinery for conducting the review and the principles adopted by the reviewing body.

4. We also have the problem of borrowing and of how powers relating to it should be dealt with. Efficiency of national fiscal policy calls for concentration of the major borrowing powers in the hands

of the national government, and provision for the formulation and execution of the borrowing programmes of all governments through either the Central Bank or a Loan Council working through that institution. Regional autonomy in the field of borrowing may undermine the country's credit-worthiness through competition worsening the terms for all governments. The time of flotation, the total issued and the terms governing it are important matters; and considerable financial expertise is needed for determining them to the best advantage of all the layers of government in the federation. Loans are best handled by the Central Bank of the country, if there is one.

III. CAUSES OF FINANCIAL CENTRALISATION IN THE NEW FEDERATIONS

It has been argued above that financial independence is generally not feasible. The percentage proportion of autonomous revenues to total revenues (including intergovernmental transfers) of any level of government is a direct index of the degree of its financial independence. For 1960–1, these figures are 65 per cent for India, 68·3 per cent for Pakistan, 59·1 per cent for Malaya and 33·3 per cent for Nigeria. For Rhodesia and Nyasaland, for 1959–60, it was 70 per cent. Thus in no federation mentioned above was the percentage proportion of intergovernmental financial transfers less than 35 per cent, the highest being 66·7 per cent. In the British Caribbean, where the general government was made to depend upon the regional governments by way of a mandatory levy on the territories, autonomous revenues of the general government formed 39·4 per cent of its total revenues in 1960–1.[16] It is interesting to observe that the corresponding figures for Canada and Australia are also within the above range of values of the index of regional financial autonomy. For the U.S.A. in 1966, federal financial transfers accounted for 40 per cent of autonomous state tax revenue[17] – which is the same thing as saying that the transfers formed 28·6 per cent of total state revenues. In the case of Canada and Australia, the percentage proportions are even higher than for the U.S.A.

This financial centralisation has been due to the fact that, with some exceptions, the major indirect taxes – customs duties, excises and sales taxation – have been federalised. The exceptions may be considered briefly. In Nigeria, customs duties were federalised; but in the light of a fortuitous regional specialisation of the production of the main exports of the country, regional sales taxation (which is the same as export taxation) was provided for. Rhodesia and Nyasaland federalised customs duties, but excise taxation of motor spirit was left to the regional governments. In the West Indies, Jamaica was loth to lose its customs revenue by lowering its tariff which, on the eve of federation, had been geared to its economic development programme; and compensation for revenue loss was an impossibility, considering that Jamaica was one of the wealthier island regions. The formation of a customs union had thus to be postponed, and justification sought for that unavoidable political necessity in terms of the relatively wide variations in inter-regional tariff rates. Customs duties were thus, in the main, a regional subject and federal powers in the field were rigidly circumscribed for the first quinquennium; the West Indies was that exceptional federation with a customs union planned to follow instead of preceding federal union. In India and Pakistan, customs and excise duties were allotted to the national governments, with minor exceptions in the field of excises on alcohol and narcotics left to the regional governments; but the policy of prohibition deprived the states in India of a considerable amount of excise revenue. (A reversal of the policy of prohibition has occurred in India in 1970, and this considerably eases the financial problems of the states.)

Sales taxation was regional in both India and Pakistan; but when inter-regional trade was found to be getting increasingly impeded by this exercise, India federalised inter-state sales taxes,[18] while Pakistan federalised all sales taxes.[19] Where national economic integration is not negligible and inter-regional trade is appreciable, these problems appear inevitable and call for at least the federalisation of the taxation of inter-regional sales so as to preserve the freedom of inter-regional trade. Since sales taxes are one of the few elastic revenue sources for regional governments, it has generally not been found possible to exclude the regional governments from that field, while the aim of inter-regional freedom of trade necessitated curtailment of the degree of regional autonomy. In Nigeria, sales taxes on a number of items like produce, hides and skins, motor spirit and diesel oil (with some qualifications) were regionalised; while in Malaysia the states were permitted to levy non-discriminatory sales taxes.

Corporate and personal income taxation as well as succession duties have generally been allotted to the general government.

However, in the interest apparently of regional autonomy, some exceptions have also sprouted up. Thus a surcharge of up to 20 per cent of the federal tax on personal incomes and corporate profits could be levied by the regional governments in Rhodesia and Nyasaland, the collection being entrusted to the general government. In Nigeria taxes on company profits are a federal subject while taxes on personal incomes are exclusively regional. In the West Indies, the constitution provided for concurrent federal–state jurisdiction over these fields; but for the initial quinquennium the general government was confined to taxing the income of its own employees. In India both corporate and personal income taxation are federal subjects.

Taxes on land, entertainments and professions, besides licence fees, are generally the exclusive fiscal jurisdiction of the regional governments, which have to share them with the local governments. (It appears eminently desirable that the constitution divide the revenue sources between the regional layer of governments and the local layer of governments.) These taxes are not elastic, and efficient land taxation calls for a complete revaluation of land in the rural areas which it is not easy to effect. There is considerable scope for taxing land in urban areas, and also capital gains because of the increases of land values due to speculation in conditions of urban growth.[20]

A very important feature of the new federations is the provision for emergencies. This marks them off from the older federations. Thus, in India, Pakistan, Malaysia, Nigeria and, indeed, even the West Indies, emergency provisions were made for increasing the financial powers of the general governments and transforming the federations into unitary polities for the duration of the emergency.[21] India and Pakistan have also provision for 'financial emergencies'.[22]

IV. BORROWING POWERS IN THE NEW FEDERATIONS

Borrowing powers give rise to an important problem. In the federations formed through 'aggregation' the units must, on the eve of the federation, have been relying each to a different extent on loans, domestic or foreign. This contributes to financial imbalance on the expenditure side, unless regional debts are assumed by the general government. Apart from this initial problem, federalisation of borrowing powers, or at least their co-ordination, is necessary for efficiency of national fiscal policy. Further, in general, all governments would be able to secure loans on easy terms when they act co-operatively instead of competitively – though big and well-known units (like Jamaica) have enjoyed this advantage even when acting alone. The Australian Loan Council is an interesting institution which has been followed only in the Federation of Rhodesia and Nyasaland. External borrowing, which is very important in an era of planning, is best left to the general government. This is so in India and Malaysia. In Nigeria, however, short-run external borrowing by the regional governments is permitted; but since such borrowing must be on the strength of external assets, the provision does not make much difference in practice. Pakistan allows external borrowing by the regional governments, subject to federal restrictions; and there is provision for special tribunals to which the provinces can appeal in case federal refusal of provincial applications is considered unwarranted. The classical mode of concurrent powers of borrowing prevailed only in the West Indies.

In the matter of internal borrowing, the National Finance Commission in Pakistan, the National Finance Council in Malaysia and the Loans Advisory Board in Nigeria are examples of agencies through which co-ordination has been sought to be achieved. In India, if the states are indebted to the Union Government, they cannot borrow without its prior consent. With the provision for the national government to make loans to the regional governments, the borrowing powers of the latter may generally be said to be restricted in the Indian federation. Considering how autonomous borrowing powers of regional governments enabled the American states to challenge the might of the federation (during the American Civil War), and also how loan co-ordination is necessary for an integrated national fiscal policy geared to economic development with stability, the provision for federal dominance in borrowing seems appropriate.

V. TECHNIQUES OF FINANCIAL ADJUSTMENT

To meet financial imbalance, devices have been built into the constitutions of the new federations. Tax sharing, revenue sharing and revenue assignment,[23] besides grants, specific-purpose and unconditional, may be resorted to.

In view of the problems attendant on federal–state concurent jurisdiction over direct taxation, tax sharing has not proved to be of much importance in these arrangements. Following American precedent, both the Australian and Canadian Constitutions provided for concurrent jurisdiction which, under pressure of the Second World War, had to modify and federalise the income tax – through tax rental agreements in Canada and pre-emptive federal legislation of the Uniform Income Tax Plan in Australia. This experience may have influenced the newer federations though in India the Constitution of 1950 seems to have relied mainly on the earlier 1935 Act which has made the income tax an exclusively federal subject.

Revenue sharing and revenue assignment are two of the several methods of fiscal adjustment in the newer federations. In the case of revenue assignment, the whole proceeds of a specified tax collected in each region are handed over to that government, the national government acting as an agency for levying and collecting the tax, thus avoiding inter-regional differences in its rates and structure.[24] Where financial imbalance is on a large scale and attempts are made to reduce it as much as possible, this technique would help reduce the cost of collection of the tax and seems best suited to direct taxation, which calls for a considerable degree of administrative expertise. Article 268 of the Constitution of India stipulates revenue assignment in respect of Union stamp duties and excises and medicinal and toilet preparations.

Revenue sharing is enjoying a wide vogue in the new federations, and indeed has come to command current attention in the U.S.A.[25] Whereas revenue assignment is the method of giving the entire proceeds of a specified tax (or taxes) to one layer of government such that the layer of government that levies and collects the tax gets none of the receipts, revenue sharing involves a share for the tax-gathering government. The shares of the two layers of government in the proceeds of the specified taxes may be safeguarded constitutionally (as was done in Australia under the Braddon Clause), or left open for determination from time to time. To reduce uncertainty in respect of revenues and to enable the governments to plan their budgets with some degree of confidence, the best arrangement seems to be one which specifies the total amount of revenue for each government; but that makes the device less useful than if the percentage shares are specified, since whatever buoyancy inheres in the tax could then be enjoyed by the participating governments.[26] The statutory grants in Canada and the capitation payments in Australia suffered from inelasticity.

The technique of fiscal adjustment through revenue sharing would be somewhat like a block (unconditional) grant, and it might be made part of a financial review by either the paying government or an independent body appointed by it for that purpose. Based partly on the Australian precedent, the Indian Constitution provides for quinquennial review of federal–state financial adjustments and recommendations of financial transfers for each Five-Year Plan period. The Constitution of Rhodesia and Nyasaland had a similar provision for quinquennial review, while the Nigerian Constitutions of 1960 and 1963 provided for the appointment of *ad hoc* commissions. In Pakistan there was an *ad hoc* commission in 1952 for instituting a 'financial inquiry regarding allocation of revenues'[27] between the national and regional governments. Malaysia furnished deviation from this normal practice of provision for periodic review: the Constitution laid down biennial and quinquennial reviews for Singapore and the Borneo states respectively, but such review by an independent commission was to be resorted to only when the interested governments could not come to an agreement. In this Malaysian case, then, financial relations were left to be thrashed out at a political level under the shadow of the Damocles' sword of independent final awards in the absence of consensus.

The basic arrangement appears to be to provide for annual review by an independent expert commission as in Australia. Continuity should be ensured by appointing the members for a term, and selection should not be dictated by considerations of representation for the states or groups of states. The commission would be able to win a reputation for impartiality by making its calculations explicit and its principles clear, while the general government (that appoints it) should establish the healthy convention of normally accepting its recommendations. These advantages could be claimed for the Australian Commonwealth Grants Commission.[28] Annual review would make it possible for federal financial transfers to be closely aligned with budgetary needs and the establishment and application of rational and uniform standards of tax effort and expenditure economy. For the commission to be of the maximum possible use, it must carry through a total review of the budgets of all the regional governments. It is not necessary that *all* federal financial transfers be channelled through it; but the quantum should be such that all the necessary adjustments for tax effort and expenditure economy can comfortably be made. In India, where the Planning Commission exists on a continuous basis, it is essential that there be close contact between that body and the Finance Commission. A permanent Finance Commission with a clear demarcation of functions from the Planning Commission seems to be quite promising; but at present the situation is somewhat clouded.[29]

Besides transfers tied to specific federal revenue heads, there is generally provision for specific-purpose grants as well as general unconditional grants to ensure the adequacy of transfers. Specific-purpose grants enable the general government to implement national development plans, enforce national priorities and national minimum standards in respect of important services, and help particular regional governments meet their special problems including national catastrophes; where demands for them emanate from the regional governments themselves, they do not appear to be subject to the objections that are otherwise generally valid against them. Thus, pursuit of federal priorities may distort the regional pattern of expenditure, upsetting regional priorities and causing overdevelopment of certain services at the expense of others of higher regional preference.[30] While this objection would be invalid if the demands for such grants emanated from the regional governments, the other problems of erecting suitable performance criteria and tailoring the rates of payments to the inter-regional inequalities in fiscal capacities are quite real. Widely varying matching requirements may be necessary, depending upon the range of variation in inter-regional fiscal capacities; and a very low percentage of matching requirements would expose them to the same political objections as unconditional grants. However, if they are conceived as an integral part of the total financial transfers, no matching requirement need be attached to them if the scheme of transfers makes allowance for inter-state differences in tax effort. Provision for continuous annual review of regional budgets in accordance with clearly enunciated rational principles, by an expert non-political commission alone, seems to be the best arrangement which, if it obtains, would make it relatively unimportant whether the composition of the quantum of transfers leans more or less heavily on this or that type of transfer. But this applies only to federations where such arrangements are politically feasible.

VI. PRINCIPLES OF FINANCIAL ADJUSTMENT

A brief account may now be given of the principles of financial transfer. The main principles are compensation, 'derivation' or 'collection' of revenues, and fiscal needs. All these appear to be important in practice.

Compensation is generally adopted to ease out the financial problems connected with the formation of federal unions and also later with federal take-over of erstwhile regional tax powers. In respect of federalisation of taxes which had previously been important sources of regional revenues, as in the case of customs and excises, this has happened in some federations; and again, in connection with the personal income tax in Canada and Australia, and in respect of federal assumption of erstwhile regional sales taxes in India.[31] It was in Australia that a concerted attempt was made to apply the compensation principle on an extensive scale; and the experience there may be summed up by saying simply that it proved impracticable. In the new federations it has enjoyed only a limited vogue. As a general principle, it is unworkable; and, even if it were practicable, 'there is something in the idea itself of compensation that runs counter to the spirit of federal union and fosters mischievous centrifugal forces'.[32]

Derivation is closely akin to compensation. In Australia, it was tried under the Braddon Clause and was somewhat more practicable than elsewhere because each Australian state has its own port (which, incidentally, is also its capital city). Generally, one has to make do with 'collections' as an index of derivation; but it can easily be a far cry from it in the face of considerable inter-regional economic integration when 'derivation' is practically impossible to determine; besides, there is extensive scope for political controversy over the choice of a suitable method of measuring it.[33] Federal financial transfers in Nigeria were based on derivation during 1954–8, but this was not found workable.[34] The Raisman Commission of 1958 limited derivation to taxes with a clearly local base and used 'needs' for the distributable pool. The experience in Pakistan, Rhodesia and Nyasaland, and India proves the unsatisfactory nature of the principle of derivation.

Fiscal needs can well be described as constituting the most important basis for federal transfers in the new federations. This is not surprising in view of the difficulties associated with other principles.

It is for this reason that the work of the Commonwealth Grants Commission of Australia proves (or ought to prove) interesting to the new federations. Population is sometimes considered an index of needs; but it would be valid only when inter-regional disparities in *per capita* income are narrow and inter-regional differences in area (or density of population) are of no material importance.[35] It seems best, therefore, to make the budgets of the regional governments the basis for arriving at fiscal needs. The Australian Commission has standardised this method;[36] but its adoption requires the availability of reliable statistics, while a modicum of uniformity of budget forms for all the regional governments would simplify the problem.

The above discussion of the principles of federal financial transfers leads up to one important consideration. If needs are recognised as basic, the general government would be underwriting the regional budgets, subject to standards of fulfilment in respect to tax effort, expenditure economy and service provision. That would logically make irrelevant all principles other than need, because then 'it is the total quanta of federal fiscal transfers to the states that are important rather than the composition of these totals'.[37] Only in respect of capital assistance to the states in connection with financing and implementing national development plans is there the problem of fixing the proportion between loans and grants; and this is very important in India and elsewhere in other federations committed to national economic planning.[38] It seems acceptable that the poorer regional governments must be given larger proportions as outright grants, to reduce the burden of service charges. A perusal of the reports of the Indian Finance Commission would show the importance of this problem in that federation.

VII. INTER-REGIONAL DISPARITIES IN FISCAL CAPACITIES

The problem of inter-regional disparities in fiscal capacities must be considered now. There is not a single federation, past or present, old or new, without this.[39] In the U.S.A. the technique of variable matching requirements in connection with specific-purpose grants is resorted to, while Australia has evolved the Special Grants (under Section 96 of the Constitution). In the latter federation, Financial Assistance Grants are themselves somewhat redistributive while the

Special Grants are very much so; while in India the Fourth Finance Commission has in the main construed grants under Article 275 of the Constitution as intended to help balance the budgets of the poorer states. In relation to state *per capita* incomes, the federal transfers in India are not redistributive.[40] However, if national standards of expenditure are erected and applied in calculating the budgetary needs of the regional governments, and federal transfers are effected to meet the calculated or 'normalised' budgetary needs based on standards of tax effort and expenditure economy, such that every regional government is put in a position to meet its standardised expenditure commitments, the totality of federal financial transfers would necessarily be redistributive; but when any one of the standards stipulated above is not duly applied, the system would prove impossible to operate. Indeed, even a flat rate of *per capita* payments to the regional governments in conjunction with a progressive federal tax structure would be redistributive, though only mildly so. However, in an underdeveloped country where the tax structure is likely to be dominated by regressive taxes, this may not be the case.

The question of measurement of tax effort must be squarely met. The Australian Commonwealth Grants Commission applies the representative tax method for assessing the 'normal' tax efforts of states, but an alternative formula based on *per capita* incomes seems simpler.[41] Wide disparities prevail in regional tax efforts in India – the only new federation for which such calculations are available – and it is interesting that some of the poorer states are generally putting forth higher tax efforts than the richer ones, as borne out by studies[42] for 1955–6 and 1960–1. But adjustment for this factor does not seem to have been made by the Finance Commission in India. The same seems generally true of the other new federations. Elsewhere I have argued the case for incorporating some degree of 'progression' in the formula for measuring the 'normal' tax efforts of regional governments. Adjustment for the degree of financial self-effort on the part of the grant-aided governments must be comprehensive and cover the financial results of their commercial undertakings, instead of being merely confined to taxation.

On the expenditure side, adjustment must be made for economy, since otherwise the system might dull the edge of husbandry, blotting the Polonian copybook of wise saws. Again, Indian experience to date is that the Finance Commission has not succeeded in finding a method of measuring this factor, but I have suggested a tentative formula for it.[43] By the norms of relative tax effort and expenditure economy, it is worth observing 'that some of the states which are in a favoured position as a result of the Finance Commission's failure to make allowance for the tax-effort factor are further favoured by the fact that the Commission does not allow for the factor of expenditure-economy either. The cumulative effect of this could be not inconsiderable.'[44] It is the lack of application of adjustments for these factors that is likely to engender a lack of financial responsibility; and once the keel is laid for a rational matrix of principles, it should not prove impossible to start collecting and improving the required statistics in any new federation. But all this is a desideratum in these countries, though it must be emphasised at once that this should not be construed as an argument in favour of modifying the intergovernmental financial relations in them in such wise as to enthrone financial responsibility through striving for financial balance by autonomous revenue sources alone.

VIII. CONCLUSIONS

The above review has revealed that the traditional principle of financial independence and responsibility is irrelevant to the new federations (as it is indeed to the older ones). Such responsibility is best achieved and preserved through the institution of review machinery which is efficient and adequate. The machinery is provided for in most of the new federations, and what is required is that it should make a good start in evolving and applying the appropriate rational principles. Periodic review seems only a second-best solution for 'ensuring financial responsibility in the broad sense of safeguarding ourselves against unpardonable waste of moneys by the aid-receiving governments'.[45] Given that all the regional governments 'are enabled to enjoy a national minimum standard of administration with no greater-than-average extravagance in the claimant states',[46] it would seem fair to say that the system has succeeded. Annual review in the place of the usual periodic review would yield the best results.[47] The Advisory Commission on Intergovernmental Relations in the U.S.A., and the Commonwealth Grants Commission in Australia, are institutions of this *basic* type, though there are major differences between them; and it is only in Canada that the Sirois Commission's recommendation for the creation of a National Finance Commission was not accepted; so that the experience of older federations may generally be claimed to point in the same direction as that of the newer ones, thus providing the basis for us to say not only that the traditional principle of financial independence and responsibility is now irrelevant in all federations, but also that the principle is now tending to be generally understood in practice in the sense explained above.

It is thus that federations can learn from one another and the experience of one federation may be claimed to be relevant to the others.[48] While differences in historical, social, political and economic factors among them are a reality, the *technical* principles of effecting financial balance appear to be the same. Progress achieved anywhere in the field of cost–benefit analysis, for example, is of relevance everywhere; advances made in respect of evolving a rational set of principles for determining the optimum quanta of federal financial transfers anywhere would be important everywhere; and individual experiences with regard to the administrative problem of setting up appropriate institutions in any federation are bound to be rewarding to all federations.

In a negative way, too, this is all true. Thus, the Canadian emphasis on political bargaining between the provinces and the Dominion Government, and the rich Australian lesson on the evils of constituting *ad hoc* review bodies haphazardly to investigate into and report on what after all is a permanent problem, have both yet to be appreciated fully in the newer federations.

A study of intergovernmental financial relations in federations does throw up a set of common principles. These are:

(1) that the traditional principle of financial independence and responsibility is invalid;
(2) that allocation of revenue sources between the two tiers of federal government (national and regional) should be guided by the doctrine of suitability;
(3) that the national government should be armed with adequate fiscal and economic powers commensurate with its commitments;
(4) that appropriate machinery should be created to ensure that federal financial transfers are effected for making all governments viable and responsible; and
(5) that provision should be made for attacking the politically

dangerous problem of wide inter-regional disparities in fiscal capacities (like that of substantial interpersonal income inequalities).[49]

In discussing the principles of intergovernmental allocation and adjustment, it is essential to draw the vital Hicksian distinction between 'tight' and 'loose' federations.[50] From the above account of the financial provisions of federal constitutions, one can see which among the new federations are 'loose' or 'tight'. The latter type has many similarities with Australia by way of recognition of the unavoidability of a high degree of financial centralisation and provision of institutional machinery sufficient for ensuring a rational approach to problems, including the problem of inter-regional differences in fiscal capacity and economic development. 'Loose' federations find it politically impossible to provide that.

It can thus be said that there are common basic principles of federal finance; and further, there are categories of federations within which there are similarities. In this connection, it has to be remembered that it is not always racial, linguistic or cultural differences alone that make for a 'loose' federation. Thus the U.S.A. is a 'loose' federation while India is a 'tight' one, the difference being due to the individualistic traditions and isolationist experience and nature of the former. The institution of the Advisory Commission on Intergovernmental Relations in the U.S.A. is a tribute to the need for a comprehensive study of the problem, while its advisory capacity reflects the vitality of the doctrine of States' Rights. Piecemeal federal aid for specific purposes (which is what characterises the U.S.A.) seems theoretically inadequate unless a rational network of grants is first planned and the individual grants then determined within this context. The late Robert F. Kennedy's scheme of the Bedford–Stuyvesant Development and Services Corporation has established that socio-economic problems can be attacked as an entity. As Sorensen has observed, 'In the past, many piecemeal programs, traditional New Deal solutions, and Federal matching grants have hurt as much as they have helped.'[51] If this awareness leads to the adoption of a unified approach to the problem of federal financial transfers in the U.S.A., the distinction drawn above between tight and loose federations would be somewhat blurred in that case; and in the light of the high degree of economic integration prevailing in the U.S.A., and of the fact that it is only socio-economic philosophy rather than ethnic and other factors that furnish the basis for federal union without unity, such a development may not be wholly inconceivable. The Kennedy philosophy seems to have initiated this change. In conclusion, one might say that there is enough in common between one federation and another to cut across the Hicksian categories.

REFERENCES

1. H. J. Laski, 'The Obsolescence of Federalism', *The Republic*, XCVIII (1939) 367.

2. K. C. Wheare, *Federal Government*, 1st ed. (Oxford U.P., 1946) chap. 12.

3. M. Beloff, 'The "Federal Solution" in its application to Europe, Asia, and Africa', *Political Studies* (1953) p. 114.

4. It appears that the Wheare definition of federalism as 'dual federalism' has erred in proceeding from the intentions of constitution-makers instead of the facts of federal government; and it is not, therefore, surprising that it is practically an 'empty box'.

5. U. K. Hicks *et al.*, *Federalism and Economic Growth in Underdeveloped Countries* (London: Allen & Unwin, 1961) p. 130. It is the general government that is best fitted to carry out policies of stabilisation and distribution. If these were handled by the regional governments there may be waste of effort, since the corrective measures taken by each government may well lead to the worsening of the problems for the others.

6. U. K. Hicks, *Development Finance: Planning and Control* (Oxford U.P., 1965) p. 119.

7. *Report of the Fiscal Commission* (1958). Cmnd 481.

8. Hicks, *Development Finance*, p. 122.

9. This terminology is due to the late Francis G. Carnell, whose classic analysis of the 'political implications of federalism' is still the best account available. See Hicks *et al.*, *Federalism and Economic Growth*, chap. 11.

10. Ibid., p. 36.

11. Subject to constraints by way of standards of tax effort and service benefits, on which more below.

12. This is subject to the obvious qualification that the degree of financial independence of the regional governments should be left unaffected by the alternative compositions of the quantum of federal financial transfers.

13. For a further consideration of this question, see Hicks *et al.*, *Federalism and Economic Growth*, pp. 131, 132. The Commonwealth Grants Commission in Australia had to abandon the principle of compensation because of its unworkability.

14. On this see ibid., chap. 3, and p. 131. Professor Musgrave has set up a series of models to analyse this problem. See J. M. Buchanan (ed.), *Public Finances: Needs, Sources and Utilisation* (Princeton U.P., 1961) pp. 97, 122; also R. A. Musgrave, *Fiscal Systems* (New Haven and London: Yale U.P., 1969) pp. 308–13.

15. See Hicks *et al.*, *Federalism and Economic Growth*, pp. 115, 130–1.

16. R. L. Watts, *New Federations: Experiments in the Commonwealth* (Oxford U.P., 1966) Appendix. The calculations are based on the data furnished there. Before the implementation of the 1961 agreement of the Constitutional Conference to abolish the mandatory levy and arm the general government with fully

independent fiscal powers commensurate with its obligations, the British Caribbean Federation disintegrated. In fact, the proposed abolition of the levy was itself a major cause of the breakdown of the Federation.

17. J. A. Maxwell, *Financing State and Local Governments* (Washington, D.C.: Brookings Institution, 1969) p. 53.

18. Sixth Amendment Act, 1956.

19. *Government of India (Amendment) Act, 1948; Government of India (Fourth Amendment) Act, 1950; Government of India (Amendment) Act, 1952.*

20. Hicks, *Development Finance*, pp. 104–6. It must be noted that Lady Hicks advocates the inclusion in the tax base (at the time of revaluation) of the increase in land prices, and does not favour capital gains taxation on rural land.

21. Watts, *New Federations*, chap. 12, sect. 6.

22. Constitution of India, 1950, Art. 360; Constitution of Pakistan, 1956, Art. 194; Constitution of Pakistan, 1962, Art. 131(2)(*a*).

23. These terms are defined in my *Federal–State Fiscal Relations in India* (Oxford U.P., 1966). They have been suggested by Lady Hicks.

24. Ibid., pp. 69–70, for a more detailed account. 'Revenue assignment' is thus distinguished from 'revenue sharing' for analytical convenience.

25. H. S. Perloff and R. P. Nathan (eds.), *Revenue Sharing and the City* (Baltimore: Johns Hopkins Press, 1968).

26. Sastri, *Federal–State Fiscal Relations in India*, p. 67.

27. The title of the report is *Financial Inquiry Regarding Allocation of Revenues.*

28. Hicks *et al.*, *Federalism and Economic Growth*, pp. 133–4; see also Lady Hicks's 'Current Problems of Federal Finance in India and Some Comparisons with Australia', *Public Finance*, XXIII 3 (1968), for an illuminating account comparing the Indian Finance Commission and the Commonwealth Grants Commission of Australia.

29. See Sastri, *Federal–State Fiscal Relations in India*, chap. 1.

30. Hicks *et al.*, *Federalism and Economic Growth*, pp. 134–5.

31. Sastri, *Federal–State Fiscal Relations in India*, p. 109.

32. Hicks *et al.*, *Federalism and Economic Growth*, p. 132.

33. Ibid.

34. Cmnd 481 (1958) paras. 11–20.

35. Sastri, *Federal–State Fiscal Relations in India*, pp. 80–1; also Hicks *et al.*, *Federalism and Economic Growth*, pp. 132–3.

36. For a description of this method, see ibid., pp. 133–4; also Sastri, *Federal–State Fiscal Relations in India*, pp. 12–13.

37. Ibid., pp. 13, 16–17, 70–1, 77–9, 100–1.

38. U. K. Hicks, 'Current Problems of Federal Finance in India and Some Comparisons with Australia', pp. 331–2.

39. Measures of inequality were computed by R. J. May, *Federalism and Fiscal Adjustment* (Oxford U.P., 1969) Statistical Appendix, Tables 1–14. The British Caribbean Federation was wrecked by inter-regional inequalities.

40. Sastri, *Federal–State Fiscal Relations in India*, chap. 3.

41. Ibid., chap. 2. After the publication of this book, I came to know (through Lady Hicks) that the Advisory Commission on Intergovernmental Relations (U.S.A.) also has a similar idea. However, the application of progression to the measure is not in their publication. See *Measures of State and Local Fiscal Capacity and Tax Effort* (Washington D.C.: A.C.I.R., 1962).

42. Sastri, *Federal–State Fiscal Relations in India*, chap. 2.

43. Ibid., chap. 1.

44. Ibid., p. 114; see also the *Report of the Finance Commission* (India), 1961, pp. 37–8.

45. Hicks *et al.*, *Federalism and Economic Growth*, p. 133.
46. Ibid., p. 134.
47. Sastri, *Federal–State Fiscal Relations in India*, p. 75.
48. Hicks *et al.*, *Federalism and Economic Growth*, p. 129.
49. There has been some difficulty in Australia and the West Indies. In the former, Western Australia threatened to secede from the Commonwealth of Australia; and in the latter, Jamaica's unsatisfied demands led to the disintegration of that federation. In fact, Jamaica felt federal union impracticable. As Bustamante said, 'To ask the creeping man and the man not started to creep and the walking man to walk together – I cannot say anything but that is nonsensical': quoted in May, *Federalism and Fiscal Adjustment*, p. 149.
50. Sir John R. Hicks, *Essays in World Economics* (Oxford U.P., 1960) chap. 10.
51. Theodore C. Sorensen, *The Kennedy Legacy* (New York: Macmillan, 1970) p. 347.

Part Four
BUDGETS AND BUDGET ORGANISATION

10

Budget Structure and Organisation in Developed and Developing Countries

RUSSELL MATHEWS

BUDGETING and accounting systems of governments must be thought of as information systems, the function of which is to provide information to parliaments and governments as a means of facilitating legislative and executive decision-making. The structure and organisation of a country's budget must therefore be related to the information needs of the legislative and executive branches for purposes of planning and executing the government's policies. These information needs depend, in turn, on the economic goals of governments, which may be expected to reflect social and political as well as purely economic objectives. In both developed and developing countries, economic goals are concerned with notions of stability, equity, growth and resource allocation, but the weights or priorities which are attached to these several objectives are likely to differ markedly between the two sets of countries.

I. THE ECONOMIC GOALS OF GOVERNMENT

In less developed countries, constitutional and institutional constraints often severely limit the freedom of action of governments in relation to economic stabilisation policies. Because their fiscal and monetary institutions, and their administrative capacity, have frequently not been developed to the point where discretionary policies can be effectively implemented in the pursuit of national objectives, they are often forced to follow balanced budget policies, to subordinate domestic economic policy to the balance of payments and, more generally, to rely on built-in stabilisers to a greater extent than developed countries.

Because the distribution of incomes and wealth in developing countries is very uneven, questions of equity cannot be ignored.

By contrast with the situation in developed countries, however, concern for equity tends to be overshadowed by preoccupation with economic development, which is regarded as the only effective means of raising incomes and wealth all round. As a goal of economic policy in developing countries, equity is thus seen in a long-term rather than a short-term perspective, while education and income growth, rather than income transfers, are considered to provide the key to long-run equity.

The dominating factor influencing the formulation and implementation of economic objectives and policies in developing countries is undoubtedly the low level of per capita income which results from rapid population growth and economic stagnation. In these circumstances, the imperatives of growth require governments to assume much greater responsibility for planning development than is the case in most highly developed Western economies. In this respect, developing countries have more in common with socialist countries, even when their economic systems are predominantly capitalistic or market-oriented. Development planning thus requires government action to determine the rate of growth which is feasible in the light of the resources available, to mobilise savings and guide the allocation of resources in the private sector, and to provide the social and economic infrastructure necessary to achieve the growth target.

As a policy objective, resource allocation in developing countries is inextricably linked with growth, since it is necessary to ensure that development plans reflect resources available rather than open-ended needs and aspirations. In developing countries, no less than in advanced economies, resources must be committed to the public sector and to private capital formation in such a way as to facilitate balanced growth, and every effort must be made to ensure that natural and human resources, savings and capital equipment are used efficiently and economically.

Taking all these influences together, it may be said that developing countries usually elevate economic development, or growth, to the position of prime importance among policy objectives. Stability and equity are usually given somewhat lower priority than in developed countries, while efficiency in resource allocation is seen as a necessary corollary of growth.

II. INFORMATION NEEDS

Differences in economic goals as between developed and developing countries may be expected to produce differences in information needs, with the latter countries placing relatively more emphasis on requirements for development planning and less on budgetary measures intended to facilitate fiscal stabilisation. Unfortunately, however, the budgeting and accounting systems of both groups of countries seem to have developed with little regard to the kind of information which is relevant for policy formulation, and it is necessary to commence this study by examining the way in which governments have traditionally interpreted their need for budgetary data.

1. *Accountability*

In countries with a British parliamentary tradition, the dominating requirement in government budgeting and accounting systems has been the necessity for the executive branch to account to parliament for the moneys which the latter body makes available through annual or standing appropriations. This may be designated the accountability requirement. The accounting information systems of governments have been designed in such a way as to facilitate parliamentary control (in a narrow financial rather than an efficiency sense) over government revenue-raising and spending activities. Appropriations machinery, classification systems, budgeting, accounting and audit procedures have all been directed primarily towards ensuring financial integrity on the part of governments.

2. *Macro-economic Policy and National Economic Planning*

If the budgetary accounts are to function effectively as an information system geared to the planning and decision-making responsibilities of executive government, however, they must do more than fulfil a stewardship role. In the first place, they must provide the government with the information needed to formulate national economic policy, and to regulate activity throughout all sectors of the economy, in the pursuit of the goals which have been specified above. This requirement we may designate the macro-economic or national planning purpose, and in order to meet it the budgeting and accounting system must record transactions in such a way as to emphasise their economic significance.

3. *Resource Management in the Public Sector*

But governments also have a responsibility to administer their own affairs efficiently, and this means that they need information which will guide them in determining priorities and making resource allocation decisions within the public sector. This requirement we may designate the resource management or efficiency purpose of accounting information systems, whereby it is necessary to relate managerial responsibility to performance, and costs of expenditure programmes and activities to accomplishments.

III. ACCOUNTING AND BUDGETING SYSTEMS

As we have seen, the accounting and budgeting systems which have evolved in response to these needs have been primarily concerned with accountability. Two distinguishing characteristics of most government accounting systems have reflected this emphasis on accountability and limited the usefulness of the budgetary accounts for other purposes. These are the fund system of accounting and the restriction of budgets and accounts to a cash basis.

1. *The Fund Structure of Budgetary Accounts*

Fund accounting is both a system of accounting and a scheme of classification; transactions are classified in accordance with funds established for financing purposes, each fund having the force of a separate accounting entity. In Australia, Commonwealth and state governments thus record transactions financed from taxation in Consolidated Revenue Funds, transactions financed from borrowing in Loan Funds, and other transactions, only some of which are handled in a trustee capacity, in Trust Funds. Superimposed on the fund basis of classification is a departmental division, whereby transactions within a fund are classified in terms of administrative responsibility. To meet the resource allocation requirement of government accounting, the classification process would need to be carried a stage further by means of functional or programme groupings, but such groupings have traditionally played a minor role.

Fund accounting is, however, more than a method of classification; it is a system of accounting which is sharply differentiated from the accounts of business enterprises and most other accounting entities. Not only is the executive branch of government as a whole allotted separate funds for which it has to account to parliament; within the executive branch of government each department is allotted funds which it must spend in accordance with the appropriations which parliament has approved. The budgeting and accounting system is thus essentially concerned with recording appropriations and expenditures made from those appropriations.

Fund accounting had its origin in the desire of parliaments, when democratic forms of government were first being evolved, to earmark revenues for particular purposes and prevent their misappropriation by the executive. These historical reasons for a fund division of budgetary accounts have long since disappeared in most developed countries, but legal and constitutional requirements have often perpetuated the use of earmarked funds and there has been a growing tendency for executive governments to use such funds as a means of circumventing parliamentary control. This development and the possibility of inter-fund transfers have destroyed the significance of separate funds even from the viewpoint of accountability.

To the extent that fund structures are rigid, they impose unnecessary constraints on governments in relation to their tasks of securing an efficient allocation of resources within the public sector and of regulating the level and pattern of activity in the national economy. If fund divisions are not rigid, on the other hand, there can be little point in maintaining them. The only types of special funds which appear justifiable under modern conditions, in either developing or developed countries, are funds of a fiduciary character relating to moneys not available for normal governmental purposes (such as Civil Service superannuation funds).

Since most expenditure transactions of governments involve the disbursement of funds provided through annual parliamentary appropriations, fund accounting may be defended as a system of budgeting and accounting (as opposed to a basis of classification), on the ground that it is better suited to the needs of general government than the so-called accrual or commercial accounting systems used by business enterprises. This is because the financial objectives of general government are different from those of business organisations. Whereas the former attempt to achieve their economic goals by using up resources, through collective consumption or capital formation, or by transferring claims over resources from one group to another, business enterprises seek to maintain a stock of resources as a basis for deriving periodic income.[1]

The funds entrusted to governments are periodically exhausted, and need to be replenished from fresh appropriations, while the funds made available to business enterprises are continuously and automatically replenished through the revenue-earning phase of the business cycle. It is therefore appropriate that the budgetary accounts should merely record the disbursement of funds entrusted to governments, whereas business enterprise accounts need to adopt accounting procedures intended to measure periodic income and funds employed.

2. *The Cash Basis of Accounting*

As a corollary to the fund system of accounting, the budgetary accounts are usually restricted to a record of cash transactions. This has several important consequences from the viewpoint of the information which they convey. The surplus or deficit which is recorded in financial statements is a cash surplus or deficit, and government budgets record cash appropriations rather than predetermined plans of performance. The accounts merely record cash receipts and outlays, not revenue receivable and costs incurred. The only assets which are recorded are cash balances and liquid investments which are held as substitutes for cash. There is no continuing accounting record of fixed capital assets or inventories, hence no depreciation charge or record of inventory consumption or accumulation. The fact that not all economic activities of governments are recorded is another factor limiting the usefulness of the accounting system for purposes other than accountability. Other problems result from the difficulty of integrating the cash accounts of general government with the accrual accounts which need to be maintained for government business undertakings. These shortcomings obstruct the task of achieving efficiency in the use of resources and at the same time make it difficult to assess the impact of the government's financial activities on the economy.

3. *Departmental Organisation*

A further corollary of fund accounting and the system of cash appropriations is the practice of classifying transactions in accordance with ministerial responsibility. Where trading departments are subject to ministerial control, the problem of accounting for their activities on a commercial basis is intensified, and even in administrative or spending departments the departmental division is likely to conflict with the classification of transactions according to programmes or activities. For purposes of controlling administrative efficiency and formulating economic policy, it is more important to be able to account for the cost of particular functions (such as the provision of social services, development of national resources, maintenance of law and order, etc.) and of particular programmes (such as an irrigation project or a road-construction programme) than it is to record parliamentary appropriations by departments.

IV. REQUIREMENTS OF A MULTI-PURPOSE SYSTEM OF BUDGETARY ACCOUNTS

A system of budgetary accounts must satisfy five requirements if it is to perform satisfactorily as an information system serving the ends of economic policy-making and resource management in the public sector, as well as fulfilling a stewardship role.

1. *Accountability*

The first requirement is the preservation of accountability as a means of legislative and executive financial control, irrespective of the modifications which may be made to the accounting system in order to serve other purposes.

2. *Functional and Programme Classification*

Government budgets need to be prepared and presented as predetermined plans of performance and not merely as cash appropriations. This implies the use of budgets classified along functional and programme lines in order to differentiate the purposes which it is intended to achieve. From the viewpoint of the executive government, such a presentation contributes to effective resource management within the public sector by making it possible to compare the costs and benefits which are expected to result from alternative courses of action, and hence to determine priorities. By fixing responsibility for performance, also, budgets classified along functional and programme lines facilitate control over the execution of policy.

3. *Trading Activities*

Departments engaged in trading activities need to be separated from administrative or spending departments and their accounts maintained on a commercial basis. The performance of trading departments, like that of public enterprises which are permitted to operate outside the day-to-day administrative control of general government, must be evaluated by reference to measures of operating results and financial position derived from commercial accounts. Only the net results of trading operations (which may be treated as cash transfers), together with net advances to the undertakings for capital purposes, need to be incorporated in the consolidated accounts of general government.

4. *Economic Classification*

If the budgetary accounts are to be used for purposes of policy formation, they need to record transactions in accordance with their economic significance. This means that a distinction must be made between resource-using (for purposes of either production or consumption) and transfer activities of government, between current and capital outlays, and between taxation and other sources of finance of government expenditures. A sector breakdown of transactions is also necessary.

5. *Comprehensiveness*

Finally, budgets and financial statements must be comprehensive in the sense that they must cover all the financial activities of the government. In addition to the net results of business undertakings (whether or not their accounts are incorporated in the budgetary accounts of general government), any activities recorded in trust or other special-purpose funds need to be brought into consolidated statements covering the whole of the government's financial activities.

V. ECONOMIC AND FUNCTIONAL CLASSIFICATION OF GOVERNMENT TRANSACTIONS

Two manuals prepared by the United Nations Department of Economic and Social Affairs have attempted to devise schemes of classification and budget organisation which will enable government accounting systems to meet these requirements. These are *A Manual for Economic and Functional Classification of Government Transactions*[2] and *A Manual for Programme and Performance Budgeting.*[3] The schemes of economic and functional classification which are developed in the first *Manual* are intended to operate alongside 'the usual budget classifications which serve primarily to ensure accountability'.[4] and are open to the objection that they fail to provide for the integration of different bases of classification within a single accounting information system. Although cross-classifications may be needed for some purposes, there is no reason why a classification scheme designed to meet accountability requirements should not be superimposed on classifications required for other purposes. What is needed, in effect, is a hierarchy of classifications forming part of a single accounting system. The primary basis might be an economic classification, the secondary basis a functional classification, the tertiary basis a programme classification and the quaternary basis an accountability classification. A decimal coding system would permit easy cross-classification, disaggregation and aggregation of data in accordance with the particular purposes for which information happens to be required. A computerised accounting system could easily handle such a scheme of classification and coding.

1. *Classification of Accounting Entities*

The *Manual for Economic and Functional Classification* made a useful distinction between what it called the government sector, financed from budget appropriations, and independent public bodies, which are established by governments but are free from the detailed accountability requirements affecting agencies within the government sector. So far as transactions are concerned, it defined economic classifications as a division 'by economic categories that are of significance for analysing the general effects of government transactions on the economy'.[5] Functional classification, on the other hand, was defined as division 'by purpose or by functional categories that are of significance for analysing the allocation of government resources'.[6]

(*a*) *Economic classification*. For purposes of economic classification, the *Manual* distinguished between the following groups of transactions: (1) transactions in goods and services; (2) payments of interest and income from property; (3) transfer payments and receipts; (4) transactions in financial claims; and (5) cash adjustments and net finance provided within the central government sector.[7]

For each accounting entity within the government sector (trading enterprises, ancillary agencies, financial enterprises and general government agencies) the *Manual* proposed that financial statements should take the form of four interlocking accounts, two main accounts and two subsidiary accounts, the latter having roughly the same relationship to items in the main accounts as subsidiary ledgers have to control accounts in the general ledger of a business enterprise accounting system. The first subsidiary account in the United Nations system records all current transactions in goods and services, the balancing item being a net surplus (or deficit) in the case of trading enterprises or 'net current expenditure on goods and services' in the case of general government agencies. The second subsidiary account records all capital expenditure on goods and services and shows net capital formation as a balance.

The first main account is also a current account, and records the balance from the current subsidiary account and all other current transactions – interest receipts and payments, dividends and current transfers. The second of the two main accounts is another capital account, and records the balance of the subsidiary capital account and all other capital transactions – capital transfers and transactions in financial claims.

Pro forma accounts for general government agencies are reproduced in Table 1. The main accounts for each accounting entity record transactions with other government agencies, but these are eliminated in a separate set of consolidated accounts for the whole of the government sector, which thus record only transactions between the government sector and the rest of the economy.

It will be seen that the subsidiary accounts are concerned essentially with transactions involving goods and services, while the main accounts are concerned mainly with transfers and financial transactions. The nomenclature used to describe the accounts is rather strange, implying as it does that transactions involving goods and services are somehow less significant in an economic sense than transfers or financial transactions. The treatment of balancing capital items in subsidiary and main accounts is also confusing. The subsidiary capital accounts record stock movements twice, once with a positive sign to record net drawings on stocks and one with a negative sign as part of the balancing item for net capital formation. Finally, the form of accounting presentation in the United Nations system makes it difficult to determine the economic significance of important aggregates and the relationship between them. No clear picture of the nature of government economic activities emerges from the accounts.

Table 1
United Nations Economic Classification Scheme for General Government Agencies

Subsidiary accounts for transactions in goods and services:

Subsidiary Current Account

Expenditure	*Receipts*
Compensation of employees	Sales of goods and services
Rental of fixed assets	Regulatory charges
Purchases of goods and services	Value of goods and services supplied free to other agencies
Net drawings on stocks	Value of own-account production of capital goods
Depreciation	*Balancing item:* Net current expenditure on goods and services
Inputed cost of fixed capital (equals interest)	

Subsidiary Capital Account

Expenditure	*Receipts*
Purchases of new capital goods	Depreciation
Purchases of existing capital goods	Sales of existing capital goods
	Net drawings on stocks
	Balancing items: Net fixed capital formation
	Net increase in stocks

Main accounts for all transactions:

Main Current Account

Expenditure	*Receipts*
Net current expenditure on goods and services	Imputed yield on fixed capital owned
Interest paid	Interest and dividends received
Subsidies	Taxes
Current transfers to other sectors	
Balancing items: Surplus on current account	

Main Capital Account

Expenditure	*Receipts*
Net fixed capital formation	Surplus on current account
Net increase in stocks	Capital transfers from other sectors
Capital transfers to other sectors	Repayment of loans and advances
Loans and advances to other sectors	Direct borrowing from other sectors
Net increase in receivables	Net sales of negotiable securities
Net increase in cash	Net increase in payables
Balancing item: Net finance provided to other central government agencies	

The accounting system which is proposed in the United Nations *Manual* is thus badly designed, from an accounting viewpoint, in relation to the principal purpose which it is desired to achieve. In order to distinguish between government transactions according to their economic significance, it is necessary to design the accounting system in such a way as to emphasise the main classes of economic activity which governments engage in, namely production, income redistribution, communal consumption, capital formation and financial capital transactions, and to record as balancing items the main aggregates which need to be measured, namely gross product (i.e. the contribution by the government to gross domestic product), disposable income (i.e. the amount available for communal consumption or saving), current expenditure on goods and services (i.e. communal consumption), government saving, capital formation and net borrowing or lending. Table 2 shows how this may be done by means of a simple set of accounts. This system has the further advantage that it may be easily combined with similar sets of accounts for other sectors to form an integrated national accounting system which comprehends, in effect, both national income accounts and flow-of-funds accounts.[8] Separate sets of accounts may be prepared for each level of general government and for public authority business undertakings, and the aggregate effect of government on the national economy may be recorded by means of consolidated production, income distribution, income disposal, capital formation and financial capital accounts for the whole of the public sector.

(*b*) *Functional classification.* For purposes of functional classification, the United Nations *Manual* distinguished between the following main groups of government transactions: (1) general services; (2) community services; (3) social services; and (4) economic services.

General services were said to 'require the use of compulsory powers and therefore have no private counterpart',[9] e.g. defence, law and order, and general administration. Community services were defined as services needed for community living, such as sanitation, water supply, fire protection and roads. Social services were defined to include education, health, welfare services and housing, while the economic services group was said to cover 'all types of activity which are carried out by the enterprise sector of the economy, or which are associated with the provision of services to those engaged in enterprise activity'.[10]

In adopting this scheme of classification, the United Nations *Manual* explained that it was not intended to differentiate between broad policy objectives of the kind discussed in the first section of this

Table 2
Economic Activity Accounts for a Government

Production Account

Purchases of intermediate goods and services from other sectors	$x	Value of government output/fees for administrative services	$x	
Gross product c/d	x	Communal consumption	x	
		Fixed capital investment	x	$x
	$x			$x

Income Distribution Account

Depreciation allowances	$x	Gross product b/d	$x
Net produce c/d	x		
Wages and salaries	$x	Net product b/d	$x
Transfer payments:		Transfer incomes:	
Interest	x	Direct taxes	x
Subsidies	x	Indirect taxes	x
Cash social service payments	x	Surplus of business undertakings	x
Disposal income c/d	x		
	$x		$x

Income Disposal Account

Government expenditure on goods and services (communal consumption)	x	Disposal income b/d	$x
Savings c/d	x		
	$x		$x

Capital Formation Account

Fixed capital investment	$x	Savings b/d	$x
Purchases of second-hand assets	x	Depreciation allowances	x
Stock accumulation	x	Sales of second-hand fixed assets	x
Capital transfers	x	Capital transfers	x
Net lending c/d	x	(Net borrowing c/d)	x
	$x		$x

Financial Capital Transactions Account

(Net borrowing b/d)	$x	Net lending b/d	$x
Increase in financial assets	x	Increases in financial liabilities	x
	$x		$x

paper, that it was not suitable for government trading enterprises (except in respect of their capital expenditures) and that it was relevant only in considering the short-run economic effects of the budget. This explanation seems to be unnecessarily restrictive. Although functional classification may have more obvious relevance in relation to questions of resource allocation within the public sector than to other policy objectives of economic stabilisation, equity and growth, the United Nations *Manual*'s own grouping indicates that a functional grouping has some significance with respect to the last two objectives. The exclusion of government trading enterprises and the concern with short-run to the exclusion of long-run purposes is also difficult to understand.

The United Nations functional classification depends to a considerable extent on a distinction between non-business and business activities; the *Manual* pointed out that services in the first three groups are provided mainly by general government agencies for consumers or for the community in general whereas economic services are provided by or for business enterprises.

But this classification suffers from a fundamental disadvantage in that it does not result in a mutually exclusive grouping of transactions. Certain economic activities of public authorities, e.g. housing construction, water supply and sewerage, are included in social or community services. Other economic activities, such as the provision of power or transport services, involve individual consumers or households as well as business enterprises, and cannot be logically differentiated from, say, water supply. The classification in different functional groups of services of similar functional significance, e.g. roads and other forms of transport, also leaves much to be desired. I have suggested elsewhere[11] that these weaknesses could be largely overcome by eliminating the community services group, by restricting the social services group to education, health and other welfare services which are not intended to be financially self-supporting, and by making an arbitrary decision to include roads in the economic services group. This would result in a functional classification along the lines of Table 3.

Although functional classification goes some way towards differentiating government financial activities in accordance with broad purposes to be achieved, it is of limited usefulness as a guide to decision-making by governments for the purpose of allocating resources within the public sector. The most promising development

Table 3
Suggested Functional Classification of Government Transactions

A. Security and Administrative Services:
1. Defence
2. Law and order
3. General administration

B. Economic Services:
4. Postal and telecommunication services
5. Transport
6. Power, fuel and light
7. Housing
8. Water supply and sewerage
9. Urban services n.e.i.
10. Rural services n.e.i.

C. Social Services:
11. Education
12. Health
13. Welfare and other

in this regard has been the emergence of a new approach to government budgeting and accounting, known variously as performance budgeting, programme budgeting and planning-programming-budgeting (or P.P.B.) systems.

2. *Programme Budgets and P.P.B. Systems*

Programme budgeting is essentially concerned with providing information for decision-making purposes. Although programme classification may generally be regarded as an extension of functional classification, with transactions classified by purpose, one basis of classification may cut across the other and programme budgeting is much more directly related to the decision-making process. The term 'performance budgeting' was used by the first Hoover Commission on Organisation of the Executive Branch of the U.S. Government in 1949, when it recommended that the U.S. federal budget should be based on 'functions, activities and projects', and that the budget should emphasise the relationship between costs and accomplishments.[12] The second Hoover Commission, reporting in 1955, recommended the adoption of the term 'programme budgeting' to indicate more clearly the objectives it sought to achieve, and more recently the term 'P.P.B. systems' has come to be used to describe both the data sources represented by the programme budgets and the decision processes themselves.

The P.P.B. approach identifies a number of distinct but interrelated phases in the budgeting, decision-making and accounting cycle. In the first place, it is necessary to identify policy objectives and programme[13] goals, the budgetary or other constraints which affect choice of goals and the alternative means which exist for achieving them.

Next, the budgeting and accounting system must be structured in such a way as to provide information which will facilitate decision-making in the pursuit of programme goals. This implies that information about the cost inputs associated with each programme must be related to the intended accomplishments or outputs of the programme. For this purpose, it is necessary not only to classify and record financial budget data along programme lines, but also to establish measures or indicators of programme outputs or accomplishments. This means not only that cost analysis must be undertaken, in order for example to derive cost–output functions, but also that the time span of the budget process must be extended, in order that decisions may be taken in a forward planning context.

The third phase of planning-programming-budgeting involves the establishment of decision criteria and the use of methods of analysis intended to choose the most effective means of achieving programme goals. This involves the use of cost–benefit analysis (if the problem is one of maximising net benefits, where both costs and accomplishments are variables), or cost-effectiveness analysis (if the problem is one of maximising accomplishments from given resource inputs, or minimising cost inputs in achieving a given programme goal).

The final element in P.P.B. systems is concerned with management control, and involves the evaluation of past performance. This implies periodic review of costs actually incurred and results achieved in each programme, relative to budgeted or planned levels of cost and performance. For this purpose, the accounting system must be organised along programme lines.

The classification of expenditures along programme lines may be illustrated by reference to the budget of a Department of Education. Classification along traditional lines would probably involve a distinction between operating or recurrent expenditure and capital expenditure, with further subdivision by inputs according to the nature of expenditures, along the lines illustrated in Table 4. A programme budget, on the other hand, would differentiate between different levels of education by regarding primary education as one programme, secondary education as another, and so on, as illustrated in Table 4. Subprogrammes, or programme elements as they are sometimes called, would then be represented by operating units such as individuals schools or universities, within which the traditional budget basis of classification, such as recurrent capital and nature of resource inputs, may still usefully be applied. In some programmes or programme elements, such as universities, a further subdivision may be made by reference to the kind of activities carried out, such as teaching, research and administration, but problems of joint cost allocation are likely to restrict opportunities for meaningful classification along these lines.

The programme budget would contain, in addition to the expenditure classification, information about educational outputs. Ideally, this should throw light on the extent to which broad educational objectives are being achieved, but in practice it may need to be restricted to such indicators as numbers of students receiving education.

For purposes of cost–benefit analysis designed to examine the case for a new educational programme, say a new kind of vocational training institution, changes in future community earnings expected to result from the educational activity might represent the output measure which would need to be compared with the costs of providing the training. For purposes of such analysis, due allowance would need to be made for imputed costs, such as earnings forgone by persons receiving the training, as well as costs directly incurred by the training institution, and time differences in respect of estimated costs and benefits would need to be allowed for by means of some kind of discounting operation.

In allocating resources between or within educational programmes or programme elements, the problem is one of cost-effectiveness. For this purpose, the use of student numbers as a measure of educational output may be modified and refined by means of cost analysis intended to throw light on the effects on costs of differences in educational structure (e.g. faculty structure within a university) or differences in the size of educational units (e.g. teaching departments carrying on similar educational tasks).[14]

It should now be clear that resource allocation decisions based on programme budgets and P.P.B. systems will be better informed than decisions based on traditional budget classifications, which tend to be related to last year's allocations with a crude budget increment

Table 4

Traditional and Programme Classification of an Education Budget

Traditional classification (one year)	*Programme classification* (by years)			
Operating expenditure	*Programmes*	*Programme elements*	*Activities*	*Input items*
Salaries				
Scholarships				
Materials and supplies	*Operating expenditures*			
Cleaning				
Electricity	Primary education	Schools	Teaching	Salaries, etc.
Maintenance of buildings			Administration	
Maintenance of grounds	Secondary education	Schools	Teaching	Salaries, etc.
			Administration	
Travel	Tertiary education	Universities	Teaching departments	Salaries, etc.
Capital expenditure		Teacher training institutions		
New buildings			Research departments	
Furniture		Other tertiary institutions		
Equipment			Administration	
	Adult education	Organisational units	Teaching	Salaries, etc.
			Administration	
	Library services	Libraries	Administration	Salaries, etc.
	Education research	Organisational units	Research	Salaries, etc.
	Central administration	Organisational units	Administration	Salaries, etc.
	Capital expenditure			
	Primary education, etc.	Building projects	–	–

criterion (e.g. a 5 per cent increase to cover rising costs) as the only (or principal) guide to this year's allocation.[15]

VI. RECENT BUDGETARY CHANGES IN DEVELOPED COUNTRIES

During recent years, the governments of developed countries have been making substantial changes to their budgeting and accounting systems in order to adapt them to the information needs of the governments. At first there was a tendency to produce the budget for two or three different purposes of accountability, macro-economic policy and resource allocation within the public sector.

In the U.S.A., for example, three separate budgets were being prepared by the Federal Government in the years before 1968, namely:

(*a*) An administrative Budget (which was the budget used for for appropriations and accountability purposes);

(*b*) a Consolidated Cash Budget (which was intended to be comprehensive by including trust funds, deposit funds and government enterprises in such a way as to show cash flows between the Federal Government and other sectors); and

(*c*) a National Income Accounts Budget (which was intended to provide an economic classification which would throw light on the economic impact of the Government's activities).

In Australia, the traditional Commonwealth (Federal) Budget, based on a fund division and used as a basis for appropriations and accountability, came to be supplemented during the 1950s and 1960s by a so-called Consolidated Cash Budget (which was not fully consolidated, in that it recorded Trust and Loan Fund transactions in total only, and did not eliminate inter-fund transactions) and a Budget in National Accounting Form.

In the U.K., the form of the traditional appropriations budget was also revised during the 1960s in order to provide a comprehensive statement of Exchequer receipts and payments, including loans to nationalised industries, local authorities and other public bodies, and a separate statement provided a National Accounts Classification of Central Government Transactions. Following the Report of the Plowden Committee on the Control of Public Expenditure,[16] annual surveys of public-sector expenditures were also prepared, which analysed expenditures for the following five years by function and by economic categories.

More recently, there has been a tendency to integrate or reconcile the different budget presentations in the three countries. This movement has proceeded furthest in the U.S.A., where it was argued that different budgets confuse understanding and impede decision-making.[17] Following a recommendation from a Presidential Commission on Budget Concepts in 1967, the Federal Government adopted a unified and comprehensive budget intended to 'enhance public and congressional understanding of the budget and [to] increase its usefulness for purposes of decision-making, public policy determination, and financial planning'.[18] The Commission endorsed the use of the P.P.B. approach to budget preparation and review,[19] the adoption of an accrual basis of accounting and the provision of estimates extending further into the future. The unified budget, which is illustrated in Table 5, is comprehensive in the sense that it includes all programmes of the Federal Government and its agencies. Only net results of government business enterprises are brought into the unified budget, but additional information about gross enterprise transactions is recorded in a supplementary statement.

The first section of the budget lists appropriations, differentiating between new appropriations requiring congressional approval and appropriations available as a result of past action. The second section is intended to measure the economic impact of the budget, by recording receipts and non-loan expenditures (leading to expenditure account surplus or deficit) followed by net lending (leading to an overall budget surplus or deficit). The third section shows how the overall budget deficit is financed.

In Australia, the process of budgetary reform has been concerned principally with the refinement of the Consolidated Cash Budget, with the intention of providing a comprehensive measure of the impact of government activities on the economy (with special reference to fiscal stabilisation) while permitting easy reconciliation with the Budget in National Accounting Form. In effect, accountability requirements continue to be met as part of the process of obtaining parliamentary approval for the Estimates within the framework of the Consolidated Cash Budget, but there has so far been no systematic attempt to reshape the budget in a programme format. (Within the executive branch, however, P.P.B. feasibility studies are being under-

Table 5
Revised U.S. Budget

	Actual 1966	Estimate 1967	Estimate 1968
I. Appropriations (classified by functions):			
Proposed for action by Congress			
Not requiring action by Congress			
Total appropriations			
II. Receipts, expenditures, and lending (receipt–expenditure account):			
Receipts	x		
Expenditures (excl. net lending)	y		
Expenditures account surplus (deficit)	(a)		
Plus: Loan account			
Loan disbursement			
Loan repayments			
Net lending	b		
Equals: Total budget:			
Receipts	x		
Expenditures and net lending	$y + b$		
Budget surplus (deficit)	$(a + b)$		
III. Means of financing:			
Borrowing from public			
Reduction of cash balances			
Total budget financing	$a + b$		
IV. Outstanding federal securities and loan, end of year			

Source: *Report of the President's Commission on Budget Concepts* (Washington: U.S. Government Printing Office, 1967) p. 85.

taken by some departments. The structure of the revised Australian Consolidated Cash Budget is illustrated in Table 6. It will be seen that it has a great deal in common with the new U.S. unified summary budget illustrated in Table 5. As with earlier forms of the Consolidated Cash Budget, however, it is not fully consolidated in so far as some inter-fund transactions (such as certain national debt sinking fund receipts) are not eliminated and net Trust Fund transactions only are recorded. The significance attached to short-term fiscal stabilisation policy is illustrated by the way in which the budget deficit is measured and by the classification of sources of

Table 6

Structure of Revised Australian Consolidated Cash Budget

	Actual 1968–9	*Estimate 1969–70*
Receipts		
Taxation receipts		
Net receipts of government enterprises		
Other receipts		
National debt sinking fund receipts		
Net increase in Trust Fund balances	——	——
Total receipts	——	——
Expenditure		
Expenditures (recurrent and capital) mainly by administrative departments		
Advances to enterprises	——	——
Total expenditures	——	——
Overall budget deficit	——	——
*Financing of deficit**		
Overseas borrowing		
Borrowing in Australia:		
Net loan proceeds		
Net issues of Treasury notes		
Borrowing from Reserve Bank		
Other (including change in cash balances)	——	——
Total finance	——	——

* Detailed estimates are not provided for this section for the budget year 1969–70.
Source: Commonwealth Treasurer's Budget Speech, 1969–70.

deficit finance. The time scale of the 1969–70 budget was limited to the current financial year, but an extension of the budget period was recently foreshadowed by the Commonwealth Treasurer.

The proposed new form of public expenditure estimates in the U.K.,[20] although presented in a separate White Paper rather than as part of the budget documents, is likely to have far-reaching significance in reshaping the U.K. budget as a tool to be used in formulating economic policy and managing public expenditure programmes. Five changes are proposed with a view to bringing out 'the main implications for resources of public expenditure plans over the period ahead'.[21] These are:

(*a*) The inclusion of rolling estimates of expenditure, covering the immediate past year, the current and the two following years for which the Government has already taken decisions (with

Table 7

United Kingdom Public-Sector Receipts and Expenditure: New Presentation

Receipts	*Survey year −1*	*Survey year 1*	*Survey year 2*	*Survey year 3*	*Expenditure*	*Survey year −1*	*Survey year 1*	*Survey year 2*	*Survey year 3*
A. Resources									
Charges for services	—	—	—	—	Purchases of resources (current and capital)	—	—	—	—
					Net expenditure	—	—	—	—
B. Transfers, taxation, etc.									
Taxes					Grants and subsidies				
Contributions					Debt interest				
Other receipts	—	—	—	—		—	—	—	—
Total	—	—	—	—		—	—	—	—
Net transfers	—	—	—	—					
C. Assets									
Taxes on capital and miscellaneous borrowing					Net purchase of land existing, buildings and financial				
Balance of asset transactions	—	—	—	—	assets	—	—	—	—
D. Total receipts	—	—	—	—	Total expenditure	—	—	—	—
E. Total balance	—	—	—	—		—	—	—	—
F. Balance of Sections A and B	—	—	—	—		—	—	—	—

Source: *Public Expenditure: A New Presentation* Cmnd 4017 (London: H.M.S.O., 1969) p. 13.

the third of these years as the main focus year in which decisions are reviewed), and two further years representing merely projections of present policies.

(*b*) The inclusion of the capital expenditure of nationalised industries.

(*c*) Similar forward projections of receipts from taxation, National Insurance contributions, charges, trading surpluses of nationalised industries and public enterprises, and other receipts accruing to the public sector.

(*d*) Classification of transactions according to whether they involve direct use of resources, transfers or transactions involving assets (including financial capital transactions).

(*e*) Adjustment for the effect on the estimates of relative price changes.

Table 7 illustrates the main summary table under the new presentation. Although the accounting design of the statement lacks elegance, it will be seen that balancing items are derived for each section, for all public-sector transactions in Section E, and for resource-using and transfer transactions together in Section F. It will be observed, however, that none of these balancing items corresponds to the budget balances or financing requirements of the revised U.S. or Australian budgets. This is because Section C includes taxes on capital, transactions in existing assets and lending transactions as well as borrowing.

Supporting tables in the new U.K. presentation provide an analysis of expenditure by function, a cross-classification by function and type of transaction, a cross-classification by function and spending authority, an analysis by economic category (all for survey years — 1 to 3), and a projection of expenditures by function for survey years 4 and 5.[22]

VII. A SUGGESTED BUDGET STRUCTURE FOR DEVELOPING COUNTRIES

As we have seen, the complex budget structures of developed countries reflect different traditions and different information needs from those of developing countries. Because of their concern with economic growth as a major policy objective, the budgets of developing countries must be cast in a development planning mould, which suggests the need for a classification of transactions by economic categories as well as by functions and programmes. Scarcity of resources in relation to likely demands on the government's budget makes it essential that budgeting and accounting systems reflect the P.P.B. approach in order to help governments determine priorities effectively and make the best use of resources. The preoccupation which advanced countries have with short-term economic stabilisation, and which results in a budget structure that emphasises measures of budget disequilibrium, is likely to be overshadowed in developing countries by the problem of finding ways and means of financing planned expenditures, or of balancing expenditures against sources of finance available.

Table 8

Proposed Budget Presentation for Central Government of Developing Country

Expenditure	*Receipts*
Current Account	
Expenditure by administrative departments on current goods and services (classified by functions and programmes)	Taxation
	Revenue from property
	Surpluses of business undertakings
Transfers:	Interest
Interest on public debt	Grants from overseas agencies
Subsidies	
Cash social service benefits	
Grants to local governments	
Surplus on current account	
Capital Account	
Expenditure by administrative departments on capital formation	Surplus on current account
	Repayment of advances
Advances to business undertakings	Overall budget deficit
Advances to other sectors	
Financing Account	
Overall budget deficit	Borrowing from public
Debt redemption	Borrowing from overseas
	Borrowing from banking system
	Reduction in cash balances

All these considerations together suggest the need for a simple budget structure along the lines of Table 8, with three accounts recording respectively recurrent receipts and expenditure (leading to a current account surplus or deficit), capital transactions other than borrowing (leading to an overall deficit) and a financing account (which shows how the overall deficit is financed by borrowing from other sectors). Within the current and capital accounts, transactions should be grouped by economic categories, functions and programmes, and for purposes of national planning a sector breakdown will be necessary. The budget must be comprehensive, in the sense that net surpluses (or deficits) of public enterprise trading activities should be incorporated in the current account, with advances to such enterprises being recorded separately in the capital account. It must be forward-looking, with rolling estimates for, say, a five-year period meshed into the development plan for the whole economy. In short, it must serve as a major instrument in the formulation of economic policy and the management of resources within the public sector, while continuing to provide accountability control within both the legislative and executive branches of government.

REFERENCES

1. Cf. J. R. Hicks, *The Problems of Budgetary Reform* (Oxford U.P., 1948) p. 16.

2. New York: United Nations, 1958.

3. New York: United Nations, 1965.

4. Op. cit., p. iii.

5. Op. cit., p. iii.

6. Ibid.

7. Ibid., chap. iv.

8. Cf. Russell Mathews, *Accounting for Economists* (Melbourne: Cheshire, 1962) p. 511.

9. Op. cit., p. 137.

10. Ibid., p. 138.

11. Russell Mathews, *Public Investment in Australia* (Melbourne: Cheshire, 1967) p. 8.

12. Commission on Organisation of the Executive Branch of the Government, *Budgeting and Accounting* (Washington, 1949) p. 8.

13. A suitable definition of a programme for this purpose is given in the United Nations *Manual for Programme and Performance Budgeting*, p. 102: 'A division of work performed by an agency which identifies that portion of work that produces an end product or service representative of the purposes for which the agency was established.'

14. See Russell Mathews, 'Resource Allocation in Universities', *Australian University* (Dec 1969), for an illustration of the derivation of cost functions in a university.

15. See Subcommittee on Economy in Government of the Joint Economic Committee, U.S. Congress, *The Planning-Programming-Budgeting System: Progress and Potentials* (Washington: U.S. Government Printing Office, 1967), statement by Otto A. Davis, p. 211, for a discussion of the influence of traditional methods of budgeting on U.S. federal budget allocations. See also O. A. Davis, M. A. H. Dempster and A. Wildavsky, 'A Theory of the Budgetary Process', *American Political Science Review* (Sep 1966).

16. Cmnd 1432 (London: H.M.S.O., 1959).

17. *Report of the President's Commission on Budget Concepts* (Washington: U.S. Government Printing Office, 1967) p. 2.

18. Ibid., p. vii.

19. A system of programme budgeting had been adopted by the Department of Defence in 1961 and was being extended to other departments and agencies following a decision to this effect by President Johnson in 1965.

20. *Public Expenditure: A New Presentation*, Cmnd 4017 (London: H.M.S.O., 1969). See also the first of the new White Papers: *Public Expenditure, 1968–69 to 1973–74*, Cmnd 4234 (London: H.M.S.O., 1969).

21. Ibid., p. 7.

22. In *Public Expenditure, 1968–69 to 1973–74*, functional classification has given way to programme classification, with twenty main programmes being distinguished in five groups as follows: defence and external relations, commerce and industry, environmental services, social services and other services.

11

Problems of Budgetary Policy in Socialist Planned Economies

MARIAN WERALSKI

I. THE GENERAL CHARACTER OF THE STATE BUDGET IN EASTERN EUROPEAN COUNTRIES

IN Eastern European countries the basic means of production have been socialised, and this has been accompanied in recent years by a considerable widening of the range of state-controlled activities, especially in the economic, social and cultural domains. At the very basis of this phenomenon is the fact that collective savings have taken the place of individual savings as a means of financing investment; also, in the field of consumption, there has been a gradual replacement of individual consumption by consumption on a collective basis.[1]

However, this should not be taken to mean that individual savings have disappeared entirely in socialist countries. On the contrary, the sustained pace of economic development and rising living standards which have been a characteristic feature of these countries over the past few years have been matched by considerable increases in savings, although their destination has undergone a fundamental change. On account of the socialisation of the basic means of production and limitations placed on the possibilities of developing capitalistic forms of productive activity, individual savings aimed at creating or increasing capital have also been limited. Private savings, whose main purpose is the development of economic activities on private account, appear in socialist countries primarily in agriculture and handicrafts, but their scope in the remaining sectors of the national economy is relatively limited. As such, individual savings take the form primarily of monetary reserves destined for consumption purposes, especially for the purchase of durable consumer goods, or to meet expenditures of an unexpected nature.[2] Savings for capital formation, as distinct from savings to meet the requirements of personal consumption expenditure, take the form of diverse pecuniary supplies collected by the state in its budget and to some extent the extra-budgetary financial resources of socialist banks and other enterprises.

In socialist countries the state has taken over the main responsibility and initiative for investment expenditure. Such investment expenditure is financed from two sources, the lion's share coming from the above-mentioned monetary reserves collected by the state, with a relatively small proportion coming from the savings of the population for consumption purposes.[3] In the latter respect some assistance is also derived from the banking sector, which in socialist countries is predominantly state-owned and controlled, although a few financial intermediaries are still organised along co-operative lines. These factors help to explain why the financing of investment by means of the private savings media forms a relatively insignificant part of total investment finance in socialist countries.

Similarly, in the field of consumption, the socialist state has pre-empted the responsibility of satisfying a large proportion of the population's needs, either on the principle of non-repayability, or alternatively against very small payments which are normally well below the costs of the goods or services in question. This is a true reflection of how citizens' participation in the national income of socialist countries is determined. Wages and salaries are based on the socialist principle 'to each according to his labour', yet the satisfaction of certain needs, particularly in the health and education fields, is recognised as essential on account of their social content and is therefore made independent of the individual's ability to pay. The principle governing the satisfaction of such needs in socialist countries derives from their collective character.[4]

This function of satisfying collective social needs is entrusted to state organs which in the performance of this function are not guided by the principle 'to each according to his labour', but rather on the basis of a principle which reflects everybody's needs. It is not he who has the necessary pecuniary means who is entitled to medical attention and medicines but rather he who most needs such attention and medicines. Similarly, the doors to educational attainment are open to all irrespective of financial means. Educational facilities are available to all citizens as a matter of right, and the higher echelons are open to all who show ability, industry and similar personal qualities. In any event, no one is barred from participation because of accidents of birth, family ties, or similar fortuitous circumstances. The above remarks are true for almost all other socio-cultural activities. The philosophical and ideological bases for the provision of social overhead capital are given practical significance in the budgetary process by which the socialist state provides these public needs either free of charge, or against a very small payment which in every instance is well below the prime cost of the service provided. This phenomenon of widespread substitution of private individual capital accumulation and the satisfaction of social needs from private individual financial resources by a process in which the state has become the prime accumulator of capital and bears the prime responsibility for satisfying these needs on a collective basis is the major factor responsible for the significant widening of the scope of the state budget in socialist countries. As a result, the share of the state budget in the redistribution of national income amounts to about 50 per cent.[5]

This large and increasing share of the state budget in national income redistribution reflects not only the widening of the scope of state administrative activities partly through changes in its financial structure, but is also related to the concentration and centralisation of economic activity. A good example of this is provided by the composition of the state budget, which includes the social insurance budget, an item which bears a close relationship to the financial ramifications governing state enterprises. At the more general level, this centralisation of financial management has proved indispensable for the procurement and establishment of a uniform financial policy and its linkages with national economic policy as set out in the assumptions of the national economic plan. The centralisation of financial and economic management does not imply that the process is undemocratic, since state financial policy is debated and decided upon every year,[6] and a definite role is assigned to local initiative and decision-making in formulating the framework for local activities.[7] In this respect, a co-ordination of state and local budgets is achieved.

The developments mentioned above have been responsible for a fundamental transformation in the structure of budget revenues and expenditures. Within recent years up to 90 per cent of budget revenues have accrued from socialised enterprises, with only a very small part indeed coming from individual sources.[8] The expenditure account has tended to follow the following approximate pattern. More than 50 per cent of the total consists of expenditure for national developmental purposes. Expenditure for social and cultural purposes accounts for more than 25 per cent of the total. The remainder has gone towards financing the miscellaneous administrative activities of the state and national defence, but these two latter categories combined account for less than 25 per cent of total budgetary expenditure.[9]

II. PURPOSES AND MEANS OF BUDGET POLICY

In socialist countries the structure of financial management is highly stratified, with the state budget playing the key role at the very top of the structure.[10] Within this framework, budgetary policy tends to play a dual role. On the one hand it is an important instrument for developing, protecting or changing socio-economic relations by means of consolidating or transforming political and constitutional institutions and their interrelationships. This function is of a very general nature, and is usually combined with the budget's more particularistic function as an instrument for ensuring protection and development of particular spheres of economic activity and for the realisation of specific changes in the national economy.[11] This generalist/particularist distinction inherent in the function of the socialist budget cuts across other distinctions based on the requisite socio-economic changes which the budget is intended to bring about. In this latter respect, budgetary policy reaches out into both the economic and non-economic spheres, the local and national levels, and is also an instrument for effecting periodic as well as permanent adjustments in the socio-economic structure. It is in such a way that the fundamental economic and socio-constitutional purposes of socialist budgetary policy become underlined.

The fundamental economic role of the budget under socialism lies in its assurance of general market equilibrium from the financial point of view in both the consumption goods and production goods sectors, and the simultaneous realisation of national income redistribution in accordance with the essential proportions established in the national economic plan, i.e. proportions receivable by the population at large and the financial system, and between accumulated income and income for consumption purposes. It is by such means that budgetary policy effectuates the overall national objectives of high economic growth rates, rising living standards and an equitable distribution of national income.[12]

The fundamental socio-constitutional objectives of budgetary policy under socialism should also be emphasised. This is achieved through the consolidation of democracy, the elimination of narrow outlook based on class and business interests, the stimulation of political activity, and the education of society in the spirit of socialism.

The methods used to effectuate budgetary policy and its implementation are closely connected with its objectives. The realisation of the economic objective is inherent in the process by which a suitable and optimal structure is given to the budget content, whereas the suitable formation of budget procedure and the definite system underlying budget administration provide for the realisation of the socio-constitutional objectives. In the economic sphere, the state authorities, who have the main responsibility for budgetary policy, have at their disposal four kinds of tools geared at achieving the first-order objectives of growth, national income redistribution and market equilibrium. These relate to the regulation of (*a*) the overall levels of budget revenue and expenditure, (*b*) the proportional distribution of budget revenues, (*c*) the proportional distribution of budget expenditure, and (*d*) the ratio of budget revenue to budget expenditure. All these measures can and should be used simultaneously, and their mutual co-ordination is absolutely necessary. The realisation of the socio-constitutional objectives is determined by certain formal and organisational considerations inherent in the manner in which budget procedure is devised, the way the budget is organised, and the system of classification.

III. METHODS AND LEGAL FORMS OF BUDGETARY POLICY

Budgetary policy methods are directly connected with the functions of the state budget, with the choice of a particular method depending on whether a specific objective will be consciously pursued. The budget's function emerges within such a perspective. It should be emphasised, however, that the existence of specific budget functions does not preclude the state authorities' directing that the budget be used in other ways, or its mere use as an instrument of budgetary policy. In this connection it is possible to discuss the functions of the budget as one would do in the case of other institutions (e.g. money), on an *a priori* basis and apart from its relationship to the ramifications of any particular budgetary or financial policy.[13] However, we cannot meaningfully discuss the methods of budgetary policy outside of a contextual framework which clearly shows how the budget and its functions are consciously organised and managed by the state in pursuance of definite objectives. Fiscal and financial commentators usually assign three important functions to the state budget, i.e. redistribution, stimulation and control. When these are applied to the methods used for the realisation of budgetary policy in the economic sphere, and in the light of experience, the interesting question arises as to which of the economic functions are the methods for realisation consciously used.

In the historical process of development, various methods of bugetary policy successively became predominant. Under capitalism the budget has been progressively used as a mechanism for government intervention. In the contemporary economic policy of capitalist countries the conscious use of financial stimulative action is so widespread that financial and budgetary policy have come to be identified with the authorities' conscious acting upon the economic process, and as a result the impression is usually conveyed that the other functions are neglected on purpose.[14] By contrast, the conscious utilisation of the stimulative function is not so important in socialist budgetary policy, in which the redistributive and control functions are paramount. The structure of socio-economic relations in socialist countries underlines the necessity for the relatively insignificant role of the state budget as a means of stimulating economic activity, and as a means of acting upon the economic process. The nationalisation of the core producers' goods sectors has provided the state authorities with the requisite facilities for direct planning of the direction of economic development and its relative proportions for many years ahead. As a result, the socialist budget has become, first and foremost, a means of national income redistribution.[15]

Different methods predominate in the various stages of socialist budgetary policy. At the stage of budget compilation, the authorities are primarily concerned with securing the general relationships that ought to exist between the budget, other financial plans, and the national economic plan.[16] The establishment of co-ordinating links between these three is of primary significance at this stage. The co-ordinating exercise tends on an *ex ante* basis to bring to light any lack of general financial equilibrium in the various plans, e.g. imbalances between the national economic plan targets and financial plans, which may call for corrections in either plan or in both.[17] This is the central function of the state budget at this stage of budgetary policy.

At the implementation stage, co-ordination between the state budget, the financial plan and the national economic plan is achieved by eliminating imbalances arising in the national economy, by means of the skilful regulation of budget revenue and expenditure. At this stage, the direct and conscious redistribution of national income becomes the main objective of socialist budgetary policy. Such a redistributive mechanism operates both on an *in tractu* basis in preventing the appearance of disproportionalities, and on an *ex post* basis in removing them once they have arisen.[18] The efficacy of this kind of budgetary policy is safeguarded by the creation and utilisation of budgetary reserves, which are provided for in the budget while it is being compiled.[19]

The methods used in the realisation of the socio-constitutional objectives of budgetary policy are closely intertwined with the conscious formulation of the budget's political functions. These political functions emerged during the period when the budget, as a legal institution, was formulated by a few state organs and to some extent by the people. However, the participation of the population and state organs in budget administration has now become firmly entrenched in the budgetary policy framework, especially in those cases relating to the realisation of socio-economic objectives.

The utilisation of both methods previously mentioned has proved indispensable to the formulation and implementation of socialist budgetary policy, which is aimed at consolidating people's sovereignty. The political process consciously sets the stage for the formulation of a suitable framework, establishes the budget's scope, the form of classification as well as budgetary procedure, both by means of direct consultation between the population and the budget administration, and indirectly via the participation of the budgetary authorities of various representative collegiate organs.[20] The interesting point about budgetary policy lies not only in the determination of its objectives and the means and the methods for their realisation, but also in the choice of legal forms of activity. Depending on the concrete situation, legal pressure or inducement may be brought to bear on the decision-making process in the form of general or particular decisions. As such, skilful utilisation of various forms of legal activity in specific cases is an indispensable factor in determining the efficiency of socialist budgetary policy.

IV. SOME POSTULATES CONCERNING STATE BUDGETARY REFORM

An analysis of the objectives, means and methods of socialist budgetary policy indicates that the outstanding legal resolutions in the sphere of budget administration are unsatisfactory. The budget is neither sufficiently elastic nor an efficient instrument for the realisation of economic objectives because of excessive rigidity and too detailed classification. As an instrument for the realisation of constitutional objectives it is also a failure because of the wide spread of state financial activity, with several essential elements remaining outside its scope and sphere of influence.

The idea of a very detailed budget classification was probably justified at the time when state financial activity was very restricted. However, under the present circumstances with a very large spread in the financial activities of the socialist state, there are no sound political or social reasons for following the traditional path of a very detailed classification. Under the present circumstances in which the state is deeply involved in the distribution of the national product, and one in which it utilises its financial machinery to determine the relative proportions of this distribution and consequently the overall direction of economic and social development, parliament in voting on the very detailed budget is likely to overlook the more important general elements of economic and social policy while concentrating on inessential details. From the social and political points of view, parliament while voting on the budget is in a position to determine the general directions of economic and social policy for the coming year.[21] But the realisation of this requires, first, the inclusion in the budget of the totality of government financial activity, and then applying to such a budget the requisite revenue and expenditure classification as will enable the determination of the general character of intended policy.

In the process of voting on the state budget, the intention and expectation is that parliament should seal the future direction of social and economic policy, and that this should serve as the major instrument for the realisation of both the economic and socio-constitutional objectives of the budget. However, once parliament has determined the basic policy directions, the government, on account of its wide discretionary powers springing from budget elasticity, should then be assigned the task of translating these policy objectives into a real and practical developmental framework. The manner in which the government sets about realising and giving practical significance to the policy objectives should be overviewed by and be subject to the control of parliament, which after receiving adequate progress reports should satisfy itself that the government is actively and satisfactorily pursuing its delegated economic and social tasks.

All state financial activity which is at present outside the budget should now be included on a *net* basis. This carries the implication that financial surpluses which emanate from definite kinds of state financial activity, but which are realised from extra-budgetary sources, should be included into the budget. Financial deficits of a similar nature should be met from budgetary sources as well. Such procedures should be related to the tasks assigned on the basis of definite kinds of ancillary plans of financial activity. These plans should be voted on by parliament simultaneously as it votes on the state budget, and should take the form of budget annexes, but nevertheless covered by the same legal sanctions governing the tasks of government in specific spheres of activity.

Thus the very detailed budget, including its revenue and expenditure accounts, should pass on to the government as the major organ for implementation, and as the organ through which the financial policy determined by parliament will be realised. In this regard, the socialist budget presupposes two kinds of legal activities or transactions. First, the budget as a bill voted by parliament should encompass the entire state financial activity in a very general economic and functional classification. It should also specify the government's obligations concerning the execution of planned financial policy. Second, and in the implementation of such a policy, the government should operate through its different departments, whose financial tasks should be clearly spelt out in a set of detailed classifications following along the lines of the traditional budget, but fixed by the government. Such a double version of the state budget would go a long way towards meeting the requirements and needs of an efficient and effective socialist budgetary policy.

REFERENCES

1. M. Weralski, *Socjalistyczne Instytucje Budzetowe* [*The Institution of the Budget under Socialism*] (Warsaw, 1966).

2. E. Wieczorek, *Oszczednosci Ludnosci w Gospodarce Socjalistycznej* [*The Savings of the Population in the Socialist Economy*] (Warsaw, 1965).

3. K. Czyzniewski, *Efektywnosc Form Finansowania Reprodukcji Srodkow Trwalych* [*Efficiency of Different Means of Investment Financing*] (Warsaw, 1966).

4. K. Szwemberg, *Spoleczny Fundusz Spozycia w Polsce* [*Collective Consumption in Poland*] (Warsaw, 1965).

5. M. Weralski, 'Na Marginesie Prawa Wagnera' ['In Connection with Wagner's Law'] (mimeo).

6. J. Harasimowicz, *Zagadnienia Uchwalania Budzetu Socjalistycznego* [*Problems of Voting the Budget in Socialist Countries*] (Warsaw, 1965).

7. A. Komar, *Finanse rad Narodowych* [*Local Finance*] (Warsaw, 1970).

8. M. Weralski, 'Les Problèmes de la fiscalité dans les états socialistes', *Revue de Science Financière*, no. 4 (Paris, 1969).

9. L. Kurowski, *Les Finances dans les états socialistes* (Paris, 1962).

10. Z. Fedorowicz, *Finanse w Gospodarce Socjalistycznej* [*Finance in the Socialist Economy*] (Warsaw, 1968).

11. M. Weralski, 'El Presupuesto en Polonia', *Revista de Derecho Finanziero y de Hacienda Publica*, no. 60 (Madrid, 1965).

12. M. Weralski, *Rola Budzetu w Planowaniu Gospodarczym*, [*The Role of the Budget in Economic Planning*] (Warsaw, 1963).

13. *Istota i Funkcje Finansow Socjalistycznych: Zagadnienia Dyskusyjne* [*Discussion of the Nature and Functions of Socialist Finance*] (Warsaw, 1965).

14. Z. Pirozynski, 'Budzet Panstwa jako Narzedzie Polityki Gospodarczej' [The State Budget as an Instrument of Economic Policy], *Ruch Prawniczy, Ekonomiczny i Socjologiczny*, no. 3 (Poznan, 1962).

15. See the figures given by M. Weralski, *Les Bases économiques et sociales des recettes budgétaires* (*Comparison and Harmonisation of Public Revenue Systems*, York, 1966).

16. L. Kurowski, 'Planowanie Budzetowe w Ramach Socjalistycznego Planowania Gospodaroczego' ['Budget Planning within the Framework of Socialist Economic Planning'], *Panstwo i Prawo*, no. 8/9 (1961).

17. M. Weralski, 'Niektore Prawno-Finansowe Aspekty Powiazan Budzetu i Narodowego Planu Gospodarczego Zwiazane z Emisja Pieniadza' ['Some Legal and Financial Aspects of the Connection between the Budget and the National Economic Plan, in Relation to the Issue of Money'], *Panstwo i Prawo*, no. 3 (1959).

18. Weralski, *Rola Budzetu*.

19. M. Kucharski, *Pieniadz, Dochod, Proporcje Wzrostu* [*Money, Income and Growth Proportions*] (Warsaw, 1964).

20. A. Gwizdz, 'Z Zagadnien Procedury Ustawodawczej: O Uchwalaniu prezez Sejm Ustawy Budzetowej' ['Some Problems of Legislative Procedure: On Voting on the Budget Bill by the Sejm'], *Panstwo i Prawo*, no. 7 (1958).

21. Z. Rajewski, 'Powiazanie Narodowego Planu Gospodarozego z systemem Finansowym Panstwa' ['The Links between the Financial System and the National Economic Plan'], *Gospodarka Planowa*, no. 7 (1958); Weralski, *Rola Budzetu*; S. Bolland, 'Ekonomiczne i Ustrojowe Aspekty Reformy Prawa Budzetowego' ['Some Economic and Political Problems of Budget Law'], *Ruch Prawniczy, Ekonomiczny i Socjologiczny*, no. 3 (Posnan, 1963).

Part Five
ECONOMIC POLICY AND PLANNING AT THE CENTRAL AND LOCAL LEVELS

12

Economic Planning, the Green Revolution and the 'Food Drive' in Ceylon

GAMANI COREA

DURING the second half of the 1960s Ceylon succeeded in raising food production very rapidly. Rice was in the main item. The success achieved in rice production is depicted in Table 1 below.

Table 1
Rice Production, 1961–70

	1961	*1962*	*1963*	*1964*	*1965*	*1966*	*1967*	*1968*	*1969*	*1970*
Output in million bushels of paddy	43	48	49	51	36	46	55	66	66	77
Index (1964 = 100)	84	94	96	100	71	92	108	129	129	151

The 51 million bushels of paddy produced in 1964 was the highest every recorded up to that date. Since then, after a drop in 1965 due to drought, production soared upwards. Between 1964 and 1970 rice production has risen by about 50 per cent, implying an average annual rate of growth of 7·1 per cent. During the same period population growth averaged 2·3 per cent annually. Most of the increases in paddy production over the 1964 level occurred after 1967. The average annual rate of increase of output between 1967 and 1970 was 11·0 per cent.

Ceylon's performance in the 'Green Revolution' in rice has surpassed the achievement of most other Asian countries, as shown by the comparative indices in Table 2.

Unlike the export staples – tea, rubber and coconut – rice is produced wholly for domestic use and is by far the dominant crop in the domestic agricultural sector. It is primarily a smallholder crop, with 92 per cent of the acreage being cultivated in holdings of

Table 2
1961 Indices of Rice Production in Selected Asian Countries
(average 1952–6 = 100)

Cylon	244	Philippines	155	China (Taiwan)	146
Laos	190	Thailand	152	Cambodia	135
South Vietnam	174	South Korea	152	Afghanistan	130
India	158	Indonesia	152	Nepal	90
Pakistan	157	Malaysia	149		

Source: Asian Development Bank, *Annual Report for 1970*, p. 4.

less than 10 acres. However, other crops produced exclusively for domestic use also registered marked increases in production. Output figures for the main 'subsidiary crops' produced in Ceylon are shown in Table 3.

Table 3
Output of Subsidiary Crops

	1964	*1965*	*1966*	*1967*	*1968*	*1969*
Potatoes (tons)	360	803	2,632	5,264	14,445	29,521
Chillies, dried ('000 cwt.)	4	9	15	36	75	133
Red onions ('000 cwt.)	325	345	385	516	680	741
Maize ('000 bushels)	354	378	363	637	452	627

Source: Ministry of Agriculture, *Draft Agricultural Development Plan, 1971–1977.*

Like rice, Ceylon's subsidiary crops are cultivated mainly by small farmers. The rise in the output of these crops as well as of rice reflected the activisation of Ceylon's domestic agricultural sector as a whole during the latter half of the 1960s. It is a mark of the success of the Government's 'Food Drive' which was one of the main planks of economic policy during the period.

II

The Food Drive was central to overall development strategy in the late 1960s. Throughout the colonial period Ceylon depended heavily on imports for providing the bulk of her food needs, including rice. The indigenous rice-growing peasantry produced little above subsistence needs. The food requirements of the population of the towns and of the plantations were met from imports that were made possible by the export of tea, rubber and coconuts. This was the basic pattern of the export–import economy that had evolved in colonial times. Indeed, colonial policy placed much emphasis on the philosophy of comparative costs and on cheap food imports.

The dependence on imported food has persisted to this day. Food imports still account for about a third of Ceylon's total import bill of around Rs. 3,100 million. But the need to step up domestic food production and reduce imports has now assumed a new significance. In the first place, domestic food production is seen as the most promising approach to the acute external payments crisis which has afflicted Ceylon in recent times. In the post-war period, and particularly after the mid-1950s, Ceylon's export staples have been in deep trouble. Rubber and coconut products were affected by competition from substitutes. Even more serious, the price of tea, which accounts for over 60 per cent of Ceylon's total exports, fell by over 30 per cent during the 1960s, the fall being particularly steep after 1965. These developments seriously undermined the foundations on which Ceylon's export–import economy was based. There was little prospect in the short run of finding new exports to offset these declines. Apart from foreign aid, which was in any case limited, import substitution in agriculture was the best means of providing relatively early relief for the payments situation. Most, though not all, of the food items in the import list are, from a technical point of view, capable of being produced locally.

Second, there is now a greater awareness of the link between domestic agriculture and industrialisation in the context of Ceylon's long-term development goals. Much of Ceylon's requirements of capital goods and industrial raw materials need to be imported. The ability to import these items remains limited as long as export earnings from tea, rubber, coconuts and other items are pre-empted by the need for consumer imports like food. Ceylon's Ten-Year Plan of Development, published as far back as 1959, spoke of turning Ceylon's existing export sector into the equivalent of a capital goods sector by the domestic production of consumer import substitutes, mainly food. In this way the growth of both industry and agriculture would be accelerated.

Third, there are the social and political aspects. The farmers, and others dependent on domestic agriculture, are a numerically large class. Whilst education and adult suffrage were making the rural population increasingly articulate, population growth and the earlier neglect of the rural economy were pressing down on rural living standards and giving rise to growing problems of landlessness and unemployment. A greater responsiveness to the needs of the rural community was one of the compulsions of the political process itself. In the political, no less than in the economic sense, the domestic agricultural sector could no longer remain peripheral to the life of the country.

III

The factors described briefly above explain the rationale of the Food Drive. Of wider interest, perhaps, are the reasons for Ceylon's success during the last five years. A rapid increase in agricultural output is today a common objective in most developing countries, and Ceylon's experience in this field is likely to be of some relevance to this common concern. The rest of the discussion is therefore largely devoted to the factors underlying the success of the Food Drive – particularly in respect of rice production.

The rapid expansion in rice production, particularly after 1965, was largely due to an increase in yields per acre. The area under rice cultivation also increased during this period, but this made only a secondary contribution to the rise in output. The post-1965 experience contrasts with trends in the previous decade when the roles were reversed and new acreages increased faster than yields. This is brought out in Table 4.

Table 4
Rice: Average Annual Compound Rates of Growth

	1952–60	*1960–70*	*1964–70*
Production	5·1	6·1	7·4
Yield per acre	2·1	3·5	4·8
Net acreage harvested	3·0	2·4	2·5

The changes shown above reflect a shift in emphasis in the government's agricultural policy. Although the Food Drive is generally taken to refer to the post-1965 agricultural programme, the goal of increased food production and of self-sufficiency in rice had earlier origins, extending back to the 1920s. In the earlier phase, however, the focus of attention fell on extensive cultivation through the reclamation of the Dry Zone by irrigation.[1] The Dry Zone had sustained Ceylon's population in ancient times and had supported an agricultural regime based on an impressive and complex network of irrigation works, some of which are over two thousand years old. But the civilisation of the Dry Zone had fallen into decay even before the colonial conquests, and the centres of government had shifted to the Wet Zone. In the later British period, Ceylonese legislators led by D. S. Senanayake made vigorous attempts to 'reopen' the Dry Zone through the restoration of ancient irrigation works, the clearing of forests and the settlement of farmers on relatively small family farms. It was this policy that was mainly responsible for extending the area under rice cultivation. Over the thirty-year period 1936–66 about 600,000 acres of land – inclusive of 'highland' not cultivated with rice – were 'colonised' under land development schemes by 83,000 allottees.[2]

The policy of Dry Zone development through irrigation and the settlement of colonists served not only to increase rice production, but also to relieve the growing pressure of population on land in the relatively crowded Wet Zone. But the policy was a relatively expensive one in terms of cost–benefit relationships. Whilst new settlement involved heavy capital costs on irrigation, land clearing, road building and housing, productivity per acre, and also per man, remained low in the new areas. Productivity was partly handicapped by the social aspects of earlier settlement policy which, in the choice of settlers, placed emphasis on need, as measured, for example, by landlessness and family size, rather than on agricultural aptitudes. But, more basically, the success of the policy was limited by the prevailing level of technology in rice farming. The new lands were provided in compact and viable units of somewhat larger size than average and were regulated by sound stipulations regarding tenure. But they were generally cultivated in accordance with the traditional techniques that were familiar at the time, which had little recourse to such practices as fertiliser application, transplanting or row seeding, and the use of improved seed. In the main, returns to investments were poor because Dry Zone agricultural development amounted to an extension at a relatively heavy capital cost of the traditional low-productivity agriculture to new areas. Perhaps government policy itself, absorbed as it was by the continuing and challenging tasks of engineering, land clearing and settlement, gave too little attention to the need for improving agricultural productivity in the settlements already established.

In the more recent period, with the growing urgency of Ceylon's external payments position, it became necessary to look to quicker and less costly ways of stepping up rice production. There was, as mentioned, a shift in emphasis. The policy of Dry Zone development, with the relatively long gestation periods and heavy capital outlays involved, was supplemented by a programme which aimed at raising productivity on lands already cultivated. The new emphasis on raising yields per acre, described in the pages to follow, does not, however, detract from the soundness of the policy of Dry Zone settlement. The cost–benefit relationship in any programme of irrigation and land development, whether old or new, changes significantly when agricultural productivity is raised. The modernisation of agricultural practices embraces not only the traditional village lands but also the lands settled under irrigation schemes. Indeed, the prospects for increasing yields are more favourable in the new areas, where water could be more readily controlled and land tenure systems are sounder, than in the old. The greater part of the total increase in rice production in the period after 1965 came from the Dry Zone. It is doubtful if the 'Green Revolution' would have produced the same results had there not been an earlier policy of Dry Zone development through irrigation and colonisation.[3]

In 1970 Ceylon inaugurated, in continuance of the policy of Dry Zone development and settlement, the first phase of its largest development project to date – the giant Mahaveli Development Scheme, which would irrigate a total of about 900,000 acres, including 600,000 acres of new land.[4] The scheme promises to be viable since it is predicted on a more modern, high-yielding agriculture. Land development must remain a plausible policy in a country where undeveloped but fertile land, capable of irrigation, is still available in a situation of growing unemployment and land hunger. The possibility of a high-yield agriculture, which recent developments have reinforced, would vindicate such a policy.

IV

The core of the post-1965 Food Drive was not, however, the continuing programme for further acreage expansion through the colonisation of new lands. Rather, it was a concerted effort at raising rice production primarily by stepping up yields and also, to some extent, by increasing the proportion of paddy lands that are cultivated each year. A sizeable proportion of 'asweddumised' land in village areas, i.e. land prepared for paddy cultivation, was invariably left uncultivated each year owing to such factors as a lack of incentive, damage to minor irrigation works and poor rainfall.[5] The increase in yields, supported by a moderate improvement in the utilisation of these lands, played the larger part in the success of the Food Drive. It is the activisation of the domestic agricultural sector in this way, and the means by which this was achieved, rather than the colonisation programme, that is of particular interest.

The factors underlying the success of the Food Drive may conveniently be grouped into three categories. These are (1) the development of a fairly extensive infrastructure of supporting services for domestic agriculture; (2) the absolute priority given to food production by the Government and the organisational steps that were taken in pursuance of this; and (3) the use of the pricing system to provide incentives in a manner unparalleled in the past. The second and third of these categories were largely developments of the post-1965 period. The first category had earlier origins.

The relatively extensive network of supporting services and facilities which the domestic agricultural sector now enjoys was not created overnight. The Food Drive did not start in a vacuum. A framework of services had been developed over a period of years, largely under the aegis of the Ministry of Agriculture. These services helped rice farmers in a number of ways and served to break down the relative isolation and neglect from which they had suffered in earlier periods. Without this framework the post-1965 Food Drive could barely have succeeded. A full description of such a framework is beyond the scope of the present paper, but its main elements were the following.

1. *A Guaranteed Price Scheme for Paddy*

The scheme had its origins during the Second World War, when there was also the compulsory acquisition of paddy surpluses by the Government. Compulsory acquisitions were terminated at the end of the war; but in 1948 farmers were offered the facility of making voluntary sales of paddy at a fixed price to government purchasing stores. The scheme originally aimed at providing farmers with an assured marketing outlet at a stable price which was around the prevailing world market price; later it came to involve a subsidy to producers when world rice prices declined whilst the guaranteed price was left unchanged.[6] The increasing effectiveness of the scheme as a marketing outlet is illustrated by the growing proportion of total paddy production sold to the Government. This proportion increased steadily from 2 per cent of the total crop in 1950 to over 60 per cent in 1966.[7] The proportion fell substantially after 1966, but this was the result of changes – which are dealt with later – in the consumer ration which raised the open-market price of rice above the support price. It is hardly possible to measure the incentive impact of the Guaranteed Price Scheme. Rice production has shown an upward trend throughout the post-war period. Whilst factors other than the price support scheme also contributed to this increase, it is reasonable to suppose that the maintenance of a stable price, in a background of falling world prices, helped to stimulate production. However, the steepest rise in production took place after 1966. During this phase deliveries of paddy to the Government under the Guaranteed Price Scheme fell significantly and the open-market price of rice rose above the guaranteed price.

2. *The Development and Distribution of High-Yielding Seed*

There can be no doubt that improved varieties of seed played a decisive role in the rise in rice production. The improved seed was developed locally by Ceylonese agronomists and was the outcome of a vigorous programme of research and experimentation.[8] Although the yield potential of these new varieties was somewhat less than that of the mircale rice developed abroad, e.g. I.R.-8, it substantially exceeded the yields of the traditional local varieties. Moreover, the new strains were suited to local conditions. The Government, through the Department of Agriculture, had established a scheme of seed production, identification and distribution.[9] Issues of certified seed paddy under the scheme rose from 130,000 bushels in 1966 to 227,000 bushels in 1969.[10] Already by 1968, nearly 70 per cent of the total acreage under rice was covered by improved varieties of seed.[11] In Ceylon, as in other countries, the Green Revolution was intimately linked to the discovery and application of high-yielding seed. Without these new varieties the rapid spurt in production could hardly have taken place. Yet these high-yielding varieties were only the technical means whereby greater production was attained. Their application depended very much on the motivation of farmers to increase output. As shown later, there were other factors which provided such motivation.

3. *Subsidised Fertiliser*

Fertiliser was made available to rice producers at a price below the market price. The fertiliser subsidy amounted to 50 per cent of market prices if payment was made in cash, and $33\frac{1}{2}$ per cent of market prices if purchases were made against credit obtained from the Government. There has been a steady upward trend in fertiliser use by rice farmers, from a total of 13,000 tons of plant nutrient in 1966 to 30,000 tons in 1968, and it is a plausible supposition that the subsidy policy contributed to this. Nevertheless, it would not be correct to conclude that the subsidy was the strategic instrument in stimulating rice production or even fertiliser use. The use of fertiliser was also influenced by such other factors as the availability of credit. Moreover, as shown later, an exceptionally strong market price situation for paddy developed in the late 1960s, and this, rather than low prices of inputs, was the major stimulus to production. In fact, fertiliser use, despite the increasing trend, still remains well below the prescribed optimum – around 30 per cent of the prescribed dosage for nitrogen, 10 per cent for phosphorus and about 16 per cent for potash.[12] Fertilisers can, for this reason, be an important means of raising output in the future. But apart from convincing farmers of the gains from fertiliser application, the extended use of fertiliser depends on improved water control and a more efficient and flexible system of fertiliser distribution than prevails today.

4. *Extension Services*

Much emphasis is usually given to the importance of extension services in improving agriculture. An agricultural extension service for paddy farmers has been operative in Ceylon for a number of years. The service, however, is not as large as might be expected in view of the priority given to food production. In 1969, at the village level, Ceylon had one extension worker per thousand farmers. This contrasts with an estimated need of about one extension worker for every 200–300 farmers. The quality of the extension service was also capable of improvement.[13] Although extension activity must have played a part in raising productivity in rice farming in the late

1960s, there was no effort at transforming the extension service into a major instrument of agricultural policy.

5. *Tenurial Reform*

Ceylon's success in raising rice production was achieved without any major changes in the pattern of land holding. Unlike tea and rubber, rice is predominantly a smallholder's crop. As Table 5 below indicates, 99 per cent of paddy holdings and 92 per cent of the area under paddy are made up of units which do not exceed 10 acres. Units of 5 acres and less account for 76 per cent of the total acreage. The average size of holding in Ceylon is slightly below 2 acres.

Ceylon's major piece of agrarian legislation was the Paddy Lands Act of 1958, which sought to provide farmers with security of tenure by making tenancy permanent and heritable and also stipulated a maximum rental of 25 per cent of the gross produce of a tenant. The Act has provisions to improve the efficiency of cultivation and to establish village-level organisations (cultivation committees) representative of paddy cultivators and vested with managerial and development functions. The Paddy Lands Act ran up against a number of difficulties in actual operation and was amended in 1970 to strengthen the provisions for the restoration of tenancies following eviction. But though the Act failed to realise fully the expectations that inspired it, it is reasonable to suppose that it played a positive part in strengthening the basis for improvements in productivity. The very existence of the Act probably reduced the displacement of

Table 5
Size Distribution of Prepared Paddy Land Holdings, 1962

Size group (acres)	*Percentage of holdings in total*	*Percentage of total area*
0 – 1	43	17
1 – 2½	31	26
2½ – 5	20	33
5 – 10	5	16
10 +	1	8
	(570,000 holdings)	(1,135,000 acres)

Note: 'Holding' = extent of land consisting of one or more parcels, forming a technical and economic unit.

Source: Department of Census and Statistics, Census of Agriculture, 1962.

small farmers by larger ones in a background of rising opportunities for profit in rice cultivation. Moreover, the cultivation committees, despite their shortcomings, proved to be useful instruments for village-level planning. It was only in the realm of planning for domestic agriculture that an attempt was made, through a process of consultation and discussion, to link up overall targets set at the national level with district- and local-level targets. The cultivation committee was the forum through which farmers were made familiar with local targets and through which assessments were made of input requirements at the village level.

6. *Agricultural Credit*

Credit facilities for farmers have increased considerably in recent times. Credit from institutional sources is channelled, almost exclusively, through co-operative societies of which, according to a survey carried out in 1962, 65 per cent of peasant farming families were members. Prior to 1963 the size of loans to individual farmers was restricted to Rs. 250, irrespective of the area cultivated. In 1965 a new Agricultural Credit Scheme was introduced which substantially enlarged the dimensions of rural credit. Under the new scheme the Peoples' Bank, a state-sponsored commercial bank, lent to co-operative societies for re-lending to farmers. The credit limits for individual loans were raised to Rs. 262 per acre up to a maximum of 10 acres. Farmers were also enabled to pledge their consumer rice ration coupons as security. The Peoples' Bank was in turn re-financed by the Central Bank of Ceylon which also guaranteed loans on behalf of the Government to the extent of 75 per cent. Under the impetus of the scheme the amount of short-term loans to farmers – the loans have usually to be repaid within the year – increased from Rs. 28 million in 1966 to Rs. 73 million in 1968. There was, however, a decline thereafter to Rs. 55 million in 1969 and Rs. 51 million in 1970. At the same time there was a disconcerting increase in defaults – from Rs. 10 million or 14 per cent in 1968 to Rs. 20 million or 40 per cent in 1970.[14] Apart from the new Agricultural Credit Scheme, the rural population is also able to obtain loans from rural banks established since 1964. These are essentially selected multi-purpose co-operative societies which are empowered to collect deposits and extend loans for specified purposes to members. The Peoples' Bank provides overdraft facilities and managerial assistance to the rural banks. The specified purposes of loans, their extent and conditions of repayment are the same as in the Agricultural Credit Scheme. By the end of 1970 there were ninety rural banks in existence, which had together made over 10,000 loans totalling Rs. 7·1 million.[15] There is also a Government-sponsored scheme of credit for subsidiary crops.

7. *Crop Insurance*

A scheme of crop insurance was inaugrated on a pilot basis in 1958 and has since been extended to cover an acreage of 200,000 in sixteen districts. The scheme has not, however, been an unqualified success up to now. Premia collected have amounted to only 38 per cent of sums due over the last ten years, and government subsidies were needed for indemnity payments. These payments have themselves been subject to delays and this in turn has undermined confidence in the scheme. A reform of the scheme is now contemplated.

As the preceding discussion indicates, domestic agriculture was served by an expanding infrastructure of services and facilities which contrasted sharply with the situation of relative neglect and isolation in the colonial period. The Food Drive in the latter part of the 1960s took place against the background of this supporting infrastructure, and would hardly have been successful without it. Nevertheless, the success of the Food Drive cannot be ascribed entirely to the factors described above. As mentioned earlier, food production, and particularly rice production, had shown a gradual upward trend in the period prior to 1965, and undoubtedly the growing network of supporting facilities for domestic agriculture played a part in bringing about this result. But these factors, by themselves, do not suffice to explain the rapid acceleration in food production that took place in the late 1960s. There was no basic change in the services provided during this latter period. What was new was the emergence of two other factors which were not quite so much in evidence before: a singular concentration by the Government of its organisational energies and administrative resources on food production, and the emergence of a situation of market scarcity which raised the prices of domestic crops to levels that had never been reached before. It is these two factors, discussed in the succeeding sections, which, together with the prevailing infrastructure, sparked off the upsurge in production in the period after 1967.

V

During the years 1965–70 the Food Drive was the main pillar of the Government's economic policy. Food production received top priority and much of the Government's administrative energies were directed towards it. Although programmes of development were implemented in other sectors of the economy, it was in the Food Drive that the Government sought the greatest economic and political rewards. One of the first acts of the Prime Minister on assuming office in 1965 was to take overall charge of the food production programme.[16] This gave political support to the programme at the highest level of government.

There were three ways in which the priority given to food production was reflected in special organisational arrangements. The first was the setting-up of special arrangements at the level of the Cabinet itself to formulate policy and watch over its implementation; the second was the gearing of the Ministry of Agriculture for extensive planning in the agricultural field; and the third was the arrangements made at the district and local level. Each of these arrangements played a significant part in bringing about the success of the campaign.

As early as 1965 a special committee of the Cabinet was set up to spearhead the food production campaign. The Cabinet Food Production Committee, as it was called, was not, however, a routine Cabinet subcommittee. It was a continuing body presided over by the Prime Minister himself. What is more, instead of making recommendations to the Cabinet – which is the usual procedure with Cabinet subcommittees – the Food Production Committee was itself empowered to take decisions. These decisions had the status of Cabinet decisions and were merely reported later to the Cabinet for ratification. The Cabinet Committee was made up of senior Ministers[17] whose departments had some connection, whether direct or indirect, with domestic agriculture. Its meetings were also attended by senior officials who participated in the discussions. The Committee met relatively frequently – about once a fortnight as a rule – and functioned with more flexibility than the Cabinet, since matters could be brought up for decision in a less formal manner.

The Committee maintained a continuing surveillance on the progress of the food production campaign, receiving regular reports on performance and on difficulties encountered. It was able to take speedy and effective action to minimise bottlenecks in implementation. Moreover, the Committee strengthened rather than weakened the role of the Minister of Agriculture, since it afforded him a more flexible forum for decision-making than the Cabinet. The Cabinet Food Production Committee, together with another body, the Cabinet Planning Committee, came to be the two most effective organs in the administration where there was a regular interchange of views between Ministers and officials. Its existence and activities were a spur to the efforts of the entire cadre of officials concerned with the food production programme. At a time when, owing to the foreign exchange shortage, critical imports were regulated by controls, it was able to assure the continuity and adequacy of equipment and supplies for the agricultural sector by ensuring adequate allocations of exchange and the speedy issue of licences.[18] Latterly, the Committee concerned itself not only with domestic food production but with the food situation as a whole, by keeping a regular watch on the flow of essential food imports.

The second of the organisational innovations was the setting-up of planning machinery with the Ministry of Agriculture. This is of some significance, since the link between plans and their implementation becomes particularly close when sectoral agencies themselves participate in the planning process. It was the Ministry of Agriculture more than any other in Ceylon which made an effective attempt at sector-wise planning. In the period immediately prior to 1965, the Ministry had gathered under its wing a group of officials of high calibre, both administrative and specialist. This group, together with the Government Agents in the districts, were the nucleus of the planning system for the domestic agricultural sector. Its work was supported by the overall planning agency in Ceylon, the Ministry of Planning and Economic Affairs, which was responsible for the allocation of resources for development, both domestic and foreign. In 1966 a draft Five-Year Plan of the Ministry of Agriculture was published setting out output targets for individual crops. These targets were not derived from any global planning aggregates for the economy as a whole, but were based largely on technical and practical possibilities. They were nevertheless consistent with general planning priorities. The Ministry of Agriculture also prepared each year a detailed Implementation Plan based on the Five-Year Plan. The Implementation Plan was the operational programme for the year. It set out targets for both outputs and inputs on a district-by-district basis. These targets were derived through consultations with the technical officers of the Ministry, the Government Agents in the provinces and the departmental personnel in the districts, and were reviewed at periodic conferences of Government Agents. The Implementation Plan was the basis for annual exchange allocations for the agricultural sector as well as for budgetary provisions.

The third of the organisational innovations related to activities at the local level. One of the first acts of the Government in 1965 was to staff the posts of Government Agents in the provinces with relatively senior officials, largely for the purpose of strengthening the food production programme.[19] Historically, the Government Agents occupied a position of pivotal importance in the entire provincial administration, but it was felt that in more recent times there had been a tendency to neglect the administration in the provinces.[20] Along with the strengthening of the provincial administration, there was a conscious attempt to involve personnel at the local level in the preparation and implementation of plans – perhaps the only example of such participation in the planning process in Ceylon. The procedure followed was broadly to discuss the district targets at meetings at the district level convened by the Government Agent and attended by the administrative personnel concerned with the agricultural programme as well as the chairmen of the cultivation committees. The previous year's performance was generally the benchmark, and assessments were made on the scope for improving upon it. The revised targets arrived at in this way, district by district, were the building blocks for the revised national target. The local targets were not broken down into targets for individual farms or even villages. But the villages' cultivation committees became a forum for assessing input requirements at the village level – fertiliser, credit, tractor services, etc. – and for transmitting these to the district and national authorities for action. In addition to all this, the communications media available to the government – the radio, film unit and press – were actively utilised to create a national consciousness of the importance of the Food Drive. Village competitions rewarded the most successful farmers, and schoolchildren were mobilised for mass paddy weeding and transplanting operations. The periodic food production inspections by the Prime Minister were also well publicised with a view to focusing public attention on the Food Drive.

The success of the Food Drive was partly due to these organisational measures. Given the large role played by government in providing services to the farmers at various points in the cultivation cycle, efficiency at the administrative level is crucial to efficiency in production. Ceylon was able to improve the scope and efficiency of its administrative services to domestic agriculture because of the singular concentration of official effort in this sector. It is interesting to speculate whether such a concentration of effort would have been practicable, given the limits on administrative resources, if food production had not been singled out for special attention and if, instead, official policy aimed at simultaneous progress over a number of sectors. In other words, had the Food Drive been supplemented by parallel pushes in other sectors – industry, transportation, education, housing, etc.– would there have been similar results in these sectors or would the dilution of organisational energies and talents have impeded the success of the Food Drive itself? In the context of the situation prevailing in Ceylon at the time, the answer may well be that a broader-based effort might have proved self-defeating. This is a consideration of some relevance in the context of the efforts of developing countries to implement overall plans with a host of multi-sector targets. It is also a consideration that needs to be taken account of in the context of the current popularity of the concept of a 'unified approach' to development. These approaches, though desirable in themselves, cannot afford to ignore the very real constraint which limitations in administrative resources place on developing countries.

VI

The expanding infrastructure of services for domestic agriculture and the priority given to the Food Drive by official policy were two of the ingredients of success. But it was, perhaps, a third ingredient – an exceptionally favourable price situation for the farmer – that proved to be the real catalyst. As far as the rice producer was concerned, the decisive change in the price situation occurred at the end of 1966. The first and second factors discussed above were already in operation by that time. Although rice production recovered rapidly in 1966 and 1967 from the setback of 1965 caused by poor weather conditions, it was only in 1968 that total production rose sharply above the level attained in 1964. By 1968 the transformation of the price situation had taken place.

The role played by a favourable price situation in stimulating rice production is of special interest since it repeats Ceylon's experience in other areas as well. At no stage did official policy in Ceylon make deliberate use, on any significant scale, of the instrument of tariff protection as a means of generating growth, whether in industry or in agriculture. This was partly a legacy of colonial policies which favoured an 'open economy', and partly a reflection of reluctance, on political grounds, to raise consumer prices. In the case of industry, in the early post-independence period, instruments other than tariff protection were preferred to assist domestic growth – tax incentives, credit and research services, and so on – but the results were minimal. In later years, industry did receive substantial protection. But this was not the result of conscious policy; it was rather a by-product of balance of payments difficulties which necessitated the curtailment, or even the total stoppage, of imports of manufactures deemed less essential. The umbrella of blanket protection proved immensely effective during the 1960s. It set in motion a process of industrial growth in Ceylon of sizeable dimensions. The particular industrial structure that emerged in this way may, of course, be questioned. But there is little doubt that it was the powerful price incentive provided by import restrictions, rather than any other measure, that became the catalyst for industrialisation.

Ceylon's balance of payments problems came to the aid of agriculture as well. But since agricultural imports were largely essential foodstuffs of mass consumption, the axe of import restrictions on balance of payments grounds could not be applied so readily. In the few instances where imports were banned, as in the case of eggs and red onions in the early 1960s, and potatoes in 1967, the response of domestic production was spectacular. But in general the domestic agricultural sector could not expect massive protection against imports to emerge as a mere by-product of foreign exchange difficulties. It had to await the emergence of some special factors which eventually made a degree of partial protection inevitable.

Although restrictions on food imports were not used as an instrument to afford general protection for domestic agriculture, the Government had for a number of years attempted to support prices through governmental purchases. The Guaranteed Price Scheme for rice was referred to earlier. Similar price guarantees were extended for a number of other crops such as chillies, onions, maize, potatoes and certain pulses. But unless the prices fixed under these schemes were no higher than the average import prices after evening out fluctuations, they would involve a government financial subsidy to producers. The Guaranteed Price Scheme for rice was in fact first introduced as a means of affording an assured market to producers at a stable price. It became a subsidy scheme only when the local buying price remained unaltered despite a decline in the world price of rice.[21] The technique of subsidies as a means of providing incentives to production could, however, be costly, especially when applied to crops like rice where production is on a large scale. In the context of the growing burden of consumer subsidies – mainly in respect of rice – on government finances, there were obvious limits to the extent to which subsidies could be provided to support production as well. The guaranteed price of rice was raised to Rs. 12 per bushel of paddy in 1962 and remained at that level until it was increased to Rs. 14 per bushel in December 1967, following the devaluation of the Ceylon rupee.

A more effective solution to the problem of a satisfactory price for the producers of rice emerged in late 1968. It was once again a by-produce of difficulties on the external front and was not designed as a deliberate instrument of protection. Since the end of the Second World War, Ceylon had been providing her people – men, women and children, farmers and non-farmers – with a weekly ration of two measures (about 4 lb.) of rice per person at a subsidised price that was below not only the guaranteed price earned by local producers, but also the world price.[22] The financial cost of this programme was heavy indeed, but all previous attempts at reducing or eliminating subsidies involved the sharpest political repercussions. Rice was a highly charged political issue. In 1966 there appeared a world shortage of rice which resulted in rice prices almost doubling in world markets. This posed serious problems for Ceylon, since the greater part of the requirements for the rice ration had still to be imported. In late 1966 these difficulties were further compounded by the non-availability of the usual quantities supplied from Burma, one of Ceylon's traditional suppliers, as well as from Thailand. The Government was placed in a position in which it was unable to supply consumers with the full quantum of the weekly ration. Some action was inevitable, and in December of that year the Government took the politically difficult and drastic decision to reduce the weekly ration by half, from two measures to one measure per person. However, in order to ease the burden on the consumer, it also decided to provide the residual ration of one measure free of cost instead of at the earlier price of 25 cents. In addition, the price of flour was also reduced. The government's decision, whilst meeting the problem of the shortage of imported rice, also resulted in a sizeable reduction in the food subsidy bill. It cost less to provide one free measure of rice per person than to supply two measures at the subsidised price of 25 cents per measure which prevailed up to that time.

More pertinent to the present discussion was the impact of this step on the price of rice received by the producer. Until the reduction in the consumer ration, the open-market price of paddy fluctuated around the official guaranteed price. The ration of two measures per person met most of the consumers' requirements and there was little demand by consumers for supplementary purchases of rice in the open market. Such additional consumer demand as existed was met by private traders who purchased paddy directly from producers. In practice, traders were able, despite the guaranteed scheme, to purchase paddy from farmers at prices below the guaranteed price. This was due to such factors as their willingness to make payments to farmers in advance of harvests, to transport paddy from the farmers' fields, and to be more flexible about quality requirements. The situation was, however, drastically altered with the halving of the rice ration. The single measure of rice now provided free on the ration fell short of consumer requirements. To some extent consumers made up for the shortfall by switching to purchases of wheat flour, which was sold by the Government at nearly cost price without restrictions on quantity. But consumers also chose to supplement the rice ration by purchasing locally produced rice in the open market. The result was a sharp rise in open-market prices.

The strengthening of consumer demand in the open market that took place after December 1966 is illustrated by the rise in the retail price of rice from around 80 cents per measure in the preceding period to about Rs. 1·00 after 1967. In off-seasons the price of rice to consumers was higher, sometimes reaching Rs. 1·50. The increase in retail prices resulted, in turn, in an increase in the price of paddy in the open market. The buoyancy in paddy prices received by farmers was reflected in the diversion of sales of paddy away from sales to the Government under the Guaranteed Price Scheme and towards sales to private traders. Deliveries of paddy to Guaranteed Price Scheme stores declined from 28 million bushels or 61 per cent of total output in 1966 (inclusive of subsistence consumption estimated at 8–10 million bushels or 20 per cent of total output) to 13 million bushels or 24 per cent of total output in 1967.[23] Deliveries to the G.P.S. stores remained at these lower levels in succeeding years up to 1969.

The favourable price for paddy, brought about by the halving of the consumer ration, provided a strong impetus to production. Paddy was now readily saleable in the open market in a bouyant price situation. Although precise data on open market paddy prices are lacking – and regional and seasonal variations in prices were common – there was undoubtedly a keen demand for paddy by the private trade, and this was reflected in stronger producer prices. Within weeks of the reduction in the ration there were countrywide reports of heightened activity in paddy production. The response of producers was visibly evident. In almost all parts of the country there were signs of efforts to cultivate as much as possible of lands that had previously been asweddumised (i.e. prepared for paddy cultivation) but left idle for one reason or another. In addition, there was a keener attempt to raise yields through more systematic cultivation, using better seed, more fertiliser and such improved cultural practices as transplanting or row seeding and weeding. Whatever the impact of the other factors on production – the infrastructure of supporting services and the administrative effort – it was essentially the transformation in the price situation that created a countrywide consciousness of the gains to be obtained by increased paddy production.

The powerful leverage effect of the price factor in stimulating production was thus demonstrated in the case of rice, as it had earlier been demonstrated in the field of industry. In both cases the degree of price advantage had to be substantial. It is a matter for doubt whether similar results would have been obtained had the price advantage been a marginal one barely calculated to give the domestic product an 'edge' over the imported substitute. The latter may be a valid prescription at an appropriate stage. But in the conditions actually prevailing, stronger medicine was clearly needed to stimulate production. In the case of agriculture, however, in contrast to industry, the problem of conflicting consumer and producer interests came to be resolved by a compromise which took the form of what amounts to a 'two-price' formula. Consumers were given partial relief through a ration provided at zero price which, however, met only a proportion of their total requirements. They were left with the option of supplementing this ration by purchasing locally produced supplies in the open market at prices that were substantially higher than world prices.[24] These higher prices benefited the local producer. But the cost of subsidising production was now borne not by the Government but by the consumer.

The dual price technique came to be applied to other agricultural products as well. Imports of chillies and onions, for example, were restricted to levels which fell short of total consumption requirements. Chillies were made available to consumers on a restricted ration at prices fractionally above the cost of imports. The balance of consumer needs was met from locally produced supplies which were disposed of in the market at prices substantially above the cost of imports. In this way some safeguards to the consumer were combined with price incentives to the producer. The average price paid by the consumer depended on the relative proportions of imported and local supplies purchased by him. The two-price formula was also applied to a manufactured product, textiles, which was also an item of mass consumption which could not readily be protected by the conventional weapon of high import duties or a drastic curtailment of imports. It is, of course, an implicit feature of the two-price technique that if imports are kept constant, the market price of local produce will fall as the increase in output outstrips demand at the prevailing level of prices. If the fall in producer prices is to be avoided, the Government will have to reduce progressively the partial ration met from imports and thereby reduce the relief to the consumer or make supporting governmental purchases of local produce for sale to consumers on the ration at import prices. This course would reduce imports, but it would also imply that the Government now bears a part of the burden of subsidising the producer.

VII

Many have expressed concern at the social implications of the Green Revolution in developing countries. It has been said that high-yielding varieties have benefited the larger farmers as against the smaller and have served to aggravate disparities in incomes and wealth in the countryside. The negative aspects of the Green Revolution are summarised in the following quotation:

> while recognising that the new technology was providing a great increase in agricultural productivity and the prospective

achievement of self-sufficiency, it was noted that at present this was confined to only a small percentage of the farmers with large acres and ample resources. It had failed to reach the vast majority of small farmers, whether owners or tenants, who for lack of resources could not apply the package of practices required. This uneven growth would in the long run affect not only social but also economic development, since the lack of effective demand among the large masses of the rural poor would inhibit the growth of industry and agriculture. Indeed, the possibility of higher yields was pushing up land values while at the same time making cultivation through hired farm labour more profitable. Consequently, a tendency was seen amongst landowners to dispense with their tenants in favour of farm labourers. As of now, the immediate impact of the 'Green Revolution' has been a sharp increase in rentals, insecurity of tenure, landlessness and polarisation in the levels of production and income which could result in increasing social tensions.[25]

There are, unfortunately, no studies as yet, or data on which to base firm conclusions, on the distributive and social aspects of the recent increase in output in Ceylon's domestic agriculture. Official surveys and reports of the food production campaign from various districts give no indication that problems of the kind referred to above have even begun to attain serious dimensions. There must, of course, be some evidence, if only to a limited extent, of the phenomena mentioned above: the rise in land values and the displacement of tenants are possible examples. But it needs to be recognised that the pattern of land holdings in Ceylon, in so far as it concerns paddy lands, is not analagous to the patterns prevailing in certain other countries, particularly in respect of wheat cultivation, where a few large-scale farmers or absentee owners possess the greater part of the arable area. Rice is predominantly a smallholder crop in Ceylon and general improvements in productivity are likely, for this reason, to be better distributed than in countries where ownership is more concentrated. Moreover, in Ceylon the numerous small farmers do have access to the supporting services provided by the Government – guaranteed prices, expanded credit and subsidised inputs – whilst tenants have at least a measure of protection through the Paddy Lands Act which was recently amended to give it further strength. The fact that nearly 70–80 per cent of the area under the main *maha* crop was cultivated with improved varieties is further evidence of the diffusion of the possible benefits from increased production.

It is nevertheless true that the Food Drive did not bring the Government of the day the electoral success that it expected. The Food Drive was the main plank of government policy and was expected to win the rural vote, precisely because it was felt that its benefits were widely diffused. The general election of May 1970 resulted in a landslide victory for the then Opposition, and this brought into critical focus the question of the political and social impact of the Green Revolution. Some critics even questioned the validity of the food production statistics, but the possibility of actual output being significantly below the reported amounts is not supported by other evidence.[26] The reason for the electoral outcome may lie in other factors. Some of these may not be related to the Food Drive: the attitudes of farmers, even when better off than before, may, for example, be influenced by grievances and expectations concerning other matters. But these are outside the scope of the present discussion.

It is important at the same time to recognise that there were also factors which might possibly have qualified or limited the immediate benefits which the rural population may have derived from increased food production. There is first the likelihood that sizeable segments of the rural population may have benefited only marginally, if at all, from the activisation of domestic agriculture. Not all rural families are landowners or tenant cultivators. The number of landless families is likely to have increased with the rapid population growth that has occurred over the last two decades. To some extent, of course, the Food Drive would have benefited groups other than direct cultivators. The fuller use of paddy lands, the application of new seed, the adoption of better cultural practices and the increase in ancilliary activities would have generated more opportunities for employment.[27] But as suggested by surveys of rural unemployment, the employment so created was largely casual and, in any case, of a lesser order of magnitude than the increase in the rural work-force. No less important, a growing proportion of the rural unemployed were young people of both sexes who, unlike their parents, had completed secondary school and in some instances were graduates of universities and other institutions of higher education.[28] Their job aspirations were not satisfied by the creation of greater seasonal and daily-paid work opportunities in paddy farming.[29]

The second factor is that the actual increase in farmers' incomes may not have been proportionate to the increase in production. Although some inputs like fertiliser and seed were subsidised, outlays on these items, together with the costs of such other services as tractor hire, credit and hired labour, may have risen at a rapid rate. The devaluation of the Ceylon rupee by 20 per cent in 1967, and the introduction in 1968 of a second premium rate of exchange of 45 per cent (subsequently raised to 55 per cent) covering over 40 per cent of total imports, resulted in a sharp increase in the general level of prices in Ceylon during this period. This, together with the relatively small size of holdings, the severe fragmentation of ownership, and the short time-span over which the increase in production was enjoyed, probably meant that the impact of the Food Drive on the living standards of farmers, though positive, was still relatively modest and fell short of aspirations.[30]

VIII

The success of the Food Drive holds out the promise of fulfilling Ceylon's long-standing aim of self-sufficiency in rice and other food crops. Ceylon has been importing rice from the time of Dutch colonial rule. Barely a decade and a half ago, over two-thirds of Ceylon's rice requirements were imported. By 1969, despite the rapid growth of population, the proportion has fallen to about 22 per cent. The figures in Table 6 illustrates Ceylon's declining dependence on imports not only for rice but for other crops as well.

Table 6
Imports as a Percentage of Total Consumption

Year	*Rice*	*Chillies*	*Red onions*	*Potatoes*
1965	56	97	27	99
1966	44	96	25	96
1967	33	89	7	78
1968	27	82	4	–
1969	22	65	–	–

These developments are also an indication of the basic structural change taking place in the Ceylon economy. The domestic agricultural sector is no longer an isolated and peripheral part of the economy. Today the performance of the sector is crucial to the performance of the economy as a whole. In the past the tempo of overall economic growth largely reflected the fortunes of the export sector. In 1968 Ceylon achieved a growth rate of 8·2 per cent in Gross Domestic Product despite negative growth in the export sector. This was a phenomenon without parallel in the past and was due, together with the growth of industry and construction, to the rapid expansion of output in the domestic agricultural sector. Today, a shortfall in domestic agricultural production can play havoc with the balance of payments of the country and have far-reaching repercussions on the availability of imports essential to the life of the economy.

What of the future? In the light of the results achieved, Ceylon's development plans confidently predict the attainment of self-sufficiency in rice within the next few years – by 1976 according to the second *Agricultural Development Proposals.* There is no reason to doubt the feasibility of the target given the fulfilment of some of the necessary conditions. The potential exists, from a technical point of view, not only for self-sufficiency but also for the production of a sizeable surplus above domestic needs should this be the object of policy. As mentioned earlier, fertiliser application is still well below the optimum. There is scope for continued improvement in seed material used. The 'miracle' I.R. varieties which produce higher yields than the locally bred H-4 and H-8 are now being utilised to an increasing extent. In addition, work is continuing on evolving new local varieties vastly superior to H-4 and H-8. The goal of self-sufficiency is capable of being reached on the existing acreages devoted to paddy by raising yields alone. But substantial extents of new land, estimated at about 1·3 million acres, are still available for development under irrigation.

The continued momentum of the rice production programme is dependent, of course, on the availability of the supporting services and on the continuance of prices favourable to the farmer. The new agricultural development proposals aim at further improving the supporting services over the next five years. Certain changes introduced by the new Government after the election of May 1970 do, however, alter certain facets of the price relationship. One of these is the restoration of the second measure of rationed rice to consumers as a supplement to the free measure. Although the price at which the second measure is sold is 75 cents, as against the 25 cents per measure charged prior to the halving of the ration in 1966, the price is below that at which rice was earlier available in the open market. This has resulted in a sharp contraction in transactions in the free market. Although the effect of this has been to increase sales to the Government under the Guaranteed Price Scheme and to reduce somewhat the additional imports needed to provide the increased ration, it remains to be seen whether incentives would at the same time be affected adversely by the weakening of the free market.[31] As shown earlier, the high free-market price was a major stimulant to paddy production after 1966.

A further raising of the guaranteed price for rice would, of course, be a possible approach to the incentive problem, but this would increase the subsidy burden on the Government. Its effectiveness would also depend on the Government's purchasing arrangements being as flexible as those of the private trade. A second change proposed by the Government is related to this. The Government has announced its intention to abolish private trade in rice, thereby making itself the sole purchaser of the commodity. Whilst this would increase deliveries of paddy to the Government and thereby reduce the need for imports to meet a part of the requirements for the rationing scheme, and also facilitate the provision of credit through the use of crops as security, it may have an adverse impact on incentives unless care is taken to meet the need of farmers for an efficient and flexible outlet for the disposal of their produce.

The policy goal for the domestic agricultural sector is not, of course, limited to the attainment of self-sufficiency. The process of expanding production involves far-reaching changes in the basic character of the sector itself. What is taking place is essentially the transformation of a traditional, largely subsistence, sector of peasant producers into a more modern system of small-scale farming producing surpluses for commercial sale. This involves a number of changes in the present system of a technical, economic and social character. One of these is a shift in emphasis away from rice growing in the rain-fed areas of the Wet Zone to the Dry Zone where conditions are technically more favourable for the raising of productivity. Much of the gains in output in the recent period have taken place in the Dry Zone, where land holdings are more compact and somewhat larger and where better control over water supplies has favoured the adoption of better cultural practices, including fertiliser use.[32] Double cropping – with two rain-fed crops in the Wet Zone, and a rain-fed and an irrigated crop in the Dry Zone – is a standard feature of rice production in Ceylon. Hitherto the major and more stable crop in both regions has been the *maha*, based on the north-east monsoon. The second crop or *yala*, has been secondary and more uncertain, depending, in the Dry Zone, on the water levels of the irrigation tanks. Yet it is the *yala* crop, dependent on irrigation, that is most amenable to improvements through a more scientific approach to cultivation based on a controlled water supply. It is therefore the *yala* crop that is now receiving special attention in the Government's programme. Another dimension to the programme is the introduction of multiple cropping, i.e. the cultivation not merely of rice but of other crops as well, as part of a more diversified and integrated system of farming. Central to all this is the effective regulation of water.[33]

No less important are the social and economic aspects. In a sense, Ceylon's agricultural system as it has evolved in the colonial period is an inherently unstable one. The plantations were predicated on cheap labour, and domestic agriculture on a traditional system which permitted little more than a bare subsistence living to the farmer. The changes that will be needed in the plantation sector are beyond the scope of the present discussion. But deep inroads have already been made into the subsistence system. For the future, Ceylon must establish a viable domestic agricultural system which offers its participants a standard and a way of living that is commensuate with the expectations generated by education and the process of social and political change. The demographic situation in the country makes it necessary that part of the increase in the work-force be found opportunities for employment or gainful living in the rural areas. Industrialisation and urban growth would not by themselves suffice to absorb the increment to the work-force. But if agriculture and agro-based activities are to succeed in providing the opportunities needed, an agrarian structure substantially different from the traditional must emerge. Higher productivity and greater diversification of crops, together with acreage expansion and other measures to relieve landlessness and population pressure, are essential ingredients of the new system. The quest for a prototype of the agriculture of tomorrow continues. New systems with different cropping patterns and with units of different sizes are being planned for the new settlement schemes – the Walawe and the Mahaveli schemes. In the process a new type of farmer must emerge, a farmer recruited from the ranks of Ceylon's growing population of educated youth, a farmer who can apply modern technology and who is supported in some degree with capital equipment. The Food Drive, up to now, can be regarded only as a beginning towards these essential goals.

REFERENCES

1. The Dry Zone occupies about 60 per cent of the land area of Ceylon. Unlike the Wet Zone, which receives the rains of both the south-west and north-east monsoons, the Dry Zone is watered only by the rains of the north-east monsoon. Double cropping in the Dry Zone is therefore dependent on irrigation.

2. *Report of the Land Utilisation Committee* (Aug 1962) p. 34.

3. The distribution of the total acreage under paddy between the Dry Zone and the Wet Zone and between systems of irrigation is as follows:

Distribution of Paddy Lands, 1964
('000 acres)

	Major and medium schemes	*Village and minor schemes*	*Rain-fed*	*Total*
Wet Zone	61	207	310	578
Dry Zone	305	163	203	671
Total	366	370	513	1,249

Source: Ministry of Agriculture, *Agricultural Development Proposals, 1966-1970.*

4. Under the Mahaveli Scheme 400,000 MW of power would also be provided. The scheme is expected to take thirty years to complete, and to cost about U.S.$4 billion – about as much as the Aswan High Dam. The World Bank is financing the first stage of the scheme.

5. The relative percentages of uncultivated 'asweddumised' land during the *maha* or major season in 1964 and 1968 are as follows:

	1964	*1968*
Major schemes	20·7	16·5
Minor schemes	23·7	17·6
Rain-fed	14·1	10·0

There was no comparable improvement in respect of the *yala* or minor season, although in both cases there was an absolute increase in the extent under cultivation.

6. The subsidy to rice producers is usually estimated by comparing the guaranteed price (in terms of the rice equivalent) with the c.i.f. price of imported rice at the official rate of exchange. To the extent that the official rate of exchange overvalues the rupee, such estimates exaggerate the subsidy to producers.

7. An estimated 20 per cent of total output is said to be consumed on the farms themselves. P. Richards and E. Stoutjesdyk, *Agriculture in Ceylon until 1985* (Paris: O.E.C.D., 1970) p. 41.

8. 'H-4' was produced by the hybridisation of the indigenous Murungakayan 302 and Indonesia Mass. 24. Cf. Asian Development Bank, *Asian Agricultural*

Survey (1970) p. 173. It is a four-month variety with a production potential of 160 bushels per acre.

9. 'The foundation seed is multiplied in departmental farms under the supervision of the Research Division [of the Department of Agriculture]. From the foundation seed registered seed is raised in departmental farms. This seed is then issued to private seed farmers who in turn multiply the seed for sale to government as certified seed at a fixed price of [now] Rs. 18 per bushel. The seed is then stored by government and sold to farmers at Rs. 16 per bushel. This means that government provides a subsidy of Rs. 2 on every bushel of certified seed sold to farmers.' Ministry of Agriculture, *Draft Agricultural Development Plan, 1971–1977*.

10. Ibid., Table 8.

11. Ibid., Table 4. The figures refer to the *maha* crop, 1967–8.

12. Richards and Stoutjesdyk, *Agriculture in Ceylon until 1985*, p. 140. The figures relate to 1967.

13. 'In Ceylon the number of agricultural graduates trained out for agricultural services since the inception, several years ago, of the University Faculty is only 100. There is not a single university graduate below that of the Agricultural Officer stationed in each district. Even some of the District Agricultural Officers are not diploma holders.' Asian Development Bank, *Asian Agricultural Survey*, p. 614.

14. 'The non-recovery of credit is one of the most disconcerting facts which will have to be faced in the future. One reason is that credit given for agricultural production is directed to consumption needs in the absence of organised credit to meet these requirements as well. Similarly . . . the credit schemes now cover uneconomic holdings, where the borrower has no prospect of repayment, even under conditions of maximum yields. In certain parts of the country the social and cultural heritage of the people has developed in a direction which treats government assistance as 'an act of charity' with no accompanying commitment of repayment. This feeling has received support from past experience where irrecoverable loans granted by government have been written off. The practical effect of such a step is really to condone the act of non-repayment and undermine the image of the conscientious borrower who was responsible enough to pay.' *Draft Agricultural Development Plan*, para. 88.

15. Central Bank of Ceylon, *Annual Report for 1970*, p. 123.

16. Mr Dudley Senanayake had at an earlier period been Minister of Agriculture.

17. Besides the Prime Minister and the Minister of Agriculture, the Ministers of State, Finance, Lands, Irrigation and Power, Education, and Home Affairs were also members of the Committee. In addition to the Cabinet Food Production Committee, an Advisory Committee on Food Production was also established in 1965 on which individuals with a special knowledge of agriculture were invited to serve. This too was chaired by the Prime Minister himself. But in practice its role was not a pivotal one, and its meetings were infrequent in the later period.

18. Tractor imports, for example, had virtually ceased by 1964. With the priority given to food production after 1965, liberal allocations of foreign exchange were made for the import of tractors and spares. Between 1965 and 1969 nearly 10,000 tractors of all types were imported.

19. The Government Agent is the chief executive of the central Government in each province.

20. In 1964, however, the Government Agent were also designated Deputy Directors of Agriculture.

21. It may be argued, as mentioned before, that in estimating the rice subsidy to producers account should be taken of the possibility of an overvalued exchange rate. But in any event, the Government will face a financial burden as long as its support prices are higher than the selling price.

22. In 1966, before the change in the rationing scheme, the price was 25 cents per measure.

23. *Draft Agricultural Development Plan*, para. 120.

24. There was no imported rice sold in the open market since rice imports, like the imports of all essential foodstuffs, were a government monopoly and were utilised for the ration.

25. *Report of the Joint F.A.O/E.C.A.F.E/I.L.O. Seminar on Land Reform Implementation in Asia and the Far East* (Rome: F.A.O., 1969) p. 4.

26. Production figures are obtained by crop-cutting surveys conducted jointly by the Departments of Agriculture and Census and Statistics. Despite the increased production of rice, there was a decline in *per capita* rice consumption following the reduction in the ration, estimated on the basis of statistics of local production and of imports. This was made up by increases in the consumption of wheat flour. Total *per capita* consumption per annum both of rice and of wheat flour, however, remained constant between 1966 and 1969, at around 128 kg. Had actual rice production between significantly short of the reported quantum, per capita consumption of rice and flour together would in fact have been below the levels of previous years, which is unlikely given the ready availability of cheap wheat flour. Vastly increased sales of consumer goods–cigarettes, textiles, sewing machines, bicycles, etc.–were also reported in the rural areas. Indeed, one of the concerns of the authorities was the possible effect on incentives of an insufficiency of consumer goods in the rural areas as a consequence of drastic import restrictions.

27. 'High-yielding varieties require more labour and capital per unit of land than the traditional varieties. The additional labour required per hectare amounts to about 30–40 per cent and increases proportionately for double-cropped land. The additional demand for labour to carry out fertilisation, weeding and plant protection is inherent in the case of high-yielding varieties.' E.C.A.F.E., *Economic Survey of Asia and the Far East* (1969) p. 35.

28. One of the notable changes revealed by rural surveys relates to the educational qualifications of the rural unemployed. In 1963, 56·5 per cent of the rural unemployed had been educated beyond the sixth standard. In 1969 the proportion had increased to 88·1 per cent. Cf. M. F. Fernando, 'Employment and Unemployment in the Rural Sector', *Central Bank of Ceylon Bulletin* (Apr 1971).

29. Ceylon has extended the franchise to those of eighteen years and above, and it is widely believed that the 'young vote' was the decisive factor which determined the outcome of the general election of 1970.

30. In any event, the rural voters may not have felt that the gains recently enjoyed by them were in any way jeopardised by an alternative Government. On the contrary, they may have expected to benefit further from the Opposition pledge to restore the second measure of rice to the consumer, bring down the cost of living in general, and transform the prospects for employment.

31. There is already evidence of a drop in rice production in 1971. Although weather conditions do not appear to have been particularly adverse, it is too early to analyse the causes of the shortfall.

32. In 1967 the Government experimented with a 'special project' whose purpose was to rehabilitate a Dry Zone colonisation scheme through the controlled introduction of a package of measures. The results of the project selected, the Elehera Project, were so successful that the programme has now been extended

to other projects as well. The colonisation schemes, being planned settlements, are particularly amenable to supervised rehabilitation.

33. 'For instance, the systematic cultivation of crops other than paddy in paddy fields during the *yala* season, when water is insufficient for making a paddy crop but sufficient for a variety of less water-consuming crops, has become an established fact of crop diversification in paddy fields in some areas of the Island . . . . A paddy field is no longer a place where only paddy is grown. Water is no longer the resource that is applied only to paddy.' ***Draft Agricultural Development Plan***, 'Perspectives and Implementation Policies', para. 10.

13

Development from Below: Aspects of Local Government and Finance in a Developing Economy – Guyana

WILFRED L. DAVID

IT has long been recognised that efficient local government must be regarded as a means of political as well as economic development.[1] Taking this as a point of departure, this paper attempts an examination of what are considered some important aspects of local government in an immature economy and in particular its historical development, organisational and institutional relationships, and some major considerations in the financial field. It is hoped that the analysis will throw some useful light on the problems faced by countries at a similar stage of development and that Guyana's experience will provide meaningful lessons for countries attempting to restructure their system of local government so that it may serve as an effective means of economic development and in time become fully integrated into the development process.

I. HISTORICAL REVIEW[2]

The abolition of slavery clearly established the need for some system of local government in Guyana, as perhaps it did in several other British colonies. After emancipation, many of the ex-slaves, who were totally disenchanted with conditions of life and work on the sugar plantations, pooled their savings and bought some abandoned plantations, thereby founding what came to be known as 'free' village settlements. The bankruptcy conditions facing many plantations and the establishment of these village settlements necessitated the development of some firm basis of association for the provision and management of a wide variety of overhead facilities required for maintenance of life on the coast. In the case of these villages, the greater part of savings having been tied up in the purchase of plantations, there were no uncommitted resources readily available for financing necessary village works.

This state of affairs came to the notice of many of the early Governors of British Guiana who strongly supported attempts, based on the spirit of self-help, to develop a system of local government by means of the voluntary type of village association. The people themselves through entirely local efforts were already making strong attempts to solve the many problems facing their villages. In this context, the typical form of village institution was the committee, consisting of a president and seven other members. These bodies were empowered to collect subscriptions for the provision of village overhead facilities, and also served the very important purpose of keeping the community alive and together. This system of voluntary subscriptions was very much in existence up to around 1864, but the funds collected were always insufficient for the proper financing of village works.

In 1856 an Ordinance was passed setting up local commissions for maintenance of roads and bridges. The Governor of the day suggested that these bodies should be extended into a general system of district councils having powers in the educational field as well. The idea was that each district should have a hospital, dispensary and workhouse and that the proceeds from a levy of house tax based on the number of inmates could be used for necessary maintenance works. These ideas were very commendable, considering the time and circumstances, but implementation proved difficult, the overriding causal factor being the lack of proper supervision of village affairs by the commissioners.

A further attempt at resolving these difficulties was made in 1878 with the passing of a Public Health Ordinance which stipulated that the entire country should be divided into three types of district for sanitary administration and regulation: Town Sanitary Districts (Georgetown and New Amsterdam), Village sanitary Districts (urban) and Country Sanitary Districts (remaining areas). This Ordinance remained in force until 1892 when a new Ordinance, providing for elected village councils with powers to vote, raise taxes, appoint village councillors and execute village works, came into force. However, the 1878 and 1892 pieces of legislation seemed to have covered the same ground with respect to spheres of influence and areas of administration, and attempts at administering them led to consequential conflicts and confusion. As a result, two separate

Ordinances – the Local Government Ordinance and the Public Health Ordinance – were enacted in 1907. The Local Government Ordinance introduced a Local Government Board with eight appointed members. This new Board replaced the Central Board of Health and the Central Board of Villages which had been in existence since 1852. Four kinds of local authorities were also created: (*a*) Urban Sanitary Districts (Georgetown and New Amsterdam); (*b*) Village Districts; (*c*) Country Districts; and (*d*) Rural Sanitary Districts (including all plantations not included in other districts). The Local Government Board which was nominated by the Governor was given some powers of supervision over Urban Sanitary Districts and extensive control over other districts.

Despite this attempt at reorganisation and consolidation in 1907, the whole approach nevertheless remained piecemeal. There was no clearly established local authority representing assembled villagers. Representation fell to either the chairman of a village committee, a leading official in the neighbourhood, a missionary, a sugar planter or a rice miller. The system threw up two major difficulties. On the the one hand, spheres of responsibility were not clearly defined for the various representatives. None of them was aware of the particular aspects of village life he had authority to supervise. On the other hand, the villagers were in a similar state of ignorance as they were generally unaware of the persons or departments they could consult for advice, guidance or assistance, and the appropriate channels through which their views could be aired.

This state of affairs continued until 1930, by which time the need for a radical change in the mode of local government administration was recognised. The existing system was clearly outmoded and could no longer meet the needs of a community which had already made considerable advances in the sociological, educational, economic, and related fields. The need for a system flexible enough to take into account immediate necessities, as well as the more important requirements and complex dynamic problems associated with future development, was clearly recognised.

It was against this background that in 1930 a local committee headed by Hector Joseph, the Attorney-General, was set up to look into various aspects of local government and administration. The Committee made two major recommendations: the introduction of a two-tier system of local government, and a system of District Commissioners. Under the two tier system of local government existing authorities were to be replaced by district councils which were to be made more viable by combining several villages into larger units. Further, there were to be county councils whose functions were to supersede those of the Local Government Board. The establishment of county councils involved the division of the country into four counties,[3] each having a District Commissioner responsible for its administration on behalf of the central Government.[4] County councils included in their membership a county engineer and a county medical officer. Provision was also made for chairmen of district councils within the county to be represented on the county council, which had overriding authority over the district council on all matters.

The Committee's recommendations on the establishment of the District Commissioner system were accepted and came into effect as from 1 January 1932. However, the recommendation on the two-tier system of local government was not accepted. The Governor argued that its implementation required the reconstruction and consolidation of all legislation pertaining to local government and expressed the view that time was not available for such an exercise. On the other hand, it can be argued with some justification that the two-tier system was rejected on account of the Committee's further recommendation that the sugar plantations and unadministered villages should be brought under local government control. The plantation owners were in firm control of the economy, parliament and political affairs generally; their opposition to the introduction of such a system was therefore expected, and it is possible that their stance carried a considerable amount of weight in influencing the Governor's decision. The introduction of the two-tier system would have brought a large number of workers still residing on the sugar estates within the wider framework and control of local government, with the inevitable consequence of a considerable reduction in the administrative, political and economic power wielded by the sugar hierarchy. In particular, it would have further impoverished the plantation owners who would now have to meet additional charges in the form of local rates and wages more reflective of free market conditions.

Thus, even by 1932, the history of local government still presented a confused and complicated picture. Farmers and labourers, dissatisfied with the exorbitant rents or rates they were called upon to pay, disappeared into the hinterland, thereby further threatening the breakdown of the rudimentary local organisation which had already been established. Inadequate finance threatened the very existence of local authorities, many of which found themselves in a position of being unable to provide a large number of necessary local services. Many of these services had to be provided by the central Government. This led to further centralisation of services, tended to whittle down the authority of local bodies, and generally militated against the development of a viable and wide network of local authorities. If the local government system is to become a meaningful part of the overall development process, then a substantial amount of decentralisation of the decision-making process becomes necessary,[5] but it is evident that circumstances prevented the development of such a process, thus causing a further setback to the development of the rural economy.

The public health functions of the Local Government Board were transferred to a re-created Central Board of Health under the Public Health Ordinance of 1934. Under this Ordinance, Village and Country Districts became Sanitary Districts, while Georgetown and New Amsterdam, the two major urban areas, became Urban Sanitary Districts and somewhat subordinate to the Central Board of Health. The powers of the Village Districts and the Country Districts were the same, except that the former were partly elected and the latter wholly nominated. In 1935 another Ordinance was passed amending the Local Government Ordinance of 1907 and providing for improved methods in the election of village councillors and for the election of a chairman by the councillors. Formerly the chairmen of the village and country councils were nominated by the Local Government Board, but under the 1935 Ordinance provision was made for secret ballot. In 1945 the Local Goverment Ordinance was revised and consolidated after consultation with local authorities.

Between 1950 and 1954 two Constitutional Commissions were appointed by the British Government, but came to different conclusions with respect to the local government system. This was probably because the terms of reference of the two commissions were different and because each was operating in a different political atmosphere. The Waddington Commission[6] appointed in 1949 was to make recommendations for central government reform. It recommended the introduction of the ministerial system of government with elected representatives, and as a result pronounced favourably on the part that local government was playing in the country, especially as a training-ground for aspirants to the central legislature. On the other hand, the Robertson Commission[7] of 1954 was appointed as a direct outcome of the suspension of the Waddington Constitution in October 1953. It came as no surprise, therefore, that the Robertson Commission openly condemned the positive recommendations of the Waddington Commission with respect to the functioning of the local government system. It was against this background that Dr A. H. Marshall, a British expert, was appointed 'to enquire and report on all aspects of local government in both rural and urban areas of the colony and to make such recommendations for reform as may be practicable and desirable'.[8]

Marshall's major recommendations covered the fields of organisation, local authority powers and finance. In the field of organisation he recommended the establishment of a Ministry of Local Government in place of the Local Government Board. As Lady Hicks comments, 'This was entirely in line with experience of what had been found useful in other countries.'[9] In the case of local authority powers and duties he recommended a single-tier system of local councils for the coastland, including unorganised areas and sugar estates, and that the coastal area should be parcelled out in not more than eighteen authorities to be called rural district councils. The municipalities of Georgetown and New Amsterdam were to be excluded from this arrangement, but it was recommended that their boundaries should be extended. The district councils were to be given additional responsibilities and authority, with a clear separation of their policy from their executive functions, as well as the engagement of more qualified officers in several fields so that local interest in development could be stimulated.[10] On the financial side he recommended a rate based on full capital values of land and buildings subject to a decennial valuation by professional valuers employed by the central Government. Because the coastlands of Guyana are below sea-level it is necessary to maintain extensive drainage and irrigation works for valuable lands in the area. For this reason it is necessary to have a drainage rate to cover some of the unearned increment on the value of such improved lands. Marshall also recommended the introduction of a well-conceived grants system which was to be equalising as well as promotional.

The Marshall recommendations were accepted by the Government of the day, and they have formed the basis of local government reform being currently implemented by the Burnham Government.[11]

One therefore wonders why it has taken nearly fifteen years for any positive attempt to be made at implementation. One explanation perhaps lies in the fact that the successful implementation required detailed spade-work and planning. As Hicks comments: 'The Marshall Plan was little more than a blueprint; it was intended that a further team of experts should go out to plan the system in detail, particularly in respect of boundaries, and of future agricultural progress.'[12] Secondly, as was the case with Hector Joseph's recommendations of 1930, the sugar plantation hierarchy were probably opposed to their being brought under the mantle of local government, as this would have meant substantial payments to local authorities in respect of rates for their considerable land holdings, with inevitable reductions in their economic, political and administrative power. Thirdly, the period up to 1964 was one of political instability and uncertainty, and within such a framework no meaningful planning could be carried out. Thus although Marshall had recommended the early implementation of a single-tier system, nothing was actually achieved until 1967.[13] The period between 1967 and 1970 saw the preparation of a large number of Bills and Acts, intended to pave the way for local government reform and elections.[14]

Several interesting conclusions emerge from this brief historical account of local government, especially within a context of the system being regarded as an instrument of economic change. Firstly, it seems that the system, from colonial times through independence and after, was never conceived as a major instrument of economic development, but rather as a relatively unimportant appendage of the political, social and economic structure. Perhaps the only attempt to perceive the system in this positive light was made by Marshall in his recommendations. In any event, even if it is argued that this conception at times existed, several variables tended to militate against progress. One of these was reflected in the piecemeal approach to finding solutions to problems, and the reluctance of the authorities to view the system in its entirety and to search for lasting solutions.

Further, the structural and institutional relationships governing the functioning of the plantation economy[15] by their very nature militated against the emergence of any efficient system suited to the needs and aspirations of the Guyanese people. This problem still exists, and unless some concerted attempt is made to integrate the plantation sector fully into the overall national economy, there can be no lasting progress in attempting development of the economy and society from below. In this regard the introduction of an efficient system of local government could be considered as both a cause and an effect of such changes, in the sense that such a system as well as speeding economic change will itself be changed for the better by the workings of a more progressive economy and policy. Finally, the problems discussed above were fully reflected in the types of institutional and organisational relationships which have emerged over time. The next section of this paper is devoted to a consideration of some major problems in this field.

II. ORGANISATIONAL AND INSTITUTIONAL RELATIONSHIPS

In this section an attempt is made to highlight some of the main organisational and institutional relationships governing the functioning of the local government system. As mentioned in the previous section, the problems in this field have been thrown up as a part of the country's curious historical development. Our primary objective is to pin-point those problems which will have to be tackled and solved if development from below is to have any meaning, and if the local development effort is to become an integral part of national development.

The local authorities in Guyana have always functioned within a highly centralised system of district administration. Their smallness in size and population, limited financial resources, and their inability to attract capable and qualified staff have always forced them to rely heavily on the central Government for supervision and administrative assistance. Further, there has always been an absence of a uniform and complete network of local authorities. Lack of uniformity could be found in the fact that there has traditionally been three types of areas – the Village and Country Districts, Unadministered Villages and Industrial Areas – with the Village and Country Districts numbering 104 at the end of 1969.[16] The Unadministered Villages are really small villages which lack formal statutory councils of management. However, because they find themselves within the boundaries of the administrative districts, they are within the jurisdiction of the District Commissioner. These villages are left on their own to provide many of the services they need, without central government facilities, and by and large village works are normally done by *ad hoc* groups working on a self-help basis.

The third class of areas falling within the local government system comprises the Industrial Areas – the coastal sugar plantations and riverain bauxite areas. In these areas the normal local government services, such as the provision of overhead facilities, refuse collection, welfare and community work and even some central government services such as health clinics, have been provided by the industrial owners. It should be mentioned, however, that the provision and administration of community services by the industrial owners, though noteworthy, has nevertheless militated against the development of solid cadres with potential experience in local government affairs. This could perhaps be considered as one of the disadvantages of paternalism.

The organisational and institutional arrangements inherent in the system have prevented the emergence of village leaders. In the first place, the property franchise narrowed the field from which leaders could be recruited. The franchise was restricted to owners of property with a value of at least G$50 per annum.[17] Of the total population of approximately 98,000 in the villages, only about 12,000 were registered voters. While the property qualification was extremely low, and appeared to give all property owners the franchise, this right to vote was even further narrowed on account of the fact that many owners were without title to their land. In any case, the property franchise excluded many young, able but propertyless citizens. As a matter of fact, the middle-aged or old who formed the backbone of the electorate were either by habit or through lack of confidence uninterested in village affairs and the local aspirations of many young people.

Further, the reservoir from which village leadership could be drawn was also somewhat limited. Occupational status has always been the criterion for prestige and influence, with the rural elite comprising a few government officers, primary school teachers, ministers of religion and persons of similar standing. Most government servants are expected to give only technical advice and as such are debarred from taking an active part in politics, thus leaving the teachers and preachers who in many instances have failed to cultivate interest in village affairs either because they were strangers or were legally debarred on account of the property qualification. While it is true to say that some members of the teaching profession have made valuable contributions to the work of village councils, their temporary stay in many areas hampered the emergence of local leaders. The large turnover of such personnel, with constant transfers and new recruits filling positions left vacant, limited the scope for village leaders to emerge.

Another causal factor was perhaps the fact that many of the persons who could have filled positions of responsibility were either uneducated or lacked the necessary initiative required for performing civic duties. However, an important factor could always be found in the uncertain conditions surrounding agriculture, which forms the backbone of rural life. There has always been very little security for the rural population engaged in farming. Because of this, successful farming families normally encourage their children to enter one of the professions or commerce. As the earnings of the father rose, so did the tendency for their children to enter occupations other than agriculture.[18] Finally, it ought to be mentioned that the situation was probably worsened by the fact that traditionally few leadership roles existed in the villages. Apart from village and country councils and a few religious organisations, there were relatively few institutions in which any continuing leadership roles were required.

A very important factor militating against the efficient functioning of the local government system has been the staff and employment practices pursued by local authorities, as illustrated by the case of the village overseer, who is supposed to be the administrative officer of the local authority, responsible to the village chairman, and whose duties include the collection of rates. His position has been aptly characterised by Marshall:

> The Overseer is frequently subject to obstruction in the performance of his duties, especially in the authorising of work and the handling of correspondence. He is often subjected to pressure to delay the collection of rates of members of the council. Ten Overseers were questioned in one area in March. Eight had members with arrears of rates for the preceding year; four claimed to have been victimised at some time or other, and six felt that their salaries had suffered because they had carried out their duties strictly.[19]

The recruitment of overseers and clerical staff is normally done by the local authorities themselves, but with the prior approval of the Local Government Board, which agrees upon salary scales. Despite this fact, the majority of councils continue to pay salaries below the scale. In 1955 Marshall reported that the pay of overseers was roughly comparable to that of messengers and clerical assistants in the central government service. The situation is more or less the same today. The low wages paid to workers in local authorities have always had the most serious disincentive effects and prevented the recruitment of high-calibre staff. Low salaries have often forced personnel to seek additional employment, collect bribes and resort to all forms of corruption, in order to eke out an existence.

The overall picture which presents itself is one of complications, confusions and problems, all militating against effective administration and planning. Local leaders, especially from among the younger generation, have failed to emerge; the scale of remuneration has been so low that only personnel of the lowest calibre could be recruited, and persons could not be enticed to make a career in the local government service. All these factors have tended to pin the system down to a low level of operational efficiency.

III. FINANCE

Local authorities cannot perform their role as organs of economic change unless they have access to adequate finance. As Lady Hicks states:

> If local bodies are to play any significant part in economic or social development, they must clearly have access to adequate finance. If they are both to act responsibly and to show initiative, some, not negligible part of this control over resources must be independent, in the context that local councils are free to choose the rates (and to some extent the conditions) of their taxes or service charges. Without this right local authorities have within their control only partial budgetary responsibility. They can arrange the priorities between different lines of expenditure and an increment of revenue. Without this second right a local authority cannot be fully responsible to its citizens; nor can the local taxes be (as they should be) the balancing factor in local budgets at the final stage of the budgetary process, when the total outlay has been decided and revenue from all other sources known.[20]

This is perhaps one of the finest statements of the responsibilities of local authorities in the financial field, and we use it as our main frame of reference in the examination of the financial operations of local authorities in Guyana.

First, a few remarks about local authority budgets and budgetary control. In Guyana the budget, commonly called an 'estimate', is a straight statement of revenue and expenditure with no subdivision of the accounts between current and captial expenditure as is the case with the national budget. Of course, experience with the compilation and presentation of budgets on a national basis has shown that it is sometimes difficult to say what expenditures ought to be classified as current on the one hand, and capital on the other, the attempt at rigorous distinction proving meaningless in many cases. However, the fact that local authorities are seen as instruments of economic change, with substantial commitments of expenditure in the development field, ought to throw up implications with respect to budgetary classification. Even on an elementary basis they should attempt to make some kind of distinction between their current and capital budgets as a means of gauging the extent to which they are making a potential contribution to the national development effort, as distinct from the allocation of funds purely for administrative and related services.

Local authorities in Guyana are not allowed to budget for surpluses except for contingencies or for projects earmarked to be covered under reserve funds. Such reserves cannot be used for any purpose other than for earmarked projects, and any decision to change such projects must in the first instance receive the approval of the Minister of Local Government. Further, any transfer of funds between any of the subheads voted in the annual estimates also requires the prior approval of the Minister. It is evident that there is therefore a very stringent system of budgetary control, centrally directed, and expenditure is tolerated only to the extent of estimated revenue. The imposition of tenets of strict financial control and accounting on local authorities could perhaps be defended on the ground that it is a means of teaching the requirements of proper financial management, but the system's inflexibility has to a considerable extent prevented them from effectively performing their role as agencies for development at the grass roots.

Within the context of budget preparation and execution, we turn to an examination of policies with respect to revenue and expenditure. Local authorities derive the greater part of their revenue from rates levied on the total appraised value of lots and buildings in their districts.[21]

The data presented in Table 1 show the major sources of revenue

Table 1
Local Authorities' Revenue by Major Sources, 1964–8
(Guyana dollars)

		Types of revenue				
Year	*Rates*	*Abattoir fees*	*Market fees*	*Water rates*	*Rents*	*Total*
1964	765,512	6.913	60,163	17,520	20,578	870,686
1965	727,513	7,463	53,304	18,041	21,129	827,450
1966	770,413	5,913	23,607	18,861	17,873	836,667
1967	891,019	6,004	35,590	27,372	45,615	1,005,600
1968	850,169	12,768	34,400	17,447	28,229	943,013
Total	4,004,626	39,061	207,064	99,241	133,424	4,483,416

Source: *Annual Reports* of the Commissioner of Local Government.

collected by local authorities between 1964 and 1968, and fully represent the normal pattern of things. It is evident that rates form the most important source of revenue, collections from other sources being relatively insignificant. This is because only a few villages can boast facilities such as markets and abattoirs. The provision of facilities of this nature can serve the twin objective of raising revenue as well as offering needed service to residents. It nevertheless remains true that if local authorities are to provide these basic services, they have to rely heavily on rates, especially since this is the most important and most stable revenue source.

The size of the annual revenue intake, both in absolute terms and as a proportion of total government revenue, has always been small, thus restricting the ability of local authorities to finance their own economic development. The smallness of revenue is to some extent explained by the poverty of rural areas, which are caught in a vicious circle of poverty and the low-level equilibrium trap. Not only is the total revenue collectable very low, but the rate of collection seems to be falling every year. Since valuation is done by carpenters, builders, farmers and persons of similar status, no scientific approach is used and this has resulted in a considerable variation in the figures from year to year and substantial differences in valuations as between areas. It is expected that the firm introduction of the Marshallised system of local government reform, with uniform valuation carried out by a trained team of valuers from the central Government, will substantially reduce this high degree of arbitrariness, and that the fixing of the rateable value of lands and buildings on a scientific basis would result in increased local revenue through the rate levy.

Under the new system each local authority will be empowered to fix its own rate to provide for that part of the expenditure included in its approved estimates. With an increase in value at the same old percentage of levy being used, revenue is expected to be greater.[22] On the other hand, if the rate is increased, assuming that the community can bear the increase, more esential services could be provided and development works undertaken.

The revenue situation is to an important extent determined by the methods of collection used, and the percentage of collectable rates which is actually collected depends on this fact. Table 2 gives a comparison between rates collected, rates collectable and arrears for the years 1964 to 1968, and reveals the large sums usually owed to local authorities.

Table 2
Rates Collected and Arrears, 1964–8
(Guyana dollars)

Year	*Collectable*	*Collected*	*Arrears*
1964	1,284,763	765,512	519,251
1965	1,211,055	727,513	483,542
1966	1,299,012	770,413	528,599
1967	1,438,187	891,019	547,168
1968	1,524,196	850,169	674,027

Authorities have always had two methods open to them for collecting rates in arrears: civil proceedings in a court of law, and parate execution, with the latter proving more effective. Many local authorities hardly use the first method because it is expensive and lengthens the time in which the defaulter is expected to pay. On the other hand parate execution enables the local authority to sell the land or building on which rates are owing. The threat of sale usually brings forth the rates due. Unfortunately pressure of work in the Law Officer's Department has always caused a considerable amount of delay in many such executions.

While some residents pay their rates promptly, a great many blatantly refuse to honour this obligation and would do so only as a last resort. There are many who are willing to pay but are prevented from doing so on account of poor financial circumstances. Others refuse to pay so that their land could be put up for sale and title acquired. Although many people have transport, there are others who are registered as owners by the local authorities for the purpose of rates, but who have no title deeds. Such persons agree to their land being put up at execution sale with the knowledge that the land will be sold for rates to the 'owner' and title thereby obtained. It is evident that such a process is both time-consuming and burdensome, and there is an obvious need for suitable and quick remedial measures to be worked out. In particular, other more efficient means should be devised for issuing titles to landowners. For example, the local authority could be empowered to pass transport with the cost being shared equally by the authority and the owner. Alternatively, further powers for effective collection could be given local authorities, which could be empowered to carry out their own parate execution, thus speeding up the rate of collection.

Grants form another source of local government revenue, and they are given to local authorities so that they may share the burden of services which are not entirely local, to make them more active, and as a means of control – the grant being withheld from local authorities which do not keep local services up to a presentable standard, and to provide for special circumstances, e.g. to meet financial expenditure of an unusual kind, or to assist weak areas. However, experience has shown that grants have been made principally to assist the weaker authorities in providing basic and essential services. For the period between 1964 and 1968 such payments amounted to around G$86,000, and the evidence clearly reveals that the relatively small amounts disbursed to the various areas could make only the most insignificant contribution to local revenue and as such to changing the quality of services provided for the better, and eliminating disparities among the various authorities. Lady Hicks[23] has made several important suggestions for improving the general system of grant disbursement, and the following considerations seem relevant in the context of Guyana.

First, consideration might well be given to the issuing of percentage grants – a type which is given for different services in order to encourage local authorities to spend more on social services and to employ more highly qualified staff to administer these services. The percentage grant is normally given after work has been completed, a safeguard to ensure that money is given for work actually completed. While the system in Guyana has been one whereby grants were given to provide for certain services, the sums disbursed have remained relatively fixed from year to year, and while the original intention might have been one of offering percentage grants, it is far from clear that the idea behind such grants was the stimulation of certain activities; on the contrary, the evidence seems to suggest that they were given for the maintenance of certain essential services.

The unit grant is another device used for stimulating activity at the local level, the grant being given to encourage the number of such units provided or persons employed. It is a means of ensuring that local authorities do not spend recklessly on inefficient services in order to obtain higher percentage grants from the central Government. Examples of unit grants are those which could be given for adult education, dispensary services, welfare and recreational facilities, etc. Local authorities might also be encouraged to provide certain services by means of the equalisation grant or subsidy. This grant is paid in recognition of the fact that the revenue to be raised for a particular essential service might be insufficient for its maintenance. The central Government therefore pays the subsidy to cover the excess of expenditure over revenue in respect of the particular service. Although this type of grant is generally unknown to local authorities in Guyana, municipal councils have at times been able to secure subsidies of a similar nature from the central Government.[24] Finally, there is the case of the block grant. While a reasonable case could be made out for this type of grant as a compensation to local authorities for revenues collected by the central Government, e.g. income tax, licences, customs and excise, it would be more advantageous if these were to be disbursed on a regional basis to Regional Development Authorities encompassing several local authorities, for major works covering these authorities, but which because of their scale would prove too costly for the purse of one authority. This argument is further developed in the concluding part of this paper.

Because of the limited sources of revenue open to local authorities, they have been forced to depend to a large extent on loans from the central government. The data in Table 3 show the extent of such loans for the period 1964–8. As in the case of grants, the system for loans is arbitrary, depending in many cases on the persuasiveness of the particular authority and even on political factors. Many local authorities have complained bitterly against the procedure for granting loans, some even alleging discrimination. Authorities are allowed to borrow from non-government sources, but only with the prior consent of the central Government. With the relatively undeveloped state of the local capital market, substantial amounts are never forthcoming from such sources. Some authorities have even complained of discrimination where they have sought government approval to borrow from such sources. Assuming that the necessary funds are available, local authorities should be given all encouragement to borrow from such external sources, as this would tend to relieve the pressure on the central Treasury. However, this should not obviate the necessity for the central Government to try as far as possible to make loans to local authorities for capital works and at a low rate of interest. This would tend to remove possible charges of discrimination and dissatisfaction, and prevent them from going to the money market at unfavourable times.

Even if grants and loans were made available to them on a rational basis, local authorities will for some time be in need of additional finances for development works and the provision of essential services. There is a wide range of such possible sources.[25] Research into such possibilities should be one of the first tasks undertaken by the new authorities being contemplated. Two possibilities readily come to mind – a cattle tax and a transportation tax. In the rural areas there are large numbers of cattle owners, and consideration should be given to the possibility of imposing a small tax on each head of cattle. While it is known that animals are mobile and owners are likely to remove them to places where they cannot be counted in order to avoid payment, experience has shown that owners are in the habit of caring for their animals in enclosed savannahs provided by the local authority or private owners. Most of these savannahs are under the control of village rangers, who could be made responsible for counting and the general administration of the scheme. The assessment or levy could be made on a yearly basis, with account being taken of any adjustments made during the course of the year. Further, local authorities might be given wide powers to prosecute owners who attempt to remove cattle in order to beat the levy.

The proposal for a transportation tax rests on the assumption of the agricultural potential of rural areas. These areas are responsible for the greater part of rice production in Guyana, and the proposal is that a small tax should be levied on every bag of paddy transported along village roads, dams or canals, based on the criterion of distance. The proceeds from such a levy could go towards road repairs, the digging and cleaning of canals or trenches, and in some cases even the provision of better drainage and irrigation. This could possibly result in a saving of revenue now being used exclusively for the maintenance of the said facilities.

Table 3
Central Government Loans to Local Authorities
1964–8
(Guyana dollars)

Administrative districts	*1964*	*1965*	*1966*	*1967*	*1968*	*Total*
East Berbice	203,871·04	204,221·04	204,221·04	173,200·00	160,200·00	945, 713·12
West Berbice	47,100·00	77,300·00	78,774·97	76,774·97	72,774·97	352,724·91
East Demerara:						
East Coast Section	252,233·00	234,133·00	234,133·00	246,133·00	241,133·00	1,207,765·00
East Bank Section	141,713·49	141,713·58	153,253·58	143,253·58	140,713·58	720,647·81
West Demerara	175,672·43	155,572·43	151,759·35	133,972·44	135,406·77	752,383·42
Essequibo Island	22,413·50	14,500·00	14,000·00	14,500·00	14,500·00	79,913·50
Mazaruni/Potaro	10,932·00	10,932·00	9,557·00	12,000·00	12,000·00	55,421·00
Essequibo	34,769·00	40,455·00	18,050·00	17,450·00	21,254·00	131,978·00
North West District	19,300·00	19,300·00	12,000·00	8,957·00	8,957·00	68,514·00
Total	908,004·46	898,127·05	875,748·94	826,240·99	806,939·32	4,315,060·76

On the expenditure side the picture is a very uninteresting one. The data contained in Table 4 show the pattern of such expenditure for the period 1964–8. The trend and pattern are similar to those noticeable for the economy as a whole, with public overhead facilities–drainage and irrigation, pure water supply and the maintenance of roads and bridges – taking the lion's share. It is within this context that the plea for bigger grants and loans to local authorities, and on a more rational basis, and also a more extensive search for new sources of revenue, comes into clear focus. The central Government should either provide some of these overhead facilities on a direct basis as a part of its overall development drive, thus releasing more local revenue for investment in directly productive activities, or if the situation remains one in which local authorities must continue to use up the greater proportion of their meagre revenue for works which are not directly productive, then it becomes incumbent upon the central Government to step up the quantity and quality of its grants and loans.

IV. CONCLUDING REMARKS

Guyana, like most other developing countries, has always presented a picture of a lop-sided dualist economic structure and society, a situation in which there exist a few small pockets of visible economic progress, with the rest of the economy (mostly rural areas) living in a state of continued degradation and poverty. Our concept of economic development is one in which visible structural and institutional changes are effected so that in time the picture would change into that of a uniform economy, with all sections playing a meaningful role in the process and progressively becoming fully integrated into it. It is within this overall context that the changes proposed for the local government system should be seen.

In the first instance, attempts should be made at instituting planning at the local level, as a part of planning at the regional level and for the entire economy. For planning purposes the entire economy should be divided up into Development Districts, each encompassing several local authorities, with a regional Planning or Development Committee being responsible for plan preparation and implementation. The membership of such Regional Planning Committees should be comprised of the relevant technicians drawn from the central Government, especially the ministry or department

Table 4
Major Items of Expenditure for Local Authorities, 1964–8
(Guyana dollars)

Types	*1964*	*1965*	*1966*	*1967*	*1968*	*Total*
Drainage and irrigation	198,761	155,294	262,579	231,915	190,064	1,038,613
	39,030	87,722	104,961	41,651	85,238	358,602
Law costs	13,761	15,354	20,442	26,314	152,451	228,322
Office	7,755	8,140	10,926	15,542	17,404	59,767
Outstanding accounts	54,605	30,372	30,777	67,422	80,253	263,429
Pure water supply	180,282	194,552	156,605	219,730	166,180	917,349
Roads, dams, bridges, etc.	153,573	103,595	150,273	216,316	143,553	767,310
Salaries	210,101	220,417	241,167	287,758	226,814	1,186,257
Miscellaneous	48,413	50,491	70,496	90,381	39,913	299,694
Total	906,281	865,937	1,048,226	1,197,029	1,101,870	5,119,343

responsible for drawing up the country's economic programme and responsible officers drawn from the various local authorities which fall within their ambit, thereby ensuring that co-ordination and dialogue are at all times maintained at the local, regional and national levels. In such a case the full-scale regional plans drawn up by these bodies will not only reflect the needs of the local authorities as set out in their own plans, but also overall national objectives.

The implementation of such a scheme will have the salutary effect of tending to upgrade the quality of local authority personnel, who will be gaining experience in the ramifications of development planning, and in time reflect in the physical economic development of local authority areas, which will now be playing an active and important role in the planning and development machinery and process, rather than being the mere appendages to the system which they are today.[26] The dynamic implications of such a scheme are obvious. Improvement in the quality of planning at the local level will, over time, reflect positively on the quality of life and development in the rural economy, which on the basis of its new viability will now be able to engage the services of more competent locally based staff, with further advantageous effects on the quality of local planning and development.

The idea also has implications in the financial field. In an earlier section of this paper reference was made to the fact that a system of block grants could be provided on a regional basis to local authorities. This could form part of a scheme whereby the central Government sets up a pool of funds from which loans could be made to local authorities, through their regional committees, for large-scale capital works covering the entire region or more than one local authority.

REFERENCES

1. See U. K. Hicks, *Development from Below: Local Government Finance in Developing Countries of the Commonwealth* (Oxford U.P., 1961).

2. For authoritative accounts of the history of local government in Guyana, see Allan Young, *The Approaches to Local Self-Government in British Guiana* (London: Longmans, 1958); also C. H. Grant, 'Rural Local Government in Guyana and British Honduras', *Social and Economic Studies* (Mar 1967).

3. For better administration of the coastlands and adjacent occupied territory, Guyana was divided into four administrative counties as follows: (1) Berbice–the area between the west bank of the Abary river and the Courantyne river, with the exception of the town of New Amsterdam; (2) East Demerara–the area between the left bank of the Abary river and Hyde Park on the Demerara river,

with the exception of the city of Georgetown; (3) West Demerara–the area between the left bank of the Demerara river and the right bank of the Essequibo river, as well as the district around Bartica and the penal settlement at Mazaruni, the island of Leguan and the district on the right bank of the Demerara river above Hyde Park; (4) Essequibo–the area west of the West Demerara administrative county to the boundary of Venezuela.

4. District Commissioners were to be responsible for the general supervision of district councils and other central government officers working within the district, with the exception of the magistracy and the police. They were also required to attend meetings of district concils and take part in the deliberations, to keep all accounts of the councils and authorise expenditure. See C. H. Grant, 'The District Commissioner System in British Guiana', *Journal of Commonwealth Political Studies* (Mar 1965).

5. United Nations, *Centralisation and Decentralisation* (New York, 1961).

6. *Report of the Waddington Commission*, Col. 280 (1951).

7. *Report of the Robertson Commission*, Cmd 9274 (1954).

8. A. H. Marshall, *Report on Local Government in British Guiana* (Georgetown 1955).

9. Hicks, *Development from Below*, p. 146.

10. *Marshall Report*, pp. 27–8.

11. See the Municipal and District Councils Act, 1969.

12. Hicks, *Development from Below*, p. 147.

13. Between 1959 (when the last local government elections were held) and 1967 the whole machinery was at a standstill. The election of village councillors scheduled to be held between November and December 1961 was postponed by the Local Government (Postponement of Elections) Ordinance No. 41 of 1961. The matter was further complicated by the decision to introduce legislation around 1962 to provide for elections under adult suffrage.

14. The period 1967–70 saw the preparation of the following pieces of legislation:

(*a*) The Local Government Special Provisions Act, No. 18, 1967.
(*b*) Local Authorities (Elections) Bill, 1968.
(*c*) Municipal and District Councils Bill, 1968.
(*d*) The Valuation for Rating Purposes Act, 1969.
(*e*) The Local Government (Amendment) Act, No. 9, 1969.
(*f*) The Municipal and District Councils Act, No. 24, 1969.
(*g*) The Local Authorities (Elections) Act, No. 23, 1969.

Marshall had recommended that the Wismar–Christianburg–Mackenzie (bauxite-mining) area be made a local authority, and this was brought into effect by Act No. 18 of 1967. The Bills of 1967 and 1968, which were mainly for informaton and comment, followed the Marshall recommendations very closely. The Valuation for Rating Purposes Act of 1969, which was also prepared with a view to implementing the Marshall recommendations, made provision for the valuation of property on which rates were to be levied in areas administered by local authorities. It made provision for a uniform valuation system and replaced the old system whereby valuations differed between areas. The Local Government (Amendment) Act of 1969 provided for the amalgamation, where it was considered necessary, of existing local authorities. The idea was to create larger local authorities to go hand in hand with the setting-up of rural district councils. Later, after much consultation and planning, both the Municipal and District Councils Act and the Local Authorities (Elections) Act were passed in November

1969. It was hoped that the provisions under these Acts would have been put into effect immediately on their passing, and elections held in December 1969. However, there was a series of administrative delays and elections for the first six areas were not held until the end of June 1970. The areas selected were Greater Georgetown, Greater New Amsterdam, Wismar–Christianburg–Mackenzie, Bartica, Sheet Anchor–Cumberland and Leguan. The expectation was that elections would have been held in the remaining areas by December 1970.

15. For an interesting account of the development of plantation economies, see L. Best, 'Outlines of a Model of Pure Plantation Economy', *Social and Economic Studies* (Sep 1968); also G. Beckford, 'The Economics of Agricultural Resource Use and Development in Plantation Economies', *Social and Economic Studies* (Dec 1969).

16. The powers of the Village Districts and Country Districts were initially similar, save that the Governing Council of the former, prior to 1959, was partly elected and partly nominated while the latter was wholly nominated. Before September 1959 the Council of the Village District consisted of not more than nine elected and appointed councillors in the proportion of 2:1, but at this time the Local Government Ordinance was amended to provide for wholly elected village councils. The Village Districts are higher in status than the Country Districts and the latter would only be elevated to the status of the former if the Local Government Board is satisfied that the people in the Country Districts are responsible enough to elect their own representatives who would form their own governing councils.

17. Under the new system being introduced, the franchise has been extended to persons of adult age with residence as the qualification for voting. See the Municipal and District Councils Act, 1969.

18. The decision taken in each case is prompted by the relatively high status of professions such as law and medicine. Professionals qualified in such fields, on return from their studies abroad, tend to live in urban areas and their interest in village politics tends to disappear. Even those who do not study for a profession tend to migrate from the villages and take up occupations in fields other than agriculture. This is an aspect of the rural–urban drift which characterises developing countries generally.

19. *Marshall Report*.

20. Hicks, *Development from Below*, p. 277.

21. They are permitted to exempt from taxes places used exclusively for religious, cultural and recreational activities. In the case of government buildings the central Government gives an administrative grant, but this has not kept pace with the number and value of buildings erected. However, under the new scheme of things the central Government is expected to get adequate rates on its property and the administrative grant will be withdrawn.

22. See Municipal and District Councils Act, 1969, Part VI.

23. Hicks, *Development from Below*, p. 408. It is rather surprising that the Municipal and District Councils Act of 1969, which is supposed to be the modern blueprint of local government in Guyana, ushering a new period of reform, contains only the vaguest reference to grants, with no statement of central government policy on this important subject.

24. In 1968 the City of Georgetown received the sum of G$142,750 from the central Government for child welfare work and G$250 for the upkeep of Vlissengen drainage. In the same year New Amsterdam received the sum of G$30,000 as a subvention towards the upkeep of its roads. As a matter of fact, these municipalities have been receiving increasing amounts of subsidy over the years. The local authorities of Kitty, Newton, Bel Air Park and Lodge are among the

few which never received any central government subsidy despite the fact that their roads, like those of the towns, were being used for general communications. But as we have mentioned, this type of grant should be extended to all local authorities as an incentive for the development of certain essential services.

25. For an authoritative discussion of possible new sources, see Hicks, *Development from Below*.

26. The arguments presented here have been developed by the present writer in a series of background papers written while he was Leader of the Development Planning Team in Guyana. In particular, see my monograph entitled *Planning from Below* (Georgetown, Guyana, 1970) Ministry of Economic Development.

Select Bibliography

Acharya, S. (1971) 'Unemployment, Excess Capacity and Benefit–Cost Investment Criteria: A Comment', *Review of Economics and Statistics.*

Andic, S., and Veverka, J. (1963–4) 'The Growth of Government Expenditure in German since the Unification', *Finanzarchiv.*

Bacha, E., and Taylor, L. (1971) 'Foreign Exchange Shadow Prices in Chile: Conflicting Theories and Comparative Evaluations', *Quarterly Journal of Economics.*

Balassa, B., and Schydlowsky, D. (1968) 'Effective Tariffs, Domestic Cost of Foreign Exchange, and the Equilibrium Exchange Rate'. *Journal of Political Economy.*

Balopoulos, E. T. (1969) 'Measuring the Effects of the Budget on Aggregate Demand and/or Balance of Payments', in A. T. Peacock (ed.), *Quantitative Analysis in Public Finance* (New York: Praeger).

Barzel, Y. (1969) 'Two Propositions on the Optimum Level of Producing Collective Goods', *Public Choice.*

Bastable, C. F. (1907) *Public Finance*, 3rd ed. (London: Macmillan).

Baumol, W. J. (1965) *Welfare Economics and the Theory of the State* (Cambridge, Mass.: Harvard U.P.).

Beckerman, W. (1968) *Introduction to National Income Analysis* (London: Weidenfeld & Nicolson).

Beckford, G. (1969) 'The Economics of Agricultural Resource Use and Development in Plantation Economies', *Social and Economic Studies.*

Beloff, M. (1953) 'The "Federal Solution" in its Application to Europe, Asia and Africa', *Political Studies.*

Best, L. (1968) 'Outlines of a Model of Pure Plantation Economy', *Social and Economic Studies.*

Bonin, J. M., Finch, B. W., and Waters, B. (1969) 'Alternative Tests of the "Displacement Effect" Hypothesis', *Public Finance.*

Brainard, W. C., and Dolbear, F. T. (1967) 'The Possibility of Oversupply of Local "Public" Goods', *Journal of Political Economy.*

Brennan, G. (1969) 'The Optimal Provision of Public Goods', *Journal of Political Economy*.

Breton, A. (1965) 'A theory of Government Grants', *Canadian Journal of Economics and Political Science*.

Bryce, M. D. (1960) *Industrial Development* (New York: McGraw-Hill).

Buchanan, J. M. (1950) 'Federalism and Fiscal Equity', *American Economic Review*.

—— (ed.) (1961) *Public Finances: Needs, Sources and Utilisation* (Princeton U.P.).

—— (1962) 'Federal Grants and Resource Allocation', *Journal of Political Economy*.

—— (1962) 'Federal Grants and Resource Allocation: A Reply', *Journal of Political Economy*.

—— (1965) 'An Economic Theory of Clubs', *Economica*.

—— (1966) 'Joint Supply, Externality, and Optimality', *Economica*.

—— (1968) 'Comment' on R. A. Musgrave, 'Approaches to a Fiscal Theory of Political Federalism', in *Public Finances: Needs, Sources and Utilisation* (1961).

—— (1968) *The Demand and Supply of Public Goods* (Chicago: Rand McNally).

—— and Kafoglis, M. J. (1963) 'A Note on Public Goods Supply', *American Economic Review*.

—— and Wagner, R. E. (1968) 'An Efficiency Basis for Federal Fiscal Equalisation', in *Universities–N.B.E.R. Conference on Economics of Public Output*.

—— (1971) 'Principles of Urban Fiscal Strategy', *Public Choice*.

—— and Goetz, C. J. (1972) 'Efficiency Limits of Fiscal Mobility: An Assessment of the Tiebout Model', *Public Economics*.

Bullock, C. J. (1898) 'Direct and Indirect Taxes in Economic Literature', *Political Science Quarterly*.

Coase, R. H. (1960) 'The Problem of Social Cost', *Journal of Law and Economics*.

Commission on Organisation of the Executive Branch of the Government (1949) *Budgeting and Accounting* (Washington, D.C.).

Copeland, M. A. (1961) *Trends in Government Financing* (Princeton U.P.).

David, W. L. (1970) *Planning from Below* (Georgetown, Guyana: Ministry of Economic Development).

Davis, O. A., Dempster, M. A. H., and Wildavsky, A. (1966) 'A

Theory of the Budgeting Process', *American Political Science Review.*

—— and Whinston, A. B. (1962) 'Externalities, Welfare, and the Theory of Games', *Journal of Political Economy.*

—— and —— (1965) 'Some Notes on Equating Private and Social Cost', *Southern Economic Journal.*

—— and —— (1966) 'On Externalities, Information and the Government-Assisted Invisible Hand', *Economica.*

Due, J. F. (1964) 'Introduction. The Issues', in Brookings Institution and N.B.E.R., *The Role of Direct and Indirect Taxes in the Federal Revenue System* (Princeton U.P.).

—— (1969) 'The Uganda Sales Tax on Importation and Manufacture', *Eastern Africa Economic Review.*

Eckstein, O. (1957) 'Investment Criteria for Economic Development and the Theory of Intertemporal Welfare Economics', *Quarterly Journal of Economics.*

Emi, K. (1963) *Government Fiscal Activity and Economic Growth in Japan, 1868–1960* (Tokyo: Kenokuniya).

—— and Shinoya, Y. (1966) 'Government Expenditures', in *Estimates of Long-term Economic Statistics of Japan since 1868* [In Japanese].

Fabricant, S. (1952) *The Trend of Government Activity in the United States since 1900* (New York: National Bureau of Economic Research).

Feldstein, M. S. (Mar 1964) 'Net Social Benefit Calculation and the Public Investment Decision', *Oxford Economic Papers.*

—— (June 1964) 'The Social Time Preference Discount Rate in Cost–Benefit Analysis', *Economic Journal.*

—— (1965) 'The Derivation of Social Time Preference Rates', *Kyklos.*

—— (1970) 'Financing in the Evaluation of Public Expenditure', in *Essays in Honour of Richard Musgrave* (forthcoming).

Frankel, S. H. (1938) *Capital Investment in Africa* (London: Oxford U.P.)

Galenson, W., and Leibenstein, H. (1955) 'Investment Criteria, Productivity, and Economic Development', *Quarterly Journal of Economics.*

Graham, J. F. (1963) *Fiscal Adjustment and Economic Development* (Toronto).

Grant, C. H. (1965) 'The District Commissioner System in British Guiana', *Journal of Commonwealth Political Studies.*

—— (1967) 'Rural Local Government in Guyana and British Honduras', *Social and Economic Studies.*

Gupta, S. P. (1967) 'Public Expenditure and Economic Growth: A Time-Series Analysis', *Public Finance.*

Haig, R. M. (1934) 'Taxation', in *Encyclopaedia of the Social Sciences*, vol. XIV (London: Macmillan).

Hansen, B. (1969) *Fiscal Policy in Seven Countries* (Paris: O.E.C.D.).

Harberger, A. C. (1965) 'Survey of Literature on Cost–Benefit Analysis for Industrial Project Evaluation', paper presented at the United Nations Inter-Regional Symposium in Industrial Project Evaluation (Prague).

Hartle, D. G., and Bird, R. M. (1969) 'Criteria for the Design of Governmental Decision-Making Units', *Canadian Economics Association Conference.*

Haveman, R., and Krutilla, J. (1967) 'Unemployment, Excess Capacity and Benefit–Cost Investment Criteria', *Review of Economics and Statistics.*

Hawkins, E. K. (1958) *Road Transport in Nigeria: A Study of African Enterprise* (Oxford U.P.).

Head, J. G. (1962) 'Public Goods and Public Policy', *Public Finance.*

—— (1968) 'The Theory of Public Goods', *Rivista di Diritto Finanziario e Scienza delle Finanze.*

—— (1969) 'Merit Goods Revisited', *Finanzarchiv.*

Hicks, J. R. (1940) 'Valuation of Social Income', *Economica.*

—— (1948) *The Problem of Budgetary Reform* (Oxford U.P.).

—— (1960) *Essays in World Economics* (Oxford U.P.).

—— (1961) 'The Nature and Basis of Economic Growth', in U. K. Hicks *et al.*, *Federalism and Economic Growth in Underdeveloped Countries* (London: Allen & Unwin).

Hicks, U. K. (1946) 'The Terminology of Tax Analysis', *Economic Journal.*

—— (1954) *British Public Finances: Their Structure and Development, 1880–1952* (Oxford U.P.).

—— (1961) *Development from Below: Local Government Finance in Developing Countries of the Commonwealth* (Oxford U.P.).

—— (1965) *Development Finance: Planning and Control* (Oxford U.P.).

—— (1968) 'Current Problems of Federal Finance in India and Some Comparisons with Australia', *Public Finance.*

Hirschman, A. O. (1958) *The Strategy of Economic Development* (New Haven: Yale U.P.).

Hochman, H. M., and Rodgers, J. D. (1969) 'Pareto-Optimal Redistribution', *American Economic Review*.

International Bank for Reconstruction and Development (1955) *The Economic Development of Malaya* (Baltimore: Johns Hopkins Press).

Jetha, N. (1966) 'Low-Income Taxation in Kenya', *British Tax Review*.

—— (1970) 'Central Government Taxes in Kenya', *Bulletin for International Fiscal Documentation*.

Kilby, P. (1965) *African Enterprise: The Nigerian Bread Industry*, Hoover Institution Studies (Stanford U.P.).

Kindleberger, C. P. (1965) *Economic Development*, 2nd ed. (New York: McGraw-Hill).

Kuznets, S. (1948) 'On the Valuation of Social Income: Reflections of Professor Hicks' "The Valuation of the Social Income"', *Economica*.

Laski, H. J. (1939) 'The Obsolescence of Federalism', *The Republic*.

Little, I. M. D., and Mirrlees, J. A. (1969) *Manual Of Industrial Project Analysis in Developing Countries*, vol. II: *Social Cost–Benefit Analysis* (Paris: O.E.C.D.).

Lotz, J. R. (1969) 'Some Economic Effects of Increasing Public Expenditures: An Empirical Study of Selected Countries', *Public Finance*.

—— (1970) 'Measuring the Effects of Fiscal Policy in Developing Countries', *Finanzarchiv*.

McLure, C. E., Jr (1970) 'Tax Incidence, Macroeconomic Policy and Absolute Prices', *Quarterly Journal of Economics*.

Marglin, S. A. (1963) *Approaches to Dynamic Investment Planning* (Amsterdam: North-Holland Publishing Company).

—— (Feb 1963) 'The Social Rate of Discount and the Optimal Rate of Investment', *Quarterly Journal of Economics*.

—— (May 1963) 'The Opportunity Cost of Public Investment', *Quarterly Journal of Economics*.

Marshall, A. H. (1965) *Report on Local Government in British Guiana* (Georgetown).

Massell, B. F. (1968) 'Consistent Estimation of Expenditure Elasticities from Cross-Section Data on Households Producing Partly for Subsistence' (mimeograph).

—— and Heyer, J. (1969) 'Household Expenditure in Nairobi: A Statistical Analysis of Consumer Behaviour', *Economic Development and Cultural Change.*

Mathews, R. (1962) *Accounting for Economists* (Melbourne: Cheshire).

—— (1969) 'Resource Allocation in Universities', *Australian University.*

Maxwell, J. A. (1969) *Financing State and Local Governments* (Washington, D.C.: Brookings Institution).

May, R. J. (1969) *Federalism and Fiscal Adjustment* (Oxford U.P.).

Michas, N. A. (1969) 'Variations in the Level of Provincial–Municipal Expenditures in Canada: An Econometric Analysis', *Public Finance.*

Minanami, R. (1965) 'Railway and Electric Utilities', in *Estimates of Long-term Economic Statistics of Japan since 1868* [In Japanese].

Morag, A. (1965) *On Taxes and Inflation* (New York: Random House).

Musgrave, R. A. (1959) *Theory of Public Finance* (New York: McGraw-Hill).

—— (1969) *Fiscal Systems* (New Haven and London: Yale U.P.).

Oates, W. E. (1972) *Fiscal Federalism* (New York: Harcourt Brace Jovanovich).

Okhawa, K. (1966) 'Capital Stock', in *Estimates of Long-term Economic Statistics of Japan since 1868* [in Japanese].

Olson, M. (1969) 'The Principle of "Fiscal Equivalence" ', *American Economic Review, Papers and Proceedings.*

Pauly, M. V. (1970) 'Efficiency in the Provision of Consumption Subsidies', *Kyklos.*

—— (1970) 'Optimality, "Public" Goods and Local Governments', *Journal of Political Economy.*

—— (1972) 'Income Redistribution as a Local Public Good', *Public Choice Society Conference.*

Peacock, A. T. and Wiseman, J. (1961) *The Growth of Public Expenditure in the United Kingdom* (Oxford U.P.).

—— and —— (1968) 'Measuring the Efficiency of Government Expenditure', in A. R. Prest (ed.), *Public Sector Economics* (Manchester U.P.).

Perloff, H. S., and Nathan, R. P. (eds.) (1968) *Revenue Sharing and the City* (Baltimore: Johns Hopkins Press).

Pigou, A. C. (1929) *A Study in Public Finance* (London: Macmillan).

Prest, A. R. (1955) 'Statistical Calculations of Tax Burdens'. *Economica.*

—— (1959) 'The Expenditure Tax and Saving', *Economic Journal.*

—— (1968) 'The Budget and Interpersonal Distribution', *Public Finance*, parts I and II.

Public Expenditure: A New Presentation (1967) Cmnd 4017 (London: H.M.S.O.).

Rao V.K.R.V. (1964) *Essays in Economic Development* (London: Asia Publishing House).

Reddy, K. N. (1970) 'Growth of Government Expenditure and National Income in India: 1872–1966', *Public Finance.*

Report of the Commission on Revenue Allocation (1951) (Lagos, Nigeria: Government Printer).

Report of the Committee Appointed to Review the Financial Provisions of the Federation of Malaya Agreement, 1948 (1955) (Kuala Lumpur: Government Press).

Report of the Plowden Committee to Control Expenditure (1959) Cmnd 1432 (London: H.M.S.O.).

Report of the President's Commissionon Budget Concepts (1967) (Washington D.C.: U.S. Government Printing Office.

Richards, P., and Stoutjesdyk, E. (1970) *Agriculture in Ceylon until 1985* (Paris: O.E.C.D.).

Rolph, E. R. (1954) *The Theory of Fiscal Economics* (Berkeley and Los Angeles: California U.P.).

—— (1968) 'Taxation', in *The International Encyclopaedia of the Social Sciences* (New York: Macmillan).

Rosovsky, H. (1961) *Capital Formation in Japan, 1868–1941*) (New York: The Free Press).

Rostow, W. W. (1960) *The Stages of Economic Growth* (Cambridge U.P.).

Rothenberg, J. (1968) 'Local Decentralisation and the Theory of Optimal Government' in *Universities – N.B.E.R. Conference on Economics of Public Output.*

Samuelson, P. A. (1954) 'The Pure Theory of Public Expenditure', *Review of Economics and Statistics.*

Sandmo, A., and Dreze, J. (1970) 'Discount Rates for Public Investment in Closed and Open Economics', CORE Discussion Paper No. 7025 (Louvain, Belgium).

Sastri, K. V. S. (1966) *Federal–State Fiscal Relations in India* (Oxford U.P.).

Schydlowsky, D. M. (1968) 'On the Choice of a Shadow Price for Foreign Exchange', Economic Development Report No. 108. Development Advisory Service, Harvard University (Cambridge, Mass.).

Scott, A. D. (1962) 'Federal Grants and Resource Allocation', *Journal of Political Economy*.

—— (1964) 'The Economic Goals of Federal Finance', *Public Finance*.

Selowsky, M. (1969) 'On the Measurement of Education's Contribution to Growth', *Quarterly Journal of Economics*.

Shoup, C. S. (1969) *Public Finance* (Chicago: Aldine).

Sidgwick, H. (1883) *Principles of Political Economy* (London: Macmillan).

Simpson, D. (1963) 'Investment, Employment, and Government Expenditures in the Highlands, 1951–1960', *Scottish Journal of Political Economy*.

Singer, H. W., and Doss, A. C. (1969) 'Technical Assistance to Kenya: Some Thoughts on Flows and Programming', *Eastern Africa Economic Review*.

Sokolski, A. (1965) *The Establishment of Manufacturing in Nigeria* (New York: Praeger).

Sorensen, T. C. (1970) *The Kennedy Legacy* (New York: Macmillan).

Steiner, P. O. (1969) 'Choosing among Alternative Public Investments in the Water Resource Field', *American Economic Review*.

Stigler, G. J. (1957) 'The Tenable Range of Functions of Local Government', in Joint Economic Committee, *Federal Expenditure Policy for Economic Growth and Stability*.

Stone, R. (1947) 'Appendix' to *Measurement of National Income and Contribution of Social Accounts* (Geneva: United Nations).

—— and Stone, G. (1961) *National Income and Expenditure*, 5th ed. (London: Bowes & Bowes).

Tiebout, C. M. (1956) 'A Pure Theory of Local Expenditures', *Journal of Political Economy*.

—— (1961) 'An Economic Theory of Fiscal Decentralisation', in J. M. Buchanan (ed.), *Public Finances: Needs, Sources and Utilisation* (Princeton U.P.).

—— and Houston, D. B. (1962) 'Metropolitan Finance Reconsidered: Budget Functions and Multi-Level Governments', *Review of Economics and Statistics*.

Tinbergen, J. (1963) *On the Theory of Economic Policy* (Amsterdam: North-Holland Publishing Company).

United Nations (1958) *A Manual for Economic and Functional Classification of Government Transactions* (New York).

Tullock, G. (1969) 'Federalism: Problems of Scale', *Public Choice*.

—— (1961) *Centralisation and Decentralisation* (New York).

—— (1965) *A Manual for Programme and Performance Budgeting* (New York).

—— (1965) *World Economic Survey*, part I: *The Financing of Economic Development* (New York).

Veverka, J. (1969) 'The Growth of Government Expenditure in the United Kingdom since 1790', *Scottish Journal of Political Economy*.

Watts, R. L. (1966) *New Federations: Experiments in the Commonwealth* (Oxford U.P.).

Weralski, M. (1969) 'Les Problèmes de la fiscalité dans les états socialistes', *Revue de Science Financière* (Paris).

Wheare, K. C. (1946) *Federal Government*, 1st ed. (Oxford U.P.).

Williams, A. (1966) 'The Optimal Provision of Public Goods in a System of Local Government', *Journal of Political Economy*.

Young, A. (1958) *The Approaches to Local Self-Government in British Guiana* (London: Longmans).

List of Works by Ursula Hicks

BOOKS

The Finance of British Government, 1920–36 (Oxford U.P., 1938; 2nd ed. with new Introduction, 1970).

The Taxation of War Wealth (with J. R. Hicks and L. Rostas) (Oxford: Clarendon Press, 1941; 2nd ed., 1942).

Public Finance (Cambridge U.P., 1947; rev. ed., 1951; 2nd ed., 1955; 3rd ed., 1968).

Standards of Local Expenditure (with J. R. Hicks), N.I.E.S.R. Occasional Papers, vol. VI (1943).

The Problem of Valuation for Rating (with J. R. Hick), N.I.E.S.R. Occasional Papers, vol. VII (1944).

The Incidence of Local Rates in Great Britain (with J. R. Hicks), N.I.E.S.R. Occasional Papers, vol. VIII (1945).

India: Public Finance Survey of Indian Finance (New York: United Nations, 1951).

British Public Finances: Their Structure and Development, 1880–1952 (Oxford U.P., 1954).

Development from Below: A Study of Local Government and Finance in Developing Countries of the British Commonwealth (Oxford U.P., 1961).

Federalism and Economic Growth in Underdeveloped Countries (with others) (London: Allen & Unwin, 1961).

Report of the Eastern Caribbean Fiscal Commission, Cmnd 1991 (London: H.M.S.O., 1963).

Development Finance: Planning and Control (Oxford U.P., 1965).

ARTICLES

'Beveridge Plan and Local Government Finance', *Review of Economic Studies*, X (1943).

'The Terminology of Tax Analysis', *Economic Journal*, LVI (1946); reprinted in *Readings in the Theory of Taxation*, ed. C. S. Shoup and R. A. Musgrave (Evanston, Ill.: American Economic Association, 1959).

'National and Local Finance', *Economic Journal*, LVI (1946).

'The Great Provisions of the Local Government Bill', *Bulletin of the Oxford Institute of Economics and Statistics* (1948).

'The Reform of Japanese Taxation', *Public Finance* (1951).

'The Search for Revenue in Underdeveloped Countries', *Librairie Générale de Droit et de Jurisprudence* (Paris, 1951).

'The Budget as an Instrument of Policy, 1937–1953', *Three Banks Review* (1953).

'The Valuation Tangle', *Public Administration* (1954).

'Direct Taxation and Economic Growth', *Oxford Economic Paper* (1956).

'The Control of Public Expenditure', *Lloyds Bank Review* (1961).

'On Teaching Public Finance', *Oxford Economic Papers* (1961).

'Choice, Efficiency and Control', in *Public Expenditure: Appraisal and Control*, ed. A. T. Peacock (Edinburgh: Oliver & Boyd, 1963).

'The Economics of Educational Expansion in Low-Income Countries', *Three Banks Review* (1965).

'Finance of the City State', *Malayan Economic Review* (Oct 1960).

'Plowden, Planning and Management in Public Services' (with Dr A. Mitchell) (1961).

'The Integration of Budget and Development Plan', *Public Finance* (1962).

'The Revenue Implications of the Uganda and Tanganyika Development Plans', *Journal of Development Studies* (Apr 1966).

'Finance of Economic Development in Malaysia', *United Malayan Banking Corporation Economic Review* (1967).

'Autonomous Revenue for Local Government', *Western Economic Journal*, VI 3 (June 1968).

'Memorandum for the Consideration of the Fifth Finance Commission', *Indian Institute of Public Opinion Monthly Commentary on Indian Economic Conditions*, X 3 (1968).

'Current Problems of Federal Finance in India and Some Comparisons with Australia', *Public Finance* (July 1968).

'Economic and Financial Problems of Metropolitan Areas', *Zeitschrift für Nationalökonomie*, XXIX (1969).

'Educational Expansion in Low-Income Countries, with Special Reference to India', *Indian Economic Thought and Development*. Nehru's Memorial Volume (Bombay, 1969).

'New Revenue Sources for Local Government: An Assessment',

Local Government Finance (May 1969; London: Institute of Municipal Treasurers and Accountants).

'La Finanza Publica nel quadro della politica economica e sociale della Gran Bretagna', *Bancaria* (1969).

'Rural Taxation and its Contribution to Development', *Development and Change*, I 3 (1969–70; The Hague: Institute of Social Studies).

'The Financing of Local Government', *Local Government Finance* (Nov 1970; London: Institute of Municipal Treasurers and Accountants).

'Can Land Value be Assessed for Purposes of Site Value Taxation?', in *The Assessment of Land Value*, ed. Daniel M. Holland (Madison: Wisconsin U.P., 1970).

'Current Experiments in Budgetary Organisation', *Malayan Bank Review* (Dec 1970).

'Experimentos acturales en Materia Presupuestaria', *La Revista de Ciencieas Administrativas del University of La Plata* (Argentina, 1971).

'Metropolitan Areas, A New Problem for Local Government', *Three Banks Review*, Dec 1971.

'City Transport and Circulation Problems in the Less Developed Countries with Special Reference to India', in *Report of a Seminar on Transport (All India) held at Dharwar, Mysore, India* (Mar 1972).

Notes on Contributors

ENOCH A. ANYANWU is an economist in the Industry Division of the World Bank in Washington and was formerly Economic Adviser at the Board of Trade, London. He has spent several years in the Government Economic Service in both Nigeria and Britain. He has served as Research Officer at the Oxford University Institute of Economics and Statistics, and also at the National Institute of Economic and Social Research, London. He has co-authored (with A. H. C. Broadbent) 'Forecasting Trade between O.E.C.D. Countries and Primary Producers', *National Institute Economic Review* (May 1970).

GAMANI COREA was Permanent Secretary to the Ministry of Planning and Development in Ceylon during the Senanayake regime, and also Deputy Governor of the Central Bank of Ceylon. He has served as a member of several national and international commissions and committees, and has made important contributions to the knowledge of planning and development in both the academic and practical fields. He is currently attached to the Institute of Development Studies at the University of Sussex.

WILFRED L. DAVID, editor of this collection as well as contributor, is Associate Professor of Economics at the University of Delaware, and did graduate work under Ursula Hicks at Oxford. He has taught at Brooklyn College of the City University of New York and at the University of Guyana, and was a Fellow at the Metropolitan Applied Research Center in New York. He will shortly be taking up a chair in Political Economy at Howard University in Washington.

CLIVE T. EDWARDS is a Senior Lecturer in Economics at the School of General Studies, Australian National University, Canberra. He is the author of *Public Finances in Malaya and Singapore* (1970), and of several articles in the *Malaysian Economic Review* and other journals.

MARTIN S. FELDSTEIN is Professor of Economics at Harvard University. He held appointments as Research Fellow and Official Fellow respectively at Nuffield College, Oxford, and succeeded Lady Hicks as University Lecturer in Public Finance at Oxford. His many papers include 'Net Social Benefit Calculation and the Public Investment Decision,' *Oxford Economic Papers* (Mar 1964); 'The Social Time Preference Discount Rate in Cost–Benefit Analysis', *Economic Journal* (June 1964); 'Opportunity Cost Calculations in Cost–Benefit Analysis', *Public Finance*, XIX 2 (1964).

JOHN G. HEAD, Professor of Economics at Dalhousie University, Canada, did graduate work under Ursula Hicks at Oxford and also worked with Professor Carl Shoup of Columbia University on the Tax Harmonisation Project. His published works include 'Public Goods and Public Policy', *Public Finance* (1962); 'Lindahl's Theory of the Budget', *Finanzarchiv* (1964); and 'Welfare Methodology and the Multi-Branch Budget', *Public Finance* (1968).

NIZAR JETHA is attached to the Latin American and Caribbean Division of the World Bank in Washington and was Planning Officer in the Ministry of Economic Planning and Development, Kenya. He has published a number of articles on Kenya's public finances.

RUSSELL MATHEWS is Professor of Accounting and Public Finance at the Australian National University, Canberra. A graduate of the University of Melbourne, he held appointments at the University of Adelaide, first as Reader in Commercial Studies and later as Professor of Commerce. During 1969 he served as a Fiscal Adviser to the Fiji Government. His major publications include *Accounting for Economists* (1962); *Public Investment in Australia* (1967); *Inflation and Company Finance*, with J. McB. Grant (1962); *Taxation in Australia* (co-author) (1965); *The Accounting Frontier* (co-editor) (1966); and *Government Accounting in Australia* (co-editor) (1967).

TETSUYA NOSSE is Director of the Institute of Economic Research at the Kobe University of Commerce, Japan, and was formerly Professor of Public Finance at that institution. He is the author of numerous professional papers, including 'A Statistical Approach to Personal Taxation', *Oxford Economic Papers* (July 1969); he has also co-authored, with Professor M. Morishimo and others, *Essays on the Working of Macroeconomic Models* (Cambridge U.P.) and is responsible for the translation into Japanese of Ursula Hicks's *Development Finance: Planning and Control.*

ALAN B. PREST, a world-renowned authority in public finance, was formerly Stanley Jevons Professor of Political Economy at the University of Manchester and has recently taken up a chair at the London School of Economics and Political Science. His published works include *Public Finance in Theory and Practice* (1960); *Public Finance in Underdeveloped Countries* (1962); and *Transport Economics in Developing Countries* (1969).

K. V. S. SASTRI is Principal, Andhra University Postgraduate Centre, Guntur, India, where he has been for some time Professor and Head of the Department of Economics. He spent the 1969–70 academic year as Fulbright Exchange Professor at the University of Wisconsin. His publications include *Federal–State Fiscal Relations in India* (Oxford U.P., 1966); and ' "Comment" on Intergovernmental Financial Relations in the New Foundations', in U. K. Hicks *et al.*, *Federalism and Economic Growth* (1961).

TARLOK SINGH is currently concerned with planning for UNICEF. He was associated for over seventeen years with the Indian Planning Commission and the preparation of India's Five-Year Plans. Since 1967 he has been Visiting Senior Research Economist at the Woodrow Wilson School for Public Finance and International Affairs, Princeton University, and Fellow and Visiting Professor at the Institute for International Economic Studies, University of Stockholm. He is an Honorary Fellow of the London School of Economics and Political Science. His many publications include *Poverty and Social Change* (1945), recently revised with 'A Reappraisal' (1969); *Planning Process* (1963); *Towards an Integrated Society* (1969); *Land Settlement Manual for Displaced Persons* (1952); and a wide variety of papers on economic problems and social planning, rural economic problems and aspects of public policy and administration.

MARIAN WERALSKI is Professor of Public Finance at Warsaw University, Poland, and Dean of the Faculty of Law. He is also a member of the Scientific Council at the Ministry of Finance. He has studied and lectured in several countries including France, Great Britain, the Soviet Union, the United States and Japan. He has published widely in several languages – French, Spanish, Russian and Polish. His most important works (in Polish) are: *Finance and Credit in Poland* (1955 and 1957); *Directions of Reforms of the Polish Fiscal System* (1960); *Budgetary Projections in the Framework of Economic Planning in Socialist Countries* (1963); *Taxation in Socialist Countries* (1965); *Socialist Budgetary Institutions* (1966); and *Some Financial Problems of Socialist Enterprise* (1969).

Index